שתזכה ללמוד וללמד ולשמור

ולעשות כל דברי תורה באהבה!

בידידות

ארי דוד קאהן

Explorations

In-depth analysis
of the weekly parashah
through the prism of rabbinic perspective

Explorations

In-depth analysis
of the weekly parashah
through the prism of rabbinic perspective

Ari D. Kahn

TARGUM/FELDHEIM

ISBN 1-56871–293–6

Published by:
Targum Press, Inc.
22700 W. Eleven Mile Rd.
Southfield, MI 48034
E-mail: targum@netvision.net.il
Fax toll-free: 888-298-9992

Distributed by:
Feldheim Publishers
200 Airport Executive Park
Nanuet, NY 10954
www.feldheim.com

Printed in Israel

To Naomi,
Matityahu, Hillel, Yishai,
Yosef, and Elisheva

This volume is dedicated

in memory of

Ruth (Rachel bat R' Chaim) Balter *z"l*

בגלל אבות תושיע בנים ומביא גאולה לבני בניהם

"In their fathers' merit their sons are redeemed and bring redemption to their children's children"

לזכר נשמת
יעקב בן שרגא פיוול פוקס ע״ה
ורעיתו שרה בת בן ציון ע״ה
Jack and Sarah Fuchs

ובתו מרת רבקה מעטל בת יעקב ע״ה
Rhoda Fuchs

אלתר יצחק בן מרדכי מאיר קעסטנבוים ע״ה
ורעיתו ליבה לאה בת חיים מאיר ע״ה
Adolph and Lily Kestenbaum

חיים יהודה בן אהרן יששכר קאי ע״ה
Henry Kaye

דבורה רחל בת יונתן טאטארקא ע״ה
Dora Tatarka

In memory of our grandparents and relatives
whose lives represented the struggle
to secure a future of Torah and Yahadus for their
children, grandchildren and all future generations.

Benzion and Deena Fuchs

In memory of

Donald Keith Adler

An inspiration and light

to all who were fortunate to know him

The Adler Family

In memory of

Rebbetzin Elisheva (Liz) Schwartz, *a"h*

לע״נ סגן **אלון אברהם חי** בביאן

נולד בירושלים בכ״ו תשרי תשל״ו

בוגר המכינה התורנית

הקדם צבאית בעצמונה

שרת בגולני כלוחם, קצין

ומפקד צוות לוחמים

נפל באסון המסוקים

בשאר ישוב בכ״ח שבט תשנ״ז

בדרכו לפעילות מבצעית

במוצב הבופור בלבנון

ת. נ. צ. ב. ה.

״כל דקה בצבא היא מצווה ובקרבי מצווה מן המובחר״

11 Nisan, 5761

Aish HaTorah has been fortunate to have Rabbi Ari Kahn as a member of our staff for the past 15 years. Ari has proven himself to be both a profound thinker and gifted communicator. These combined talents have made him uniquely successful in communicating the depth and relevance of Torah to thousands of uninitiated Jews from all over the world.

His impact has grown beyond Aish HaTorah through his weekly discussion on the *sedra* that is received by thousands of subscribers via the Internet.

I am sure that his book on the weekly *sedra* will be highly effective in inspiring Jews of all backgrounds.

I hope that this is only the first of many *sefarim* that he will publish להגדיל תורה להאדירה.

Sincerely,

Rabbi Noah Weinberg

Rabbi Nachman Bulman
Yeshivat Ohr Somayach
Ohr Lagolah

הרב נחמן בולמן
ישיבת אור שמח
אור לגולה

בס"ד

י"ט טבת תשנ"ט
January 6, 1999

Parashat Hashavua is for all times a magnet for Torah students — both learned and "beginners." Every age has its emphasis, and reflects the "spirit of the age," while attempting to fathom the insights of our earlier sages.

Each new attempt is suspect. Is it the new author who reads himself into the Divine text? Or is it the new author in whom the resonance of the Divine text evokes a new echo?

Yet another work on the parashah has come to the attention of the writer of these lines — *Explorations* by Rabbi Ari Kahn of Givat Ze'ev, Yerushalayim. In the humble judgment of the undersigned, it passes the above test brilliantly, and with integrity. It also capitvates the reader-learner. It focuses the teachings of Midrash masterfully on a wide range of the existential intellectual dilemmas of our time. With the help of Hashem, the present work will illuminate many seekers of Torah truth.

הכותב לכי התורה — לומדי' ומלמדי'

נחמן בולמן
Nachman Bulman

Nachman Bulman
ירושלים ת"ו

בס"ד

ירושלים ת"ו י"ט בטבת תשס"א

In our daily acknowledgment of the privilege of having been commanded to study Torah, we include the prayer והערב נא — May the words of Torah be made sweet to the taste — for ourselves — for our children — and for all of Israel. An emotional appreciation of the beauty of the Divine wisdom is an essential element both in facilitating an internalization of the truths of Torah as well as the fostering of an emotional relationship with the נותן התורה — Hashem Himself. (See Rambam, *Yesodei HaTorah* 2:2.)

In our sages' accounts of the most elevated moments of Torah study, we read of an intellectual dance from one area of Torah to another — to the point of a reenactment of the ecstasy experienced at the revelation at Sinai.

My friend and colleague Rabbi Ari Kahn is gifted with the natural ability to extract-combine-create Torah that provokes mind and heart to reach new levels of awe and appreciation of the beauty of the intertwining of the totality of Torah with itself.

May the author continue to inspire us all with his beautiful, creative works of Torah.

Yitzchak Berkovits

Yitzchak Berkovits

לשכת הרבנות
גבעת זאב

ב"ה כ"ה אדר א' תש"ס

לכבוד
יקר תפארת ורב פעלים לתורה ולהפצתה
אציל הרעיון וזך המחשבה, המשיב רבים מעוון
הרה"ג כמוה"ר רבי ארי דוד קאהן שליט"א
גבעת זאב.

שלום שלום.

מכובדי,

אחד"ש כת"ר, הנני להביע את שמחתי הרבה והתפעלותי עד מאד לטובה, על מה שראיתי בגליונות ספרו היקר באנגלית Shiurim on Parashat Hashavua עבור דוברי השפה האנגלית, מעשי ידי אומן, מלא יראת ד', כולו מחמדים, כי כולו עשוי בטוב טעם ודעת אמת לאמיתה של תורה, הכל בשפה ברורה ונעימה להשאיר את הקורא בהרגשה נכונה על פרשנות התורה מתוך אספקלריא של חכמינו זכרונם לברכה, השאובים מהתלמודים בבלי והירושלמי, מדרשים ואף מן הזוהר הקדוש לחזק את האמונה ואהבת השם יתברך מתוך תורתה של ארץ ישראל שעליה נאמר "וזהב הארץ ההיא טוב מאוד" - (משלי כה, יא) אין תורה כתורת ארץ ישראל - כתפוחי זהב המשכיות כסף, דבר דבור על אופניו.

יישר כחך וחילך לאורייתא על פעליך המבורכים הבאים להגדיל תורה ולהאדירה בישובנו גבעת זאב אשר בצפון יהודה יע"א ובמקומות רבים אחרים בארץ ובחוץ לארץ, תוך עיסוק בזיכוי הרבים ובקירוב לבבות ישראל כולל אלה הדוברים עדיין בשפה אנגלית. ועתה עמלתה ויגעתה יגיעה רבה, לערוך חיבור ערוך ומסודר על סדר פרשיותיה של תורה מ"בראשית" עד "וזאת הברכה", בכדי לזכות את הרבים במצוה חשובה ביותר של לימוד התורה על סדר פרשיותיה.

הנני מברך על כן את כת"ר המחבר את הספר "שיעורים על פרשת השבוע", שיפוצו מעיינותיו חוצה להגדיל תורה ולהאדירה וירחיב גבולו בתלמידים לאורך ימים ושנות חיים טובים.

ויהי רצון שיהיו דבריו מקובלים ורצויים לפני אבינו שבשמיים לעשות נחת רוח ליוצרנו לעילא מן כל ברכתא. ה' ישלח עזרו מקודש, להמשיך ולקרב את ישראל בארץ ובתפוצות לאביהם שבשמים ולהמשיך בפעולותיו הכבירות לקרב רחוקים וללמד קרובים תורה ויראת שמים.

בצפיית ראיית הישועה השלימה על עמו ונחלתו.

ובכבוד ויקר.
יוסף טולידאנו
הרב המקומי

יוסף טולידאנו
הרב המקומי גבעת זאב

לשכת הרבנות גבעת זאב, ת.ד. 907 מיקוד 90917 טל' 02-5362755/6

Acknowledgments

There are many people I need to thank. Without their help it is difficult for me to imagine that this work would have been undertaken, and certainly not completed.

Foremost, I would like to express my thanks to my parents, who raised my sister, brothers, and me in a house permeated with Torah. Words are really inadequate to express my love and appreciation for all they have done for me. I hope I can have a similar impact on my children's lives.

My father is more than a father; he is my first rebbe, and so much of his outlook can be found in these pages. It was he who opened up for me the world of Midrash, skillfully combining Torah knowledge, analytical ability, and psychological insight. I hope this book inspires him to write his own words of Torah in order to share them with a larger audience. I wish my parents many years of health and productivity, and *nachat* from their children and grandchildren.

My in-laws, the Linders, have treated me as a son, and I pray they have many years of health and happiness.

My brothers, sister, brothers-in-law, and sisters-in-law have all been incredibly supportive. Many of them have read the manuscript and offered numerous comments and suggestions.

My father also introduced me to the person who was the major intellectual and spiritual influence of his life, my revered master Rabbi Yosef Dov Soloveitchik, of blessed memory. The Rav, as he was known to his followers, was a Torah giant of unfathomable proportions. The Rav is cited numerous times on these pages, but more importantly his *derech*, his approach, is in my mind at all times. The greatest compliment I received from readers was when people said they heard the voice of the Rav in the background. I was thankful for this comment despite the obvious exaggeration.

Other *rabbanim* with whom I have been privileged to study include Rav Yisrael Zev Gustman, of blessed memory; *l'havdil bein chaim l'chaim*, Rav Aharon Lichtenstein, *shlita*; and Rav Dovid Miller, *shlita*. The latter found time in his busy schedule to read parts of the manuscript and encourage its publication. A little part of each of these incredible people found its way into my soul and into this book.

I especially wish to thank Rav Nachman Bulman, *shlita*, who kindly read the entire manuscript and strongly encouraged me to publish these insights. He was also gracious enough to write a *haskamah*. May Hashem grant him many years of health and productivity.

Rav Yitzchak Berkovits, *shlita*, also strongly encouraged me to write down my *shiurim*; he has heard many of the ideas and encouraged me to have confidence in my original explanations.

Rav Yehoshua Shimon (Shia) Brizel, *shlita*, heard almost the entire *sefer* during our car rides together and also gave me a great deal of encouragement.

There are a number of people who helped make this book a reality: Alisa Adler and family, the Babayan family, Rabbi Chaim and Chaya Balter, Jerry Berlin, Howie and Susan Chusid, Ben Zion and Deena Fuchs, Adam and David Lieberman, the Miller family, Rabbi Yehudah Yakov Schwartz, and the Young Israel of Oceanside. I thank all of these individuals and pray that God care for them in a special way. May they have the strength and the means to continue to support Torah projects.

I especially wish to thank the many students I have taught over the past decade in Bar Ilan University and Yeshivat Aish HaTorah (and numerous other institutions), friends and neighbors in Givat Ze'ev, and the tens of thousands of people I have had the incredible privilege to teach in person or via *shiurim* on the Internet. It is in the merit of these students that these classes were prepared, delivered, and eventually written.

The incomparable Rav Noah Weinberg, *shlita*, who has accomplished more in one lifetime than other men could dream of in many lifetimes, has given me the opportunity to teach countless people over the past fifteen years. His boundless energy, creativity, and dedication to *klal Yisrael* serve as a daily reminder of what we can accomplish if we dare try. I thank him for his inspiration and friendship and for allowing me to be part of the team. May God give him the strength and resources to make his dreams come true.

The administration of Bar Ilan University, especially Mr. Arye Arzi and Professors Yossi Yeshurun, Ella Belfer, and Stuart Cohen, have all been tremendously supportive and allowed me to create a situation in which I can teach and impact upon young people. Special mention also goes to my *chavruta* in all aspects of my position in Bar Ilan, Rav Chaim Tabaski, who has been a wonderful friend and colleague. My assistant, Alyta Pitaru, has proven invaluable; without her I would be unable to attempt to direct a program and teach in the university.

All of the articles in the present work were circulated under the name "*Mi'oray Ha'aish*" on aish.com. Special thanks go to Rabbi Nechemia Coopersmith, David LeVine, and Uriela Obst, who oversaw various levels of the Web project.

The present work would not have come to fruition had it not been for Rabbi Moshe Dombey, Chaya Baila Gavant, and D. Liff of Targum Press who produced, edited, and designed this book.

The process of research has been transformed in recent years with the availability of data research via computers. Sources that in previous years had been obscure can today be found with the push of a button. While this technology provides the researcher with easier access, it requires the researcher to consider far more raw source material than would have been imagined by previous generations, with the exception of those great luminaries who, due to their erudition, had instant access to all rabbinic literature. I utilized for this project the digital archives of the Bar Ilan Responsa project, DBS, and the Soncino archives of Davka Corporation. I believe that this work could have been completed without these tools, but it would not have been as well developed and would certainly have taken far longer. Any scholar who takes his learning seriously should certainly avail himself of these incredible tools; in fact, I would suggest that once these tools have become available, the student and scholar are required to make use of them.

Many years ago, a young woman told me that her idea of the study of Torah is a pursuit of revelation. Her comment was so simple yet so profound, for at times those of us who spend many years in yeshivah run the risk of focusing on the ideas and losing sight of the revelation. In all Torah learning one should experience what Rav Soloveitchik described as "feeling the breath of eternity on your face." I wish to thank that young woman for helping me focus my learning and teaching, for making sure that I never lose sight of the rendezvous with the Divine. I would like to thank her for editing and proofreading my writings, for being my best critic and greatest fan. I would like to thank her for marrying me, for raising our children, for creating a home of Torah and *chesed*. I would like to thank her for encouraging me to write (even on *erev Shabbat* when the house could have used an extra hand!) and teach (all over the world — even if it meant long travel and weeks apart), and for sharing with me the excitement of a new idea — at any hour of the day or night.

Naomi, thank you for inspiring me and helping me inspire others.

May the merit of this Torah protect us and our children. May our children and descendants be among those who study Torah, fear God, follow His commandments, and bring *nachat* to their grandparents, parents, and the entire community of Israel.

Ari Kahn
Givat Ze'ev
Tevet 5761

Introduction

With awe, trepidation, and most of all thanks to the Almighty I write these words of introduction.

This book emerged after years of study, research, teaching, and various editions of an e-mail *shiur*. I didn't set out to write a book; the writing resulted from a dual objective of not wishing to forget my own Torah and a desire to share it with more people.

Over the years my students pushed me to write my *shiurim*. After a number of years I acquiesced. My primary motivation was to maintain contact with students whom I no longer had the opportunity to teach personally. These essays were mostly written while sitting for many hours in front of my computer at home; some were written on the road — in airports, on planes, in army bases during a lull in reserve duty. What began as an e-mail list to students, family, and friends proceeded to grow exponentially, starting with some fifty readers. As I write these words, some six thousand subscribers, along with countless others (who read the aish.com Web site or read copies printed out or forwarded by e-mail) have read my essays. It is an incredible privilege to have been blessed with this opportunity to teach Torah. We can feel the light of the Messianic Age when we contemplate that a person can almost instantly produce a work that reaches literally all over the world.

The present work represents an attempt to understand Torah. There are many types of Torah study and many levels of understanding the Divine text. One manner is *peshat* — the "simple" or straightforward meaning of the text. Despite the term, the process of learning *peshat* is not simple. In this book I have attempted to explore other levels, primarily *drash*, rabbinic associations, and occasionally *sod*, mystical tradition. I tried to learn and teach the Torah through the prism of the interpretations of our tradition, our Sages. While *peshat* was not the objective, I tried to offer only interpretations consonant with the straightforward meaning of the text. In my research I utilized *midrashim*, relevant passages in Talmud, *Zohar*, the classical commentaries found in the *Mikraot Gedolot*, and the major chassidic commentaries. As I indicated above, often the conclusions were original. I tried to focus on major themes in the narrative; occasionally I presented studies of major theological issues that emerge from a particular section.

In my lectures I attempted to provide deep, meaningful studies based on Torah sources. I attempted to do this for audiences of both beginners as well as students who were advanced and well versed in the biblical narrative and who enjoyed a familiarity with the various commentaries. Two teachers in particular came to mind when I began this project. One was my incomparable rebbe, Rav Yosef Dov Soloveitchik, *zt"l*; the other was the immensely popular contemporary phenomenon, Rav Mordechai Elon, *shlita*. What both of these men had in common was an approach which, while sensitive to the text of the Torah, had an eye focused on rabbinic literature, particularly Midrash. While the methodological style was adapted and modified, for the most part the essays contained in this volume are original; on the occasions I was (knowingly) influenced, acknowledgment is given.

For reasons best discussed in another forum, over the past fifty years there has been a tendency among yeshivah students and teachers to avoid novel explanations — *chiddushim*. More energy has been invested in collecting older ideas. However, as many who have been involved in learning can attest, *ein beit midrash beli chiddush* — there can be no study without creative understanding or applications. This work is full of creative ideas, but there may be cases where I heard or read an idea and forgot the source. I offer sincere apologies for any unattributed ideas mentioned.

The need to record one's novel explanations may be an absolute halachic requirement. A difference of opinion exists among the major rabbinic authorities regarding the precise nature of an individual's requirement to learn Torah. The Baal HaTanya says that the biblical prohibition of forgetting Sinai applies to forgetting any learning (*Shulchan Aruch HaRav, Hilchot Talmud Torah* 2:4; see *Avot* 3:8). This opinion has potentially major implications for how Torah should be taught and studied.

However, Rav Chaim of Volozhin states that the prohibition of forgetting Sinai applied only in the days when learning was done orally. Now that books are used this prohibition does not apply (*Keter Rosh*, section 67). Apparently Rav Chaim understands that the prohibition applies only to Torah which will be lost from the entire Jewish community. Hence, once Torah was committed to writing, the prohibition disappeared. However, it seems to me that this would apply only to Torah ideas made known to others; hence, if someone has a novel interpretation he would be obligated to write it in order to insure that it is not forgotten. This would require people to retain a notebook of their own original interpretations as they learn.

While it is possible to rely on students to insure that ideas are passed on and trust in oral transmission, this would depend on the skill and dedication of the students. Furthermore, the process of writing as a means of clarifying, crystallizing, sifting, and selecting ideas would be foregone. As Rav Yitzchak Berkovits told me (in the name of a leading *rav*), many people are willing to say all sorts of things in the classroom — but only the ideas that they really believe get written down.

I offer you my "notebook." I hope you find the ideas worthy. As I studied, taught, and wrote, I often felt a *siyatta diShmaya* (a particular Divine assistance), but I have little doubt that any success which these ideas have is in the merit of the audience. Therefore I offer the ideas back to *klal Yisrael*, the true, rightful owner of Torah.

Contents

Sefer Bereishit

Parashat Bereishit

The First Argument

> In the beginning God created the heaven and the earth.
>
> *(Bereishit 1:1)*

The Torah begins with a description of the events unfolding at the dawn of history. It has long been the understanding of the Rabbis that, as important as the literal text may be, the primary importance of the Torah lies in its theological teachings. The Torah is a book of theological truth which is the word of God, and, therefore, it is historically accurate as well. The Rabbis of the Talmud, Midrash, and *Zohar* were well aware of this idea. Consequently, verses which may seem mundane or simplistic to the uninitiated reader often contain the most profound teachings and secrets of the Torah.[1]

The Midrash in this week's parashah makes an inference, not from what is said but by noting what is missing:

> Why is [the phrase] "that it was good" not written in connection to the second day? Rabbi Yochanan explained in the name of Rabbi Yosi bar Chalafta: Because on it the Gehenna [Hell] was created.... Rabbi Chanina said: Because on it schism

1 This is especially found in the *Zohar*. The list of kings of Edom in *Bereishit*, ch. 36, is one example of this phenomena.

> came into the world, [as it is written,] "[God said, 'Let there be a firmament in the midst of the waters, and] let it divide the waters from the waters' " (*Bereishit* 1:6).
>
> *(Bereishit Rabbah 4:6)*

The Midrash teaches that this act of separation of waters is the power which allows dissension to enter into the world. However, readers familiar with the text will note that the term *vayavdeil*, "He divided," was used on the first day as well, when God separated between light and darkness. Why, then, is the power of dissension only expressed on the second day? Apparently, argumentation can only take place when two things or two people do not have clearly defined boundaries. The separation between light and darkness is absolute; they are opposites, and therefore no dissension follows their separation. However, the separation between water and water, which are ostensibly the same, is where the power of dissent originates. God separated the higher waters from the lower waters — two items which seem to be the same. On this day, dissension was created.

This *midrash* serves as an introduction to one of the most tragic events recorded in *Sefer Bereishit.* Chapter 4 records the birth of Kayin and Hevel, their difference of opinion, and finally the horrifying murder of Hevel.

> Adam knew Chavah, his wife. She conceived and gave birth to Kayin, and [she] said, "I have acquired a man from the Lord." She gave birth again [to] his brother, Hevel. Hevel was a keeper of sheep, and Kayin was a tiller of the ground.
>
> *(Bereishit 4:1–2)*

These two verses lack symmetry. When Kayin is born, his name is immediately explained, but when Hevel is born, no rhyme or reason is given for his name. At the outset, Hevel is described simply as a brother — "and she gave birth again [to] his brother."

Let us consider the name given to Kayin. The section began "Adam knew Chavah, his wife." Immediately preceding this section was the expulsion of Adam and Chavah from the Garden of Eden due to their improper partaking of the fruit of the Tree of Knowledge. Immediately afterward, we are told that Adam knew Chavah. Evidently, they took the knowledge, distilled from the "Tree of Knowledge," and applied it. When she names her son Kayin, which has the root of the word *acquisition*, Chavah seems to be seeking a way to rekindle her relationship with God, which had deteriorated.

In the Garden of Eden, God's presence was felt. God is the Creator (with a capital "C"). Adam, too, creates by giving names to the animals, by categorizing the animals. Adam uses speech to be creative (with a lowercase "c"). The fact that Adam creates with speech is quite significant: We find that when God creates, He creates via speech — "God said, 'Let there be light' " (*Bereishit* 1:3). Surely God could have created by simply willing something into being, but instead He decided to create with speech. When the Torah tells us that man was created in the image of God (ibid. 2:7), the *Targum* explains that this means God endowed man with speech. Thus, God creates with speech, and man creates with speech. God's creation is ex nihilo, creating something from nothing, while man's creative act is in categorizing and understanding God's creation. When man is expelled, he is told that he must work the land, engaging in a different type of creative activity. Chavah, for her part, seeks to repair her damaged relationship with God and sees in the birth of Kayin a reacquisition of her own partnership in Creation.

We are given no explanation of Hevel's name. His birth seems to be an afterthought. The very name *Hevel* means "nothingness." It is difficult to interpret what significance Adam and Chavah saw in the arrival of Hevel, but it does not seem to inspire the same fanfare as the arrival of Kayin.

> Hevel was a keeper of sheep, and Kayin was a tiller of the ground.

Kayin becomes a farmer. He is relating to God as per the rules of exile; he is working the land. Hevel, however, becomes a shepherd; he seems to ignore the rules of exile and tries to relate to God in the way his father did before the sin.

The Midrash tells us something interesting about the births of Kayin and Hevel. Kayin, we are told, was born with a twin sister; Hevel, however, was born along with two sisters (*Bereishit Rabbah* 12:2).

Perhaps this is the origin of the friction between Kayin and Hevel. Kayin is the older brother, the "golden child." Chavah's hopes and aspirations rest upon him. Kayin may question the propriety of God's giving the younger brother two sisters, when he himself had only one. After all, if anyone should have received a double share, it should have been Kayin, the firstborn. This sets the stage for the rest of *Sefer Bereishit*, where the younger brother consistently achieves superiority over the older brother who inevitably fails.

Kayin, however, sets about his task, works the land and brings an offering to God. Hevel, too, offers from his flock.

> Hevel also brought of the firstlings of his flock and of the fat of it. God turned to Hevel and to his offering. [But] to Kayin and his offering, He did not turn.
>
> Kayin was very angry, and his countenance fell. God said to Kayin, "Why are you angry and why is your countenance fallen? If you do well, shall you not be accepted? And if you do not well, sin lies at the door. To you shall be its desire, and yet you may rule over it."
>
> *(Bereishit 4:4–7)*

Kayin repeatedly compares himself with his brother, Hevel, and finds himself with the short end of the stick. First, he felt slighted that his brother had two sisters, and now Hevel's offering is accepted by God and his own offering is not. Kayin defines himself in terms of his relationship with his brother. He judges his accomplishments by comparing them with his brother's. When Kayin sees that he has not been as successful as Hevel, he becomes bitter, angry, and depressed.

Kayin's mistake was that he assumed that he and his brother were the same and were, therefore, deserving of equal opportunities and success. This reminds us of the second day of Creation, when God separated between the waters. When two things are assumed to be equal, dissension follows.

> Kayin talked with Hevel, his brother; and it came to pass, when they were in the field, that Kayin rose up against Hevel, his brother, and killed him.
>
> God said to Kayin, "Where is Hevel, your brother?"
>
> He said, "I do not know. Am I my brother's keeper?"
>
> [God] said, "What have you done? The voice of your brother's blood cries to me from the ground. Now you are cursed from the earth, which has opened her mouth to receive your brother's blood from your hand. When you till the ground, it shall not henceforth yield to you its strength; a fugitive and a wanderer shall you be in the earth."
>
> *(Ibid., 8–12)*

Although the Torah reports that Kayin speaks to Hevel, it does not record what he said. Hevel does not answer. He is apparently not involved in this argument; it is one-sided. Although Kayin is haunted by the competition, Hevel is merely concerned with tending his flock, offering gifts to God, trying to relate to God. Again, there is a lack of symmetry. We are told that the earth, which had already been cursed and was now to be worked by man, opened up its mouth and swallowed the blood of Hevel. The earth will now be cursed again, and Kayin will be forced to wander the earth, finding no respite.

The tragic relationship between Kayin and Hevel created the spiritual power for other arguments that take place in the future. We are told of one such argument in *Sefer Bemidbar*:

> They [Korach and his followers] gathered themselves together against Moshe and Aharon and said to them, "You take too much upon yourselves, since all the congregation is holy, ev-

> ery one of them, and God is among them. Why then do you lift yourselves up above the congregation of God?"
>
> *(Bemidbar 16:3)*

Korach was a populist with an attractive philosophy which he conveyed to the masses. He claimed that all people are holy and all people are equal, and they should all have the same opportunities and the right to do the same tasks. The origin of such thought dates back to the second day of Creation, before God separates the upper and lower waters. Korach's argument is the same as Kayin's. The Kabbalists, based on a tradition from the Arizal, explain this similarity by teaching that Korach is a reincarnation of the soul of Kayin.[1]

Ironically, the punishment which Korach receives is that the earth "opens up its mouth" and swallows him (*Bemidbar* 16:32). The only other time in the Torah that this terminology appears is when the earth swallowed the blood of Hevel (*Bereishit* 4:11). Now Korach, who follows in the footsteps of Kayin, receives the appropriate punishment. The earth "opens up its mouth" and swallows him.

The similarity between Korach and Kayin is not the only one; there is also a striking similarity between Moshe and Hevel. As we have seen, the name *Hevel* means nothingness. We are told that Moshe was the most modest of men (*Bemidbar* 12:3). We may assume that Moshe, like Hevel, did not think too much of himself. Moshe's position was not attained through political maneuvering; he was chosen directly by God. Although Moshe tried to decline, God impressed upon him that his destiny, his unique task, was to lead the Jewish people.

When Kayin argued with Hevel, Hevel did not respond. Similarly, *Pirkei Avot* describes the argument of Korach as "the argument of Korach and his followers," not as "the argument between Korach and Moshe."

---

1 *Shaar HaGilgulim, hakdamah* 33, and see *Sheim MiShmuel* in *Parashat Korach.*

> Every controversy that is for the sake of Heaven is destined to result in something permanent; but one that is not for the sake of Heaven is not destined to result in something permanent.
>
> What is [an example of] a controversy that is for the sake of Heaven? The controversy between Hillel and Shammai. And what is [an example of] a controversy that is not for the sake of Heaven? The controversy of Korach and his entire congregation.
>
> *(Avot 5:17)*[1]

Moshe, the faithful shepherd,[2] cared for each of his flock. He was aware of the uniqueness of each inidividual. Korah, however, tried to blur the differences between people.

One of the profound teachings of Judaism is that not all people are created equal. Each person certainly has an inalienable right to his or her dignity, but not all people possess equal roles and destinies.

---

1 The *Zohar* goes even further in highlighting the nature of dispute:

> The dispute between Shammai and Hillel was composed on the pattern of the supernal dispute, becoming more and not less worthy as it proceeded and perpetuating itself rightfully. The Holy One, blessed be he, approved of their dispute, because its motive was lofty and it therefore resembled [the dispute] which took place at the Creation. Hence, like the latter, the dispute between Shammai and Hillel has survived to this day.
>
> Korach, on the other hand, denied the Creation, fought against Heaven itself and sought to confute the words of the Torah. He certainly was of the following of the Gehinnom, and therefore remained attached to it...
>
> Shammai conducted his dispute in that spirit of calm which should follow on the first burst of passion; it therefore became a quarrel of love and obtained the approval of Heaven. This is indicated by our text. It says first: "Let there be a firmament in the midst of the waters, and let it divide" (*Bereishit* 1:6). This refers to the beginning of quarrel, the outburst of passion and violence. There was a desire for reconciliation, but meanwhile the Gehinnom arose before the wrath and passion cooled down. Then "God made the firmament"; that is, there emerged a quarrel of love and affection which made for the permanence of the world. In this category is the dispute between Shammai and Hillel, which resulted in the Oral Law approaching the Written law with love, so that they mutually supported each other.
>
> (*Zohar, Bereishit* 17b)

The commentaries on the *Zohar* in this passage contain the elusive tradition of the Arizal that in the future the law will follow the rulings of Shammai. See *Mikdash Melech* ad loc.

2 This appellation for Moshe is often utilized in the *Zohar*.

My rebbe, Rav Yosef Dov Soloveitchik, illustrated this idea with an insight regarding the verse, "*Shema Yisrael, Hashem Elokeinu, Hashem echad* — Listen Israel, God is the Lord, God is One." Rav Soloveitchik commented that he would prefer to translate the word *echad* (one) as "unique." Jewish monotheism does not differ from polytheism purely in numeric terms. Our belief in God is not just that He is one, but that He is unique.

Man is created in the image of God, which means that each and every man is unique as well. The challenge of life is to find our uniqueness and develop it — not to define ourselves in comparison with others, but to search within ourselves and find our uniqueness, our image of God.

When the Torah commands us to love our neighbor as ourselves, one can ask, "How can we possibly love others?" The secret to loving others is to discover their uniqueness and appreciate it. A mother loves all her children, for she appreciates the uniqueness of each child. We are commanded to find the uniqueness in each person and to love him or her for it. When a person identifies his own uniqueness and develops that uniqueness, he truly manifests the image of God within himself.[1]

Sefer Bereishit begins with one brother murdering the other, with one brother focusing only on the unequal treatment each receives. The horrific act of fratricide is the result of Kayin's depression as he is haunted by his brother's successes. On the other hand, *Sefer Shemot* begins with Moshe wandering out of Pharaoh's palace to help his nation.

> It came to pass in those days, when Moshe was grown, that he went out to his brothers and looked upon their burdens. He spied an Egyptian beating a Hebrew, one of his brothers.
>
> *(Shemot 2:11)*

Moshe seeks brotherhood, going to see his brothers' suffering. He is not jaded by his status as prince of Egypt. Quite the contrary,

1 We will return to the idea of loving others in *Parashat Kedoshim*.

he senses the brotherhood that exists between all Jews.

> [Moshe] looked this way and that way, and when he saw that there was no man, he slew the Egyptian and hid him in the sand.
>
> *(Ibid., 12)*

This act is profoundly different from the act of Kayin. While Kayin was motivated by jealousy, Moshe's motivation is to protect his kinsman.

The Arizal explains that the soul of Hevel transmigrated into Moshe. Moshe knew that each person has a unique task. Moshe never defined himself in terms of others. In fact, the first brothers that we find in the Torah who truly relate to one another with love and respect are Moshe and his brother, Aharon.

> God said to Aharon, "Go into the wilderness to meet Moshe." He went and met him on the mountain of God, and he [Aharon] kissed him [Moshe].
>
> *(Ibid. 4:27)*

The Midrash stresses the importance of this kiss:

> When it says "Kindness and truth met; righteousness and peace kissed" (*Tehillim* 85:11), "kindness" refers to Aharon, of whom it is said: "To Levi [Aharon's tribe] said, 'Your *tumim* and *urim* will be with Your man of kindness' " (*Devarim* 33:8), while "truth" refers to Moshe, of whom it says: "My servant Moshe...is trusted in all My house" (*Bemidbar* 7:7). Hence "kindness and truth met" when "He went and met him on the mountain of God."
>
> "Righteousness" refers to Moshe, of whom it is said, "He executed the righteousness of God" (*Devarim* 33:21), and "peace" refers to Aharon, of whom it says, "He walked with Me in peace and uprightness" (*Malachi* 2:6). "Kissed," as it says..."and he kissed him." Why? Each one rejoiced at the other's greatness.
>
> *(Shemot Rabbah 5:10)*

Throughout *Sefer Bereishit*, we do not find harmony among brothers. The unity of these two brothers, Moshe and Aharon, is what enables them to lead the people from Egypt and to bring them to Mount Sinai and accept the Torah. In order to leave Egypt, the Jewish people had to first become a nation. In order to receive the Torah they needed unity; the core of this unity was the love and mutual respect exhibited by Moshe and Aharon for one another. "Each one rejoiced at the other's greatness." Each appreciated the greatness and uniqueness of the other.

Unfortunately, Kayin and Hevel never did.[1]

1 See my discussion in *Kedoshim*, where the comments of the Vilna Gaon are cited, linking the command of *shaatnez* with the fratricide perpetrated by Kayin.

Parashat Noach

Was Noach a Tzaddik?

> These are the generations of Noach. Noach was a righteous man. He was perfect in his generations.
>
> *(Bereishit 6:9)*

The saga of Noach is well known. However, Noach himself remains an elusive personality. What was the nature of his righteousness? The description of Noach as a righteous man, perfect in his generation, sounds like a back-handed compliment. Why the limitation "in his generation"? Rashi brings two opinions.

> Some of the Sages expound this positively: Certainly if he had been in a generation of righteous people, he would have been more righteous. Other Sages expound it negatively: In his generation, he was righteous, but if he had been in the generation of Avraham, he would have been considered worthless.

There is a lack of symmetry in the words of Rashi. Why does he speak of "a generation of righteous people" in one statement, and of "the generation of Avraham" in the other? Could Avraham's generation not have served as the model for both opinions?

Let us return to the generation of Noach. In order to understand Noach's righteousness, we must first understand the generation in which he lived.

> It was when men began to multiply on the face of the earth and daughters were born to them, the sons of the powerful men saw the daughters of man for they were pretty, and they took wives for themselves all those whom they chose.... The earth became corrupt before the Lord, and the earth was filled with violence. The Lord looked upon the earth, and, behold, it was corrupt; for all flesh had corrupted its way upon the earth. The Lord said to Noach, "The end of all flesh has come before Me, for the earth is filled with violence through them. I will destroy them from the earth."
>
> *(Bereishit 6:1–2, 11–13)*

The Torah describes the generation of Noach as people of corruption and thievery. Powerful men took any women they wanted to, fitting the description of corruption, which has sexual overtones, and thievery.[1] It was a generation whose moral boundaries had broken down. The very fabric of society and its social contract was nonexistent.

So what was the nature of Noach's righteousness? Apparently Noach did not practice the sexual immorality and thievery of his generation, nor did he commit evil acts. On the other hand, we are not taught that he performed good deeds, either.

In a sense, Noach was an island — neither hurting others nor helping them. This is the greatness of Noach, as well as the tragedy of Noach.

According to the *Zohar*, the following conversation took place between Noach and God after the flood:

> [Noach] began to cry before God, and he said, "Master of the universe, You are called compassionate. You should have been compassionate for Your creation."
>
> God responded, "You are a stupid shepherd. Now you say this! Why did you not say it when I told you that I saw you were righteous among your generation, or afterward when I

---

1 See the comments of Ibn Ezra to *Bereishit* 6:11.

> said that I would bring a flood upon the people, or afterward when I said to build an ark? I constantly procrastinated and said, 'When is he [Noach] going to ask for compassion for the world?'... And now that the world is destroyed, you open your mouth to cry before Me and to ask for supplication?"
>
> *(Zohar HaShmatot, Margoliot edition, Bereishit 254b)*

Noach, as leader of the generation, had responsibilities. He was given the task of building the ark; yet he did not save even one person outside his immediate family. As a shepherd of God, Noach had the responsibility to lead the people, but he didn't, failing miserably as a leader. He was like a shepherd who sees his flock straying from the proper path, wandering in the proximity of dangerous wolves, and concludes that the sheep deserve to be eaten because they have strayed from the path. Instead of trying to save them, he mourns their loss after they are killed. God called Noach a "stupid shepherd," for he was guilty of "malpractice."

The *Zohar* continues:

> Come and see the difference between the righteous among the Jews after Noach and Noach. Noach did not defend his generation, nor did he pray for them, as Avraham did. When God told Avraham that the outcry of Sedom and Amorah had become great [i.e., they deserved destruction], Avraham immediately began to pray in front of God until he asked God if He would forgive the entire city if ten righteous people were found [in it]. Avraham thought that in the city which had Lot and his wife and children, there must have been ten righteous people. Therefore, Avraham did not pray any further.
>
> Afterwards, Moshe came, and he prayed for and protected his generation when God said to him, "They have turned away quickly from the way in which I commanded them" (*Shemot* 32:8).... It is said that Moshe did not leave God alone until [He forgave the Jewish people]. Moshe was willing to give his soul for the people in both this world and the next....
>
> What was Noach thinking, that he did not ask for mercy for

his generation? He said to himself, "Perhaps I won't escape."

The great religious leader after Noach was Avraham. When hearing of the horrific acts of the populations of Sedom and Amorah, Avraham pleaded with God not to kill the righteous along with the wicked. Noach never engaged God in a similar dialogue.

Moshe went even further. After the Jewish people committed the terrible sin of worshiping the golden calf, God was prepared to destroy the entire nation. Despite the people's guilt, Moshe pleaded with God to have mercy on them, since they had just left Egypt and had not yet had time to develop spiritually. Moshe is referred to in the *Zohar* as a "faithful shepherd." He even had the audacity to tell God that if He would wipe out the entire people, He should wipe Moshe out as well.

Noach, on the other hand, accepted the decree of God. If the people were guilty, there was no argument. Avraham tried to save the cities from annihilation, or at least exonerate some of the people living there.[1] Moshe, despite the unquestioned guilt of his people, was prepared to sacrifice himself in order to save them. Had he been in Noach's place, perhaps he would have refused to board the ark, demanding that God have mercy on the people.[2]

The Torah records that Noach built the ark over a period of 120 years. Not one person was brought under the influence of this great religious personality during this time. Why not? In a word, Noach was an island. The name *Noach* means "comfortable." He was comfortable and self-satisfied in his own righteousness. The sad truth is that Noach was a spiritual misanthrope.

It is fascinating that the next person in the Torah we see in an ark is Moshe.[3]

---

1 According to the *Zohar,* Avraham thought there were ten righteous people. Therefore, he stopped arguing, thinking he had won the case.

2 The story is told that the Brisker Rav refused to comply to the last wish of a condemned man, for he understood that such compliance would seal the man's fate. In the end, the man's life was saved due to the Brisker Rav's action.

3 Perhaps this is telling us that Moshe's destiny is to rectify the sin of the previous inhabitant of an ark.

> A man of the house of Levi went and took as his wife a daughter of Levi. The woman conceived and bore a son. When she saw that he was good, she hid him for three months. And when she could no longer hide him, she took for him an ark made of reeds and daubed it with loam and with pitch. She put the child in it, and she laid it in the rushes by the bank of the river. His sister stood at a distance to see what would be done to him.
>
> The daughter of Pharaoh came to wash herself at the river, and her maidens walked along by the side of the river. When she saw the ark among the reeds, she sent her maid to fetch it.
>
> *(Shemot 2:1–5)*

Moshe, as an infant floating in an ark in the Nile River, seemed destined to begin his mission where Noach ended his own. Moshe's entire career would be filled with self-sacrifice for his flock. Moshe's lifespan would be 120 years, perhaps in order to rectify Noach's failure in his 120 years of building the ark. Moshe was the "faithful shepherd."

The Arizal explains that Moshe was chosen to complete the task which Noach failed.

This idea is borne out by a verse in Yeshayahu in this week's haftarah:

> For this is like the waters of Noach to Me [God]; for just as I have sworn that the waters of Noach should no more go over the earth, so have I sworn that I will not be angry with you [the Jewish people] or rebuke you.
>
> *(Yeshayah 54:9)*

The *Zohar* explains the term "waters of Noach":

> Why is the expression "waters of Noach" and not "waters of the flood"? This is because when mankind is sinful and there is a righteous man in the world, God speaks to him so that he can pray for mankind and obtain forgiveness for them. God first promises to save him alone and destroy the rest. The

> proper thing for a righteous man to do at such a time is to forget himself and espouse the cause of the whole world in order to appease God's wrath against them, as Moshe did when Israel sinned.
>
> However, when God said to Noach, "The end of all flesh has come before Me," Noach replied, "And what will You do to me?"
>
> God replied, "I will establish My covenant with you. Make for yourself an ark of gopher wood."
>
> So Noach did not pray for the world, and the waters came down and destroyed mankind. Therefore, they are called "the waters of Noach."
>
> *(Zohar, Vayikra 15a)*

The *Zohar* is blaming Noach for the waters that fell. The Hebrew term for "waters of Naoch" is *"mei Noach."*

Moshe exemplifies the faithful servant in no instance more valiantly than when he offers his own life for his people:

> Now, if You will forgive their sin, [good,] and if not, blot me, I beg You, from Your book which You have written.
>
> *(Shemot 32:32)*

The Hebrew word for "blot" is *micheini* (מחני) — the same letters as *"mei Noach"* (מי נח)!

The Arizal stresses that the moment which Moshe prayed and said the word *micheini*, Noach's error was corrected.[1]

After Noach left the ark, he saw the destruction of the world and recognized that he and his family were the only survivors. How did he cope with this? The Torah tells us that one of the first things that Noach did was plant a vineyard, make wine, and become intoxicated.

> Noach began to be a farmer, and he planted a vineyard. He drank of the wine and became drunk, and he lay uncovered inside his tent.
>
> *(Bereishit 9:20–21)*

---

1 Arizal, *Shaar Pesukim Bereishit, drush* 4.

Noach could not deal with the enormity of the destruction that he had witnessed. Perhaps he sensed that he had failed; that his passivity had led to the destruction of an entire civilization. The Torah records that one of Noach's sons, Cham, discovered Noach's nakedness while his father was intoxicated.[1]

> Cham, the father of Canaan, saw the nakedness of his father, and he told his two brothers outside. Sheim and Yafes took a garment and laid it upon both their shoulders. They went backward and covered the nakedness of their father [with] their faces backward, and they did not see their father's nakedness.
>
> Noach awoke from his wine and knew what his younger son had done to him.
>
> *(Ibid., 22–24)*

The Sages explain that not only did Cham reveal his father's nakedness, but he also took advantage of it to abuse his father. There are two opinions of what actually transpired:

> Rav and Shmuel [differ,] one saying that he castrated him, while the other says that he sexually abused him.
>
> *(Sanhedrin 70a)*

Noach's children were saved from the flood not for their own righteousness, but by the merit of their father. Yet this did not prevent Cham from committing a terrible outrage against his father. It would seem that Noach failed even in educating his own children.

Let us consider Cham's worldview. Cham was involved in the culture of violence, thievery, and sexual licentiousness. His father caused the destruction of this world through his passivity. The Talmudic opinions that Cham raped or castrated his father seem to be an expression of Cham's disdain for that passivity. In a sense, Noach's nakedness was his passivity.

---

1 See my comments to *Parashat Shemini* for a Kabbalistic understanding of the wine that was drunk.

Noach lived for 350 years after the flood, witnessing the birth of numerous descendants, countless future generations. What message does Noach impart to his descendants? It seems that Noach remains passive; he has nothing to say. It is as if the rest of his life remained clouded by intoxication.

> The whole earth was of one language and one speech. It came to pass as [the people] journeyed from the east that they found a plain in the land of Shinar, and they lived there.
>
> They said one to another, "Come, let us make bricks and burn them thoroughly." They had brick for stone and loam for mortar.
>
> They said, "Come, let us build us a city and a tower whose top may reach to Heaven, and let us make for ourselves a name, lest we be scattered upon the face of the whole earth."
>
> God came down to see the city and the tower that the sons of man built. God said, "Behold, the people are one, and they have all one language, and this they begin to do? Now should nothing be withheld from them, all that they have schemed to do?"
>
> *(Bereishit 11:1–6)*

All the people of the world were gathered in Shinar, building the Tower of Bavel. The Sages tell us that Noach was still alive at this time.

> We find that Noach lived for ten years after the dispersion [which resulted from the Tower of Bavel].
>
> *(Seder Olam, ch. 1)*

Noach was still alive, but he was silent. This is the tragedy of Noach. It was not just his own generation that he did not try to protect and educate, but even his own children and grandchildren were deprived of the influence of this righteous man. One would imagine that Noach would have exemplified wonderful leadership, sharing insights to life and displaying courage and religious zeal for the future generations. But tradition reports nothing.

There was another prominent individual present in Bavel. His name was Avraham.

> Avraham was forty-eight years old at the dispersion [which resulted from the Tower of Bavel].
>
> *(Ibid.)*

These two spiritual giants met at the tower where all the people of the world had gathered. Yet it appears that Noach has nothing to share with Avraham. Whatever greatness Avraham would achieve would be without the insight or tutelage of Noach.

Some commentaries see this meeting of Noach and Avraham as a potential watershed in human history. The Torah hints at the opportunity:

> God came down to see the city and the tower that the sons of man built. God said, "Behold, the people are one, and they have all one language, and this they begin to do?"
>
> *(Bereishit 11:5–6)*

A spirit of unity had swept the world, Noach was there with his experience, and Avraham was there with his idealism.[1] The time and place were ripe for a religious renaissance. If these leaders would merge, the world could be elevated and saved. They could have reached Heaven even without the aid of a tower. But alas, Noach was silent and Avraham will have to start anew, alone.[2]

This is what Rashi means when he comments on the verse "Noach was...a perfect man in his generations." We noted at the outset the lack of symmetry. Rashi commented that

> Some of the Sages expound this positively: Certainly if he had been in a generation of righteous people, he would have been more righteous. Other Sages expound it negatively: In his generations, he was righteous, but if he had lived in the genera-

1 See the comments of Alshich to *Bereishit* 11:1.

2 When Noach dies, Avraham is fifty-eight years old, which is the numerical value of *Noach*. This is understood in terms of responsibility — now Avraham will have to become Noach, the righteous man of *his* generation.

tion of Avraham, he would have been considered worthless.

The Talmudic source which Rashi draws from makes no mention of Avraham:

> "Noach was a righteous man. He was perfect in his generations." Rabbi Yochanan said: In his generations, but not in other generations. Reish Lakish maintained: [Even] in his generations — how much more so in other generations.
>
> *(Sanhedrin 108a)*

The Midrash also addresses the righteousness of Noach:

> Rabbi Yehudah said: Only in his generations was he a righteous man [by comparison]; had he flourished in the generation of Moshe or Shmuel, he would not have been called righteous. In the street of the totally blind, a one-eyed man is called clear-sighted, and an infant is called a scholar. It is like a man who had a wine vault. He opened one barrel and found it vinegar, [and opened] another and found it [also] vinegar. But the third [he opened], he found turning sour. "It is turning," people said to him. "Is there any better here?" he retorted. Similarly, *in his generations* [Noach] was a righteous man.
>
> Rabbi Nechemyah said: If he was righteous even in his generation, how much more righteous he would have been [had he lived] in the age of Moshe.
>
> *(Bereishit Rabbah 30:9)*

The reference to Moshe is understood — Moshe succeeded in leadership, responsibility to the point of self-sacrifice, where Noach failed. By why did Rabbi Yehudah choose to mention Shmuel from among all the prophets? Shmuel was the one who anointed David HaMelech. If Noach could not lead as Moshe had, then he should have at least assumed an auxiliary role of anointer — teaching Avraham. But the Torah does not record Noach communicating to Avraham or to any of the rest of his descendants.

Rashi is interpreting the Talmudic passage in his inimitable way. It seems strange that Rashi should ignore the leaders mentioned in the Talmud and the Midrash in favor of his own example — Avraham. Obviously Rashi is attempting to convey a message with this subtle change. He is telling us that the authorities are not in conflict. Both opinions are true. Had Noach lived in a greater generation, he would have been greater; and had he lived in the generation of Avraham, he would have been considered worthless. But of course, Noach did live in the generation of Avraham, and, despite his greatness as an individual, he was worthless to his generation.[1]

The image of Noach left for posterity is of a righteous man, a calm in the face of turbulent waters, withstanding the incredible decadent social pressures. Noach's greatness was a self-absorbed greatness which ignored the outside world crumbling around him. Surely he should be commended for ignoring the seductive depravaity of that world. Certainly he was greater in the better generation. Yet his was an isolationist philosophy. He did not see his future merged with others.

Noach is therefore remembered as a righteous person in his generation, but one who did not forge a positive relationship with subsequent generations. He remained alone, floating in his ark, forming no relationships and forging no change. Alone, in silence.

---

1 See Rav Yonatan Eibeshitz in *Tiferet Yonatan*, p. 14 (*Parashat Noach*), for a similar observation.

Parashat Lech Lecha

Avraham's Discovery

> God said to Avram, "Go for yourself from your country, from your birthplace, from your father's home, to the land which I will show you...."
>
> *(Bereishit 12:1)*

Parashat Lech Lecha begins with God's command to Avraham to leave the home to which he had become accustomed and to set out an unknown destination. The Torah, however, does not tell us why God chose Avraham. What was special about Avraham? Why was he destined to become the first of the patriarchs, the founder of a nation? Who was Avraham? What were his accomplishments? What would his resume look like? Regarding all these questions, the Torah is silent.

Of course, the Midrashic literature ably fills in all the gaps, recounting Avraham's trials and tribulations. We are told of his lonely explorations and his eventual discovery of God. While we have no question about the authenticity of our oral tradition, if these stories of Avraham's youth are to be taken literally, why does the Torah itself not share them with us? Why was it left to our Sages to inform us of Avraham's past? While these questions could be posed about any section of Midrash, in this instance the complete lack of explanation of Avraham's special status leaves us with no apparent reason for the revelation of God to man. Why is this information found exclusively in the Oral Tradition?

Let us consider the picture of Avraham that is painted by our Sages. Avraham was born into a world of polytheism. His father, Terach, is described as a sculptor and purveyor of idols. When Avraham is asked to mind the store, he engages various customers in theological debate.

> Terach was a manufacturer of idols. He once went away somewhere and left Avraham to sell them in his place. A man entered and wished to buy one.
>
> "How old are you?" Avraham asked him.
>
> "Fifty years," was the reply.
>
> "Woe to such a man!" he [Avraham] exclaimed. "You are fifty years old and would worship a day-old object!"
>
> At this, [the man] became ashamed and departed.
>
> On another occasion, a woman came with a plateful of flour and requested him, "Take this and offer it to [the idols]."
>
> [Avraham] took a stick, broke [all the idols], and put the stick in the hand of the largest.
>
> When his father returned, he demanded, "What have you done to them?"
>
> "I cannot conceal it from you," he [Avraham] rejoined. "A woman came with a plateful of fine meal and requested me to offer it to them. One claimed, 'I must eat first,' while another claimed, 'I must eat first.' Thereupon the largest arose, took the stick, and broke them."
>
> "Why do you make sport of me?" [Terach] cried out. "Have they then any knowledge?"
>
> "Do your ears hear what your mouth is saying?" [Avraham] retorted.
>
> *(Bereishit Rabbah 38:13)*

Avraham's challenge is a theological one which undoubtedly was the result of many long hours of painstaking analysis and critical thinking. We are told that Avraham considered the various forms of worship which were extant in his region,[1] rejecting one after the other through the use of critical thinking. Avraham used pure logic to conclude that the world must have had a beginning:

> "We have a little sister, and she has no[t developed] breasts" (*Shir HaShirim* 8:8). [This hints to Avraham:] "Little" — even as a young person he stored up pious acts and good deeds. "She has no[t developed] breasts" — no breasts suckled him.
>
> *(Bereishit Rabbah 39:3)*

> From where did Avraham learn Torah? Said Rabbi Shimon bar Yochai, "His two kidneys became like pitchers of water, from where Torah gushed forth."
>
> *(Ibid. 95:3)*

These obscure *midrashim* describe Avraham's theological development, stressing that he arrived at his conclusions on his own; he had no teacher. He reasoned that there must be some great force this world; there must be a First Cause, there must be a God. After shattering his father's idols, Avraham argued with Terach, "If you recognize that the idols do not have the power to help or harm one another, how can you possibly base all of your dreams, hopes, and aspirations on the power of these impotent stones?"

Avraham is persecuted for his beliefs. Nimrod, a wicked tyrant, attempts to lead Avraham toward the worship of idols or nature — anything concrete.

> Thereupon he [Terach] seized [Avraham] and delivered him to Nimrod.
>
> "Let us worship the fire!" [Nimrod] proposed.
>
> "Let us rather worship water, which extinguishes the fire," replied [Avraham].
>
> "Then let us worship water!"
>
> "Let us rather worship the clouds which bear the water."
>
> "Then let us worship the clouds!"

---

1 See *Shabbat* 156a.

> "Let us rather worship the winds which disperse the clouds."
>
> "Then let us worship the wind!"
>
> "Let us rather worship human beings, who withstand the wind."
>
> "You are just bandying words," [Nimrod] exclaimed. "We will worship naught but the fire. Behold, I will cast you into it, and let your God whom you adore come and save you from it."
>
> *(Ibid. 38:13)*

With each suggestion, Avraham forces Nimrod to recognize that the object of his worship can be reduced to a previous form or vanquished by something more powerful. In this dialogue we can discern Avraham's philosophical position: There must be a First Cause — a God.

Eventually, Nimrod hurled Avraham into the fire. Avraham was saved and miraculously left the furnace unscathed. We witness the incredible heroism of Avraham, who was willing to sacrifice all for the ideas and ideals in which he had come to believe. Why does the Torah omit these impressive stories of religious searching and discovery, persecution, and heroism? Surely the image of Avraham withstanding the torments of his persecutor would have served as an impressive example for future generations.

Apparently God preferred to begin the tale of Avraham with revelation:

> God said to Avram, "Go for yourself from your country, from your birthplace, from your father's home, to the land which I will show you...."

For all of Avraham's genius, his decisions and behavior are based on logic — wonderful logic, compelling logic, but nevertheless human logic. There are limits to the human mind, to man's understanding. When man analyzes the world around him, he is limited by his subjectivity.[1] Did Avraham know that he was right?

1 See *Kuzari* 4:27.

All the logic that he could muster pointed in the direction of the truth of his conclusions. Of course, he must have felt with every fiber of his being that he had uncovered the truth, he had found God. But could he know with complete certainty that he was, indeed, correct?

Avraham was so convinced of the merits of his argument that he was literally prepared to die for them. He was not satisfied with merely embracing his new Weltanschauung for himself; he endeavored to teach and inspire others to follow the same path. The Sages in the Midrash leave us with an image of a spiritual giant who arrives at a conclusion based on careful, compelling logic, of a man who is so intellectually honest that he is willing to die for his convictions.

Perhaps now we can understand why the Torah starts the saga of Avraham with a revelation. The Torah is a document which describes the covenant between God and His people, between the people and their God. Such a commitment can only be based on revelation. Human logic has its limits, but revelation is beyond logic. The Torah is replete with commandments, yet such commandments can only exist if there is a command. Revelation is the vehicle through which God commands us.[1]

Let us consider: When Avraham was willing to enter the furnace, did he know that was the proper mode of behavior? Prior to God's revealing Himself, did Avraham know the proper response for each situation, or was he merely using logic? Of course, every one of Avraham's decisions was correct. Avraham was so spiritually sensitive that he had the ability to discern God's will; this is the reason that our Sages have recorded and preserved Avraham's trials and tribulations in the Midrash. The belief in monotheism is eminently logical, and Avraham's behavior was heroic. However, in the absence of a Divine command — of any Divine communication — Avraham's behavior took on a subjective cast. Although he was

1 See *Torat Chaim*, p. 145, for Rabbi Chaim Soloveitchik's understanding of the distinction between faith and knowledge.

correct, the story of the Jewish people only begins with the revelation.

> [Avraham] may be compared to a man who was traveling from place to place when he saw a building in flames. "Is it possible that the building lacks a person to look after it?" he wondered. The owner of the building looked out and said, "I am the owner of the building."
>
> Similarly, because our father Avraham said, "Is it conceivable that the world is without a guide?" the Holy One, blessed be He, looked out and said to him, "I am the Guide, the Sovereign of the Universe".... Hence, "God said to Avram, 'Go for yourself from your country, from your birthplace, from your father's home, to the land which I will show you....' "
>
> *(Bereishit Rabbah 39:1)*

Avraham believes in God — a God who is involved in history, a God who controls human destiny. What led Avraham to his discovery? Perhaps the Torah wishes to teach us that belief in One God is ultimately such a simple concept that anyone, even a child of three, can conceive of it.[1] However, spiritual greatness does not exist in a vacuum. The Biblical text leaves us a hint about the source of Avraham's inspiration — it was none other than his pagan father, Terach.

There is something unique about Terach:

> Nachor lived twenty-nine years, and fathered Terach. Nachor lived after he fathered Terach 119 years, and fathered [more] sons and daughters. And Terach lived seventy years, and fathered Avram, Nachor, and Haran.
>
> *(Bereishit 11:24–26)*

We find that Terach, son of Nachor, named one of his sons after his father. He is the first person recorded in the Torah to do so. Every day of Avraham's youth, when he looked at his brother Nachor, he was reminded of his roots and of his father's roots. Per-

1 See *Kovetz Maamarim* of Rav Elchanan Wasserman, p. 11–16.

haps this is what started Avraham wondering about the origins of other things. This approach, taken to its extreme, eventually led Avraham out of the pagan mindset and into the concept of monotheism.

If so, we can ascribe to Terach the nascent belief in One God. However, Terach was unable to take the idea to its conclusion. Apparently Terach was derailed somewhere along the way. Another instance of this same phenomenon is to be found at the end of *Parashat Noach*:

> Terach took Avram, his son, and Lot the son of Haran (his son's son), and Sarai, his daughter-in-law (his son Avram's wife), and they went out with them from Or Kasdim to go into the land of Canaan. They came to Charan and dwelt there.
>
> *(Ibid., 31)*

Terach was on his way to Canaan — the Land of Israel — but he never arrived there. Instead, he settled in Charan. Terach knew that he must leave the place of his birth, his homeland, his people, and he knew that his destination was Israel. But he never quite accomplished his mission. The revelation with which our parashah opens commands Avraham, in a sense, to continue that which his father began but lacked the ability to complete.

> God said to Avram, "Go for yourself from your country, from your birthplace, from your father's home, to the land which I will show you...."

Based on logic, Avraham understood that there must be something beyond logic, something beyond nature. Avraham sought an elusive, higher wisdom. God's revelation was his answer — confirmation that Avraham had been correct in his logic. Both the medium and the message were revelation: The fact that God communicated directly with man and the content of that communication would shape Avraham's personal destiny.[1]

The closing section of the parashah is equally instructive, for it is here that Avraham is given the commandment of circumcision:

> The Lord said to Avraham, "You shall keep My covenant, you and your seed after you throughout their generations. This is My covenant which you shall keep between Me and you, and your seed after you: Every male child among you shall be circumcised. You shall circumcise the flesh of your foreskin, and it shall be a sign of the covenant between Me and you. Every eight-day-old male shall be circumcised among you, every male child in your generations, he who is born in the house or bought with money from any stranger who is not of your seed."
>
> *(Bereishit 17:9–12)*

The basic concept of circumcision is that nature is not perfect and that man can "improve" on nature. Circumcision declares to man that he can control his sexual urges. He can go beyond nature. This is a concept which necessitated a revelation. It is the logical conclusion, or perhaps the metalogical conclusion, that Terach and his generation were unable to find. After Avraham's lonely, logical search led him to realize that there was something beyond nature, God revealed Himself and His commandments to Avraham, and to his children, specifically with the commandment to circumcise, to go beyond nature, and to rise above nature in a way that could never have been possible through pure logic, devoid of revelation.

---

1 The progression of Avraham's spiritual growth is described in the *Zohar, Bereishit* 80a.

Parashat Vayeira

The Trial

Parashat Vayeira contains the tenth and last trial of Avraham: the binding of Yitzchak. Avraham was commanded to sacrifice his beloved son Yitzchak. Avraham did not complain. He did not engage God in dialogue. He did not negotiate with God, as he had on other occasions. It seems that Avraham sensed that this was something that he had to set out to do. The most obvious question which faces us is, What was the purpose of the test?

Numerous scholars over countless generations, Jewish and non-Jewish alike, have studied this text and attempted to penetrate the lesson of the passage. Soren Kierkegaard, a Danish philosopher, in his book *The Fear and Trembling*, describes Avraham as a "knight of faith." He concludes with labeling the act as a "leap of faith." This term of Kierkegaard has entered into the lexicon of virtually all contemporary religious thinkers. It is interesting that in Jewish sources, Avraham is not described as one who excelled in faith, per se, as much as he is described as one who loved God.

> It is written, "You loved righteousness and hated wickedness" (*Tehillim* 45:8), and it is further written, "Avraham who loves me" (*Yeshayah* 41:8). Avraham is said to have loved God because he loved righteousness; this was Avraham's love of God in which he excelled over all his contemporaries.
>
> *(Zohar, Bereishit 76b)*

Based on Jewish sources, then, perhaps we should label Avraham's action as a "leap of love," rather than a "leap of faith." His love of God allowed Avraham to respond with enthusiasm when called upon to perform this superhuman task.

Let us consider the *akeidah* (binding). What was the essence of the challenge of the *akeidah*? At first glance this question seems absurd. On the one hand, Avraham was being asked to sacrifice his son, and the very notion of child sacrifice is abhorrent to modern man. However, on a conceptual level, the idea of an individual who is willing to sacrifice his child for his own ideals may not be completely alien to us. Even enlightened, modern society is often prepared to sacrifice children for its ideals. Indeed, if this were not so, there would be no war. As difficult as sacrificing one's child is, it would seem that it may be justifiable when it is done for the sake of one's beliefs.

Perhaps the challenge of the *akeidah* lay in the fact that Avraham had previously been told that Yitzchak would be his spiritual heir. If Yitzchak died, how could he inherit Avraham's position? This would place the problem within the realm of logical inconsistency. A dead Yitzchak could not lead. Yet this is more than a technical problem; Yitzchak's death would indicate that the word of God could not be trusted. The theological problem was compounded by the personal pain Avraham must have felt. He would not abort his mission, but his life's mission would lose its luster, its very meaning, with Yitzchak's demise. Philo of Alexandria suggested that the sacrifice of Yitzchak would mean the eradication of all laughter from the world, for the name *Yitzchak* means "laughter." Certainly for Avraham, the death of his beloved son would mark the death of his relationship with his God, whose word would be proven as fickle.

Midrashic and Kabbalistic sources offer a deeper understanding of the dilemma: In Midrashic and Kabbalistic sources, Avraham is described as the individual who excelled at the trait of *chesed* (kindness). Avraham, in his understanding of monotheism, knew that

God is all-powerful, that God has no needs, that there is absolutely nothing one can do for God. What is left for man is to try to emulate God. Therefore, Avraham tried to impress upon his pagan neighbors that God did not need their sacrifices; He only desired them to treat one another with kindness, just as God had created the world with incredible kindness and love.

Chesed was Avraham's credo. Now, God was calling upon Avraham to go against the very basis of his life's mission. Viktor Frankl, in his classic work *Man's Search for Meaning*, describes the need for meaning as one of the most profound needs within the hierarchy of human existence. What God was asking of Avraham was not merely to sacrifice his son Yitzchak, but to sacrifice his own life's meaning. We can clearly appreciate that had the test been to entertain fifty, a hundred, or two hundred guests for dinner, Avraham would have risen to the challenge heroically, with a smile on his face and gladness in his heart. That would not have been a challenge. That would have fit within Avraham's worldview as an act of *chesed*. Instead, God asked Avraham to perform an act which was the very antithesis of *chesed*, to sacrifice his son. Perhaps this was the most difficult aspect of the *akeidah*, for with one stroke of the knife Avraham would be conceding to all his pagan neighbors that their human sacrifices had been correct after all.

Let us consider the pagan world, in which gods were created in the image of man. Judaism teaches that man is created in the image of God. Perhaps Avraham, after all these years of Divine service, during which he excelled in the performance of *chesed*, was open to the challenge of his pagan neighbors that he was, in fact, no different from them. They could claim that Avraham, who was so interested in *chesed*, had also created a God in his own image — a "kinder, gentler" God than theirs, but one of Avraham's creation nonetheless. If he were ever called upon by God to perform an act which was not an act of *chesed*, would Avraham succeed?

When God calls upon Avraham and demands the sacrifice of Yitzchak, Avraham sets out to obey God's command. Only when we understand that the greatness of Avraham was his *chesed* are we able to appreciate the significance of this test. The first step toward religious development is taking one's capabilities, one's natural gifts, and utilizing them for a divine mission. But God wanted Avraham to gain from the *akeidah* the appreciation that man can go beyond his natural tendencies and skills. Therefore, He calls upon Avraham to perform an act which is the complete opposite of his natural instinct. Avraham excelled in *chesed,* but could he perform *din* (justice)?

This understanding is buttressed by an analysis of the Name of God used in this text.

> It came to pass after these things, that the Lord [*Elokim*] tested Avraham. He said to him, "Avraham."
>
> He [Avraham] said, "Here I am."
>
> [The Lord] said, "Take your son, your only son Yitzchak, whom you love, and go to the land of Moriah. Offer him there as an offering upon one of the mountains which I will tell you."
>
> *(Bereishit 22:1–2)*

The Name of God used at the outset is "*Elokim,*" the Name associated with judgment. At the conclusion of the ordeal, the text states:

> An angel of God called to him from Heaven, and said, "Avraham, Avraham."
>
> He said, "Here I am."
>
> [The angel] said, "Do not lay your hand upon the lad, and do not do anything to him; for now I know that you fear the Lord, seeing that you did not withhold your son, your only son, from Me."
>
> *(Ibid., 11–12)*

Here an angel, speaking in the name of God, states that it is now known that Avraham has the ability to relate to "*Elokim*" — judgment, as well as kindness.[1] When Avraham was prepared to

---

1 See *Michtav Me'Eliyahu,* by Rabbi Eliyahu Dessler, for a full discussion of this point.

sacrifice his son, he passed the test, and the sacrifice itself became unnecessary. Avraham's tenth test, therefore, was to relate to God in a manner which was contrary to his instinct. Greatness is found in not merely using your skills in the service of God, but in developing new skills for the service of God.

This test was not for God; He knew Avraham's potential. This test was for the benefit of Avraham, to elevate him to a level of Divine worship which he could not previously have imagined. Our Sages teach us that according to the difficulty is the reward. Avraham most probably received more reward for the *akeidah* than for any of his other acts.

However, there is another player in the *Akeidah* — namely, Yitzchak. According to tradition, Yitzchak was thirty-seven years old at the time of the *akeidah* (*Bereishit Rabbah* 56:3).

According to the Midrashic and Kabbalistic sources, Yitzchak represents *din*. What was Yitzchak's role in the *akeidah*?

> Avraham rose early in the morning, and he saddled his donkey. He took two of his young men with him and Yitzchak, his son.... Avraham took the wood for the kindling and put it on Yitzchak, his son. He took in his hand the kindling and the knife, and they both went together.
>
> *(Bereishit 22:3,6)*

Avraham and Yitzchak, we are told, traveled together on this mission. It would seem that the togetherness denotes more than mere traveling companions. They were "in on this together."

> "And they both went together" — one to bind and the other to be bound, one to slaughter and the other to be slaughtered.
>
> *(Bereishit Rabbah 56:3)*

What follows is a unique dialogue. It is the only time in the entire Biblical literature that Avraham and Yitzchak speak to one another:[1]

---

1 Rabbi Mordechai Elon (author of *Techeilet Mordechai*) made this observation.

> Yitzchak spoke to Avraham, his father, and said, "My father."
>
> He said, "Here I am, my son."
>
> He said, "Here is the kindling and the wood. Where is the lamb for the offering?"
>
> Avraham said, "God will provide for Himself a lamb for an offering, my son." And both of them walked on together.
>
> *(Bereishit 22:7–8)*

We must recall that Yitzchak was an adult at this point. He was aware of the neighboring pagan practices. He walked together with his father, completely dedicated to his father's wishes. After all, Yitzchak embodies *din*. He follows the law as set down by his father. Yitzchak's relationship with God is through his father's teachings. They walk together, two people on one mission.

On the third day of traveling, Avraham lifts up his eyes and sees the mountain from afar. He tells his young men to wait with the donkey while he and Yitzchak go to make the sacrifice.

Interestingly enough, God initially told Avraham, "Take your son...and offer him as an offering upon one of the mountains which I will tell you." He did not tell Avraham upon which mountain he should sacrifice Yitzchak. That information would follow. But later we are told, "Avraham lifted his eyes and saw the place from afar" (*Bereishit* 22:4). The Midrash expounds on this:

> "And saw the place from afar." What did [Avraham] see? He saw a cloud enveloping the mountain, and said, "It appears that that is the place where the Holy One, blessed be He, told me to sacrifice my son." He then said to [Yitzchak], "Yitzchak, my son, do you see what I see?"
>
> "Yes," he replied.
>
> Then he said to his two servants, "Do you see what I see?"
>
> "No," they answered.
>
> [Avraham told them,] "Since you do not see it, stay here with the donkey."
>
> *(Bereishit Rabbah 56:1–2)*

Only Avraham and Yitzchak saw the cloud, or the spiritual entity, hovering above the mountain. When Avraham tells his two servants (the young men referred to earlier in the text) to remain with the donkey, we note that the Hebrew word for donkey is "*chamor,*" which is related to the word *chomer* (physical). He is saying, "If you cannot see the spiritual cloud hovering on the mountain, your perception is exclusively of the physical, and you have no choice but to remain here with the physical."[1]

When Avraham and Yitzchak reach the designated spot, Yitzchak is tied down to the altar. Avraham was never commanded to tie Yitzchak. The Hebrew word for "binding" is *akeidah,* and the offering of Yitzchak has been called throughout the ages "*akeidat Yitzchak,*" the binding of Yitzchak. Why did Avraham bind Yitzchak if God had never asked him to do so?

Again, the Sages in the Midrash fill in the missing information. According to the Midrash, Yitzchak is a willing, enthusiastic participant in this event. He lies down on the altar, stretches out his neck, and says to his father,

> "Father, the soul is willing, but the flesh is weak. Tie me down in order to restrain me, to prevent me from flinching upon seeing the blade."
>
> *(Bereishit Rabbah 56:8)*[2]

According to the Midrash, the idea of the binding was completely Yitzchak's. Perhaps this is why throughout history it has been called *akeidat Yitzchak,* the binding of Yitzchak, and not simply the "tenth test."

As the knife is about to make its mark on Yitzchak, a voice calls from Heaven, instructing Avraham to stop. Yitzchak will be saved; there will be no human sacrifice that day or any other day in the Jewish tradition. A ram is sacrificed in Yitzchak's stead. After Avraham is blessed by an angel, we are told,

---

1 The *Zohar* and Maharal have expanded teachings on this topic. We will return to this concept in our discussion of *Chayei Sarah.*

2 See *Tanchuma,* section 46.

> Avraham returned to his young men, and they rose and went together to Be'er Sheva.
>
> *(Bereishit 22:19)*

But what about Yitzchak? Why does the Torah not tell us about his descent? Did Yitzchak come down from the mountain?[1] Did he want to come down from the mountain?

The next time we see Yitzchak, it is three years later. He is standing in a field, eyes gazing Heavenward, praying to God.

> Yitzchak went out to pray in the field toward evening. He lifted up his eyes and saw, and behold the camels were coming.
>
> *(Ibid. 24:63)*

Later in his life, Yitzchak became blind. The Sages explain that the origin of his blindness was the tears of the angels which were shed during those moments on the mountain, when it appeared as if his father's knife would kill him.[2] Evidently, Yitzchak was in some way affected by that experience on the mountain. His sight or perception was forever altered by the events on the mountain.

If the test for Avraham was to perform an act which was against his nature, he surely passed with flying colors. But what about Yitzchak? If his personality is identified with the concept of *din*, perhaps his test was in coming down the mountain, joining the rest of the world, relating to God through the attribute of *chesed*. Did Yitzchak succeed in passing his test?

Our Sages relate the following scene which will take place in the future:

> What does the verse mean, "You are our father, for Avraham did not know us and Yisrael did not recognize us. You, God, are our Father, our Redeemer; forever is Your Name" (*Yeshayah* 63:16).

---

1 See the remarkable comments of Ibn Ezra on this verse — specifically the concept that he is rejecting, that Yitzchak may have actually died.

2 *Bereishit Rabbah*, 56:8.

In the future, God will say to Avraham, "Your children have sinned against Me."

Avraham will say to Him, "Master of the universe, wipe them out for the sake of the sanctification of Your Name."

God will say, "Perhaps Yaakov, who experienced difficulty raising his children, will ask for mercy for the Jewish people." God will say to him, "Your children have sinned against Me."

[Yaakov] will say to Him, "Master of the universe, wipe them out for the sake of the sanctification of Your Name."

God...will then say to Yitzchak, "Your children have sinned against Me."

[Yitzchak] will say to Him, "Master of the universe, my children? My children, and not Your children? When the Jews said, 'We will do and we will listen,' You called them 'My first-born son,' and now You call them my children, and not Your children? Besides, how much did they sin? How many years are the years of a man's life — seventy? Subtract twenty, for which a person is not punished [a person is not punished for the sins of the first twenty years of his life]. You are left with fifty. Subtract twenty-five, which are evenings, and You are left with twenty-five. Subtract twelve and a half which a person uses to pray, eat, and answer nature's call, and You are left with twelve and a half. If You can tolerate all of this, then good; if not, then let us split it, half for You and half for me. If you want to say that all of the years of their sins are on me, remember that I sacrificed my soul for You."

[Thereupon,] they shall commence and say, "For you [Yitzchak] are our father." Then Yitzchak shall say to them, "Instead of praising me, praise the Holy One, blessed be He," and Yitzchak shall show them the Holy One, blessed be He, with their own eyes. Immediately they shall lift up their eyes on high and exclaim, "You, God, are our Father, our Redeemer; forever is Your Name."

(Shabbat 89b)

In this amazing passage, we are told that in the future, Avraham and Yaakov will not stand in defense of the Jews who have sinned. Their response to God is "wipe them out." Yitzchak, however, engages God in negotiations reminiscent of Avraham's conversation with God regarding the fate of the cities of Sedom and Amorah. Yitzchak will not tolerate the Jews' being punished. He argues, he negotiates, and finally pulls out his trump card: in the merit of his being willing to sacrifice himself, God must forgive the people.

In this passage, Yitzchak displays an incredible amount of understanding and *chesed* for his people. Why is it that Yitzchak displays more *chesed* than his father Avraham, whose very nature was *chesed*? Apparently the trait of *chesed* which was acquired by Yitzchak is stronger than the trait of *chesed* which came naturally to Avraham. Yitzchak becomes a *baal teshuvah* vis à vis *chesed*, with the elevated stance ascribed to *baalei teshuvah* by our Sages (see *Berachot* 34b and *Sanhedrin* 99a). Apparently, a trait acquired is stronger than a natural trait.

At the end of the day, Yitzchak does descend the mountain. He does develop the trait of *chesed*, and when he does, he surpasses even Avraham himself. Such is the merit of a trait acquired. It was not easy for Yitzchak to acquire this trait, but the Gemara tells us that once he does, the entire Jewish people will be saved on its merit.

Parashat Chayei Sarah

The First Matriarch

Parashat Chayei Sarah marks the transition of matriarchs from Sarah to Rivkah. A great deal of the narrative is devoted to the death and burial of Sarah on the one hand, and the search for wife for Yitzchak on the other. Rabbi Yosef Dov Soloveitchik, *zt"l*, once noted that with the death of Sarah, "Avraham takes leave of the world stage." Despite Avraham's relative longevity, subsequent to Sarah's demise, Avraham seems to disappear. He ceases to be a major player; the mantle of leadership passes to Yitzchak — and Rivkah. Avraham and Sarah were apparently complete partners, and therefore the death of the one causes the focus to be removed from the other. Avraham was keenly aware of this partnership. Hence, as soon as the burial and mourning period ended, a replacement for Sarah was sought.

The fact that Avraham and Sarah were indeed partners can be discerned from the very outset. In *Parashat Lech Lecha*, we are told that when Avraham and Sarah headed toward the Land of Canaan, they brought with them "the *nefesh* which they made in Charan" (*Bereishit* 12:6), which is understood as the people whom they converted while in Charan. Rashi explains:

> Avraham converted the men and Sarah converted the women.

Avraham and Sarah were equals, each working in his or her own realm.

This observation gives us some insight into the spiritual greatness of the patriarchs and the matriarchs. Upon Sarah's death, Avraham eulogizes Sarah, explaining to the world who this woman was and what had been lost with her death. Who was Sarah? She was obviously more than just the woman who prepared the food for Avraham's guests. She clearly took a much more proactive role in educating and inspiring other women.

Of all of her students, one stands out in particular: Hagar. Hagar is introduced in chapter 16 of *Bereishit* as an Egyptian servant of Sarah. The Midrash (cited by Rashi) gives us some biographical information about Hagar:

> Hagar was Pharaoh's daughter. When Pharaoh saw what was done on Sarah's behalf in his house, he took his daughter and gave her to Sarah, saying, "Better that my daughter should be a handmaid in this house than a mistress in another house."
>
> *(Bereishit Rabbah 45:1)*

When it became apparent to Sarah that she would be unable to bear children, she sought an appropriate partner for Avraham, one with the most illustrious lineage that she could find. A lesser woman than Sarah might have been afraid to bring in such "competition," but Sarah felt that if Avraham was to have a child, that child must be the greatest child possible. In an act of complete self-sacrifice, Sarah invites the beautiful Egyptian princess to become a partner with her husband.

> "Sarai, Avram's wife, took Hagar the Egyptian..." (*Bereishit* 16:3). She persuaded [took] her with words: "Fortunate are you to be united to so holy a man."
>
> *(Bereishit Rabbah 45:3)*

Hagar, who had been the primary disciple of Sarah, became pregnant and bore a child. She concluded from this that God now favored her, and not Sarah, and that Sarah was an unworthy partner for Avraham. She began to conduct herself as the wife.

> Hagar would say, "My mistress Sarah is not inwardly what she is outwardly; she appears to be a righteous woman, but she is not. She has not merited to conceive all these years, whereas I conceived in one night."
>
> *(Ibid., 4)*

One can understand and perhaps even sympathize with the position of Hagar. She had been born into a family of aristocracy, but the search for truth had led her away from her father's pagan world. Avraham's genius enraptured her, and she came to believe that it was better for her to serve in that house than to rule Egypt. But now she was given the opportunity to rule in Avraham's house. She believed that she had received a Divine sign that she, who was born to be queen, would indeed be the queen — of Avraham's nascent movement.

Hagar's mistake was in assuming that Avraham alone led the people, that he alone was a spiritual giant. She failed to recognize that it was a partnership, the combination of Avraham and Sarah, which was the basis for the great spiritual movement she herself had become a part of.

Sarah did understand: Sarah responds, not out of selfishness, not out of jealousy. Sarah understands that she and Avraham are partners and equals. At the point where Hagar gets carried away, Sarah pushes her aside and causes her pain. This is not the petty action of a hurt woman, but rather a calculated act by a great woman. Later, when Hagar's son, Yishmael, also exhibits negative behavior, Sarah informs Avraham it is time to send Hagar away. Avraham finds this quite difficult. But, of course, Sarah was right. God says to Avraham:

> Whatever Sarah, your wife, says you shall listen.
>
> *(Bereishit 21:12)*

The partnership was between the two of them. Without Sarah, there cannot be an Avraham. The covenantal community requires two leaders, a man and a woman, Avraham and Sarah.

We can further appreciate the greatness of Sarah by exploring a second passage in the Midrash, cited by Rashi to explain a verse at the end of our parashah:

> Yitzchak brought her [Rivkah] to the tent of his mother, Sarah. He took Rivkah and she became a wife for him. He loved her, and he was consoled after his mother.
>
> *(Ibid. 24:67)*

Rashi explains, based on the Midrash,

> "To the tent of his mother, Sarah" — as long as his mother, Sarah, was alive, there was a candle lit from one Friday night to the next. Her dough was blessed, and a cloud was tied to her tent. When Sarah died, all these things ceased. When Rivkah entered the tent, all these phenomena returned.

The reference to "a cloud tied to her tent" is obscure. It is the only time this usage appears in Midrash. There is, however, a description of a cloud tied to something else — a mountain. As Avraham headed toward the *akeidah,* he looked up and saw a mountain with a peculiar cloud tied to its top. Yitzchak shared this vision, but the others who accompanied them saw only the mountain (*Bereishit Rabbah* 56:1–2).

Since the two young servants saw only the mountain, the physical reality, and not the cloud which represents the metaphysical, Avraham told them to remain with the *chamor*, the donkey. The word *chamor* comes from the word *chomer*, physical. Only Avraham and Yitzchak see the cloud tied to the mountain, and only they will continue the spiritual journey up the mountain.

Again, the concept of a cloud tied to a mountain makes its only appearance in Midrashic literature with regard to Avraham and Yitzchak. No one else ever sees such a cloud. Interestingly, Avraham is described in the Midrash as one of three people who rides on a donkey, and the other two are Moshe and Mashiach.

The prophet Zecharyah describes Mashiach as a poor man riding on a donkey. Citing this teaching, the Gemara teaches that there are two possible scenarios of the coming of Mashiach:

> Rabbi Yehoshua contrasted two verses: It is written, "Behold, one like the son of man came with the clouds of heaven" (*Daniel* 7:13), and [elsewhere] it is written, "[Behold, your king will come to you...] lowly, and riding upon a donkey" (*Zecharyah* 9:9). If they [the Jewish people] are meritorious, [Mashiach will come] with the clouds of Heaven; if not, [he will be] lowly and riding upon a donkey.
>
> *(Sanhedrin 98a)*

Either clouds or on a donkey; either sooner or later. The choice is ours. The *Zohar* explains that the role of Mashiach is to ride on the *chamor*, to subdue the physical.

> Those of the right are all merged in one called "donkey," and that is the donkey of which it is written, "You shall not plow with an ox and a donkey together" (*Devarim* 22:10). That is also the donkey which the King Mashiach shall control.
>
> *(Zohar, Bemidbar 207a)*

In Jewish thought, there is ideally no tension between the physical world and the spiritual world. The physical is to be elevated and used in spiritual contexts. The physical is a means toward an end. The tragic error of so many people and nations is seeing the physical as an end unto itself. Therefore, Mashiach is described as the one who rides on top of the *chamor*, the physical, subdues the physical, and thus ushers in the Messianic Age. Similarly, Avraham, who knows how to subdue the physical, transcends the physical and ascends the mountain. He and Yitzchak see the cloud, for they are in touch with something beyond the physical.

The case of the matriarchs is similar. Sarah and Rivkah had a cloud tied to their tent, like the cloud tied to the mountain in the *akeidah*. They, too, had a metaphysical experience, but within their own tents. Despite the fact that they lived in a physical world, they were tied or connected to the spiritual world. Avraham and Sarah,

Yitzchak and Rivkah were equals — all of them, spiritual giants.

But what was the specific greatness of Sarah? We are told that Sarah died at the age of 127. Rashi (to *Bereishit* 23:1) comments, based on the Midrash, that when she was one hundred, she was like a twenty-year-old regarding sin. Just as a twenty-year-old is free of sin, for one is not held responsible for his actions until the age of twenty, so, too, was Sarah clean of all sin at one hundred years of age.

When she was twenty, the Midrash continues, she was like a seven-year-old in regard to beauty. Here, the Midrash is somewhat difficult to understand. If anything, it should have been the other way around — as sinless as a seven-year-old and as beautiful as a twenty-year-old! Rabbi Shamshon Refael Hirsch explains that in truth, a seven-year-old is quite beautiful — perhaps not in a sexual or sensual sense, but with the beauty of a child. We would think that the idea of sinlessness would be more appropriate for a seven-year-old than for a twenty-year-old. But Rabbi Hirsch points out that a seven-year-old simply does not have the opportunity to sin in the manner that an adult of twenty years does.

Rabbi Yosef Dov Soloveitchik, *zt"l*, explained[1] that the greatness of Sarah and her role within the covenantal community can be culled from the words of Rashi: She was one hundred, she was twenty, she was seven. Most people pass from one stage of their lives to the next, leaving the previous stage behind, perhaps taking with them some fond memories. But Sarah retained something from every stage of her life even after she moved on to the next one. Each one of these ages — one hundred, twenty, seven — has something unique about it. A seven-year-old has innocence; a twenty-year-old has strength; a hundred-year-old has wisdom. The secret of the greatness of Sarah was that throughout her entire life she was one hundred and twenty and seven.

Rashi comments on the words "the years of the life of Sarah"

---

1 See Rabbi Abraham Besdin, *Man of Faith in the Modern World — Reflections of the Rov*, vol. 2, p. 83ff.

that "all were equal for the good." At every point in her life, Sarah remained the same. She was always as innocent as a seven-year-old, with the strength, determination, and idealism of a twenty-year-old, and with the wisdom of a one hundred-year-old.

Let us take a deeper look at each of these traits.[1] Innocence is a quality necessary for prayer — in order for a person to pray, he needs to feel that God is really listening. Adults often become cynical and lose the ability to stand before God and share their innermost secrets and aspiration. A child, on the other hand, has not developed such cynicism and thus still possesses the ability to pray. When we pray, we need to feel that God is our Father in Heaven; we are His children. Sarah always felt that way.

The greatness of a twenty-year-old is physical strength and idealism. A twenty-year-old feels that he can change the world. He feels that he can do just about anything. There are no limits, no rules, only potential. This is how Sarah retained the strengths of a twenty-year-old — by always remaining idealistic, never feeling limited.

A one-hundred-year-old possesses wisdom. After many years of living, a person gains the perspective which only experience can give. Great sages are almost always older people whose skills have not diminished over the years. Quite the opposite: they possess wisdom that transcends "book knowledge." Sarah always had this wisdom. Similarly, Rivkah even at a tender age was able to transcend her station and relate to others as a person far beyond her years.[2]

Sarah was always one hundred, and twenty, and seven. Throughout her life she possessed all these skills. This is the greatness of Sarah, the greatness which made her our first matriarch.

---

1 These ideals are also Rabbi Yosef Dov Soloveitchik's, although Rabbi Besdin's book presents them in a somewhat truncated form (compared to Rav Soloveitchik's lecture on the topic).

2 This was observed by my *chavruta*, Shlomo Simkin.

Parashat Toldot[1]

Yaakov and Eisav

In *Parashat Toldot* we confront two brothers, Yaakov and Eisav. Since we are descendants of Yaakov, we know which brother we are supposed to be "rooting" for, yet our identification with Yaakov raises some questions: The Torah tells us that Yitzchak loved Eisav, which is very difficult for us to understand or accept. Why would Yitzchak love Eisav? We are told that God Himself hated Eisav!

> "I loved you," said God, "yet you say, 'For what have You loved us?'
>
> "Was not Eisav Yaakov's brother?" says God. "Yet I loved Yaakov, and I hated Eisav, and laid waste his mountains and gave his heritage to the jackals of the wilderness."
>
> *(Malachi 1:2–3)*

When Yitzchak grew older, why did he wish to bless Eisav, who was even hated by God? We would have thought that Yaakov would receive the blessing.

The key to understanding the relationship between Yitzchak and Eisav, as well as the relationship between Eisav and Yaakov,

---

1 Many of the ideas discussed in this parashah and next one are based on ideas which I first heard from Rabbi Mordechai Elon. However, the formulations and conclusions are my own.

may be found in the beginning of the parashah.

Rivkah was pregnant, and she was experiencing extreme, perhaps unnatural, pain.

> God said to her, "Two nations are in your womb, and two peoples shall be separated from your bowels. One people shall be stronger than the other people, and the elder shall serve the younger."
>
> *(Bereishit 25:23)*

Rivkah alone was informed of the different destinies of her children. Apparently, Yitzchak was unaware of their duality, and, consequently, of their separate missions.

> The first [baby] came out red all over like a hairy garment; and they called his name "Eisav." After that his brother came out, his hand grasping Eisav's heel, and he [Yitzchak] called his name Yaakov.
>
> *(Ibid., 25–26)*

It is interesting that both parents name the firstborn, while only the father names the second. In fact, nowhere in the Torah does Rivkah refer to her second son as Yaakov. She always calls him "my son." Perhaps this is because she knows that his identity is not determined by his relationship with his brother. Perhaps she realizes that he will receive a different name.[1]

> The boys grew, and Eisav became a skillful hunter, a man of the field, while Yaakov was a pure man, living in tents.
>
> *(Ibid., 27)*

We would have thought that the father of the Jewish people would prefer the man of the tent to the hunter. Why, then, does Yitzchak prefer Eisav?

The Torah tells us:

> Yitzchak loved Eisav, because he ate of his venison; but Rivkah loved Yaakov.
>
> *(Ibid., 28)*

1 Rabbi Mordechai Elon made this observation.

Yitzchak loved Eisav because *"tzayid b'fiv"* (literally, "the hunting was in his mouth"), while Rivkah loved Yaakov. It is strange that Yitzchak's love for Eisav is conditional, *"talui b'davar,"* while Rivkah's love for Yaakov is unconditional. Yitzchak's love is directly connected to Eisav's hunting — he loved the meat that Eisav fed him. A most perplexing relationship; it would seem that the adventurous Eisav caught Yitzchak's fancy. Can this be the entire story?

The story of how Yaakov surreptitiously took the blessings from his father that were destined for Eisav is well known. This, coupled with the Torah's declaration of Yitzchak's love for Eisav, lead many to assume that Yitzchak loved Eisav more than he loved Yaakov, and that Yitzchak had felt that the legacy of Avraham would be manifest in Eisav. This is not the case. When Yaakov goes in to his father's room to take the blessing intended for Eisav's, Yitzchak says:

> God will give you from the dew of the heavens and the fat of the earth, and the fullness of grain and wine. Nations will be subservient to you, and peoples will bow to you. You will be your brother's master, and the sons of your mother will bow to you. Those you curse shall be accursed and those you bless shall be blessed.
>
> *(Ibid. 27:28–29)*

The blessing is certainly a beautiful one. It speaks of wealth and power. What it neglects to mention is a spiritual mission or message. When Eisav stands before his father and understands that his brother, Yaakov, has taken the blessing intended for him, Eisav says to Yitzchak, "Bless me as well, Father" (ibid., 34).

> He [Yitzchak] said, "Your brother came in deception and took your blessing."
>
> *(Ibid., 35)*

It would seem that Yitzchak has "run out" of blessings. However, when Yaakov is about to leave home, Yitzchak summons

Yaakov and blesses him:

> The Almighty God will bless you and make you multiply, and you will become a great nation. He will grant you the blessing of Avraham, for you and your descendants, to inherit the land of your sojournings which the Lord gave to Avraham.
>
> *(Ibid. 28:3–4)*

Evidently, Yitzchak did have another blessing to give. This "blessing of Avraham" and the Land of Israel, a spiritual blessing, was always intended for Yaakov, while the blessing of power had always been intended for Eisav. However, because of Rivkah's intervention, Yaakov received both blessings.

Yitzchak apparently felt that his spiritual son needed only spiritual blessings, while his physical son needed the physical blessing. Rivkah's understanding was quite different; she felt that the spiritual cannot subsist without the physical. Divine providence agreed with Rivkah.

Perhaps Yitzchak pitied Eisav, and he felt that if Eisav would be a hunter, absorbed in the physical world, he would be better off prospering by God's hand than trying any of his own unsavory tactics. What we can conclude is that the love of Yitzchak for Eisav was, indeed, conditional, and therefore limited.

The Sages hint at a deeper understanding of the text. When Yaakov stands before his father to receive the blessing, Yitzchak is under the impression that he is Eisav.

> [Yaakov] came near and kissed [his father], and [Yitzchak] smelled the scent of his clothes and blessed him. He [Yitzchak] said, "Behold the scent of my son is like the scent of a field that is blessed by God."
>
> *(Ibid. 27:27)*

What is Yitzchak smelling?

> There is no harsher scent than the stench of goats that was on his clothing, yet the text says he "smells the scent of his

clothes and blesses him"! Rather, when the patriarch Yaakov entered to his father, Gan Eden entered with him.... And when Eisav entered to his father, Gehinnom entered with him.

(Bereishit Rabbah 65:22)

The observation of the Midrash is striking: Yaakov enters in clothing saturated with blood and sweat, and Yitzchak speaks of "the scent of a field that is blessed by God," meaning Gan Eden. We noted earlier that Yitzchak's spiritual identity is somehow related to "the field." After the *akeidah*, the text does not describe the descent of Yitzchak from the mountain. We do not see Yitzchak in the next number of sections in the *Chumash*. He is absent from the description of the death and burial of Sarah. Even when Avraham's servant searches for a bride for him, Yitzchak is absent. The next time we see Yitzchak is when

Yitzchak went out to pray in the field toward evening.

(Bereishit 24:63)

Yitzchak, who was last seen on an altar, ready and willing to be sacrificed to God, now stands in a field and gazes Heavenward. Specifically from a field, Yitzchak searches for God. What was Yitzchak trying to accomplish in the field? The answer lies in the scent of Gan Eden, which emerged from a time prior to the sin of Adam, before man is cursed to work the field.

If the physical realm can be elevated in the service of God, then the sin of Adam can be rectified. When Yaakov enters and Yitzchak smells Paradise, Yitzchak believes that his son has succeeded in mending the world, returning that scent of Gan Eden to the world. Of course, when the real Eisav enters, the gates of Hell are opened, and Yitzchak sadly realizes how far the world is from perfection. Yaakov, who sat and learned in the tents, and not Eisav, who hunted, had the scent of Paradise on him. Perfection will not come from the man of the fields; it will come from the *ish tam*, the "complete man," Yaakov.

Bringing perfection to the world will not be an easy task.

Yaakov's odyssey will take him on a circuitous route far from the tents which he has called home. He is forced now to leave the tents, to become a man of the field. Just as Avraham had to grow in a trait against his nature, so too, Yaakov will have to leave his natural habitat and become a worldly man — a man of the field. As we have seen, the greatness of the patriarchs was in creating new aspects of self, new avenues toward the worship of God.

> Yaakov came out of the field in the evening, and Leah went out to meet him.
>
> *(Ibid. 30:16)*

Things have now come full circle; Yaakov, the pure man of the tents, has now become a man of the field. He has taken the responsibility of Eisav, in addition to his own mission.

As a result of this meeting with Leah in the field, two children enter the world — Yissachar and Zevulun. These two sons will have a different type of relationship: They will succeed where Yaakov and Eisav failed.[1]

> Zevulun was involved in business, while Yissachar was involved in Torah.
>
> *(Bereishit Rabbah 99:16)*

> Zevulun comes before Yissachar [in the blessings Yaakov gave before his death] though surely Yissachar was older than Zevulun, since their birth is thus recorded: Yissachar Zevulun. When then is it so? Because Zevulun engaged in commerce, while Yissachar studied Torah, and Zevulun came and provided him with sustenance.
>
> *(Ibid., 9)*

Despite their differences, Yissachar and Zevulun were partners, working together toward one common goal. Perhaps this was Yitzchak's dream, that his two sons work together to mend the world. The dream was not realized by Yitzchak's children, for Eisav

---

1 See *Sefat Emet, Toldot* 5651.

did not accept the responsibility of serving God. Only Yaakov's children are therefore able to bring their grandfather's dream to its fruition.

With this in mind, we can turn to another difficult section of the parashah:

> Yaakov cooked pottage, and Eisav came from the field, exhausted. Eisav said to Yaakov, "Give me, I beg you, some of that red pottage; for I am exhausted." Therefore his name was called "Edom."
>
> Yaakov said, "Sell me this day your birthright."
>
> Eisav said, "Behold, I am at the point of death. Why do I need this birthright?"
>
> Yaakov said, "Swear to me this day." He swore to him, and he sold his birthright to Yaakov.
>
> Then Yaakov gave Eisav bread and pottage of lentils. He ate and drank, and rose and went on his way.
>
> Thus Eisav despised his birthright.
>
> *(Bereishit 25:29–34)*

This negotiation seems strange; how can Yaakov be so petty as to demand the birthright from his hungry brother? The text, however, did not say that Eisav was hungry, but exhausted. This exhaustion indicated to Yaakov, and to his mother, Rivkah, that Yitzchak's vision would not be realized. Yitzchak believed that his two sons would join forces, Eisav in the field and Yaakov in the tents — as Yissachar and Zevulun would later do — but Rivkah knew better. God had spoken to her, and she knew that only her younger son would achieve greatness.

> God said to her, "Two nations are in your womb, and two peoples shall be separated from your bowels. One people shall be stronger than the other people, and the elder shall serve the younger."
>
> *(Ibid., 23)*

When Eisav came in from the field tired and asking for food,

Yaakov realized that his mother had been correct: His father's dream would not come true. Eisav was tired of his role and no longer wished to fulfill his part in the partnership. If Yaakov had to provide food for Eisav, then Eisav was undeserving of his birthright. Yaakov would adopt both roles.[1]

Was Yitzchak wrong in his expectations for his two sons? In theory, this type of an arrangement could work, though not between Yaakov and Eisav. At least, not at that point in time. Yitzchak saw things in an idealistic, pure manner. He saw the world from his own particular vantage point, at the top of an altar high upon a holy mountain. Yitzchak's vision was forever affected by his awesome experience:

> [Why did Yitzchak become blind?] As a result of that event [the *akeidah*]; for when our father Avraham bound his son, Yitzchak, the ministering angels wept, as it says, "Behold, the valiant ones cry outside; the angels of peace weep bitterly" (*Yeshayah* 33:7). Tears dropped from their eyes into his and left their mark upon them, and so when he became old his eyes dimmed.... Another interpretation of "[Yitzchak's eyes became dull] from seeing" is: [He became blind] through [seeing] that event [the *akeidah*]; for when our father Avraham bound Yitzchak on the altar, he lifted up his eyes Heavenward and gazed at the *Shechinah*.
>
> *(Bereishit Rabbah 45:10)*

The name *Yitzchak* means "will laugh," implying the future tense. Yitzchak's entire perspective is in the future. He sees only the future, the way that things should be. Eisav's superficiality apparently escaped him. The vicissitudes of experience which his son Yaakov would have to endure while fulfilling both roles eludes him. But Yitzchak's vision will be realized one day, at the end of history, and Eisav will indeed join Yaakov in a joint mission:

[Yaakov promised Eisav he would join him in *Sei'ir*, but] we

1 Rabbi Mordechai Elon made this observation.

have searched the whole Scriptures and we do not find that Yaakov ever went to Eisav in Mount Sei'ir. Is it possible that Yaakov, the truthful, had deceived him [Eisav]? [Certainly not.] When would he come to him? In the messianic era, as it says, "The liberators will ascend Mount Tzion to judge the Mountain of Eisav..." (*Ovadyah* 1:21).

(Bereishit Rabbah 78:14)

Either the descendants of Eisav will join us of their own volition or we will have to seek them out, either a partnership or a judgment:

> God shall be King over the whole earth; on that day God shall be One and His Name One.

(Zecharyah 14:9)

In any event, at the end of days laughter will fill the world; the laughter and joy of Yitzchak, the joy of a world perfected, as the verse says, "Then our mouths will be filled with laughter" (*Tehillim* 126:2).

Then, but not now, will we experience the laughter.

Parashat Vayeitzei

Antecedents of a Nation

Yaakov leaves Be'er Sheva and heads toward Charan. He leaves laden with blessings, but he has no place to sleep. Ironically, all the blessings which he possesses do not provide him with any shelter from the elements. He uses stones for a pillow. There, on the ground, he dreams of a ladder which reaches into the Heavens, with angels of God ascending and descending. Then God appears to Him and promises to give him the Land of Israel and protect him wherever he goes.

When he awakens, Yaakov is afraid:

> He said, "How awesome is this place! This is none other than the House of God, and this is the gate to Heaven."
>
> When Yaakov awoke in the morning, he took the stone that was under his head, set it up as a monument, and poured oil over it. And he called the name of the place "Beit El" [House of God]; however, Luz was its original name.
>
> Yaakov vowed, "...This stone which I have put up as a pillar will become a House of God."
>
> *(Bereishit 28:17–22)*

Yaakov encounters God, perhaps for the first time. His immediate response is to erect a monument, a *matzeivah*, which he vows to transform into a House of God upon his return to the Land of Israel.

His behavior is understandable: He is but one individual, despite the many potential blessings bestowed on him. His vow is an expression of his aspirations. He hopes that upon his return he will realize this potential and the blessings bestowed upon him will come to their fruition, just as this one rock will become an entire House of God.

A subtle theme running through *Parashiyot Vayeitzei* and *Vayishlach* is illustrated by the building of the *matzeivah* and the subsequent building of an altar. The underlying issue of these two parashiyot is the transformation of Yaakov from a solitary, lonely individual on the run to the leader of a clan which will in turn become a great nation. The pillar symbolizes the individual's spiritual quest, while the "House of God" symbolizes a nation's place of worship.

However, there is a problem — a technical and legal problem, but a problem nonetheless. The Torah states:

> You shall not set up any pillar [*matzeivah*] which God, your Lord, despises.
>
> *(Devarim 16:22)*

Rashi notes that a *matzeivah* is made of but one stone, while an altar is made of many. The former was despised because of its identification with Canaanite idolatry.

> Even though it [the making of *matzeivot*] was a beloved practice during the time of the patriarchs, it is now despised.
>
> *(Rashi, Devarim 16:22)*

If a *matzeivah* is something despised by God, why does Yaakov erect one? While it is interesting to analyze the religious behavior displayed by the forefathers, it would certainly be unfair to judge them through the prism of contemporary religious practice. Nonetheless, it is still disturbing to find Yaakov doing something that is "despised by God."

The halachic issues raised here are certainly of interest, but beyond our present scope: How is an acceptable practice metamorphosized into an unacceptable one? How does something beloved by God become contemptible?

The answer to this question lies in the essence of the religious practice on the one hand and the identity of the practitioner on the other. A *matzeivah* made of one stone was an acceptable form of practice before the emergence of the Jewish nation. When the patriarchs lived, they were essentially individuals who encompassed national aspirations and potential. Therefore, one stone reflected their individuality. However, once the nation comes into existence, relating to God must be via an altar of many stones gathered together, reflecting the unity which forms a nation out of many individuals.

After Yaakov's eleven children are born and Yaakov heads back home, God appears to him with the following command:

> Go up to Beit El and dwell there and build an altar to God, who appeared to you when you fled from Eisav, your brother.
>
> *(Bereishit 35:1)*

Here God commands Yaakov to build an altar; evidently, the change in status from individual to nation has occurred. The construction is no longer with a single, individual rock, but with many small ones. Upon analysis of the section preceding God's command, we find that Yaakov was not completely aware of the impending change, or of the fact that it perhaps should already have taken place.

Yaakov had traveled to Charan to marry and start a family. He returns to Israel with his wives and eleven children after extricating himself, with great difficulty, from Lavan's house. This separation is permeated with great theological significance, as is. This idea may be illustrated by a celebrated passage in the Haggadah, where Lavan is compared unfavorably to Pharaoh:

> For Pharaoh sought to annihilate only the males, while Lavan sought to uproot everything.

What did the Sages see in the text that elicited this shocking contrast? The Biblical text does not recount any attempt by Lavan to kill his own children or grandchildren, Yaakov's wives and their sons. Quite the opposite is the case: Lavan seems truly wounded when Yaakov takes his leave. And yet, Yaakov recognizes that he must leave Lavan's house, make a clean break, and return to the Land of Israel. The sinister act of Lavan, then, was not attempted murder; rather, it was the seduction of Yaakov to assimilate. Yaakov recognized that he must flee Lavan's house and return to the Land of Israel if there was to be any hope of fulfilling his destiny.

> Yaakov outwitted Lavan the Aramite, by leaving without a word.
>
> *(Bereishit 31:20)*

When Lavan catches up with him and confronts him, Yaakov explains himself:

> "Because I was afraid; for I said perhaps you would take by force your daughters from me...."
>
> Lavan answered Yaakov, "These daughters are my daughters, and these children are my children...."
>
> *(Ibid., 31–43)*

Lavan's perspective was that Yaakov and his family were in fact Lavan's family, and they were therefore one people. Yaakov's desire to take leave seems somewhat strange, elitist. Lavan was within his rights to charge Yaakov with creating differences between them; this same charge, in fact, follows the Jews through many generations.

By separating himself, Yaakov expresses his separatist religious or nationalistic aspirations. Removing his family from Lavan's house is a declaration of independence: It is Yaakov's family, not Lavan's. Different destinies await Yaakov and Lavan respectively. The time had come for Yaakov to recognize his family as a nation.

Yaakov should have returned to Beit El immediately and built the House of God, but before he does this the episode of Dinah unfolds. Let us look at the text:

> Dinah, the daughter of Leah, whom she bore to Yaakov, went out to see the daughters of the land. Shechem the son of Chamor the Chivi, prince of the land, saw her. He took her and lay with her and abused her.
>
> *(Ibid. 34:1–2)*

Dinah goes out to befriend the neighbors, a natural impulse; upon moving to a new land, she seeks companionship. Apparently, Dinah does not feel any limitations, and she has no qualms about leaving her family. If her action is understood as that of an individual girl going to visit her neighbors, we would not have given it a second thought, had it not been for the unfortunate results. However, if the Jews are now a nation, then her step constitutes a breaking of barriers, a totally unacceptable action.

Dinah is described as a daughter of Yaakov. Shechem is described as the son of Chamor, prince of the land. If these two descriptions are intended to be parallel, then the incident must be viewed as the daughter of Yaakov, leader or king of the Jewish nation, being abused by the son of the leader of the Chivi. If the son of a leader attacks the daughter of another leader, the result is not a simple family squabble; it is, at least, an international incident, and, at worst, war.

Yaakov seems to view the episode as no more than an unfortunate incident, on a personal or familial level. His children, on the other hand, see Shechem's actions as a declaration of war. They seem to sense that which eludes Yaakov.

> Yaakov heard that his daughter, Dinah, had been defiled.... The sons of Yaakov came from the field when they heard. The men [Yaakov's sons] were saddened and greatly incensed, for [they felt] a disgrace was brought upon Israel by lying with the daughter of Yaakov, a deed which should not be done.
>
> *(Ibid., 5,7)*

Yaakov hears that his daughter has been defiled; his sons hear that Israel has been disgraced. The sons see the act in a national context.[1] For the first time, the term *Israel* is used to describe what was heretofore Yaakov's family. The shift from private, individual life to national existence and experience has occurred in the minds of the sons. Hadn't their father led them out of the house of their grandfather in order to set them apart, to form a separate entity? To them, their unique national destiny, which was clear and unequivocal, was already playing itself out.

Ironically, Yaakov seems unaware that the time has come to be a nation. His response to the sons' call for action is instructive: as individuals, as a family, we are out of our league, he explains. Perhaps in the future, when we become something more, we will have the wherewithal to respond differently, but now is not the time. How different is the viewpoint of the sons, who see themselves already as part of the future, possessing a responsibility to the coming generations of the Jewish people who will look to their actions for spiritual guidance. The text contains their impassioned response:

> Can we let our sister be taken for a whore?
>
> *(Ibid., 31)*

Targum Yonatan (Yerushalmi) reads between the lines of their response:

> What will future generations of the Jewish people understand when they read about these events in their synagogues each year?!

"What sort of role models are we to be?" the brothers are saying. "Shechem has committed an act of war, and we have a responsibility to answer that challenge and to set national standards."

Immediately after the Dinah episode, God calls upon Yaakov to go to Beit El and build the altar, thus fulfilling the vow he made when he fled from Eisav. God Himself sees Yaakov's family as the people of Israel; at this point, worship must be formalized. Perhaps the entire incident with Dinah might have been avoided had

---

1 Rabbi Mordechai Elon made this observation.

Yaakov understood this new status earlier, at the point where the term *nation* was used for the first time: immediately prior to the incident with Dinah, after leaving the house of Lavan, when Yaakov prepared for his meeting with Eisav.

> Yaakov was greatly afraid and distressed, and he divided the nation that was with him.
>
> *(Ibid. 32:8)*

There is another change of identity which runs through *Parashat Veyeitzei.* Let us return to the beginning of the parashah.

> And he called the name of the place "Beit El"; however, Luz was its original name.
>
> *(Ibid. 27:19)*

Upon Yaakov's return, the text goes to great lengths to describe his destination.

> So Yaakov came to Luz, which is in the land of Canaan, that is, Beit El — he and all the nation which was with him. He built an altar there, and called the place "El Beit El"; because there God appeared to him when he fled from his brother.
>
> *(Ibid. 35:6–7)*

The altar is built in Luz, which Yaakov himself had earlier renamed Beit El. However, even on his deathbed, Yaakov still refers to this place as Luz:

> Yaakov said to Yosef, "God Almighty appeared to me in Luz and blessed me."
>
> *(Ibid. 48:3)*

Why does Yaakov revert to the city's original name? Perhaps the change from Luz to Beit El was not definitive, paralleling the Yaakov-Yisrael duality, the individual-nation duality.

What was Luz? Our Sages teach:

> This is the Luz where they dyed the *techeilet* (blue dye). This is the Luz which Sancheiriv invaded but did not conquer, and

which Nevuchadnetzar did not destroy. This is the Luz where the Angel of Death had no power.

(Bereishit Rabbah 69:8)

Luz seems to be a city with quite a formidable spiritual personality. Demonic forces have no control within its boundaries. Death was unknown there. In another context, the Sages tell us that a particular part of the spine, called the *luz*, will be the tool for the Resurrection of the Dead in the Messianic Age:

> Hadrian...asked Rabbi Yehoshua ben Chananyah, "From which part of the body will the Holy One, blessed be He, cause man to sprout forth in the future?"
>
> He [Rabbi Yehoshua] answered, "From the *luz* of the spinal column."
>
> *(Vayikra Rabbah 18:1)*

Luz seems to be indestructible, whether it be the *luz* of the spine or Luz the city. Similarly, Yaakov is indestructible. The Gemara states:

> Rabbi Yochanan said, "Yaakov our Patriarch is not dead."
>
> They said to him, "Was he not eulogized, embalmed, and buried?"
>
> Rabbi Yochanan answered, "...He is connected to his descendants. Just as his descendants live, so he lives."
>
> *(Ta'anit 5b)*

The Gemara tells us that Yaakov lives on. Such a declaration is not made about Avraham or Yitzchak. Why is Yaakov alone said to live on? Rabbi Yochanan refers to the nation of Israel, and not to Israel, Yaakov, himself. It is through his descendants that Yaakov lives. Specifically, the aspect of Yaakov expressed by the name *Yisrael* is eternal. The eternal nature of the Jewish people emanates from Yaakov's first encounter with the Almighty under the stars in the city of Luz.

We can further appreciate the uniqueness of Luz by looking more closely at the tradition cited in the *midrash* quoted earlier:

The Midrash stated that the *techeilet*, the dye used to make tzitzit, was manufactured in Luz.

There are two colors on the tzitzit: white and *techeilet*, blue. In another context, the Gemara reports:

> Why was blue chosen from among all the other colors? *Techeilet* resembles the sea, and the sea resembles the sky. The sky, in turn, resembles the Divine Throne.
>
> *(Menachot 43b)*

Just as the blue of the ocean or the sky is elusive in nature, so are the Heavens themselves and the Divine Throne elusive, beyond man's grasp. Rabbi Yosef Dov Soloveitchik, *zt"l*, explained that the white represents logic or clarity. Alternatively, the blue represents "metalogic" — the divine breath which energizes man spiritually.[1] With the mitzvah of tzitzit, Jews are commanded to conduct their everyday lives surrounded by white and blue, the logical and the heavenly. The Yiddish and Hebrew word *tachlis* is actually another application, or an alternative vocalization, of the word *techeilet*. *Tachlis* means "the purpose," for while Jews surely operate based on logic, there is a second thing which motivates them: *tachlis*, the essence or purpose of creation. At times, when we are involved in the mundane, we lose sight of the purpose of our existence. At those times we are commanded to look at the *techeilet* in order to remind us of our lofty destiny.

The Gemara teaches that in the morning, we can only recite Shema, accepting God's kingship, after it is possible to distinguish between white and blue. Only someone who can sense the blue which reflects the throne of God can truly accept God's dominion. The *techeilet*, then, is a means of connecting to Heaven. This was, in a sense, the purpose of Yaakov's dream, the meaning of his vision of the "ladder set on the ground with its head reaching the heavens" (*Bereishit* 28:12).

---

1 See Rabbi Abraham Besdin, *Man of Faith in the Modern World — Reflections of the Rov*, vol. 2, p. 25ff.

In this light, Yaakov's encounter with Lavan gains greater significance. The threat of assimilation presented by Lavan seems curious when regarded in purely logical terms: Logically speaking, is there really a difference between one man and the next? Lavan's argument makes perfect sense. Perhaps that is why he was called "Lavan," which means white!

The only way a Jew can withstand the threat of assimilation is if he is connected to Heaven. Only the Jew who can see beyond the logical can be free of Lavan. Only a Jew who sees himself as part of a great nation, with a mission and a destiny, will be liberated from Lavan's arguments. For this reason, Yaakov stopped in Luz: The vision of the ladder, a singular experience, will be permanently represented by the *techeilet*, which will serve as a permanent ladder for every Jew who wishes to connect with Heaven. The secret of the eternity of the Jewish people has its origins in the city of Luz, for that was where Yaakov, and thus all Jews, learned how to lie on the ground but still look up to the Heavens.

Parashat Vayishlach

The Struggle

When Yaakov returns from Charan, as he is preparing for his epic showdown with his estranged brother, Eisav, he has a bizarre confrontation:

Yaakov remained alone, and a man wrestled with him until daybreak. When he saw that he could not [defeat] him, he touched the joint of his thigh. Yaakov's hip became dislocated from wrestling with him.

[The man] said, "Release me, for dawn is breaking."

He said, "I will not release you unless you bless me."

He said, "What is your name?"

He said, "Yaakov."

He said, "Your name shall no longer be called Yaakov, but rather Yisrael, for you have struggled with God and with man and [you] have been victorious."

Yaakov asked, "Please tell me your name."

He said, "Why are you asking for my name?" And he blessed him there.

Yaakov called the place "Peniel" [face of God], "For I have seen God face to face, and my soul was saved."

The sun rose as he left Penuel, and he was limping because of his thigh.

> Therefore, the Children of Israel do not eat the *gid hanasheh* which is on the thigh [of an animal] until this very day, for Yaakov's thigh was afflicted on the *gid hanasheh.*
>
> *(Bereishit 32:25–32)*

The text seems deliberately enigmatic and contradictory. If Yaakov is by himself, how can a man wrestle with him? Each verse seems to contain its own difficulties and ambiguities.

> When he saw that he could not [defeat] him, he touched the joint of his thigh.

Who is "he" and who is "him"? This verse cannot be understood on its own; only by reading the next verse can we understand the meaning. Why is there so much confusion? What is the identity of Yaakov's adversary?

> He said, "What is your name?"
> He said, "Yaakov."

Does the adversary not even know with whom he is struggling?

> He said, "Your name shall no longer be called Yaakov, but rather Yisrael, for you have struggled with God and with man and [you] have been victorious.

The adversary, who does not even know the identity of his foe, declares that the one with whom he has been wrestling has been victorious in his struggle with God and man!

> Yaakov asked, "Please tell me your name."
> He said, "Why are you asking for my name?"

Why does Yaakov wish to know the identity of this person?

Despite the complexity of the verses, the Midrash and commentaries are relatively unified as to the identity of the assailant: It is none other than the divine protector of Eisav, the angel of Eisav. As Yaakov prepares to meet his brother after all these years, Eisav's angel comes down from Heaven in order to "have a go" at Yaakov first. It is interesting to note that Yaakov reaches an understanding with Eisav, yet he is unable to avoid battle with the angel.

What are the Sages trying to teach us with this suggestion as to the identity of the mysterious assailant? The text reads:

> Yaakov remained alone, and a man wrestled with him until daybreak.

Our problem is that if Yaakov is truly alone, who can he be wrestling with? One possible answer is — no one! Yaakov was actually wrestling with himself. This would explain the ambiguity in the passage. However, by solving the textual problem (if indeed we are correct), we have raised an even greater problem: Why would a sane man wrestle with himself? A careful reading of the text may give us some insight.

> Yaakov remained alone, and a man [*ish*] wrestled with him until daybreak.

Can the term *ish* possibly refer to Yaakov? The word *ish* means "man"; we are told that Yaakov wrestled with a man. There is, however, another verse in which the term *ish* clearly refers to Yaakov:

> The man increased exceedingly, and he possessed many flocks and maids and servants and camels and donkeys.
>
> *(Ibid. 30:43)*

Here, Yaakov has finally succeeded financially. The blessings which he took surreptitiously from Eisav have come to fruition. Yaakov has "made it." The text calls him *ha'ish*, "the man." Yaakov has completed a metamorphosis from being a man of the tent — a yeshivah student, if you will — to becoming a successful entrepreneur.

Yet Yaakov struggles with his success. It was one thing to take the blessings destined for Eisav; it is quite another to live with the results of those blessings. As Yaakov prepares to meet his brother, he looks at all the wealth he has accumulated and he is worried. He separates all his possessions and his beloved family into different camps, and he is left alone.

Previously, the text described Yaakov as alone when he was fleeing from Eisav and he spent an awesome night under the stars and saw the vision of the ladder to Heaven. Now, again, Yaakov is alone as he prepares to meet his brother. When he fled to Charan, he didn't even have a place to rest his head and he was forced to use a rock for a pillow. He asked God for the bare minimum — food and clothing. Now, Yaakov returns with riches. At this point, he asks only one question: *Who am I? Yaakov or Eisav?* As Yaakov crosses the river and sees his reflection, he questions his identity. Had he begun to look like Eisav? Had the fulfillment of the stolen blessings actually turned him into Eisav?

It would seem that Eisav thought so. When Eisav was last mentioned, he swore to kill Yaakov. Now when they meet, Eisav indeed comes prepared for war, bringing an army of four hundred men (ibid. 33:1). But when he sees the size of Yaakov's camp, Eisav asks Yaakov to travel together with him — quite an unexpected response from someone who has sworn to kill.

Eisav's anger should naturally have been exacerbated by the sight of Yaakov's great wealth; after all, this blessing of wealth was rightfully his own. What brought about Eisav's sudden change of heart? Yaakov did offer Eisav gifts, but why settle for gifts when he could have killed Yaakov, taken his revenge, and walked off with everything?

Eisav must have seen something in Yaakov which he had never seen before. Eisav saw the "new" Yaakov, the man who had seemingly abandoned his spiritual pursuits in favor of material wealth. In Eisav's mind, Yaakov had become Eisav, and as far as Eisav was concerned, there was no longer a reason to hate his brother. The barriers which had divided them had disappeared; they could now join forces. Eisav thought he had achieved an ideological victory, which was far sweeter than any revenge he could have exacted.

This was precisely the cause of Yaakov's inner struggle. He, too, saw what Eisav thought he saw.

Yaakov remained alone, and a man wrestled with him until

> daybreak. When he saw that he could not [defeat] him, he touched the joint of his thigh. Yaakov's hip became dislocated from wrestling with him.
>
> He said, "What is your name?"
>
> He said, "Yaakov."
>
> He said, "Your name shall no longer be called Yaakov, but rather Yisrael, for you have struggled with God and with man and [you] have been victorious."

All night long, Yaakov struggles with his success. His spiritual self and his physical self collide as he tries to determine his true identity. But Yaakov was unable to resolve this conflict.

> When he saw that he could not [defeat] him, he touched the joint of his thigh. Yaakov's hip became dislocated from wrestling with him.... And he was limping because of his thigh.
>
> Therefore, the Children of Israel do not eat the *gid hanasheh* which is on the thigh [of an animal] until this very day, for Yaakov's thigh was afflicted on the *gid hanasheh*.

In the resolution that was finally achieved, the physical realm was forced to yield, to move at a slower pace. Laws, like that of the *gid hanasheh*, would create spiritual boundaries within physical experience, making possible the elevation of the physical world to a spiritual plane. This was Yaakov's resolution. Yaakov might have looked like Eisav; in truth, he was no longer the same Yaakov. The very name *Yaakov*, which connotes a relationship with Eisav (see *Bereishit* 25:26), would now be superseded by the name *Yisrael*, which speaks of his relationship with the physical and spiritual realms.

When the Sages said that Yaakov's adversary was the angel of Eisav, they referred to the power of Eisav within himself with which Yaakov was struggling, this power which Yaakov feared had taken over his life.[1]

1 More on the similarity between Yaakov and Eisav and their struggle can be found in *Parashat Acharei Mot*.

> Eisav said, "Let us travel and I will walk alongside you."
>
> [Yaakov] said to him, "My master knows that the children are young and the sheep and cattle weigh heavily on me. If I should overdrive them one day, all the sheep would die."
>
> *(Ibid. 33:12–13)*

When Eisav suggests to Yaakov that they travel together, joining forces, Yaakov begs off, explaining that for him, his possessions are a burden which slow him down. Just as Yaakov's leg slows him down after his confrontation, so too is he slowed down here. The physical bounty with which he has been blessed is cumbersome for Yaakov. It holds him back from reaching his true stride, from realizing his spiritual potential. For Eisav, this physical plenty is the goal, the sought-after prize, and he believes that Yaakov has abandoned his earlier pursuits in favor of attaining the wealth that he sees before him.

> On that day Eisav returned to his way to Sei'ir. Yaakov went to Sukkot and built for himself a house and made booths [*sukkot*] for the cattle. Therefore, the name of the place was called Sukkot.
>
> *(Ibid., 16–17)*

At the conclusion of the confrontation, Yaakov and Eisav travel in two different directions. Eisav returns to Sei'ir, while Yaakov travels to Sukkot. Yaakov's new home is called Sukkot because of the booths he made for his animals. This is interesting, because Yaakov also built a home in this place, presumably for his family. Why would he prefer to name the place for the booths made for the animals?

The image conjured up by these booths is, of course, the festival of Sukkot. During Sukkot, Jews are required to leave the comforts of their homes and live in a temporary abode, reminding us that the physical world is a temporary one. Therefore, Yaakov building *sukkot* for his animals is an appropriate conclusion to the section: Yaakov recognizes that his blessing of physical bounty is transitory. Even more so, he sees it as a means to an end, one which is not defined by the physical but rather elevates the physical. In order to stress this message, he names his first stop after meeting Eisav and coming to terms with his material existence "Sukkot."

While Yaakov headed toward Sukkot after his confrontation with Eisav, Jews yearly head to Sukkot immediately after Yom Kippur.

In attempting to explain the concept of the Yom Kippur scapegoat, the *sa'ir la'azazel*, Ramban (on *Vayikra* 16:8)[1] explains that in offering this peculiar sacrifice on Yom Kippur, the Jews would give a bribe to Samael in order to appease him and facilitate his testimony before the Heavenly Court on behalf of the Jewish people.[2] Who is Samael? The Midrash, commenting on our parashah, writes:

> "Yaakov remained alone and a man wrestled with him" — this is Sama'el, the guardian angel of Eisav, who wished to kill him.
>
> *(Midrash Tanchuma, Vayishlach 8)*

We can trace the emergence of a pattern or theme: On Yom Kippur, every Jew must struggle with who he is or who he has become. The Torah commands us on Yom Kippur to offer a scapegoat, to "give the devil his due," as it were. This process enables man to keep his physical aspect in perspective. When Yaakov met up with Eisav, he, too, gave gifts. The *Zohar*, apparently aware of this connection, writes:

> "On that day Eisav returned to his way, to Sei'ir." When did this happen? At the hour of *ne'ilah* [the concluding prayer service of Yom Kippur].
>
> *(Zohar, Vayikra 100b)*

According to the *Zohar*, the confrontation between Yaakov and

---

1 The idea expressed by *Ramban* is based on a teaching found in *Pirkei D'Rabbi Eliezer*, ch. 45.

2 See Rav Soloveitchik's commentary on this *Ramban* in "On Repentance" (edited by P. Peli), 317ff. Without the Rav's explanation, this *Ramban* is almost impenetrable.

Eisav does indeed take place on Yom Kippur, and is resolved at *ne'ilah*, at which point Yaakov sets off to build his *sukkah*, his temporary abode. Therefore, the gifts which Yaakov gives Eisav serve as the prototype for the yearly gift, offered on Yom Kippur, which is offered to the power of Eisav in the world: the scapegoat, the bribe offered Samael.

If the confrontation between Yaakov and Eisav takes place on Yom Kippur day, then, by extension, the confrontation with his anonymous opponent takes place the previous night — *Kol Nidrei* night, Yom Kippur Eve.[1] All that night, Yaakov struggled with the Eisav within him: Was he still Yaakov or had he become Eisav?[2] Had his possessions and his preoccupation with acquiring those possessions changed him? By taking Eisav's blessing, had he in fact taken on Eisav's persona? By daylight, the time when the *kohein gadol* would begin the service in the Holy Temple, the struggle must be resolved.

The Torah said that Yaakov and the angel wrestled with one another. The Gemara comments:

> This teaches us that the dust from their [the combatants'] feet reached the Divine Throne.
>
> *(Chullin 91a)*

The *Zohar* elaborates on this:

> The identity of the angel was the Guardian of Eisav. And who is he? Samael. It is appropriate that the dust of their feet went up to the Divine Throne, for that is the place of judgment.
>
> *(Zohar, Bereishit 170a)*

The *Zohar* understands that judgment filled the air that night. Would the angel of Eisav be able to attest to Yaakov's innocence as he would for generations of Jews in the future?

---

1 It is interesting to note that Yaakov's first *neder* (vow) in Beit El was that upon his return to Israel he would build a sanctuary. Now the time to fulfill this vow has arrived.

2 See *Zohar, Bemidbar* 203a. The question "Who are these?" (i.e., are we behaving like Yaakov or Eisav?) is asked every Yom Kippur, by the Satan.

> He [Yaakov] said, "I will not release you unless you bless me."

Yaakov wants the blessing. In the end he receives it, as the verses tell us:

> And he blessed him there. Yaakov called the place "Peniel" [face of God], "For I have seen God face to face, and my soul was saved." The sun rose as he left Penuel.

This section is closed with Yaakov naming the place Peniel, for Yaakov's profound self-analysis and inner struggle bring him "face to face" with God. Real *teshuvah* (repentance), which results from profound introspection, leads to a rendezvous with God.

> Great is repentance, for it reaches up to the Throne of Glory, as it says, "Return, O Israel, to God, your Lord" (*Hoshei'a* 14:2).
>
> *(Yoma 86a)*

That is what Yaakov feels as he takes leave in the morning. Real *teshuvah*, we are told, reaches the very throne of God.

> The sun rose as he left Penuel, and he was limping because of his thigh.

Yaakov limped away from that confrontation, physically weaker but spiritually transformed and empowered. Now Yaakov knew how to respond to challenges which awaited him from both this world and the other. His identity would no longer be defined or determined exclusively by his relationship with his brother Eisav. He had now become Yisrael. The physical and spiritual were no longer at odds. Together, they accompany Yaakov-Yisrael with every step he takes as he moves toward his destiny — at a slower pace physically, but spiritually invigorated.

Parashat Vayeishev

The Light of Mashiach

The parashah begins with the following statement:

> Yaakov settled in the land in which his fathers dwelled.
>
> *(Bereishit 37:1)*

Yaakov had come to the point in his life when he could finally settle down. The Hebrew term for "settled" is *vayeishev,* while the term for "dwelled" is *migurei,* from the word *gur,* from the same root as the word *ger* or stranger. Yaakov succeeded in settling while his father and grandfather before him only managed to dwell. The juxtaposition piques our interest. Interestingly, when Yaakov himself is brought before Pharaoh and the latter asks him his age, Yaakov answers:

> The days of my dwellings are one hundred and thirty years, few and bad have been the days of my life....
>
> *(Ibid. 47:9)*

Here Yaakov uses the word dwellings — *migurei* — as opposed to the term we encounter in the beginning of our parashah, *vayeishev,* settling. Did Yaakov, in fact, settle, or did he merely dwell?

Rashi cites a *midrash* which explains the meaning of Yaakov's "settling."

> Yaakov wished to settle in tranquillity, but the episode of [lit., *the anger of*] Yosef confronted him. The righteous wish to live in tranquillity. God says, "It is not sufficient for the righteous what is awaiting them in the next world; they [also] wish to live in tranquillity in this world!"
>
> *(Rashi, Bereishit 37:2, based on Bereishit Rabbah 84:3)*

This concept is quite puzzling. What does it mean that Yaakov wished to live in tranquillity? Did Yaakov wish to "retire" from active patriarchal service and enjoy the "golden years"? Certainly Yaakov's life was difficult, but was this a reason to abandon his mission and enjoy the "good life"?

There must be a deeper meaning to the idea of "tranquillity" which Yaakov was seeking. Rav Yosef Dov Soloveitchik, *zt"l*, suggested that what Yaakov was seeking was spiritual tranquillity. Yaakov anticipated the onset of nothing less than the Messianic Age. This would explain the comparison with the World to Come. Yaakov sought spiritual utopia here on earth, as reflected in God's comment — this is the wish of tzaddikim, who are not satisfied with what God has waiting for them in the World to Come and desire perfection here and now as well.

But how could Yaakov possibly think that perfection or tranquillity could be manifest at that particular juncture in history? Did God not promise Avraham that his descendants would be enslaved for four hundred years?

> [God] said to Avraham, "You shall know that your descendants will be strangers in a land which is not theirs. They will be slaves and abused for four hundred years. The nation which enslaves them will be judged by Me. They will subsequently leave with great fortune. The fourth generation will return here, for the sin of the Emori will not be complete until then."
>
> *(Bereishit 15:13–16)*

How could Yaakov ignore the four hundred years of slavery stipulated in the Divine decree?

In reality, the Jews never were slaves for four hundred years. In the Haggadah we note that God was lenient in the calculation, and after a mere 210 years the Israelites were liberated. As the Jews leave Egypt the Torah states, "At the end of four hundred and thirty years, the Exodus took place" (*Shemot* 12:41).

The Midrash asks, which is it? Four hundred years, four hundred and thirty years, or four generations? The answer given by the Midrash reconciles the seeming contradiction by explaining that God's revelation to Avraham took place thirty years prior to the birth of Yitzchak, and the calculation of the four hundred years begins with Yitzchak's birth. What, however, is the significance of the four generations?

> The Holy One, blessed be He, said, "If they do *teshuvah* I will redeem them [after four] generations, if not I will redeem them [after four hundred] years."
>
> *(Mechilta D'Rabbi Yishmael, Bo 14)*

The promise to Avraham was not etched in stone. There was a flexibility to it. The central idea was that Avraham's descendants would be enslaved, be abused, and eventually leave the place of their oppression with great wealth. Apparently, Yaakov believed that this sequence had already occurred, that all these elements of God's promise had been fulfilled in his own life story. He must have thought that his oppression at the hands of Lavan and the years of labor which ended in his return to Israel with tremendous material wealth had fulfilled God's words to Avraham, and redemption could now take place. And then, out of the blue, Yaakov's worldview was derailed by the saga of Yosef and his brothers. "The anger of Yosef" shatters his illusions of tranquillity and fulfillment.

When the enemy was Nimrod, Yishmael, Lavan, or Eisav, confrontation was understood — even anticipated. But an internal struggle such as this did not seem to be part of the Divine Plan. Yaakov was certain that all the adversaries had been neutralized, and that the era of spiritual tranquillity was dawning. With his sons at his side, Yaakov was confident that the Messianic Age had arrived. There was, however, this last, unanticipated struggle. The Messianic Age could not begin (nor could *Sefer Bereishit* come to an end!) before this final intrigue within the family of Israel was played out. Later, toward the end of *Bereishit*, when Yaakov meets up with Pharaoh, Yaakov relates that, in retrospect, he had in fact "dwelled" but did not succeed in "settling." He had never achieved this sought-after tranquillity.

The narratives of *Bereishit* are more than stories. The vicissitudes of the forefathers are far more than ancient tales; they are spiritual realities pregnant with meaning, which form the woof and warp of Jewish history. In order to understand the significance of the teachings in *Bereishit* in general and this week's parashah in particular, we must introduce the concept of *ma'aseh avot siman labanim* (see *Tanchuma*, section 9, and Ramban to *Bereishit* 12:6), which literally means "the actions of the forefathers serve as a portent for their descendants." Put another way, history repeats itself, or, in theological terms, Jewish history is Jewish destiny.

When Yosef and his brothers fight, the spiritual power for future domestic disputes is unleashed. It is no accident that the festival of Chanukah, with its tragic fratricidal overtones, always falls during the weeks when the portions regarding Yosef and his brothers are read. The destruction of the Second Temple is attributed to the *sinat chinam*, the unwarranted hatred between brothers, that is the plot of these Torah portions, and the civil war fought by the Maccabees is seen as a repercussion — in the most literal sense of repercussion, the repeated beating of the same drum — of the conflict in *Vayeishev*. The *midrash* in the Yom Kippur liturgy which describes the demise of the ten martyrs in the days of the *Tannaim* is another far-reaching echo of Yosef's story.

Once the problem of internal conflict is presented, a new type of solution is required. This is the lesson of *Vayeishev*. Not only would tranquillity not be achieved in Yaakov's life, but also the insidious power of internal conflict would haunt future generations.

In order to understand this phenomenon, we must delve into

the text of the Torah. Ancient and modern scholars alike have noted a difficulty in the text: The last verse of Chapter 37 and the first verse of Chapter 39 are almost identical.

> The Midianites sold him [Yosef] to Egypt, to Potifar.
>
> *(Bereishit 37:36)*

> Yosef was brought down to Egypt, where he was purchased by Potifar.
>
> *(Ibid. 39:1)*

Between these two verses, time seems to stand still in the life of Yosef, while Chapter 38 recounts the life of Yehudah over many years. Yehudah marries and raises a family, and his children marry and die. The Torah finds it necessary to take us into the life and character of Yehudah before it can proceed to tell us about Yosef's fate. Why?

To understand this peculiar ordering of the text, we must first recall the setting: Yosef was sent by his father to look for his ten older brothers. When they see Yosef coming from afar, the brothers plot to kill him. Reuven, who, as the eldest, would be held most responsible, suggests that they throw him into a pit, for he planned to rescue Yosef later and return him to his father. In one of the harshest scenes in the Bible, the brothers sit down to break bread as Yosef languishes in the pit. At this point, Yehudah speaks (for the first time in the entire Torah):

> "What will we gain if we kill our brother and cover his blood? Let us sell him to the Yishmaelites and let not our hands be upon him, for he is our brother and our flesh." His brothers acquiesced.
>
> *(Ibid. 37:27)*

Yehudah takes responsibility and displays leadership; on the other hand, he also displays callousness and an almost-Machiavellian cynicism. His conclusion, "Let us not kill him, for he is our brother and our flesh," while he suggests in the same breath that they sell him as a slave, is shocking.

With Yosef gone, the brothers are presented with a new problem: How are they to inform their father, Yaakov, of Yosef's disappearance? They dip his coat of many colors in the blood of a slaughtered goat and say to their father:

> We have found this. Do you recognize it? Is it your son's coat?
>
> *(Ibid., 32)*

The brothers didn't actually lie to Yaakov; they merely deceived him. According to the Midrash, Yehudah was still the leader, and it was he who spoke. Yaakov, who immediately recognized the coat and assumed the worst, began to mourn for his son in a way that only a bereaved father can.

Now the Yehudah narrative begins. We are told:

> It came to pass, at that time, that Yehudah parted ways with [literally, *went down from*] his brothers.
>
> *(Ibid. 38:1)*

Rashi explains that Yehudah's descent was the result of the lowered esteem in his brothers' eyes. The brothers blamed Yehudah for their father's bereavement, and therefore for Yosef's disappearance.

> They said, "You are the one who said to sell him! Had you said, 'Return him to his father,' we would have listened to you."
>
> *(Rashi, Bereishit 38:1)*

The Midrash, in an attempt to explain this seeming tangent in the narrative, explains:

> "It came to pass at that time" — The brothers were occupied with the selling of Yosef, Yosef was occupied with his sackcloth and fasting, Reuven was occupied with his sackcloth and fasting, Yaakov was occupied with his sackcloth and fasting, Yehudah was occupied with taking a wife for himself, and God was busy creating the light of the King Mashiach.... Before the first enslavement occurs the final redeemer is born.
>
> *(Bereishit Rabbah 85:1)*

The Midrash is in effect asking a question: Where was God during the sale of Yosef? The answer is amazing. God was busy creating the light of Mashiach. What are we to make of this bizarre response? The result of the sale was that the Jews would all make their way to Egypt. Slavery will ensue, causing incredible suffering for countless people, all because of this sale of Yosef.

Yaakov did not anticipate this entire episode. He sought tranquillity, yet God had a different plan. Even though the slavery and eventual redemption promised to Avraham had not taken place yet, God was busy planning for the final redemption, a plan which began with the sale of Yosef and was crystallized with the "descent of Yehudah."

Yosef recognized the Divine Hand involved in the events of his life. When he went to seek his brothers in Shechem as per his father's instructions, he was informed that his brothers had in fact left Shechem and were headed toward Dotan.

> A man found him [Yosef] wandering, lost in a field. The man asked him, "What are you seeking?"
>
> He [Yosef] said, "I am seeking my brothers. Tell me, please, where they are grazing [their flocks]."
>
> The man said, "They left here, for I heard them say, 'Let us go to Dotan.' "
>
> Yosef went after his brothers and found them in Dotan.
>
> *(Bereishit 37:15–17)*

Yosef would never have found his brothers and would have returned to his father had this man not found him. But God made sure that, one way or another, Yosef would find his brothers, he would be sold, he would end up in Egypt, and his brothers would follow. Yaakov's tranquillity would have to wait.

Yosef eventually came to understand this interlude with the mysterious man in the field as an act of Divine Will:

> Now do not be saddened and do not be angered that you have sold me here, for the Lord has sent me ahead to be a source of

> sustenance. For these two years there is famine in the land, and for another five years there will be no sowing and harvesting. The Lord sent me ahead of you to set aside for you a remnant of the land and to save your lives by great deliverance. And now, it is not you who has sent me here but the Lord....
>
> *(Ibid. 45:5–8)*

Fate took the form of this mysterious man in the field. This seemingly insignificant event in the life of Yosef was in actuality the Divine Hand guiding him to his destiny in Egypt. While this does not exonerate the brothers for their nefarious behavior, the will of God is ultimately apparent in the world. Rashi tells us that the anonymous person in the field was none other than the angel Gavriel, whose very name denotes *gevurah* (strength), the aspect of *din* (justice).

As we saw in the *midrash*, at the moment of the sale of Yosef into slavery God was occupied with weaving the mantle of Mashiach, while Yehudah was involved in his own family life. What is the meaning of this *midrash*?

When Yehudah's oldest son, Eir, dies, one would expect Yehudah to gain some insight into his own father's pain. He now knows intimately, firsthand, what his father feels and what it means to mourn one's own child. When Yehudah's second son, Onan, dies, we would expect Yehudah to be tormented with guilt; it would be a natural response for him to blame his own actions for the tragic deaths of his sons. We would expect Yehudah to approach his father, admit his guilt, and tell him, "Yosef is alive!" But Yehudah seems cold and indifferent.

When Tamar, Yehudah's daughter-in-law, approaches Yehudah, he callously tells her to wait for his third son, despite having no intention of giving him to her for a husband. Some time later, Yehudah's own wife dies, and he seeks comfort in the form of a woman standing on the side of the road, Tamar. She has come to realize that Yehudah has not been honest with her. Therefore, she takes initiative and disguises herself as a prostitute as Yehudah is about to cross her path.

When she becomes pregnant as a result of this union, Yehudah, unaware of his paternity, orders her to be killed. She has, however, the ring, staff, and coat of Yehudah, which she received as collateral, in lieu of the goat she was to receive as her wages.

The Midrash questions why she asked for a goat, and answers:

> God said to Yehudah, "You deceived your father with a goat. By your life, Tamar will deceive you with a goat."
>
> *(Bereishit Rabbah 85:11)*

Tamar finally confronts Yehudah, sending him a message that she was impregnated by the owner of these personal effects.

> She said, "Do you recognize who owns this ring, staff, and coat?"
>
> *(Bereishit 38:25)*

The Midrash explains,

> God said to Yehudah, "You said to your father, 'We have found this. Do you recognize it? Is it your son's coat?' (*Bereishit* 37:32). By your life, Tamar will say to you, 'Do you recognize...?' "
>
> *(Bereishit Rabbah 85:2)*

The Midrash understands that the relationship between Yehudah and Tamar is directly related to the relationship between Yehudah and his father; the sin of Yehudah will be rehabilitated by Tamar. When Tamar says the words, "Do you recognize who owns this ring, staff, and coat?" Yehudah hears the echo of his own words all those years before, when he looked his father in the eye and shattered his father's world by saying, "Do you recognize it? Is it your son's coat?"

The next verse says:

> Yehudah recognized, and said, "She is more righteous than I."
>
> *(Bereishit 38:26)*

With those words, the idea of Mashiach was created. The power of man to recognize his sin and take responsibility for it is the concept of Mashiach. From this point on, Yehudah is a changed person, perhaps the first true *baal teshuvah*. From this relationship between Yehudah and Tamar, kings will emerge — David and his descendant, Mashiach.

The Midrash explains why Tamar asked for Yehudah's staff:

> The staff [is the scepter] of the King Mashiach.
>
> *(Bereishit Rabbah 85:9)*

When Tamar asked Yehudah to identify his staff, she was asking him to manifest the greatness which she saw nascent within him: the courage to admit guilt and take responsibility, to change. This is the lesson that Mashiach will one day teach the world. Man controls his destiny. No matter what mistakes he has made, man can fix them.

As a result of the episode of Yosef, the Jews were destined to be enslaved in Egypt. As a result of the *teshuvah* of Yehudah, the Jews are destined to be redeemed at the End of Days. A spirit of change will permeate the world, spearheaded by a descendant of Yehudah. History will reach its apex, and the light of Mashiach, created all those years ago at the sale of Yosef, will shine bright. At that time, all the children of Yaakov, and indeed the entire world's population, will live in tranquillity.

Parashat Mikeitz

Yosef HaTzaddik

The story of Yosef is well known: Yosef, the favorite son, becomes the object of the jealousy and derision of his brothers. He is sold into slavery, and after many trials and tribulations he rises to the second most powerful position in Egypt. Many years later he confronts his brothers, and finally the visions of his youth come true.

The stories told in the *Chumash* are often quite compelling, and this saga is truly great literature. For Jews, however, these stories contain much more than a "good read." There are many levels of understanding of every text, and here in particular I would like to delve into the theological and mystical implications of Yosef's life.

> These are the generations of Yaakov: Yosef was seventeen years old....
>
> *(Bereishit 37:2)*

The Torah connects Yaakov with Yosef. Of all his sons specifically Yosef holds the key to Yaakov's legacy. The fulfillment or completeness of Yaakov will take place through Yosef; the generations of Yaakov will be fulfilled in Yosef.

> Yisrael loved Yosef more than all his sons.
>
> *(Ibid., 3)*

Yaakov's mission was a spiritual one; if he favored Yosef, it was because he believed that Yosef was best suited to fulfill that mission. It is interesting that here the text uses the name *Yisrael*, implying that the love he felt was on a national level, not merely a sentimental love.

> Yosef dreamed a dream.
>
> *(Ibid., 5)*

We are told that Yosef is a visionary. Perhaps this was one of the reasons that Yaakov loved Yosef — he had the ability to dream and to understand the meaning of dreams.

Avraham, Yitzchak, and Yaakov were not merely three highly accomplished spiritual individuals. They formed a dynasty, in Hebrew a *shalshelet* (the root being three, *shalosh*).

The dynasty begins when God speaks to Avraham, using the Name *Keil Shakai*.

> When Avraham was ninety-nine years old, God appeared to Avraham. He said to him, "I am the Almighty God [*Keil Shakai*]; walk with Me and be complete. I will make a covenant between Me and you and multiply you exceedingly.... Your name shall be Avraham.... This is My covenant which you shall keep between Me and you, and your seed after you: Every male child among you shall be circumcised. You shall circumcise the flesh of your foreskin, and it shall be a sign of the covenant between Me and you. Every eight-day-old male shall be circumcised among you...."
>
> *(Ibid. 17:1–12)*

This conversation takes place prior to the birth of Yitzchak. Avram becomes Avraham, the new name signifying a new identity. He is at the same time commanded to circumcise all his descendants. As a result of these changes, Yitzchak will come into the world and the chain will continue. The dynasty has begun.

There is another significant element in this section. It is the first time the Name *Shakai* is used in the Torah.

When Yitzchak sends Yaakov away and orders him not to take a wife from among the local women, he blesses his son,

> The Almighty God [*Keil Shakai*] shall bless you and make you fruitful and multiply you, and you will become a large nation. He will give the blessing of Avraham to you and to your descendants with you.
>
> *(Ibid. 28:1–4)*

When the blessing, or nationhood, of Avraham is passed on, the Name of God invoked is again *Shakai*.

When Yaakov's name is changed, the Torah writes:

> The Lord said to him, "Your name is Yaakov. No longer should your name be called Yaakov, but rather Yisrael shall be your name." He named him Yisrael. The Lord said to him, "I am the Almighty God [*Keil Shakai*]. May you be fruitful and multiply; a nation and a congregation of nations shall descend from you, and kings will emerge from your loins."
>
> *(Ibid. 35:10–11)*

We see a pattern developing. When God blesses the patriarchs with many descendants, He uses the Name *Shakai*. We should also note that the passages cited constitute the only usage of this Divine Name until this point in the Torah. The name is not used in other contexts. Instead, the more familiar *Yud-kei-vav-kei* or *Elokim* are used.

The next time the Name *Shakai* is used is in this week's parashah, when Yaakov finally agrees to send Binyamin to Egypt. Yaakov says,

> May the Almighty God [*Keil Shakai*] give you mercy before the man [the leader of Egypt]. May He send your brother [Shimon] and Binyamin back, and as I mourned [for Yosef] I will mourn [for Binyamin].
>
> *(Ibid. 43:14)*

Here Yaakov is tormented at the prospect of losing Binyamin.

However, if we view this dialogue as Yaakov speaking not only as a father but as the leader of a nation, the statement takes on a different meaning. He fears for the future of his nation, as his children's lives are endangered.

In the last days of Yaakov's life, the Name *Shakai* is used twice, both times in discussions with Yosef. The first time takes place when Yaakov is recounting certain events of his life to Yosef:

> Yaakov said to Yosef, "The Almighty God [*Keil Shakai*] appeared to me in Luz and blessed me."
>
> *(Ibid. 48:5)*

Again, the topic is children or descendants. Here Yaakov is about to bless his grandchildren, the sons of Yosef — the only grandchildren to receive his blessing directly.

The last time the Name *Shakai* is used in *Sefer Bereishit* is in the blessing which Yaakov gives Yosef on his own deathbed.

> May the God [*Keil*] of your father help you, and the Almighty *Shakai* shall bless you, blessings of the Heavens above, blessings of the depths which crouch below, blessings of the breast and womb. The blessings of your father are potent beyond those of my ancestors, to the utmost boundary of the everlasting hills. They shall be on the head of Yosef, and on the crown of the head of he who was separated from his brothers.
>
> *(Ibid. 49:25–26)*

Here Yaakov passes on to Yosef the powerful blessings which he has received from God directly and from his own father and grandfather. Again the Name associated with this blessing of progeny is the Name *Shakai*.

The passages cited above are the only uses of this Name of God in the entire *Sefer Bereishit*. We can draw two conclusions: 1) The Name *Shakai* is connected with having children, and 2) This blessing becomes the domain of Yosef. It encapsulates that which Yosef inherited from Yaakov.

The first time the Name *Shakai* is used in *Shemot* is also of interest:

> The Lord spoke to Moshe, and said to him, "I am God. I appeared to Avraham, Yitzchak, and Yaakov as *Keil Shakai*, and My Name God [*Yud-kei-vav-kei*] I did not make known to them."
>
> *(Shemot 6:2–3)*

In order for Moshe to fulfill his mission, he will need a different type of relationship with God than the one enjoyed by the patriarchs.

In order to understand the essence of Yosef, we must probe into the meaning of the Name *Shakai*.

> What is the meaning of "I am *Keil Shakai*"? I am He who told the world, "Enough!" Reish Lakish taught: When the Holy One, blessed be He, created the sea, it kept on expanding until the Holy One, blessed be He, chastised it, and it stopped.
>
> *(Chagigah 12a)*

The Gemara teaches us that the Name *Shakai* comes from the word *enough* or *stop* (*dai* in Hebrew homiletically similar to the ineffable pronunciation of "*Shakai*"). When Creation is unleashed it needs to be stopped or the process of creation will overwhelm that which is created. Nature must be restrained from running amok.

The Name of God used in the description of creation is *Elokim*, the Almighty. The name implies omnipotence. According to Kabbalistic tradition, God's Name *Elokim* does not describe the essence of God, but rather it is indicative of an aspect of God. In Kabbalistic texts, the Name *Ein Sof* is the preferred way to describe the essence of God. *Ein Sof* means "no limits," or infinite. One would think that by calling God "the Almighty" we are ascribing to Him a great role in the cosmic drama. Why would the Kabbalists prefer the Name *Ein Sof*?

The problem confronting the Kabbalists is that the essence of God is transcendental, completely beyond man's grasp or ability to categorize, and therefore beyond articulation. Consequently, even the term *the Almighty* is in effect an anthropomorphism. The *Zohar* even goes so far as to suggest that the first verse in the Torah should be translated as "In the beginning *Elokim* was created [by the Transcendental *Ein Sof*]" (*Tikunei Zohar, Tikunim Chadashim HaIdra Kadisha*).

The name *Elokim* has the same numeric value as *hateva* (the nature).[1] In the Kabbalistic description of creation, the world's emergence is the result of the Transcendental God "holding back" His transcendence and allowing a world to spring forth. This process is known as *tzimtzum* (literally, contraction); the result is the creation of nature.

Avraham came to recognize God through nature;[2] God's response is to give Avraham the mitzvah of circumcision, which implies that man must control his natural instincts. In order for the Jewish people to emerge, Avraham must first acquire an ability to control nature. A "kingdom of priests" will have to be holy, not by allowing nature to control them, but rather by controlling nature. This is the symbol of the eighth day: There are seven days of the week in the process of creation, while the eighth day is beyond the natural, beyond the physical.

The Name *Shakai*, then, denotes limitations on nature. Therefore, the Jewish people could not emerge as a nation until the mitzvah of circumcision was commanded. It is, in a sense, the prerequisite for the existence of the nation. For this reason, the Name *Shakai* accompanied the blessings for children. It is the foundation of a holy nation.

Yosef, specifically in his relationship with the wife of Potifar, displays the ability to control his nature, or instincts, better than anyone else in Scripture. Therefore, Yosef is often known as "Yosef the Tzaddik." The Kabbalistic term associated with Yosef is *yesod* (foundation), as in "*Tzaddik yesod olam* — A tzaddik is the foundation of the world" (*Mishlei* 10:25). Alternatively, Yosef is the foundation of the Jewish people. Had Yosef disappeared from the Jewish

---

1 Ramchal's commentary to *Sefer Yetzirah*, and numerous other later writers.
2 See my comments to *Lech Lecha*.

community, the foundation of the nation would have been missing as well.

Perhaps now we can understand another episode in the *Chumash*. When the Jews finally leave Egypt, the masses head for their neighbors' homes, in order to borrow possessions which they will take with them, in fulfillment of the promise made to Avraham, "Your children will leave with great possessions" (*Bereishit* 15:14). However, Moshe, their leader, heads to the Nile River in order to recover Yosef's remains and fulfill the promise to bring them out of Egypt. Why would Moshe himself occupy himself with recovering Yosef's remains?

We know that Moshe was hidden in an ark in the Nile as an infant. He was found by Pharaoh's daughter and thus saved from death. Moshe's sister, Miriam, offered to find a nurse for the baby, and Pharaoh's daughter agreed. Thus, Moshe was returned to his parents' home for two years, until he was weaned. Then he went back to Pharaoh's place, where he was raised as Pharaoh's daughter's son (*Shemot*, ch. 2).

Moshe's parents had a brief opportunity to educate their son prior to his return to the daughter of Pharaoh and to life in the palace. What sort of things did they teach him? He certainly was aware his Jewish identity:

> It was in those days, when Moshe was grown, that he went out to his brothers and looked on their burdens.
>
> *(Shemot 2:11)*

His parents surely taught him to retain his own Jewish identity in the palace, and no better example than Yosef could be mustered. Who else spent long years in the palace, with the upper echelon of Egyptian society, and, despite all its depravity and seductiveness, kept his identity? The example of Yosef the Tzaddik is surely that which inspired Moshe. Therefore, Moshe himself lifts Yosef from the Nile and out of Egypt, as thanks for Yosef's example which uplifted Moshe in the palace and created the foundation for the Exodus from Egypt.

When the *Zohar* describes Moshe's retrieval of Yosef's remains, it says,

> "Moshe took the remains of Yosef with him" (*Shemot* 11:19) — the tzaddik, the foundation of the world, the level of Yosef the Tzaddik.
>
> *(Zohar, Bemidbar 236a)*

The *Zohar* sees the relationship on its spiritual level: it was not merely Moshe's great-uncle, it was Yosef the Tzaddik, the foundation, whom Moshe liberated. It was the symbol of man's ability to control his own nature, the human manifestation of *Shakai*. That is who Moshe brings out.

If Moshe identified with Yosef, we can now understand God's words to Moshe:

> The Lord spoke to Moshe, and said, "I am God. I appeared to Avraham, Yitzchak, and Yaakov as *Keil Shakai*, and My Name God [*Yud-kei-vav-kei*] I did not make known to them."
>
> *(Shemot 6:2–3)*

The concept of *Shakai* is a powerful one, and surely no holy nation of Jews could have come into existence without it. God, however, has many more plans for the Jews — standing on Mount Sinai, receiving the Torah, entering into the Land of Israel, and eventually mending the world. For these missions, more Divine Light will have to be shed, and other aspects of God will become known and manifest in this world. Yosef represents *yesod*, the foundation — *Shakai* — but the building which will stand on this foundation has yet to be built. That will require Moshe's ascent to Mount Sinai, an event that goes considerably beyond the foundation laid thus far.

Parashat Vayigash

The Beauty of Yosef

Parashat Vayigash begins with Yosef and Yehudah nearing a showdown: Soon Yosef will reveal himself and send for his father. Throughout the generations, scholars have been perturbed by Yosef's seeming callousness. Why did it take Yosef so long to orchestrate this reunion? One could argue that the primary victim of this delay was Yaakov, who spent twenty-two years in needless mourning. One might excuse Yosef's desire for vengeance against his brothers for their perfidy, but this seems to be inconsistent with Yosef's reputation as a tzaddik. Certainly, when vengeance impinges on Yosef's filial responsibilities and leaves Yaakov mourning and in hunger — when Yosef could easily solve both problems — any delay seems inexcusable.

In his commentary on the Torah, Ramban poses this question, which, in a sense hovers over the last three parashiyot: Why didn't Yosef try to contact his father? After all, the distance between Israel and Egypt only takes six days (*Ramban, Bereishit* 42:9). Why didn't Yosef send a letter to his father, informing him that he was alive and well? When Yosef became the head of Potifar's household he should have had the ways and means to contact Yaakov. Certainly, once he became the second most powerful man in Egypt he should have had all the connections necessary to send a message to his father. All those years of Yaakov languishing in Israel, mourning for his favorite son, could have been avoided. Didn't Yosef return his father's love? How could he leave his father for all those years?

The answer which Ramban offers is that Yosef could not contact Yaakov until Yosef's dreams had come true. Yaakov and his sons would come to Egypt and bow to Yosef; only then would the visions come true and Yosef vindicated.

Other commentaries have taken issue with this response. Dreams are in the domain of God, they say; let Him worry about dreams. It is man's job to do that which is ethical, and the ethical thing for Yosef to do would have been to inform Yaakov that he, Yosef, was indeed alive and well.

A contemporary commentator, Rabbi Yoel Bin Nun,[1] has suggested that perhaps the question is unfair. Instead, we should ask the reverse question: Why did Yaakov not contact Yosef? The answer seems straightforward; Yaakov thought that Yosef was dead. But did Yosef know that Yaakov thought he was dead? The sequence of events, from Yosef's perspective, may suggest a different conclusion. Yaakov was surely aware of the enmity which existed between Yosef and his brothers. Why would Yaakov send Yosef to his brothers? Was Yaakov involved in the plot?

Let us consider the family history: Whenever brothers do not get along, the solution is to separate. One can see this from the behavior of Avraham and Lot; though they were not actually brothers, when they saw that they could not coexist, they separated. The same is true with Yishmael, sent away from Avraham's house so he would not influence Yitzchak, and with Eisav, whom Yaakov separated from when it became clear that Eisav wanted to kill him. Perhaps Yosef felt that because of all the dissension he had stirred up in his father's house, Yaakov decided to send him away. Rabbi Bin Nun suggests that only upon hearing Yehudah quote his father as saying that his son Yosef "was ripped apart by beasts" (*Bereishit*

---

1 *Alon Shevut LiBogrim* (Alon Shevut Journal for Alumni), vol. 5 (Kislev 5755), p. 29–39.

44:28) did Yosef realize that his father was under the assumption that he, Yosef, was dead. Therefore, at that point Yosef reveals himself to his brothers and sends for his father.

While this interpretation is certainly highly original, it lacks support from the Sages. Moreover, it paints Yosef as a maladjusted individual who is highly insecure in his father's love. The commentators teach us that one of the major lessons of *Sefer Bereishit* is *"ma'aseh avot siman labanim"* — history repeats itself. The stories in the Torah create spiritual realities which will be repeated at other junctures in Jewish history. There must be deeper significance to these episodes than the insecurities of Yosef.

Rabbi Shimshon of Sens, one of the authorities in the school of Tosafot, suggested,

> Had Yosef sent a message about everything which happened, his brothers would have scattered in every direction, because of the embarrassment. Therefore, Yosef worked slowly to bring them back, and therefore avoid embarrassing them. His intention was good.
>
> *(Tosafot HaShalem)*

According to Rabbi Shimshon, the dreams of Yosef's youth had nothing to do with his plan. Rather, he had a problem. How do you inform your father that you have had an extended stay in Egypt because your brothers sold you as a slave? This idea is further developed in the comments of Rabbi Shamshon Refael Hirsch.

> If I am not mistaken, Yosef's consideration in not sending a letter to his father in his years of success was, what would Yaakov gain in getting one son back, if in the process he would lose ten?... Therefore Yosef used all the subterfuge, and in my mind this was certainly worthy of the wisdom of Yosef.
>
> *(Rav Hirsch, Bereishit 42:9)*

According to this approach, Yosef's consideration was completely selfless. To have been reunited with his father would clearly have been a great personal occasion, but it would have had tragic consequences. Therefore, Yosef chose to remain on his own.

Other commentaries believe that Yosef was motivated by the desire to help his brothers do *teshuvah*. Yosef orchestrated the series of events which brought Binyamin to Egypt and provided his brothers with the opportunity to defend Binyamin.

These last interpretations are not necessarily mutually exclusive; in both cases, Yosef's goal is beyond the personal. Both also indicate the great spiritual level on which Yosef operated.

A close reading of the text, on the one hand, and a survey of the Midrashic and Kabbalistic sources on the other, will foster a deeper understanding of Yosef and shed light on this issue.

Let us return to the text. The Torah's comments on Yosef's physical appearance are interesting:

> Yosef was handsome and of fine appearance.
>
> *(Bereishit 39:6)*

This comment is not made in Yosef's youth or, in the most logical context, the first time that he is introduced in the text. Rather, this information is supplied much later, after Yosef has endured the ridicule of his brothers, sale, and enslavement. The simple understanding is that this is merely an introduction to the scene with Potifar's wife, where for the first time Yosef's physical appearance becomes relevant.

However, the very verse which describes Yosef's looks is the same verse which Ramban alluded to above:

> He [Potifar] left all that he had in the hands of Yosef...and Yosef was handsome and of fine appearance.
>
> *(Ibid.)*

This would have been the first time that Yosef had the ability to contact his father, and here, in the same verse, the Torah chooses to speak of Yosef's looks! Perhaps there is a deeper meaning to this section, and to Yosef's beauty.

What is the source of Yosef's good looks? The last person the Torah described as possessing beautiful looks was Rachel, Yosef's mother:

Rachel was beautiful and of fine appearance.

(Ibid. 29:17)

We may therefore conclude that Yosef looked like his mother. In fact, both the Midrash and the *Zohar* allude to this connection.

Throw a stick to the ground, and it will land near the place you found it. For it says, "Rachel was beautiful and of fine appearance." Therefore, [the text says] Yosef was handsome.

(Bereishit Rabbah 86:6)

As the modern saying goes, an apple doesn't fall far from the tree, and the source of Yosef's beauty was Rachel's. The *Zohar* goes a bit further in its description:

Whenever Yosef would walk by Yaakov, he would look at Yosef and his soul would be restored, as if he was looking at Yosef's mother, for the beauty of Yosef was similar to the beauty of Rachel.

(Zohar, Bereishit 216b)

Yosef's beauty was inherited from his mother.

On the other hand, there are sources which indicate implicitly and explicitly that Yosef looked just like his father!

His [Yosef's] face was like [Yaakov's].

(Bereishit Rabbah 84:8)

The *Zohar* also stresses the resemblance between father and son:

Whoever would look at Yosef would see the image of Yaakov.

(Zohar, Bereishit 180a)

The similarity between father and son gives us insight to the comments of the Sages regarding Yosef's reaction to the seductive advances of the wife of Potifar:

"She [Potifar's wife] grabbed him by the clothing..." — At that moment the image of his father appeared to him in the window.

(Sotah 36b)

When Yosef looks in the window, he sees his own reflection, which looks just like his father. This is what strikes Yosef and saves him from temptation.

If Yosef looked like his father, what does it mean that his beauty was the beauty of his mother? What was the essence of the beauty of Rachel? Surely the Torah is not speaking about a trait which is only skin deep. Rachel's beauty must also represent some spiritual characteristic.

In a lengthy Midrashic discussion of the Heavenly response to the destruction of the First Temple, God summons Avraham, Yitzchak, Yaakov, Moshe, and Yirmiyahu to Him. Each offers an argument as to why God should rebuild the Temple. God, however, is unmoved by all of their arguments. The Midrash then states:

> At that moment, our mother Rachel broke forth into speech before the Holy One, blessed be He, and said, "Master of the universe, it is revealed before You that Your servant Yaakov loved me exceedingly and toiled for my father on my behalf for seven years. When those seven years were completed and the time arrived for my marriage with my husband, it came to my attention that my father was conspiring to switch my sister for me. It was very hard for me, because the plot was known to me and I disclosed it to my husband; and I gave him a sign whereby he could distinguish between me and my sister, so that my father would not be able to make the substitution.
>
> "After that I relented, suppressed my desire, and had pity upon my sister so that she should not be exposed to shame. In the evening they substituted my sister for me with my husband, and I delivered to my sister all the signs which I had arranged with my husband so that he should think that she was Rachel.... I performed *chesed* for her, was not jealous of her, and did not expose her to shame.
>
> "If I, a creature of flesh and blood, formed of dust and ashes, was not envious of my rival and did not expose her to shame and contempt, why should You, a King who lives eternally and

is merciful, be jealous of idolatry in which there is no reality, and exile my children and let them be slain by the sword, and their enemies have done with them as they wished?"

Forthwith the mercy of the Holy One, blessed be He, was aroused. "For you, Rachel, I will return Israel to their place." That is [the meaning of the] verse, "Thus says God, 'A voice in Ramah is heard — a bitter cry, Rachel crying for her children. She refuses to be comforted for her children, for they are gone,' " and it says, "Thus says God, 'Refrain your voice from weeping and your eyes from their tears for your work shall be rewarded,' " and it says, " 'And there is hope in the future,' says God, 'and your children shall return to their borders' " (*Yirmiyahu* 31:14–16).

(Eichah Rabbah, introduction, section 24)

The beauty, the greatness of Rachel is her ability to sacrifice her personal needs or desires for the sake of her sister. Yosef displays this same trait, but only when he is older, in Egypt. The same verse which describes his beauty describes his dominion over the house of Potifar. This was the first time that Yosef had the ability to contact his father; for the first time, the "beauty" of Yosef, the self-sacrifice he took upon himself, shone through. Yosef's beauty, inherited from his mother, became apparent at exactly this point, so it is described precisely in this verse.

In the words of the Midrash, the reward for Rachel's sacrifice was the building of the Second Temple. What was the reward for Yosef's sacrifice? We have touched upon the idea of "*ma'aseh avot siman labanim*," history repeating itself through the spiritual forces unleashed by the events of our forefathers' lives. The Jews were destined to be enslaved, but their enslavement was set in motion by the sale of Yosef, by the spiritual dynamic of *sinat chinam* (groundless hatred) which would one day cause the destruction of the Second Temple. The Second Temple was built upon the foundation of the love and *chesed* of Rachel; when her children ceased to act in a similar way, when hatred became a part of their lives, the Second

Temple crumbled to the ground. Extending this idea, we see that, had the potential of *sinat chinam* not been created, the Second Temple would not have been destroyed and the ten martyrs would not have been killed. Once the power of *sinat chinam* had been unleashed on the world by the brothers, Yosef endeavored to create a spiritual antidote.

A closer look at the original confrontation between Yosef and the brothers will clarify this concept: Yosef dreamed that his brothers would all bow down to him. The brothers understood that the leader among the brothers, and for that matter of the entire nation, was Yehudah. Thus, Yosef's dream constituted a capital offense — *meridah b'malchut* (treason). The brothers misinterpreted Yosef's dreams as a rejection of Yehudah's leadership. Yosef, however, understood that the brothers must rally around him, a son of Rachel, as well as around Yehudah, the son of Leah, before *Sefer Bereishit* comes to an end. There must be a power of unity established as a spiritual precedent.

When the brothers come to Egypt searching for food, Yosef confronts them. The Torah describes the scene:

> Yosef saw his brothers and recognized them. He acted like a stranger to them and spoke to them harshly, saying, "From where have you come?"
>
> They said, "From the land of Canaan to buy food."
>
> Yosef recognized his brothers, but they did not recognize him.
>
> *(Bereishit 42:7–8)*

The text is puzzling: Why does the Torah need to tell us twice, in subsequent verses, that Yosef recognized his brothers? We recall that the metamorphosis of Yehudah took place when "Yehudah recognized and he said, 'She is more righteous than I' "(ibid. 38:26).[1] Now, again, the Torah uses the same words to indicate that Yosef also acts with pure motives, for the sake of Heaven.

---

1 See my notes to *Vayeishev*.

Yosef continues to interrogate his brothers, accusing them of being spies. They reply,

> "Your servants are twelve. We are brothers, sons of one man from the land of Canaan. The youngest is with our father, and one is missing."
>
> Yosef responded, "That is precisely what I meant [literally, *he is the one I spoke of*] when I said you are spies."
>
> *(Ibid. 42:13–14)*

The dialogue is quite obscure. What is Yosef trying to get out of his brothers? What does he hope their response will be? The answer is remarkably simple. He wants them to admit to being spies and confess that they are seeking their missing brother. He wants the brothers to rectify their perfidy. The truest *teshuvah* will be if they seek out Yosef and rally around him as a brother, not as a replacement for Yehudah, but as a son of Rachel. Yosef all but tells them his wishes:

> That is precisely what I meant [literally, *he is the one I spoke of*] when I said you are spies.

The brothers miss the opportunity, so Yosef creates a second, albeit lesser, opportunity for rectification: Binyamin. If the brothers can rally around Binyamin, a son of Rachel, they can be forgiven. This is precisely what happens. Consequently, Binyamin becomes the unifying force in the Land of Israel. The Temple will stand in his territory. When the people become disunited, the unifying factor which is its foundation crumbles, and the Temple falls, destroyed by *sinat chinam*. The unity of the brothers was incomplete; it revolved around Binyamin, and not around Yosef, as it should have. For their *teshuvah* to be complete, they would have had to face the same situation as they had the first time and this time refrained from sinning, as *Hilchos Teshuvah* (2:1) teaches.

Since the rectification for the brothers' sale of Yosef took place when they rallied around Binyamin, and not around Yosef, their *teshuvah* was incomplete. The Second Temple will one day fall; the *teshuvah* involving Binyamin was not sufficient to eradicate the sin of the brothers. Only *teshuvah* involving Yosef himself could have provided the complete antidote for the power of *sinat chinam* the brothers had unleashed. We can now understand the comment of Rashi, when Yosef and Binyamin embrace:

> "He fell on his brother Binyamin's shoulder and cried" — [Yosef cried] about the two Temples which would stand in the portion of Binyamin and be destroyed.
>
> *(Rashi, Bereishit 45:14)*

The brothers' *teshuvah* was enough to allow the Temple to be built on the territory of Binyamin, but it was not enough to prevent its eventual destruction. Yosef understood that one day the Jewish people would have to rally behind him, not as a substitute for Yehudah but as a preparation for Yehudah's kingdom. Apparently, Ramban's comment that Yosef waited for the fruition of his dreams before contacting his father referred to the creation of spiritual precedents for the Jewish people. This is the idea of Mashiach ben Yosef, who prepares the way for Mashiach ben David (himself a descendent of Yehudah).

According to tradition, Mashiach ben Yosef will unite all the Jewish people in preparation for the arrival of Mashiach ben David, but he will die in the process (*Sukkah* 52a), in an act of self-sacrifice for his people. Just like his ancestress Rachel, whose self-sacrifice allowed the building of the Second Temple, his self-sacrifice will allow the building of the Third Temple. The spiritual model is Yosef, who chose not to contact his father even though it would have made life much pleasanter. In each case, the ultimate goal could not be achieved without the self-sacrifice of Rachel and her descendants.

Yosef, the dreamer, the visionary, the interpreter of dreams, saw that which his brothers could not. He dedicated his life to others; he was the great provider for others. He decreed a sentence of loneliness on himself so that others would have the chance to be redeemed.

Just like his mother, he was truly beautiful.

Parashat Vayechi

The Death of Yaakov

Parashat Vayechi is different from the other parashiyot in the Torah. The beginning of every parashah is delineated by a new paragraph or at least an indentation in the text of the Torah, except for *Vayechi*, which is *satum* (closed). Rashi quotes the Midrash, which explains this idiosyncrasy.

> Why is this portion closed [*satum*]? The death of Yaakov caused a closing of the eyes and hearts of Israel, due to the troubles of the oppression which began [with Yaakov's death]. Alternatively, [Yaakov] wished to reveal the end of days to his children, but it was closed to him.
>
> *(Rashi to Bereishit 47:28, based on Bereishit Rabbah 96:1)*

The death of Yaakov represents the end of an era. With his demise, the patriarchal age comes to a close and a new generation begins. *Parashat Vayechi* is the end of *Sefer Bereishit*, literally as well as ideologically. Rashi's comments establish *Vayechi* as not only the close of a book, but as a closed book. Yaakov felt that the end of *Bereishit* was the perfect time to reveal to his children what awaits them and their descendants in the future. But at the moment that this revelation was to take place, Yaakov's prophecy eluded him.

Yaakov called to his sons and said, "Gather, and I will tell you

> what will happen to you in the end of days.... Reuven, you are my firstborn."
>
> *(Bereishit 49:1,3)*

Yaakov gathers his children, his stated intention to inform them of events in the future. Instead, he proceeds to bless each of them. What happened?

> Yaakov wished to reveal the end of days but the *Shechinah* [God's presence] left him, so Yaakov began to say other things.
>
> *(Rashi, Bereishit 49:1, based on Pesachim 56a)*

Yaakov's response to the loss of his vision is fear. The Gemara describes the scene:

> Yaakov wished to reveal the end of days, but the *Shechinah* left him. He said, "Perhaps there is a defect in my bed [i.e., with my children], Heaven forbid, like there was with Avraham, who fathered Yishmael, and with my father, Yitzchak, who fathered Eisav."
>
> His sons said to him, "*Shema Yisrael, Hashem Elokeinu, Hashem Echad* — Hear, Yisrael, God is Lord, God is One.... Just as in your heart there is only One [God], so, too, in our heart there is only One."
>
> At that moment, Yaakov responded, "*Baruch Sheim kevod malchuto l'olam va'ed* — Blessed be the honorable Name of His Kingship forever and ever."
>
> *(Pesachim 56a)*

When Yaakov's desire to share his knowledge with his children was frustrated, he feared that this was indicative of some lack in his children and therefore in himself, and, by extension, a deficiency within *knesset Yisrael* (the congregation of Israel). As we have seen in earlier sections (particularly *Vayeitzei*), the children of Yaakov are no longer individuals; they represent the nation of Israel. If something is lacking in Yaakov's children, the repercussions will be felt by the entire nation. For Yaakov, the situation is frightening: On his deathbed, it seems to him that he has failed his mission.

The Gemara connects Yaakov's fear to the errant offspring of his father and grandfather. How could Yaakov expect his children to be greater than his revolutionary grandfather's or his saintly father's? If Avraham could father a Yishmael and Yitzchak could father an Eisav, why would Yaakov expect that all his own children be righteous? This question is closely related to the Kabbalistic discussion of the three *avot* (forefathers), specifically the importance of the number three. Why were there three patriarchs and not two or, for that matter, six? What delineates the era of the patriarchs, which, as we have noted, comes to an end in our parashah?

According to Kabbalistic thought, each of the three patriarchs created a spiritual awareness in the world. Each established one of the three pillars necessary to support the establishment of the nation. Avraham, who is identified with *chesed* (kindness), brought the Godly aspect of *chesed* into this world. Yitzchak represents *gevurah* or *din* (justice). The *din* of Yitzchak is, in a sense, antithetical to *chesed*, but each is required as a counterbalance for the other. Yaakov represents *tiferet* (beauty), a synthesis between *chesed* and *gevurah*. To borrow the Hegelian model, the patriarchs represent thesis, antithesis, and synthesis. Once synthesis is achieved, the nation can emerge.

There is, however, another side to this coin, for in addition to the synthesis, another philosophical thread is woven through our history. Avraham also fathered Yishmael. What was the spiritual makeup of Yishmael? According to Rabbinic teaching, Yishmael was the counterfeit of Avraham. Instead of truly emulating his father or establishing his own spiritual legacy, Yishmael imitated his father in a superficial, external manner. Avraham represents *chesed*, and the main trait of *chesed* is giving. Although the act of giving is Godly, giving, too, must have its limitations. *Chesed* taken to an extreme can lead to immorality and sexual licentiousness. In fact, when the Torah describes the prohibition of sexual relations between siblings, it is labeled *chesed*.

If a man takes his sister, daughter of his father or daughter of

> his mother, and sees her nakedness, and she sees his nakedness, it is "*chesed.*" They shall be cut off before their nation. His sister's nakedness he uncovered, and he shall bear his sin.
>
> *(Vayikra 20:17)*

Chesed is the act of giving, but even the giving must be governed by some type of moral system. Herein lies the Sages' indictment of Yishmael; Yishmael made cynical use of his father's teachings.

> "Sarah saw the son of Hagar the Egyptian" (*Bereishit* 21:9) — [he was guilty of] sexual immorality...this teaches us that our matriarch Sarah was aware that Yishmael conquered young maidens and hunted married women and abused them.
>
> *(Bereishit Rabbah 53:11)*

How is it possible that Avraham raised a son like Yishmael? The answer is that Yishmael twisted the great teachings of Avraham. We can imagine Yishmael's arguments. "My father teaches that *chesed* is what is important. If you are really dedicated to the idea of *chesed*, then you should certainly give your body." Avraham taught the idea of love, Yishmael taught "free love." If Avraham taught that people should "love their neighbors as themselves," Yishmael taught that people should love their neighbors' wives or husbands. The counterfeit — or, in the language of the mystics, the *klipah* — of *chesed* is sexual immorality. This was the domain of Yishmael.

Yitzchak endeavored to create a spiritual balance to his father's *chesed*. His greatness was *gevurah*, strength, a second aspect of God. The Jewish teaching of *gevurah* is encapsulated in the words of the Sages:

> Who is strong? He who controls his desires.
>
> *(Avot 4:2)*

As God controlled His infiniteness to create a finite world, man must control himself, and a beautiful world will emerge. The *klipah* of *gevurah* is the individual who tries to control or dominate others. The "worst-case scenario" of this is when the desire to control actually leads to bloodshed. This was Eisav's forte, as is suggested by his coloring and his name, Edom.

> "He was red" — this is a sign that he will spill blood.
>
> *(Rashi, Bereishit 25:25)*

Eisav, like his uncle Yishmael, was superficial. He did not deeply understand his father's teachings. He twisted the idea of *gevurah* into a mandate to control, and ultimately to take life. The fact that Eisav married the daughters of Yishmael should come as no surprise: These two had more in common than mere ancestry, and the result was the combination of their negative forces.

Yaakov, on the other hand, internalized the positive aspects of the teachings of Avraham and Yitzchak, and he came to represent the combination of their two traits, *chesed* and *gevurah*, in the third philosophical pillar, *tiferet* (beauty). The trait of *tiferet* sees beauty in all things, in differences and distinctions, and is able to create a harmonious synthesis. Yaakov, who becomes Yisrael, the nation, must be able to combine all sorts of ideas, experiences, and outlooks. This is in contradistinction to Avraham or Yitzchak, whose traits represented spiritual building blocks, but not the spiritual building.

Once this synthesis is in place, the nation should emerge. Yaakov's children should be complete, and in them we do not find any counterfeit. The *klipah* of the newly emergent Jewish nation is the *eirev rav*, those responsible for the worship of the golden calf, people who were not the descendants of Yaakov, but rather Egyptians who had joined the Jewish people in their victorious march out of Egypt.

The *eirev rav*, too, had a superficial grasp of the philosophical underpinnings of Judaism. To them, the trait of *tiferet*, this all-inclusive outlook, encompassed all types of worship. Their perversion of Yisrael's ability to synthesize allowed them to embrace idol-worship; their error was in assigning such worship any meaning at all. *Tiferet* is the inclusion of many different attributes in the service and worship of the One God; idolatry is the inclusion of other gods, which are, in fact, nonentities.

Time and again throughout our history, this perversion of *tiferet* has resurfaced, and the books of the prophets tell of many "movements" within Judaism which attempted to synthesize worship of the Ba'al (a type of idol) with Jewish worship. This motif begins at the foot of Mount Sinai and continues through the Hellenistic period to modern times.

The spiritual negativity created by Yishmael, Eisav, and the *eirav rav* is the power of the *klipot* of our patriarchs' teachings. Herein lie the sources for sexual immorality, murder, and idolatry, which eventually caused the destruction of the First Temple. When the Jews follow the counterfeited teachings of their forefathers instead of internalizing the true messages presented by the pillars of our nationhood, their mandate to lead by example comes to an end. The Temple is destroyed, the Jewish commonwealth laid to waste, and the Jewish people scattered.

We may now understand Yaakov's fear; he thought that perhaps he had misunderstood the spiritual dynamics of the nascent Jewish nation. Perhaps among his children there was someone who was counterfeit. If this was the case, perhaps it was not time for the nation to be formed. Yaakov's sons, recognizing their father's fear, respond by saying Shema; they accept one God. There is, however, a deeper meaning behind their choice of declaration. By saying Shema, they were actually referring to an earlier episode in their father's life and trying to communicate something very specific to Yaakov.

According to the Midrash, during the entire period that Yaakov thought Yosef was dead, Yaakov was devoid of prophecy; the *Shechinah* left him. When Yaakov thought that Yosef was dead, he also thought that he had failed in his mission, for it had earlier been revealed to him that if none of his sons died in his lifetime he would be spared from Hell (*Rashi, Bereishit* 37:35). With Yosef apparently dead, Yaakov spends his years awaiting his bitter fate in the World to Come.

When the message arrives that Yosef lives, the Torah comments:

> The spirit of Yaakov, their father, lived.
>
> *(Bereishit 45:27)*

Rashi adds,

> The *Shechinah* which had left him returned.

When Yaakov and Yosef reunite after twenty-two years, the Torah describes their embrace:

> [Yosef] saw [Yaakov], and fell on his neck and cried on his neck.
>
> *(Bereishit 46:29)*

After twenty-two years, father and son are reunited. We understand why Yosef cried, but what was Yaakov doing?

Rashi explains:

> Yaakov did not fall on the neck of Yosef, and he didn't kiss him. Our Sages explain that he [Yaakov] was saying Shema.

Yaakov's response to seeing his long-lost son was the recitation of Shema. At first glance this seems strange; he has not seen his son in all these years, and now, at the moment of reunion, Yaakov feels that it is time to say Shema! A closer look at the words of Shema will explain Yaakov's response.

A statement of faith in One God, or even a statement of praise and thanks to the Almighty for reuniting him with his beloved son, could have consisted of only the words "*Hashem Elokeinu, Hashem echad.*" But Yaakov added something more: "*Shema Yisrael.*" Years later, when Yaakov's sons respond to him on his deathbed with the words "*Shema Yisrael,*" it is clear that they are addressing their father. But why does Yaakov say "*Shema Yisrael*"? Can he be addressing himself, or are these words superfluous?

In fact, Yaakov addresses Yisrael — not himself, but the entire *knesset Yisrael*, the totality of the Jewish people, who are at that moment reunited. Upon seeing Yosef alive, Yaakov knows that *knesset*

Yisrael is complete, and he recites Shema. He realizes that his children are indeed complete, that the *Shechinah* is once again with him, that the nation of Israel may now emerge.

With this background, we understand why his children say Shema when, on his deathbed, he loses the *Shechinah* again. They wish to assure him that they all accept One God, that they are complete, and that he should not fear. They repeat his own prayer, echoing his reference to a united *knesset Yisrael* while at the same time referring directly to their father.

However, there is another aspect of the recitation of Shema. The Midrash teaches:

> The Jewish people say, "*Shema Yisrael, Hashem Elokeinu, Hashem echad* — Hear, Yisrael, God is Lord, God is One;" and the Holy Spirit [*Ruach HaKodesh*] cries out and says from Heaven, "Who is like Your nation Israel, a unique nation on earth" (*Divrei HaYamim* I 17:21).
>
> *(Mechilta, Beshalach 3)*

When we recite Shema, there is a response in Heaven. We accept God's Oneness, and God declares our oneness — our uniqueness.

The Gemara entertains the possibility that God wears tefillin, as it were. The question is then posed, what is the content of God's tefillin? Surely it is not Shema, as in man's tefillin. The Gemara (*Berachot* 6a) explains that again it is the verse, "Who is like Your nation Israel, a unique nation on earth."

Just as the Jewish people are dedicated to God, God is dedicated to the Jewish people. Yaakov understood this, and therefore when his sons said Shema he responded, *"Baruch Sheim kevod malchuto l'olam va'ed."*

This declaration is said in the Temple on Yom Kippur by the people, after they hear the Ineffable Name uttered by the *kohein gadol*. The utterance of the Ineffable Name is in itself a manifestation of the *Shechinah*, which lead the assembled masses to prostrate themselves and declare, *"Baruch Sheim kevod malchuto l'olam va'ed."*

When the children of Yaakov say Shema, the Heavens respond, "Who is like Your nation Israel, a unique nation on earth." Yaakov then realized that his children were complete, God's unique nation. He responded with praise for having seen the *Shechinah*, just as the entire nation will respond to the *Shechinah* in the future: "*Baruch Sheim kevod malchuto l'olam va'ed.*"

According to the Midrash, the slavery in Egypt could not commence until the Jews were a unified, independent nation. Otherwise they stood the risk of assimilation (see *Tanna D'Vei Eliyahu Rabbah* 21). Now *Sefer Bereishit* may come to its end; the slavery and eventual Exodus will follow, leading up to the giving of the Torah on Mount Sinai. Shema will remain the "pledge of allegiance" of this nation.

Over the generations, many will say Shema in all sorts of situations, and the *Shechinah* will always take notice. Perhaps the most famous Shema of all also took place in a death scene:

> When [the Romans] took Rabbi Akiva out to be executed, it was time to say Shema...he prolonged the word "One" until his soul departed in [saying] "One."
>
> *(Berachot 61b)*

When the Romans tortured Rabbi Akiva, the Gemara notes it was "time to say Shema" — it was time to uplift the nation from the oppression of the Romans and infuse it with a sense of nationhood. The *Shechinah* had been exiled with the destruction of the Second Temple, and now the glimmer of hope of rebuilding the Temple had been extinguished. Rabbi Akiva's Shema echoes throughout the generations. It was heard by Jews in countless situations, giving them the strength to make the most difficult decisions. It is fascinating that the name *Akiva* is derived from the name *Yaakov*; both were married to women named Rachel, who in turn both excelled in self-sacrifice. The Shema of Rabbi Akiva is certainly connected to the Shema of Yaakov.[1]

God chose not to have the end of days revealed by Yaakov. This was not an indication of unworthiness, either on the part of Yaakov or on the part of his children. Rather, it was an indication that some books must remain closed. Rabbi Akiva was also involved in speculation about the end of days. He tried to orchestrate the speedy arrival of Mashiach, which heralds the end of days, or the Messianic Era. Although he failed, this did not discourage him from saying Shema loud and clear, so that it was heard both in this world and in Heaven.

The above Gemara continues,

> A voice came from Heaven and said, "Fortunate is Rabbi Akiva whose soul departed in [saying] 'One.' ".... A voice came from Heaven and said, "Fortunate is Rabbi Akiva, for you are invited to the World to Come."

---

1 See Rav Yonatan Eibeshitz, *Yaarot Devash* 1:2. Yaakov Avinu and Rabbi Akiva are interrelated on a soul level.

Sefer Shemot

Parashat Shemot

Moshe: The Emergence of a Leader

Parashat Shemot tells the story of the enslavement of the Jews in Egypt and the beginning of their liberation. There are many traditions regarding the nature of the Jewish community at the time. The Midrash describes how the people had sunk to the "forty-ninth level of impurity." The general picture which emerges is of a people who had strayed from the path of their forefathers. Our Sages teach us that even circumcision had been abandoned, and Moshe had to force it upon the people prior to the Exodus.

> "A new king arose over Egypt" (*Shemot* 1:8) — the Rabbis commenced this discourse with the verse, "They have betrayed God for they have given birth to strange children; now the new moon shall devour them with their portions" (*Hoshea* 5:7). This teaches that when Yosef died, [the Jews] abolished the covenant of circumcision, saying, "Let us become like the Egyptians."
>
> *(Shemot Rabbah 1:8)*

Nonetheless, we are told that some aspects of tradition did remain intact: The Jews retained distinct dress, names, and language.

The *Meshech Chochmah* explains that the retention of these three practices was based on a tradition passed on by Yaakov himself, who had anticipated a deterioration in Jewish life due to the exile. Yaakov instructed his children that, come what may, they must always keep these three basic identifying customs, in the hope that this would curtail the process of assimilation. The *midrash* which is the source for this teaching is somewhat obscure; a more accessible *midrash* teaches that the Jews were redeemed because they didn't change their names or language, speak *lashon hara,*[1] or engage in sexual immorality. The source which mentions clothing in place of the latter two items is *Midrash Shocher Tov,* and this is the version which has entered into the consciousness of the Jewish community.

When we consider these three behaviors, it is fascinating to note that Moshe himself, the leader and savior, seems to be deficient specifically in these areas.

First and foremost, the name *Moshe*: Moshe was born into a family from the tribe of Levi. At that time there was an edict that all baby boys born be thrown into the Nile River. Moshe was put into an ark by his mother and found by the daughter of Pharaoh.[2] Pharaoh's daughter adopts Moshe and names him.

> The child grew, and she brought him to the daughter of Pharaoh. He became a son to her, and she named him "Moshe," saying, "For from the water I drew him out."
>
> *(Shemot 2:10)*

Although Moshe was given a Jewish name by his parents, he was called from this point onward by the name given to him by the Egyptian princess. Moshe's name, however, contains an element which is far more insidious than simply a non-Jewish origin. The Gemara poses the following question regarding Moshe's name:

1 Or, in an alternative text, "reveal their mystery."

2 The last time we saw someone in an ark, it was Noach. Regarding the comparison between Noach, who was indifferent to the plight of his fellow man, and Moshe, who was willing to sacrifice all for his fellow man, see my comments to *Parashat Noach.*

> Where is [the name] *Moshe* indicated in the Torah?
>
> *(Chullin 139b)*

When the daughter of Pharaoh named Moshe, what was she trying to communicate? In order to understand the depth of her action, we must first understand who this woman was and, for that matter, who her father thought he was. In the book of *Yechezkel* the following passage appears:

> Thus says God, "Behold I am against you, Pharaoh, king of Egypt, the great crocodile that crouches in the midst of the streams, who says, 'The Nile River is mine, and I created it.' "
>
> *(Yechezkel 29:3)*

Pharaoh believed that he was god of the Nile, that he has created the Nile. The edict decreeing that all male Jewish children be thrown into the Nile becomes more significant in this light: When the midwives refused to kill the males in a clear act of murder, Pharaoh suggests to his nation that they throw the children into the water instead. Why would this have been more palatable than simply killing the children? When we appreciate that Pharaoh declared himself god of the Nile, in effect he was saying, "Cast the children into the Nile, and the god of the Nile shall decide who will live and who will die," as if the midwives would not be performing the act of murder. This will also give us insight into the first plague, blood. Turning the waters of the Nile into blood was perceived by the Egyptians as an act of war, as if someone had stabbed their god.

Not only did Pharaoh think that he was god of the Nile, but he named his daughter "Bityah," which means "daughter of god."

> These are the children of Bityah, daughter of Pharaoh.
>
> *(Divrei HaYamim I 4:18)*[1]

This was the woman who saved, and named, Moshe. Her father was "god of the Nile," she was daughter of "god," and she pulls a

1 See *Kallah Rabbati* 3:23 and *Vayikra Rabbah* 1:3. We have a tradition that Bityah later converted, but we have no reason to believe that the name is a post-conversion name. Later on, *Bityah* takes on a different meaning — "daughter of God."

son out of the Nile and names him Moshe, "For from the water I drew him out."

Bityah, in naming Moshe, was making a claim which had theological meaning as well as political implications. She was claiming that the Nile had given birth to her son. Of course, she knew rationally that one of the Hebrews had in fact given birth to Moshe, but we must recall that casting the children into the Nile was not seen as murder, but rather as some type of judgment, perhaps reminiscent of the children left to die in Sparta. Moshe emerges from the Nile alive, which has theological significance for Bityah. He is therefore declared "son of the Nile." She is obviously priming him to become the next Pharaoh, or at least to take his place among the pantheon of Egyptian gods. Moshe's name is not merely Egyptian; it is steeped with idolatrous connotations.

This insight also gives us a greater appreciation of Moshe, for we now understand what it must have meant for him to leave the palace and to "seek out his brothers" (*Shemot* 2:11). When Moshe killed an Egyptian striking a Jew, he was in effect rejecting the entire way of life that was laid out for him. Moshe's heroic act — which had its spiritual antecedent in the behavior of his grandfather Levi — was an act of self-sacrifice for the sake of a fellow Jew. By killing the Egyptian, Moshe forfeited his role in Egyptian society; he would no longer be seen as a god, but only as a Jew, and his chances of one day ascending the throne dissipated. This self-sacrifice was the first step toward assuming the mantle of leadership of the Jews, but of course such considerations were quite foreign to Moshe. In any case, we cannot overlook the irony in Moshe's name: the savior of the Jews, who retained their distinction in their naming practices, was considered to be a god by the Egyptians, and his name reflected this status and role.

The second factor which contributed to the liberation was distinct dress. Here, too, Moshe was deficient. When it is revealed to Pharaoh that Moshe has killed an Egyptian, Moshe escapes Egypt and makes his way to Midyan, where he is described as "*ish Mitzri* —

an Egyptian man" (ibid., 19). What was it about Moshe that made him seem Egyptian?

> Was Moshe an Egyptian? Rather, his clothes were Egyptian, but he was a Hebrew.
>
> *(Shemot Rabbah 1:32)*

Finally, the Jews retained a different language, preserving Hebrew as their mother tongue despite the long years in exile. In contrast, Moshe's credentials seem lacking. The Torah tells us that Moshe had difficulty with speech:

> Moshe said..."I am not a eloquent man...I am slow of speech and slow of tongue."
>
> *(Ibid. 4:10)*

Later, Moshe describes himself as *"aral sefatayim"* (ibid. 6:12), which literally means "uncircumcised lips," referring to some other sort of impediment. Taken literally, it emerges that Moshe does not feel that he has the right to represent the Jewish people because his tongue is "uncircumcised": Moshe's speech is too Egyptian.

If, indeed, the Jews were saved because they retained these three basic identifying practices, then Moshe seems an unlikely savior. Why is Moshe chosen? As we saw by Moshe's response to the oppression of his fellow Jew, he certainly did possess leadership qualities. The model of leadership in the Jewish tradition is not the individual who subjugates others, but rather the individual who is willing to sacrifice for others. Moshe, the most modest, self-effacing man, would make the finest leader and teacher that our nation ever had. Furthermore, despite Moshe's upbringing, he rejected his role in Egyptian society, as well as the culture and beliefs of Egypt. This is evidenced by the fact that, after leaving Egypt, we are told:

> Moshe was the shepherd of his father-in-law's flock.
>
> *(Ibid. 3:1)*

This seemingly innocent statement speaks volumes when we recall Yosef's warning to his brothers upon their arrival in Egypt:

They must find a delicate way to inform Pharaoh of their occupation,

> For every shepherd is considered an abomination in Egypt.
> *(Bereishit 46:34)*

Moshe has become a shepherd, the most detestable occupation in the value system of Egypt. God reveals Himself to Moshe for the first time, at the burning bush, precisely when he is occupied with the sheep. The rejection of Egyptian life and values is what seems to allow the Divine Revelation.

We can begin to understand why Moshe deserved to be leader: He possessed incredible spiritual integrity. From what sources did Moshe draw the strength to change his life? What inspired Moshe to begin a spiritual quest, an odyssey which would transform him from heir to the Egyptian throne to caring shepherd, freedom fighter for the disenfranchised slaves, vanquisher of the Egyptian empire, leader of the Jews, and ultimately the one to receive and transmit the Torah, fulfilling the destiny of Avraham, Yitzchak, and Yaakov?

We can discern within Moshe the traits of his illustrious forefathers. Moshe embodies the *chesed* of Avraham, the *gevurah* of Yitzchak, and the *emet* of Yaakov.[1] All this can be seen in Moshe's reaction to the Jewish slave who was being beaten. Moshe felt for the victim, acting with *chesed*, and he displayed *gevurah* by holding back personal considerations and involving himself in the altercation. Finally, he displayed *emet* by immediately discerning which side was right. Moshe's parents obviously did a very good job educating him in the short time he was in their home before being taken to the palace.

Moshe certainly earned his leadership role, but why did God choose a Jew brought up in Pharaoh's palace as the leader? Evidently, in order for the Exodus to take place, precisely a person like Moshe was needed. There is a powerful lesson about the nature of

---

1 See *Zohar, Shemot* 276a, where the term *emet* is equated with *tiferet* and attributed to Yaakov.

the Exodus to be learned here. Had He so desired, God surely could have simply "willed" the Jews out of Egypt. Why go through the entire process of plagues and negotiations with Pharaoh?

The purpose seems to be twofold: It was necessary for both the Jews and the Egyptians. After spending all those years in Egypt, the beliefs of the Egyptians had made inroads into the Jewish community. What better way to show the bankruptcy of the Egyptian belief system than having one of the Egyptian "gods" revealed as a Jew? For the Jews, this would eradicate any nascent belief in Egyptian mythology. Of course, some Jews did find it difficult to totally reject these influences, as can be seen by the sin of the golden calf, but for most Jews the message was loud and clear. While Moshe saw himself as unworthy to lead the Jews, God found no one more worthy, specifically because of the attributes Moshe enumerated as his own "faults."

On the other hand, the message was also important for the Egyptians; they too needed to know that their religion was false. What better teacher than Moshe, the ultimate "insider"? At one point he had dressed like them and talked like them, and they had even been prepared to worship him. This theme of educating the Egyptians is articulated in the haftarah of *Vayeira,* where we are told that one day all the nations of the world will recognize God.

> All the inhabitants of Egypt shall know that I am the Lord, because they have been a staff of reed to the house of Israel.... And I will scatter Egypt among the nations and disperse them among the countries, and they shall know that I am God.
>
> *(Yechezkel 29:6, 30:26)*

The redemption from Egypt, which serves as a prototype for our final redemption, had universal concerns; it was not merely the removal of the Jews from this foreign land, but a powerful polemic against the greatest civilization in the world at that time. Each of the plagues was designed to convince the Jews of God's existence and sovereignty, on the one hand, and demoralize the Egyptians, on the other. But as the Egyptian mythology was revealed as a bankrupt, self-glorifying system, the Egyptian people should have realized the superiority of Jewish thought. Instead, they remained convinced of the strength of their god-Pharaoh and followed him into the sea to their deaths. Amazingly, even after ten plagues, they still believed that they had a chance of victory. We can only imagine the Egyptian leadership encouraging the support of the army, insisting that the Jewish God's power was limited to dry land, while Pharaoh's power over the sea was absolute and victory was certain....

When the final redemption comes, it will not be of parochial, Jewish concern. It will be the greatest event in the history of the world, and it will convince all the people of the world of the error of their ways. This Jewish concept of redemption has its antecedent in the redemption from Egypt. Moshe, the unlikely hero, emerges from the very epicenter of the civilization which must be rejected: As the crowning glory of Egyptian culture, Moshe's rejection of Egyptian life spoke volumes to all who knew him or of him. Though Moshe was himself hesitant to assume the role of savior, his very reluctance made him an even more attractive choice, especially when we recall that a crucial element of the Exodus was the eventual Revelation at Sinai.

> [God] said [to Moshe], "I certainly will be with you; and this shall be a sign to you that I have sent you — when you have brought forth the people out of Egypt, you shall serve the Lord upon this mountain."
>
> *(Shemot 3:12)*

Moshe is remembered for posterity not so much as redeemer — his name is virtually absent from the Haggadah which tells the tale of the redemption — but rather as *rabbeinu* (our teacher). Although the redemption was certainly political and geographic, it was also, more importantly, theological, and here is where Moshe stands out, as the greatest teacher in our history. Similarly, when Mashiach arrives, part of his task will be political in nature, but his main task will be to teach the world the truth and power of God.

Parashat Va'eira

A Touch of the Divine

Sefer Shemot represents a new beginning for the world. While the book of *Bereishit* discusses the creation and early history of the world, in many ways *Bereishit* represents failure. From the appearance of man in Gan Eden through the death of Yaakov, we observe so many lost opportunities. In Kayin and Hevel, in the generation of the flood, we find tragic examples of man's failure. Uniformly the younger brother succeeds where the older brother fails, and uniformly brothers seem unable to coexist peacefully.

There are numerous literary and theological connections between these two books which lead us to the conclusion that in order to understand *Shemot*, comparisons and contrasts with *Bereishit* must be considered:

- *Bereishit* opens with creation and the command for man to procreate, whereby man becomes a partner in creation. *Shemot* opens with Jews multiplying at an impressive rate — enough to alarm the Egyptians.
- *Bereishit* begins with a horrific act of murder — fratricide. *Shemot* begins with Moshe seeking his brothers and killing to protect his brother.[1] This alone should suffice to alert us that this *sefer* will be different from the previous *sefer*.

---

1 See my comments on *Bereishit*.

- *Bereishit* describes Noach in an ark, while *Shemot* begins with Moshe floating in an ark. Where Noach failed as a leader, Moshe will succeed, in an unparalleled fashion.

In the theological realm, a major change takes place in the transition between the two *sefarim*. This week's parashah begins with a declaration from God that while the patriarchs related to Him in a particular manner, there are aspects of the Divine which eluded them, and Moshe alone is privy to this particular revelation:

> The Lord spoke to Moshe, and said to him, "I am God. I appeared to Avraham, Yitzchak, and Yaakov as *Keil Shakai* [God Almighty], and My Name God [*Yud-kei-vav-kei*] did not make known to them."
>
> *(Shemot 6:2–3)*

The Ineffable Name of God which indicates God's complete transcendence was not revealed to the patriarchs. Rather, the Name *Elokim* or *Keil Shakai* was used when God revealed Himself in *Bereishit.*

Let us take a closer look at the various Names of God. The Name *Elokim* means All-powerful, or Almighty. It is the Name used to describe the drama of creation:

> In the beginning *Elokim* created heaven and earth.
>
> *(Bereishit 1:1)*

The Name *Elokim* implies a dominance over nature; the Kabbalists point out that the numerical value of *Elokim* equals the numerical value of *hateva* — the natural world, or nature.[1] This name is indicative of one particular relationship which God has with man, but it does not describe the essence of God on His terms. One could argue that from our perspective, this is the only aspect which is relevant. We, as created beings, can only relate to God as a Creator. This seems to be the aspect of God which the *avot* related to: Avraham came to "know" his Creator by recognizing this aspect of the Divinity.

---

1 See my comments on *Mikeitz*.

Moshe, however, comes to understand God on a different level; he perceives an aspect which had eluded the patriarchs. He relates to the aspect of God which is, by definition, beyond human understanding: the transcendent God, described by the Ineffable Name, the Name which is so holy that man is not even permitted to pronounce it. Yet the verse at the opening of our parashah which introduces this Name is somewhat unclear, for the name of God spelled *Yud-kei-vav-kei* has already been revealed to Moshe. When Moshe witnessed the burning bush, God instructed,

> This is what you shall say to the Jewish people: "God [*Yud-kei-vav-kei*], the Lord of your fathers, the Lord of Avraham, Yitzchak, and Yaakov, sent me to you. This is My Name forever; this is My memorial from generation to generation."
>
> *(Ibid. 3:15)*

This is precisely what the burning bush symbolized. A closer look at the portion of the burning bush clarifies the underlying issue:

> Moshe was a shepherd of his father-in-law's flock...and he came to the mountain of *Elokim* in Choreiv.
>
> *(Ibid., 1)*

Moshe is seeking the God of his fathers, *Elokim*.

> An angel of God [*Yud-kei-vav-kei*] appeared to him from the midst of the fire within the bush. He saw that the bush was burning, but it was not being consumed. Moshe said, "I will turn and look at this great sight. Why is the bush not being burnt?"
>
> God [*Yud-kei-vav-kei*] saw that Moshe turned to look. The Lord [*Elokim*] called to him from within the bush and said, "Moshe, Moshe."
>
> He said, "Here I am."
>
> *(Ibid., 2–4)*

While Moshe was seeking the God of his fathers, the ineffable, transcendent aspect of God revealed itself to Moshe. Moshe apparently did not understand the significance of the revelation. The tradition which he possessed, passed down from the patriarchs, concerned the aspect of God which we call *Elokim*, the God over Nature.

The burning bush itself is an intrinsic symbol of eternity, the idea of something which is burning but not being consumed. It is a representation of the metaphysical, a statement of infinity. Moshe turns to see but does not grasp the meaning, and at that point *Elokim* calls out to Moshe. Moshe is then told that the land upon which he stands is holy, and he is instructed to remove his shoes.

This is the first time in the *Chumash* that we are told of holy land. This is a concept which we have come accustomed to, but at this point in the text the idea is new. What is "holy land"? For that matter, what is the meaning of "holy"?

We are taught by the Sages that holiness is separateness.[1] If that is the case, then this land is separate, different from other lands. The only other such case hitherto in the *Chumash* is Gan Eden. Once again, we should not miss the parallel between the books of *Bereishit* and *Shemot*: In the beginning of *Bereishit*, man was expelled from Eden, and ethereal guards are stationed at its gates to prevent man from entering. Now, Moshe stands at the foot of this holy mountain and sees a sight which is not of this world. In both places God's transcendence is felt, as it says in *Bereishit*,

> They [Adam and Chavah] heard the voice of God, the Lord, walking in the garden in the breeze of the day.
>
> *(Bereishit 3:8)*

There is, however, a further, deeper connection between these awesome places, which becomes apparent when we consider the meaning of this burning bush. The first association drawn is a connection with Sinai, and therefore the giving of the Torah. Both Sinai and the burning bush are places of revelation — Sinai on the macro level for the entire nation and the burning bush a

1 See *Rashi, Vayikra* 19:2.

microrevelation directed exclusively toward Moshe. This association begins with the verse:

> He [God] said [to Moshe], "When you have brought the people out of Egypt, you shall worship *Elokim* on this mountain."
> *(Shemot 3:12)*

Here Moshe is clearly told that he will return to this very place in order to worship God.

The purpose of leaving Egypt, then, will not be merely political; the culmination of the Exodus would take place here on this same mountain — when the Torah is given.

The Sages see the connection on another level as well. The revelation of the burning bush took place on Mount Choreiv, as we read above. The Midrash comments:

> From the day that heaven and earth were created, the name of the mountain was Choreiv. At the time that God revealed Himself from the midst of the bush [*sneh*], [the name was changed and as a] result of *sneh* the mountain was named "Sinai." It is actually the same place as Choreiv. How do we know that the Jewish people received the Torah at Choreiv? It says, "The day you stood in front of God at Choreiv" (*Devarim* 4:10).
> *(Pirkei D'Rabbi Eliezer 40)*

The connection between the burning bush and Sinai, the place of the giving of the Torah, is established. The connections, however, run even deeper. The image of the bush is replicated at the giving of the Torah, where we are told that God reveals Himself from the midst of the fire:

> The mountain was burning in fire to the very heart of Heaven.
> *(Devarim 4:11)*

We can now appreciate that the burning bush is a microcosm of the Revelation at Sinai. But why a bush? The symbolism of a tree connected with Torah is obvious: We know of the "Tree of Life" from Gan Eden, and we are taught in *Mishlei* that the Tree of Life is Torah.

> My son, do not forget my Torah.... It is a tree of life to those who hold onto it.
>
> *(Mishlei 3:1, 18)*

The Talmud explains:

> Let him study the Torah, as it says, "Desire fulfilled is a tree of life" (*Mishlei* 13:12), and the tree of life is naught but the Torah, as it says, "It is a tree of life to those who hold onto it."
>
> *(Berachot 32b)*

The Tree of Life symbolizes Torah. Long after man's expulsion from Gan Eden, Moshe approaches the flaming bush. This bush is the conduit between Eden and Sinai; it is none other than the Tree of Life.

In *Bereishit* man failed in his mission and was expelled from the Garden prior to approaching the Tree of Life — Torah. Man's error was in partaking from the Tree of Good and Evil, often called the Tree of Knowledge. If we recognize that the other tree — the Tree of Life — was the tree of Torah, we must reevaluate our understanding of the Tree of Knowledge, the Tree of Good and Evil, called in Hebrew *"Eitz HaDaat."*

Immediately following the episode of the expulsion from Eden we are told that Adam *yada,* "knew," his wife (*Bereishit* 4:1). Apparently, the word *yada* implies an experience. Similarly, the Tree of Knowledge was a tree of experience. Had Adam obeyed the commandment given to him by God, he would have partaken of Torah first, and then he could have turned to experiences. The problem was that the snake used its seductive, destructive power to lead man away from the Tree of Life.

The idea of the snake in Gan Eden is the concept of the death wish, man's desire to avoid life.

> The [evil] inclination of a person attacks him every day and attempts to kill him.
>
> *(Sukkah 52a)*

The Sages teach us that the Angel of Death, the evil inclination, and Satan are all in fact one force (*Bava Batra* 16a), and this is the domain of the snake. The antidote for this force is the Torah.

> If you meet that disgusting one [the evil inclination] drag him into the study hall.
>
> *(Sukkah 52a)*

The cure for the temptation represented by the snake existed before the malady: God's intention, his commandment to Adam, was to arm mankind with Torah before opening them up to experience.

Now, all these years later, a new day has dawned. *Shemot* is a new beginning, a new creation. Moshe stands in front of this burning bush, a tree which represents Torah and, later, Sinai. At this very moment, Moshe questions God regarding His essence; he seeks His name. Finally, he asks:

> Behold, when I come to the People of Israel, and say to them, "The God of your fathers has sent me to you," and they say to me, "What is His name?" what shall I say to them?
>
> *(Shemot 3:13)*

God's transcendence is obvious, yet Moshe, while aware that he is on holy ground, is still unsure of the significance of the revelation.

> Moshe answered, "They [the people] won't believe me, nor will they listen to my voice, for they will say, 'God [*Yud-kei-vav-kei*] didn't reveal Himself to you.' "
>
> God said to him, "What is in your hand?"
>
> He said, "A staff."
>
> He [God] said, "Throw it to the ground." He [Moshe] threw it to the ground and it became a snake. Moshe fled from it [the snake].
>
> God said to Moshe, "Put out your hand, and take hold of its tail."
>
> He put out his hand and held on to it, and it became a staff in his hand.
>
> *(Ibid. 4:1–3)*

The staff, which was only a piece of wood, became a snake. When Moshe sees this snake he becomes justifiably frightened, not just because a snake is dangerous, but because it symbolizes sin. Mankind's previous encounter with a snake had disastrous consequences for the world. Now, however, things are different. Standing in front of the burning bush, or the "tree of life," Moshe is shown that he can control the snake.[1] The antidote is in his hands. Evil can be countered. When one connects with the Transcendent God, via Torah, evil can have no hold.

Now we can better appreciate the opening declaration of our parashah, when God again reveals Himself to Moshe. Immediately preceding this, at the end of last week's parashah, Moshe had posed a serious question to God.

> Moshe returned to God [*Yud-kei-vav-kei*], and said, "Master, why have You done evil to this people? Why have You sent me? From the time I came to speak in Your Name, evil has befallen this people...."
>
> *(Ibid. 5:22–23)*

Once Moshe has understood the idea of an infinite, compassionate God who will redeem His people, Moshe questions the suffering of his people. Why does evil still prosper? If we look back at the revelation at the burning bush, we can discern that God has already answered the question, albeit in a hidden manner.

> The Lord further said to Moshe, "This is what you shall say to the Jewish people: 'God [*Yud-kei-vav-kei*], the Lord of your fathers, the Lord of Avraham, Yitzchak, and Yaakov, sent me to you. This is My Name forever; this is My memorial from generation to generation.' "
>
> *(Ibid. 3:15)*

Here, the name of God is revealed, and God says, "This is My Name forever." The word *forever, "olam,"* normally spelled *ayin vav*

1 See *Zohar, Bereishit* 27a. The same staff at times represents the evil inclination (embodied by the serpent), as well as the Torah.

lamed mem, is missing the *vav*. Thus, what is pronounced *"olam"* [עולם] is written *"elem"* [עלם], meaning "hidden" (see *Pesachim* 50a). Even at the moment of revelation, God's Name must remain hidden, and we are reminded of our Sages' prohibition against pronouncing His Name. It remains ineffable, even when it is revealed.

In this world the Name of God remains hidden, but there will be a time when God's Name will become clear and known.

> "God shall be King over the whole earth. On that day God shall be one, and His Name one" (*Zecharyah* 14:9). Is He not One now? Rabbi Acha bar Chanina said: The future world is not like this world. In this world, for good tidings one says, "Blessed is the One who is good and does good," while for bad tidings one says, "Blessed is the true Judge." In the future world, it shall be only "Blessed is the one who is good and does good."
>
> "And His Name one" — what does "one" mean? Is His Name not one now? Rabbi Nachman bar Yitzchak said: "Not like this world is the future world. [In] this world [God's Name] is written with *yud-hei* and read *alef-dalet*. But in the future world it shall all be one: it shall be written *yud-hei* and read *yud-hei*.
>
> *(Pesachim 50a)*

The word *olam* is not the only word in the above sentence which is written in a defective manner; "generation to generation" is also written with a *vav* missing, as if to say, "Here is My Name, but realize that it cannot yet be fully manifest."

What is it that we are waiting for, that will bring about the end of evil? The term "from generation to generation" is found in another context: the battle with Amaleik, the embodiment of evil in history.

> God [*Yud-kei-vav-kei*] said to Moshe, "Write this as a remembrance in a book...."
>
> He [Moshe] said, "Because God has sworn by His throne that God will have a war with Amaleik from generation to generation."
>
> *(Shemot 17:16)*

Here the words "generation to generation" are again written without the *vav*. In addition, the word *throne*, normally pronounced *"kisei"* and spelled *"kaf samech alef,"* is written without the *alef*. God's throne, as it were, is incomplete from generation to generation, just as His Name is incomplete. Amaleik, the living representative of evil, thrives, preventing God's Name from being one. In other words, this is what prevents God's Oneness from being manifest in this world.

As we have seen, the antidote to evil is Torah. Amaleik attacked the Jewish people prior to the giving of the Torah, just as the snake attacked prior to man's eating from the Tree of Life (see *Shemot*, ch. 17).

This is what disturbed Moshe at the end of last week's parashah. His understanding of God as compassionate and transcendental led him to believe that all evil would be eradicated as soon as God made Himself known in Egypt. In response, God returned to the lesson in the beginning of this week's parashah: All promises will be fulfilled, the Jews will leave Egypt, and they will enter their own land. But for evil to be destroyed, something else must take place: The Torah must be received and kept. This is the Tree of Life.

There is a Kabbalistic tradition, cited by Ramban in the introduction to his commentary on the Torah, that the entire Torah, written with black fire on white fire, is in fact the Name of God.[1] This Name of God is also hidden. The *Zohar* teaches that there are 600,000 letters to the Torah,[2] and that every soul has its own connection with Torah. But an actual count of the letters in the Torah yields a result of only 304,805 — half the number we seek! However, we must take into account both the black fire and the white: The Torah consists of elements which are easily discernible — the letters, the black fire; as well as material which is elusive — the white fire. God's Name is hidden in this world; the task of revealing that Name is given to us, the Jewish people.

---

1 Chavel, Hebrew edition, p. 6–7. See *Yerushalmi Shekalim* 6:1.

2 *Zohar Chadash, Shir HaShirim* 74d.

Moshe had a mission which differed from that of the forefathers. They understood God's greatness through nature; they connected to *Elokim*. Moshe, on the other hand, was destined to bring the Torah from Heaven down to this world; therefore, Moshe needed to understand the idea of transcendence in order to accomplish his mission.

For God's Name to be completely revealed on earth, all the parts of the Torah must become known. This is the secret of the 600,000 letters: Every Jewish soul must complete its task, must realize its unique connection with Torah. Then and only then will evil have no existence. The Jewish people are woven together with the Torah, and God respectfully. If the people are incomplete in their actions, then the Torah is incomplete in its teachings, and God remains incomplete in His manifestation in this world. But the time will come when man, through his actions, will allow the Torah, and by extension God's Name, to become revealed. The world will then regain its innocence and become Eden-like; the serpent will be slain. God's Name will then become known and celebrated universally:

> God shall be King over the whole earth. On that day God shall be one and His Name one.

Parashat Bo

Time for Freedom

> God spoke to Moshe and Aharon in the land of Egypt, saying, "This month is the first of the months for you; it shall be the first of the months of the year for you. Speak to the entire congregation of Israel, saying, "On the tenth of this month each person shall take a lamb....' "
>
> *(Shemot 12:1–3)*

These verses mark the first commandments given to the entire congregation of Israel. The Midrash, cited by Rashi on the very first verse in the Torah, questions why the Torah begins with so much narrative. One would have assumed that the Torah, being a book of laws, would have begun with a legal section. Rashi specifically asks, "Why didn't the Torah begin with '*Hachodesh hazeh* — This month is the first...' "

A different *midrash* raises the same question:

> The Torah did not need to be taught except from, "This month is the first of the months for you." Why then did God reveal to Israel what was on the first day, and what was on the second day, up to the sixth day? As a reward for their saying, "Everything that God has spoken we will do and obey" (*Shemot* 24:7).
>
> *(Shir HaShirim Rabbah 1:28)*

We must conclude that ultimately the narratives of *Bereishit* and the beginning of *Shemot* are quite important, and it is certainly no accident that they are included in the Torah. Nonetheless, the verses cited above ostensibly should have been the beginning of the Torah, or, had they been the beginning, they would have been an appropriate one.

What is so unique about this section that it should have marked the beginning of the Torah? The simple answer would be that, as we mentioned earlier, it marks the first commandment given to the entire community. But in a sense, this answer begs the issue. Why was this the first commandment? Surely God had at least 613 choices with which to start the Torah or at least lead off the commandments. Furthermore, why was this commandment given in the land of Egypt? Why couldn't the Jews wait until Sinai for this mitzvah? We might say that in a sense the commandment regarding the new moon is a prerequisite for the holiday of Pesach, which would be celebrated in Egypt. In order to separate a lamb on the tenth of the month, one needs to know when the tenth of the month is. In order to have a seder on the eve of the fifteenth, we need to know when the fifteenth is.

Rabbi Yosef Dov Soloveitchik, *zt"l*, explained the rationale for this mitzvah being taught here and now: The Jews in Egypt were slaves and, like all slaves, lacked a sense of time. In order to be truly liberated, they had to acquire a sense of time, and thus be transformed from objects to independent people. The concept of time, indeed the ability to legislate time, is part and parcel of the transition from slavery to freedom.

While this explanation certainly gives us insight into the concept of *kiddush hachodesh* (the sanctification of the new month), one could argue that many, if not all, of the mitzvot contribute to the religious personality of the Jew. It is hard to see why this commandment could not have waited some two months until Sinai. God could have simply told Moshe, "In ten days have the people prepare a lamb, and in two weeks we are leaving."

An analysis of the seder which the Jews celebrated in Egypt will help us understand the importance of this mitzvah, and why it was indeed commanded at this particular point in time.

The Jews were commanded to take a lamb, slaughter it, and smear its blood on the doorposts and doorframes. This would certainly be liberating, considering that many animals were worshipped in Egypt; to kill the animals and smear the blood where it could be seen by all would be perceived as an act of defiance and a rejection of the Egyptian deity. The next part of the commandment was

> They shall eat the meat [of the sacrifice] that evening, roasted; they shall eat it with matzah and *maror* [bitter herbs].
>
> *(Shemot 12:8)*

At first glance, this verse seems unexceptional; for thousands of years Jews have observed this rite, eating matzah and *maror* on the first night of Pesach, either with the sacrifice (during the time of the Temple) or by itself. Therefore, it should come as no surprise that the Jews in Egypt ate the Pesach sacrifice with matzah and *maror*. Yet upon contemplation, a problem arises: Why do we eat matzah and *maror*? The Mishnah explains the symbolism of each of these three elements of the Pesach seder:

> Rabban Gamliel used to say: Whoever does not mention these three things on Pesach does not discharge his duty, and these are they: the Pesach offering, matzah, and bitter herbs. The Pesach offering is [sacrificed] because the Omnipresent passed over the houses of our fathers in Egypt, as it says, "You shall say, 'It is the sacrifice of Pesach for God, who passed over...' " (*Shemot* 2:2). The matzah is [eaten] because our fathers were redeemed from Egypt, as it says, "They baked unleavened cakes of the dough which they brought forth out of Egypt..." (ibid., 39). The bitter herbs are [eaten] because the Egyptians embittered the lives of our fathers in Egypt, as it says, "They made their lives bitter..." (ibid. 1:14). In every generation a man is

> obligated to regard himself as though he personally had left Egypt.
>
> *(Pesachim 116b)*

If so, it indeed seems strange that the Jews in Egypt — prior to the Exodus — needed a memorial, a symbolic reminder, as if they had already forgotten what it was like to be slaves to Pharaoh in Egypt. Perhaps today we need to eat bitter herbs in order to remind ourselves of the bitterness of slavery, but why would the slaves need such a reminder? The matzah poses an even more difficult challenge. The reason we eat matzah is also taught in the Mishnah: The Jews left Egypt in such haste that they did not even have time for their dough to rise or become leavened.

> The people took their dough before it could leaven.... They baked the dough that they took out of Egypt into matzot, for it did not leaven, for they were exiled from Egypt and they could not tarry, and they had not made any [other] provisions.
>
> *(Shemot 12:34, 39)*

The obvious problem here is with the matzah which the Jews ate at the very first seder: Why did they eat matzah in Egypt? Let us consider the sequence of events. God speaks to Moshe prior to the first day of Nissan, telling Moshe that there is a concept of new moons, months, and years. He further instructs Moshe to tell the people to prepare lambs for sacrifice by the tenth of the month. The celebratory, festive dinner takes place on the night of the fourteenth (leading into the fifteenth). At midnight that night, the firstborns of the Egyptians die, and God "passes over" the homes of the Jews, who escape unscathed. Sometime after midnight Pharaoh comes looking for Moshe, and subsequently the Jews are quickly sent out of Egypt. The actual Exodus takes place in the morning, at which point the Jews leave so quickly that there was not even time for the bread to rise — hence the introduction of matzah.

Again, why eat matzah the previous evening? When the Jews ate matzah that evening, what was their religious experience while eating it? Of course, the reason for eating the matzah was that God had told them to, and we know today that we eat it in order to remember the haste in which we left Egypt. But why ask the Jews in Egypt to eat unleavened bread when the concept of matzah did not, as of yet, exist?

A passage in the Gemara may shed light on this issue. There is an argument in the Gemara concerning the proper order of the prayers in *ma'ariv.*

> Rabbi Yochanan says: Who inherits the World to Come? One who [recites the blessings of] redemption immediately before the evening prayer. Rabbi Yehoshua ben Levi says: The prayers were arranged to be said in the middle [with Shema after the evening prayer].
>
> What is the ground of their difference? If you like, I can say it is [the interpretation of] a verse, and if you like, I can say that they reason differently. For Rabbi Yochanan argues that though the complete deliverance from Egypt did not take place until the morning, there was some kind of deliverance in the evening; whereas Rabbi Yehoshua ben Levi argues that since the real deliverance happened in the morning, [that of the evening] was no proper deliverance.
>
> *(Berachot 4b)*

Rabbi Yochanan says that in our evening prayers we should first recite Shema, then the blessings of redemption, and then *Shemoneh Esrei.* Rabbi Yehoshua ben Levi says that first *Shemoneh Esrei* should be recited, and then Shema. The halachah follows the opinion of Rabbi Yochanan. This passage has two more points of interest. The first is the comment cited in the name of Rabbi Yochanan, which serves as the introduction to this passage:

> Who inherits the World to Come? One who [recites the blessings of redemption] immediately before the evening prayer.

The blessing referred to here is the one recited after Shema ("Blessed are You...Redeemer of Israel"). Obviously, only if you say

Shema before *Shemoneh Esrei* can you juxtapose the blessing said after it to *Shemoneh Esrei*. The reward seems disproportionate for such a mechanical action. After all, how difficult is it to say Shema with its blessing prior to *Shemoneh Esrei*?

The second interesting point is the philosophical reasoning offered in the Gemara as the underpinning for the difference of opinion between Rabbi Yochanan and Rabbi Yehoshua ben Levi. The Gemara tells us that the legal argument is based both on exegesis and *sevara* (logic or philosophy): Rabbi Yochanan is of the position that even though complete redemption did not take place until the morning, there was still a partial redemption in the evening. Rabbi Yehoshua ben Levi opines that complete redemption did not take place until the morning, and only complete, actual redemption concerns us.

According to both sides of the argument, the redemption from Egypt did not take place until the morning. The question which remains is, how do we view the "darkness before the dawn"? Not only does Rabbi Yochanan believe that the partial redemption is significant, he states that whoever succeeds in articulating it is deserving of the World to Come. I heard Rav Nissan Alpert, *zt"l*, (son-in-law of Rav Chaim Pinchas Scheinberg and *talmid muvhak* of Rav Moshe Feinstein) explain Rabbi Yochanan's position beautifully: A share in the World to Come, *Olam HaBa*, is not a reward for juxtaposing the blessing of Shema with *Shemoneh Esrei*. Rather, in so doing, a person is a *"ben Olam HaBa,"* a member of the World to Come. He lives here in the present, but his existence is connected with the future. The individual who can see or experience the redemption in the darkness of the evening is a member of the World to Come, here and now.

Dawn is a time of clarity, stability. The blessing we say after Shema in the morning begins, *"Emet v'yatziv* — true and stable." In the evening, the blessing begins, *"Emet v'emunah* — true and faithful." In the dawn, when things are clear, faith is simple. In the darkness of the night, faith is much more difficult to maintain. Despite the fact that the redemption did not take place until the morning, a Jew can still trust in God to the point that he can literally feel the redemption despite the darkness of the night.

The archetype of this behavior took place in Egypt. The night before redemption, while they were still enslaved to Pharaoh, the Jews smeared the blood of the Paschal lamb on their doors and then sat down to celebrate the redemption, because at that point they were free! Although the redemption had not actually taken place, they were liberated from the oppression of Pharaoh: They believed so completely in the redemption that they were literally able to taste it. Their trust in God was complete. They were still in Egypt physically, but they were miles away psychologically. This was God's purpose on that awesome night.

Once the Jews felt liberated, they needed to eat from the bitter herbs in order to remind them of the oppression. They were even able to eat the matzah, which served as the symbol of their rapid exodus — which would take place only the next morning. They knew that they would be leaving so quickly that they would not have time for the bread to rise. Because they trusted in God so completely, they were able to literally taste the future. How ironic, then, is the commandment on the night of Pesach that we are to envision ourselves as if we have personally left Egypt (*Pesachim* 116b). The Jews in Egypt did just that: They, too, envisioned themselves as if they had personally left Egypt, only they accomplished this by looking into the future, while we must look into the past.

The selection of *kiddush hachodesh* as the first commandment for the nation of Israel reflects upon the very nature of Redemption. Redemption is not merely political or geographical. True redemption brings with it complete liberation, physical and psychological. Even if Mashiach would come today, bring all the Jews to Israel, and cause all the nations "to beat their swords into plowshares" (*Yeshayah* 2:4), all this would not suffice if we were still psychologically enslaved. For example, if we were still tormented by the horrors of the Holocaust, not understanding the ways of God, we would in effect still be enslaved.

The Gemara teaches:

> Rabbi Acha bar Chanina said: The future world is not like this world. In this world, for good tidings, one says, "Blessed is the One who is good and does good," while for bad tidings one says, "Blessed is the true Judge." In the future world, it shall be only "Blessed is the One who is good and does good."
>
> *(Pesachim 50a)*

We see that redemption has a psychological aspect as well. True liberation means freedom from the things that haunt our minds, not just from our physical torment. This is what God wanted to teach us in Egypt: how to become truly free. There is an old saying that it is easier to take a Jew out of exile than to take the exile out of a Jew. Later on in the Torah the Jews suffer many setbacks during their sojourn in the desert, more often than not due to the inability to free themselves from their past. But God in Egypt gave them one glorious lesson on the "art of liberation."

We find this lesson taught by Rabbi Akiva in a celebrated passage:

> [Rabbi Eliezer ben Azaryah, Rabbi Yehoshua, and Rabbi Akiva] were coming up to Yerushalayim together, and...when they reached the Temple Mount they saw a fox emerging from the Holy of Holies. They began to cry and Rabbi Akiva began to laugh. They said to him, "Why are you laughing?"
>
> He said to them, "Why are you crying?"
>
> They said to him, "A place of which it was once said, 'The common man who draws near shall be put to death' (*Bemidbar* 1:51) is now the haunt of foxes. Should we not weep?"
>
> He said to them, "That is why I am laughing. It is written, 'I [God] will take for Myself faithful witnesses, Uriyah the Kohein and Zecharyah ben Yevarechyahu' (*Yeshayah* 8:2). What is the connection between Uriyah the Kohein and

Zecharyah? Uriyah lived during the period of the First Temple, while Zecharyah lived [and prophesied] during the Second Temple; but the verse linked the [later] prophecy of Zecharyah with the [earlier] prophecy of Uriyah.

"In the prophecy [in the days] of Uriyah, it is written, 'Therefore because of you Tzion shall be plowed as a field...' (*Michah* 3:12). In Zecharyah it is written, 'Thus says the Lord of Hosts, "There shall yet be old men and old women sitting in the streets of Yerushalayim" ' (*Zecharyah* 5:4). So long as Uriyah's [threatening] prophecy had not had its fulfillment, I was afraid that Zecharyah's prophecy might not be fulfilled. Now that Uriyah's prophecy has been fulfilled, it is quite certain that Zecharyah's prophecy will also find its fulfillment (lit., *is also fulfilled*)."

They said to him, "Akiva, you have comforted us! Akiva, you have comforted us!"

(Makkot 24b)

What did Rabbi Akiva see that eluded his contemporaries? The stark vision of the Temple in ruins was surely enough to dampen the spirits of even the most enthusiastic optimist. But even at the darkest moment, Rabbi Akiva saw the hand of God and the impending redemption. It is fascinating to note that Rabbi Akiva speaks in the present tense; he sees that the prophecy of Zecharyah "is fulfilled" — taking place here and now. For Rabbi Akiva, the dark of the night is the moment before dawn. Where others saw darkness, he saw the glory of redemption. He lived in the present while being a *ben Olam Haba*, for he had the unique ability to experience the potential of redemption as a reality. He truly connected redemption to prayer.

Rabbi Akiva's uplifting approach had its antecedent in Egypt on the night of the first seder. This is precisely the lesson which God gave the Jews, a moment prior to their redemption. With the instruction to eat the matzah and *maror*, the Jews were encouraged to taste the impending redemption.

We can now understand why the Torah begins this section with the commandment to master time. We are commanded to anoint the seasons, to decide when the new moon has arrived. We are entrusted with the task of determining the nature of time. Will it be sacred or mundane? At the same time we are taught a powerful lesson: The Jew has the ability to control time, and thus to rise above it; to trust in God so completely that the problems of the present are resolved when considered in the larger context of eternity. Will the night be a time of fear, or the final moment before dawn?

The ability of the Jews to trust in God was the final act that ushered in the redemption from Egypt. For when a Jew truly trusts in God, he becomes part of the World to Come, tasting redemption.

Parashat Beshalach

From the Sea to Sinai

When the Jewish people began their journey from Egypt, they must have been on top of the world. The question, of course, would be, "What comes next?" Simply leaving Egypt was never the objective; when God revealed Himself to Moshe, He said:

> When you take the people out of Egypt, you shall serve the Lord on this mountain.
>
> *(Shemot 3:12)*

The Jews are meant to arrive at Sinai, where the Torah will be revealed. There they will receive their mandate, which will instruct, inspire, and guide them throughout history. From Sinai the Jews are to enter the land promised to Avraham, Yitzchak, and Yaakov, the Land of Israel. But something happened on the way to Israel, and the Jews took a detour which left them wandering in the desert for the next forty years.

This detour has its origins in this week's parashah. In the first verse of *Beshalach* we are told that the Jews are but a short distance from Israel, near the land of the Philistines, but despite this proximity, a different path was chosen.

> It was when Pharaoh sent the nation, the Lord would not let

> them travel via the route of the land of the Philistines, for it was quite close, for the Lord said, "Lest the nation have second thoughts if they see war, and return to Egypt."
>
> *(Ibid. 13:17)*

The people were not yet ready to enter the Promised Land, and we may venture to say that the tragedies and disappointments of the ensuing forty years are foreshadowed in this week's parashah. Because the people displayed a lack of preparedness, the Divine plan took a detour. This detour represents one of the great tragedies of Jewish history.

God knew that the Jews were simply not prepared psychologically to enter the Land, nor were they ready to fight for it. We may see this as an archetype of Divine behavior: God desires that man's potential be fulfilled, but man at times is unable or unwilling to respond to God's call. Analysis of the parashah will illuminate an educational philosophy, the lessons which were meant to transform the Jews from slaves to Pharaoh into partners with God.

The Jews had just witnessed the greatest display of God's power the world had ever seen. This power, however, was a double-edged sword. On the one hand, it provided the Jews with an awesome lesson in monotheism; on the other hand, it set standards of a relationship with God which could not, for man's sake, be sustained. Miracles would have to be replaced with a different way of appreciating, understanding, and connecting to God. For this transformation to occur, one last glorious plague would befall the Egyptians: the splitting of the sea.

While the splitting of the sea is not enumerated with the ten plagues, the Jews' response to it was stronger than their response to any other plague. Here the Jews break into song; here they finally realize that their enslavement by the hated Egyptians is truly a thing of the past. Here we are told that the Jews truly believed in God and Moshe. Why was the response so strong? We may answer this question by posing a different question: What possessed the Egyptians to chase the Jews into the water?

We have seen in previous parashiyot that Pharaoh saw himself as god of the Nile. Perhaps the Egyptians rationalized that on dry land the "Jewish" God was able to prevail but that the water is the domain of Egypt. This mode of thought may have inroads into the Jewish community as well. To see the Egyptians die in the water confirmed for all God's utter superiority. In a sense, the miracle at the sea was like seeing the god of Egypt die. The first plague drew first blood, as it were, and the splitting of the sea was the completion of the theological lesson. For this reason, the splitting of the sea was considered so momentous:

> A maidservant at the sea had a greater vision than Yechezkel ben Buzi.
>
> *(Mechilta, Beshalach 3)*

Or in the words of Rashi:

> In His glory, [God] revealed Himself to them.... A maidservant on the sea saw that which eluded the prophets.
>
> *(Rashi, Shemot 15:2)*

This type of supernatural relationship is wonderful — God attacks all those who wish to harm us. But it is an unnatural relationship. Man needs independence of these miracles in order for his free will to become operational. The plagues which have been the basis of the recent relationship between God and the Jews will have to come to an end.

The splitting of the sea marks the point of departure from the previous plagues.

> [God said to Moshe,] "Lift your staff and stretch your arm out over the sea and divide it [the sea]."... Moshe stretched his hand out over the sea.... God said to Moshe, "Stretch your arm out over the sea, and the water will return over the Egyptians, on their chariots and their horsemen."
>
> *(Shemot 14:16, 21, 26)*

Moshe is told to take his staff, the same staff which had performed so many miracles, and to hold it up, but to use his arm — not the staff! This marks a departure from the manner in which miracles were performed in Egypt — via the staff. Another important element is that the splitting of the sea takes place as the wind blows the entire night.

> Moshe stretched his hand out over the sea; and God drove the sea back by a strong east wind all that night. He made the sea dry land, and the waters were divided.
>
> *(Ibid. 14:21)*

The result is not immediate. The hand replaces the staff and the wind replaces the "instant miracles" which happened time and again in Egypt. Nonetheless, the people experienced God. In the minds of the people, the revelation of God is specifically identified with the sea, for here the glory of God was fully experienced.

The Jews leave the sea after this experience and continue their march toward the desert.

> Moshe brought Israel from the Yam Suf, and they went out into the wilderness of Shur. They went three days in the wilderness, and they found no water. When they came to Marah, they could not drink of the waters of Marah, for they were bitter. Therefore, its name was called "Marah." The people complained against Moshe, saying, "What shall we drink?"
>
> *(Ibid. 15:22–24)*

Nowhere does the text say that the people were, in fact, seeking water or that they were thirsty. Rather, it says that they did not find water. When they arrive at Marah, they find water, but it is unsatisfying; the water is bitter. How strange: Had they been truly thirsty, even bitter water should have quenched their thirst. But, as noted, the text did not say that they were thirsty. They wanted the water for a different reason: They wanted to experience God again, as they did at the sea. In this light we can understand God's response:

> He [Moshe] prayed to God. God showed him a tree which he

> cast into the water, and the water became sweet. There He gave him rituals and laws.
>
> *(Ibid., 25)*

While the second part of the verse may seem completely disconnected from the first, a profound educational philosophy is embedded in this short verse. The people thought that what they wanted was water, while their real desire was to experience God again. The response was to give them Torah. This would be the new way that the people would relate to and experience God. If this is the case, what is the nature of this tree which is cast into the water? The Sages teach us that the tree is the "Tree of Life" which is identified with Torah (see *Mechilta, Bahir,* and the list of sources cited by Rav Kasher in *Torah Sheleimah*).

The people thought they wanted water, but God knew what they really needed. He turned their complaining into a positive educational experience, which sets the stage for the next episode. When the people complain about the scarcity of food in the desert, God responds by giving the people *man* (manna). On the surface it appears that the purpose of the manna was simply to provide the people with nourishment. The Torah, however, informs us of an ulterior motive. The people gather the same amount of manna for the first five days, while on the sixth they receive a double portion. The people question Moshe as to the meaning of this phenomenon. The answer is:

> This is what God spoke of. A day of rest, a Shabbat sanctified to God, will take place tomorrow.
>
> *(Ibid. 16:23)*

The people think they want food, but God gives the people what they really need: Shabbat. Once again, a positive educational response. We see that the former slaves, who are moving toward Mount Sinai, are being primed by God, prepared for the type of spiritual experiences which will become part and parcel of Jewish life. The staff, the symbol of God's miracles, is no longer employed.

Even at Marah, the tree is utilized. This is the "natural" form of the staff. Ramban notes that the tree turned the water sweet "in a natural way."[1] This is the new agenda: A free nation will become dedicated to the teachings of a supernatural God in the most natural way. Nature can lead to a deep understanding of God, and God's teachings are meant for this world, the natural world. As it says in *Devarim*, "It is not in heaven" (*Devarim* 30:12).

The manna was a tangible lesson in Shabbat. The desire for food is obviously quite real and cannot be ignored, but the purpose of food is not simply to fill our stomachs. Rather, it facilitates our relationship with God. The purpose of Judaism is to take the mundane and sanctify it. When the people thought they wanted food, God gave them food from heaven. But isn't all food really from heaven? We must take the food from heaven and process it into a relationship with God. This is our role on earth. The best example of this lesson is Shabbat, when God ceased creating, as it were, and made the seventh day holy. That was the lesson of the manna: Food can be used in the service of God, and this entire world may be used as a catalyst to allow us to relate to God.

Therefore, the Jews traveled from Egypt to the sea, where there were liberated from the Egyptians, who had haunted them all those years, and from the Egyptian gods. The next stop is Marah, where the Jews received some basic teachings of Torah. At the next stop the Jews experienced Shabbat and learned a lesson in sanctifying this world. The next stage, though, is a reversal. Here we are told that the Jews were thirsty, and they fought with Moshe. Worst of all, the Jews questioned God.

> They tested God, saying, "Is God among us or not?"
>
> *(Shemot 17:7)*

The people seem to be going in the wrong direction, suffering a relapse. Theoretically, they should have already learned a lesson at Marah, the lesson that Torah is their connection to God. Now the text says that they are thirsty; now they challenge the existence of

1 *Ramban, Shemot* 15:25.

God. At this point, God's response is different.

> God said to Moshe, "Pass before the people, and take with you some of the elders of Israel; and take in your hand your staff, with which you struck the river, and go. Behold, I will stand before you there upon the rock in Choreiv; and you shall strike the rock and water shall come out of it, so that the people may drink." Moshe did so in the sight of the elders of Israel.
>
> *(Ibid. 17:5–6)*

Here the staff is employed again. The people, who were supposed to be moving away from the plagues, toward Sinai and Torah, are now taking a step backward toward Egypt. Therefore, the response which is used is taken from the repertoire of the plagues. The movement away from blatant supernatural miracles to the next stage in the spiritual development of the Jewish people has been arrested. God must revert back to supernatural signs and symbols, repeating a lesson taught earlier, but not fully internalized. Even worse, though, was the nation's questioning the existence of a living God among them. The response to such questioning was the appearance of Amaleik. Whereas the parashah opens with the Jews detouring around the lands of the Philistines in order to avoid war, by the end of the parashah they find themselves engaged in battle when they are attacked by the Amaleikites.

Amaleik represents the philosophy which rejects a living God, and instead ascribes everything to coincidence and happenstance. In *Devarim*, as we are commanded to remember Amaleik, the Torah writes:

> Remember what Amaleik did to you, on the road when you left Egypt. How they happened upon you....
>
> *(Devarim 25:17–18)*

Rashi explains that the term "happened upon" means "coincidence."

One of the great Chassidic masters, Rav Tzaddok HaKohen, explained: Amaleik believes that everything in this world is coincidence, that there is no *hashgachah* (Divine Providence) in the world, or, in other words, that nature is god. The Jews became vulnerable to the attack of Amaleik when they questioned if God was really with them. The Jews needed yet another lesson in the power of God. Now, during the battle, we are told that Moshe took the staff of God with him.

> Moshe said to Yehoshua, "Choose for us men and go out, fight against Amaleik. Tomorrow I will stand on the top of the hill with the staff of the Lord in my hand."
>
> Yehoshua did as Moshe had said to him, and fought against Amaleik. Moshe, Aharon, and Chur went up to the top of the hill. When Moshe held up his hand, Israel prevailed; and when he put down his hand, Amaleik prevailed.
>
> *(Shemot 17:9–11)*

The Mishnah questions this verse:

> Did the hands of Moshe wage war or crush the enemy? [Certainly not.] Only the text signifies that so long as Israel looked upwards and humbled their hearts before their Father in Heaven they prevailed, and if not they fell.
>
> *(Rosh HaShanah 29a)*

The hands of Moshe helped focus the Jewish people on their Father in Heaven. In a sense, the battle with Amaleik is similar to the splitting of the sea, for there, too, Moshe brought the staff but used his hands. In this case the relationship between the hands of Moshe and victory is even more clear: The function of Moshe's hands was to bring the people in touch with the fact that there is a God, that He sees all and is all-powerful. Amaleik was able to attack through the chink in the Jewish people's armor of belief. When the Jews doubted God's involvement in their history and destiny, in their everyday lives, and took the lessons of nature to improper conclusions, Amaleik and its philosophy of random happenstance could make inroads into Israel. The lessons which God had taught them were not learned in proper sequence, and some needed repetition.

This, then, is the tragedy of *Parashat Beshalach*: Lessons had to be repeated, and opportunities were not realized. The battle which was avoided with the Philistines became a reality with Amaleik. The battle of Amaleik was not part of the utopian Divine plan. Had the Jews internalized the lesson at Marah and succeeded in maintaining their relationship with God via Torah, Amaleik and the philosophy it represents would have been powerless. But the behavior of the Jews in the desert created the necessity for a "plan B." Other lessons not properly learned will bring upon them plans C and D. For while God provides the lessons and allows for the growth needed at each stage, it has been our task throughout history to learn the lessons, internalize them, and utilize them.

God and His methods are perfect. Man, in his rebelliousness from time immemorial, has rejected the beauty of God's plan. From Gan Eden onwards, man's actions have necessitated revisions of the Divine plan; each time such revisions are made, man suffers the painful feeling of being distanced from God. God, for His part, offers the precise educational message needed at each stage to ensure the proper growth, and the tools needed to close the gap between man and God. It is incumbent upon us to realize these opportunities and seize the moment, lest more distancing result. To paraphrase a modern-day icon: In life, man does not always get what he wants, but God always provides what he needs.

Parashat Yitro

The Ten Commandments: Part 1

In this week's parashah, the greatest moment in the history of the world transpires: the Revelation of God at Mount Sinai. Despite the magnitude of the event, the nature and content of the Revelation remain somewhat obscure: From God's perspective, what was revealed. On the receiving side, what was man's response to this epic event?

The Torah introduces the Ten Commandments with the following declaration:

> The Lord spoke all of these things, saying....
>
> *(Shemot 20:1)*

Rashi, citing the *Mechilta*, explains:

> This teaches that the Holy One, Blessed be He, said the entire decalogue in one expression, that which a person cannot possibly articulate. If this is the case, why does it subsequently say, "I am the God who took you out..." (ibid., 2), [and] "You shall have no other..." (ibid., 3)? [God] returned and explained each commandment independently.

According to Rashi, the entire Ten Commandments were revealed simultaneously, in a manner "which a person cannot possibly articulate," or, to use the language of the Midrash:

> That which a mouth could not say and ears could not hear is what was revealed.
>
> *(Mechilta, Shemot 20:1)*

According to Rashi and the *Mechilta*, this verse is not merely an introduction to the Revelation, it describes the essence of the Revelation itself! This communication by God, independent of its content, is qualitatively different from any other.

This being the case, we must examine the message itself before attempting to understand its content. An obvious question emerges: What is the purpose of a Revelation which cannot be cognitively understood? If indeed God spoke all Ten Commandments at once, no one could possibly have understood a word. Why should God speak in a manner which man cannot hear? What did the people hear, or experience, when God spoke to them in this manner?

Perhaps the people did not hear at all! The verse immediately following the Ten Commandments states:

> The entire nation saw the voices and the thunder and the sound of the shofar, and the mountain consumed with smoke. The people saw and were frightened; therefore, they stood at a distance. They said to Moshe, "You speak to us and we will hear, but the Lord shall not speak to us lest we die."
>
> *(Shemot 20:15–16)*

Here the Torah does not say that the people heard the Word of God. Quite the opposite: The people saw the sounds, and this frightened them. They ask Moshe to speak, so that they might hear. Moshe counters:

> Moshe said to the nation, "Do not be frightened. The Lord comes to uplift you and so that fear of God will be upon you, so that you will not sin."
>
> The people stood from afar, and Moshe approached the

> mist where the Lord was.
>
> *(Ibid., 17–18)*

The idea that the people saw, rather than heard, the sounds is further confirmed by the following verse:

> God said to Moshe, "Thus tell the people: 'You have seen that from Heaven I have spoken with you.' "
>
> *(Ibid., 19)*

Rashi explains that when the Torah states that the people "saw the sounds" (ibid., 15), they actually saw that which is usually heard, that which was impossible to see under different circumstances.

Again the term "seen" is used instead of "heard," and the image we have is one in which God spoke in a miraculous way, in which the people could see, but could not hear. When God invited them to listen, they were so awestruck that they recoiled.

Thus far, our understanding is that God spoke in a manner which was unmistakable. The Revelation was completely supernatural. No one could doubt that the sounds they saw emanated from God. However, the people did not know what God had said, because they could not hear, only see. Therefore, God began to repeat the commandments in a manner that the people could hear. It was at that point that the people failed to seize the moment and missed their historic opportunity. Instead of continuing their rendezvous with God, they requested an intermediary:

> The people saw and were frightened; therefore, they stood at a distance. They said to Moshe, "You speak to us and we will hear, but the Lord shall not speak to us lest we die."

Our Sages teach that the first two commandments were repeated by God prior to the people making the plea to Moshe:

> "I am [God]" and "You shall have no [other gods]" we heard from the mouth of God.
>
> *(Makkot 24a)*

To make matters even more complicated, we are taught in next week's parashah:

> God said to Moshe, "Ascend to Me up the mountain, and be there. I will give you the Tablets of Stone, the Torah, and the commandment, which I have written to instruct them."
>
> *(Shemot 24:12)*

This verse seems to indicate that the Torah, which Moshe received at Sinai, was more than simply Ten Commandments. Rashi on the above verse explains:

> All 613 mitzvot are subsumed in the Ten Commandments.

This teaching complicates matters even more, for if all of our mitzvot are embedded in the Ten Commandments, the nature of their Revelation is truly perplexing: Did God communicate all 613 commandments at Sinai, despite the fact that the people could not hear even one word? Midrashic, Kabbalistic, and chassidic sources all develop and discuss the idea that the communication at Sinai consisted of all 613 mitzvot. If this is what we mean by "Torah from Sinai," then perhaps this may also explain the nature of the Revelation. For if all 613 commandments are included in the Ten Commandments, then when God said all ten simultaneously, He actually communicated all 613 commandments at one time! If this is the case, we further understand why the people were unable to hear.

The Sages explain that Moshe received the totality of Torah at Sinai — everything from the Ten Commandments to questions raised by an "established student, commenting in front of his master" millennia in the future (*Yerushalmi Pe'ah* 2:4 17a).

> What is the meaning of the verse, "I will give you the Tablets of Stone, the Torah, and the commandment, which I have written to instruct them"? "Tablets of Stone" refers to the Ten Commandments. "The Torah" refers to the Written Torah [*Chumash*]. "The commandment" refers to the Mishnah. "Which I have written" refers to the [books of] *Nevi'im* and

> *Ketuvim*. "To instruct them" refers to the Gemara. This teaches that all these things were given to Moshe on Sinai.
>
> *(Berachot 5a)*

This was certainly more information than the people could possibly have assimilated at one time, in terms of both quantity and substance.

In that case, we return to our previous question: What was the purpose of a Revelation of Torah that the people could not have heard? Let us consider the fundamental difference between seeing and hearing: A person can see an incredible amount of material at once, but may only hear and comprehend one sound at a time. The nature of the Revelation at Sinai should be seen in this context: The primary significance of the Revelation was the unmistakable fact that the ineffable, transcendent God was communicating with man. In order to accomplish this, the nature of the communication had to be fundamentally different from any other ever known. The reversal of the senses, or the suspension of the boundaries between vision and hearing which make up our perceptions, established this as a completely supernatural experience.

The second aspect of the Revelation was the presentation of the entire Torah as one organic whole. This required that vision be employed instead of normal hearing. Only if the people saw what would otherwise have been heard could they take in the entire Torah in the way God wanted it presented.

The third aspect was that God wanted the people to hear all the details. After the entire Torah was presented at one time, God began to enumerate the commandments one by one.

The first objective was clearly accomplished, and the Revelation at Sinai was so powerful an experience that it has served as the basis of belief for millennia. The second objective was accomplished as well, and the people received a complete, organic vision. However, without the details that constituted the next step, this second level could not have been appreciated. The difference between seeing the beauty of Judaism and listening to the details is ultimately the difference between an appreciation of Judaism and observance.

Perhaps we can make a leap, and say that had the Jews been willing to listen to the details they would never have been able to worship a golden calf. Once the details break down, the whole system becomes deficient. The people flinched, as it were, and were not prepared to accept the Torah that God wanted to give at Sinai. This is precisely what Moshe said to the people:

> Do not be frightened. The Lord comes to uplift you and so that the fear of God will be upon you, so that you will not sin."

The inability of man to hear and directly receive the word of God at Sinai leads to the sin of the golden calf. The people allowed their relationship to be based on the general, amorphous "big picture" which they viewed, while what they actually needed was to hear and internalize the details. This big picture is a wonderful mosaic which consists of 613 interlocking pieces. It was essential for the people to see the big picture in order to be focused on the ultimate objective of Torah.

The people saw this wonderful image, but they failed to appreciate that they needed to learn for themselves how to bring the Torah down to earth. In order to build their own edifice, to forge their own way to God, they required tools — the details which God wished to impress upon them. But alas, the people preferred the beautiful, aesthetic view over the details needed to perfect the world.

God provided a second opportunity to bring all the details to earth:

> God said to Moshe, "Ascend to Me up the mountain, and be there. I will give you the Tablets of Stone, the Torah, and the commandment, which I have written to instruct them."

Again, God offered the people all the details of Torah, wrought by God's own hand. When God spoke to them at Sinai, the information was "compacted" in a supernatural manner. Here, too, when God writes, the transmission of information is supernatural. But when Moshe descends with the Tablets of Stone, which were written by the hand of God and contained all 613 commandments, he sees the Jews worshipping the golden calf and throws the Tablets to the ground. The Midrash relates that the letters then returned to Heaven:

> Moshe looked at the Tablets, and he saw the letters flying up in the air [toward Heaven]. The stones then became heavy and fell from his hands.
>
> *(Yalkut Shimoni, Ki Tisa 393)*

The Beit HaLevi explains (*drashah* 18) that the letters which returned to Heaven were the 613 mitzvot and the Oral Tradition. There were, then, two occasions on which God desired to give man far more than Ten Commandments, but man was simply not ready to accept that gift from God. Our path to the Torah becomes a circuitous route, a route filled with sin and the resultant distance from God, a route not at all resembling the one God originally planned for us.

God desires that man accept the Torah, both its numerous details and the magnificent mosaic, which results from embracing those details bit by bit. For when man does succeed in accepting the Torah, he becomes a partner with God, and a beautiful perfected world results.

Parashat Mishpatim

The Ten Commandments, Continued

Last week, we studied the portion dealing with the Revelation of the Torah at Sinai. We learned that while only ten commandments were revealed at that time, the people actually saw the entire Torah. When presented with the possibility of having God explain to them the Torah in detail, they failed to rise to the challenge. This week, in *Parashat Mishpatim*, the people receive many more commandments; in fact, the core of Jewish judicial law is presented in this parashah.

At the end of *Parashat Mishpatim*, Moshe is invited to ascend Mount Sinai in order to receive the content of the Revelation:

> God said to Moshe, "Ascend to Me up the mountain, and be there. I will give you the Tablets of Stone, the Torah, and the commandment, which I have written to instruct them."
>
> *(Shemot 24:12)*

Rashi's comments on this verse clarify that this occurred after giving of the Torah. We can therefore surmise that the sequence of events was as follows: Moshe goes up to Mount Sinai for forty days, subsequent to the Revelation on the mountain which all of Israel witnessed. But what was the purpose of Moshe's ascension, if he had already witnessed the Revelation? According to Rabbinic understanding, Moshe received far more than the "Tablets of Stone" when he ascended Mount Sinai. The verse itself indicates a much broader Revelation: "I will give you the Tablets of Stone, the Torah, and the commandment [*hamitzvah*], which I have written to instruct them.

This verse is clearly pregnant with meaning. Aside from the problem of defining each term, there is the additional problem of a dangling participle: "Tablets of Stone" seems a clear reference to the Ten Commandments etched in stone by God, but what are the "Torah" and the "mitzvah," and which of these is referred to by the phrase "which I have written"?

In the Gemara we are taught:

> What is the meaning of the verse, "I will give you the Tablets of Stone, the Torah, and the commandment, which I have written to instruct them"? "Tablets of Stone" refers to the Ten Commandments. "The Torah" refers to the Written Torah [*Chumash*]. "The commandment" refers to the Mishnah. "Which I have written" refers to the [books of] *Nevi'im* and *Ketuvim*. "To instruct them" refers to the Gemara. This teaches that all these things were given to Moshe on Sinai.
>
> *(Berachot 5a)*

According to this passage, the entire corpus of what we call Torah was given to Moshe at Sinai. The *Talmud Yerushalmi* (*Pe'ah* 2:4, 17a) continues this teaching: Even that which a "*talmid vatik*" (an established student) will someday ask was already given to Moshe at Sinai.

While this teaching seems quite clear and straightforward, some immediate questions arise. Moshe ascends Sinai in the first months following the Exodus, yet the Five Books of Moses — the *Chumash* — contain narrative which will unfold over the course of the ensuing forty years. We may simply say that Moshe was a prophet, and therefore was privy to information which the intellect is incapable of grasping. While this is surely the case, in this particular instance, knowledge of the entire *Chumash*, particularly the narrative which had yet to occur, leaves us with questions which are anything but simple.

For example, had Moshe been aware of the disastrous results of sending the spies, why would he have sent them? Why would Moshe strike the rock if he was aware of the results? Moreover, if we would posit that Moshe had no choice, that he had to "play out the script," how could he be held responsible for his actions? To rephrase the question: The Torah consists of both narrative and law; how could Moshe have received narrative of events which had not as of yet transpired, and need not necessarily have transpired? Had the Jews not sinned in the incident of the spies, they would not have wandered in the desert for forty years, which would then call into question the necessity for the entire *Sefer Bemidbar*. Obviously, the same question may be posed regarding the books of the Prophets — *Nevi'im* and *Ketuvim*. Regarding the Mishnah and Gemara, it is likewise difficult to understand how Moshe could have received these documents in totality, replete with names of later authorities, millennia before their birth.

> Moshe turned and descended from the mountain, with the two Tablets of the Testimony in his hand. The Tablets were written on both their sides; on the one side and on the other were they written. The Tablets were the work of God, and the writing was the writing of God, engraved upon the Tablets.
>
> *(Shemot 32:15–16)*

Here there is no reference to any information other than the "Tablets of Stone." Likewise, when Moshe descends the second time, the verse says,

> He was there with the Lord forty days and forty nights, and he did not eat bread or drink water. He wrote upon the Tablets the words of the covenant, the Ten Commandments. It was, when Moshe came down from Mount Sinai, with the two Tablets of Testimony in Moshe's hand when he came down from the mountain, that Moshe did not know that the skin of his face

shone [as a result of God's] speaking with him.

(Ibid. 34:28–29)

Moshe does not descend the mountain holding a Torah scroll. What, then, is the meaning of the passage cited above, which describes Moshe's knowledge and revelation as having been complete?

It is worthwhile to note that the text does describe additional information as having been imparted to Moshe:

> Afterward, all the Children of Israel came forward, and he [Moshe] commanded them all the things which God spoke with him on Mount Sinai.
>
> *(Ibid., 32)*

This verse clearly indicates that while perhaps in written form all that Moshe received was the Ten Commandments, there were other things taught to Moshe orally.

Thus far we have focused on the school of thought which teaches that Moshe received the entire corpus of Jewish knowledge on Mount Sinai, but another view is expressed in the Midrash. Immediately preceding the golden calf episode, the Torah states:

> [God] gave Moshe, when He finished speaking with him on Mount Sinai, two Tablets of Testimony, Tablets of Stone, written by the finger of the Lord.
>
> *(Ibid. 31:18)*

The Midrash focuses on the word "finished," *k'chaloto*:

> Did Moshe [finish] learning the entire Torah? It says in the Torah [that the Torah is] "longer than the land and broader than the sea" (Iyov 11:9). Did Moshe learn all this in forty days? Rather, God taught Moshe principles (כללים). This is what the verse means [when it says] *k'chaloto* (ככלתו).
>
> *(Shemot Rabbah 41:6)*

This Midrash implies that Moshe learned the principles of Torah, and not all of the Torah in a literal sense. However, we need not conclude that these two schools of thought are contradictory. They may, in fact, be complementary! The question of foreknowledge of events, for example, may be answered when we combine both schools of thought: Perhaps Moshe indeed learned the entire corpus of Jewish knowledge, but not in the detailed form; he knew the principles of theological truth which the biblical narratives teach, without knowledge of the details of future events.

It is an axiom in Torah that all teachings must conform with the teachings of Moshe. If any later prophet were to contradict Moshe, that latter teaching would be invalid, even heretical. All later teachings that are accurate are in accordance with the principles that God taught Moshe at Sinai. When it comes to practical law, God taught Moshe many details, but the *midrash* teaches that in some instances God taught Moshe principles without going into every application of the law which could, or would, arise in the future.

This insight will help us understand the formulation by Rambam in his introduction to *Mishnah Torah*:

> All the mitzvot which were given to Moshe at Sinai were given with explanations, as it says, "I will give you the Tablets of Stone, the Torah, and the *mitzvah* [commandment], which I have written to instruct them." The Torah is the Oral Torah and the "*mitzvah*" is the explanations. We are commanded to fulfill the Torah according to the *mitzvah*. This *mitzvah* is called the "Oral Torah." The entire Torah was written by Moshe Rabbeinu, prior to his death, by his hand. A copy was given to each tribe, and a copy was placed in the ark.... The *mitzvah*, which is the explanations, was not written, but rather it was taught to the elders, Yehoshua, and the rest of Israel.

Rambam is clearly conceptualizing the Talmudic passage cited above: Moshe indeed received far more than the Ten Commandments. He received the entire Oral Tradition. What is fascinating about Rambam's explanation is that Moshe received the Oral Tradition at Sinai, even though the Written Torah was not written until just prior to his death — long after the original Revelation. "The entire Torah was written by Moshe Rabbenu, prior to his death, by his hand." The Written Torah as we know it was "produced" before Moshe's death, not at Sinai, even though the Oral Torah, which is obviously interconnected with the Written Torah, was given to Moshe at an earlier juncture.

The nature of the interrelationship of the Written and Oral Torahs is a topic in and of itself, one that is beyond our present scope. Nonetheless, we have seen that Moshe descends the mountain with only the Tablets of Stone in hand, yet when invited to ascend the mountain he was promised much more. The Beit HaLevi (*drashah* 18) presents an incredible teaching: The original Tablets written by the hand of God indeed contained far more information. As we recall, the verse stated:

> I will give you the Tablets of Stone, the Torah, and the commandment [*hamitzvah*], which I have written to instruct them.

The Beit HaLevi says that the original Tablets indeed contained all this information. According to his understanding, had it not been for the sin of the golden calf, there would never have been a distinction between the Oral and Written Torahs. The Midrash recounts that when Moshe came down and saw the golden calf, he smashed the Tablets, and the letters floated Heavenward. As we saw above, when Moshe writes the second Tablets, it is now his own writing, not that of "the finger of God." Only when the second Tablets are given is a distinction created between Oral and Written Torah. At this point we saw that the verse states:

> He was there with the Lord forty days and forty nights, and he did not eat bread or drink water. He wrote upon the Tablets the words of the covenant, the Ten Commandments. It was, when Moshe came down from Mount Sinai, with the two Tablets of Testimony in Moshe's hand when he came down from the mountain, that Moshe did not know that the skin of his face shone [as a result of God's] speaking with him.

According to *Yalkut Shimoni,* the glow on Moshe's face was from the "leftover ink in his quill." The Beit HaLevi explains that the "leftover ink" refers to that which was included in the first Tablets but was missing from the second ones, namely the Oral Torah.

Now we can also understand the "dangling participle."

> I will give you the Tablets of Stone, the Torah, and the commandment [*hamitzvah*], which I have written to instruct them.

God had, in fact, transmitted both the Oral and Written Torah, but as a result of our own actions we never received the Torah in that complete form. The dangling participle, then, refers to all of Torah, written supernaturally on the Tablets of Stone.

We should recall what we learned in *Parashat Yitro*: God wished to give the people the entire Torah at Sinai, including all 613 commandments. Alas, the people "flinched" and did not seize the moment. Here again we see the continuation of the same idea: God wished to give the people the entire Torah directly, but once again they were not ready. In this vein, Shavuot is referred to as the day the Torah was given — "Yom Matan Torateinu" — and not as the day the Torah was received by man — "Yom Kabbalat Torateinu." According to the Midrash, the real day of receiving the Torah is the day Moshe came down from the mountain the second time, none other than Yom Kippur. The day the Jews accept the Torah is the day of forgiveness on the part of God.

Of course, every day can and should be for us "Yom Matan Torah." The Midrash teaches that we are always to remember Sinai and view every day as if it were the day the Torah was given (*Pesikta* 6:6). Moreover, we should see every day as the day the Torah will be received by us. That was God's original intention: that He give us the entire Torah, and that we receive it and live it. For truly receiving Torah brings about forgiveness and elevation.

Parashat Terumah

Innocence Lost and Found

Parashat Terumah represents somewhat of a departure from the theme of the previous sections of the Torah. While the other sections were mainly concerned with narrative, and *Mishpatim* introduced what may be seen as an extension of the Ten Commandments, *Terumah* virtually ignores narrative and instead gives instructions for building the Mishkan.

On the face of it, building the Mishkan is a strange thing to do. God, who is transcendent, certainly has no need of a "home," and it would be a mistake to understand the Divine decree as an attempt to build a haven for the ineffable, transcendent God. A careful reading of the text indicates the objective of the construction:

> Make Me a sanctuary, and I will dwell among them.
>
> *(Shemot 25:8)*

As a result of the building, God declares, He will live within the Jew or the Jewish nation, rather than the more obvious result of God "residing" in the Sanctuary. Clearly, the objective of the building was not to provide God with shelter, but to provide an avenue for man to bring God into his life.

The decree to build the Mishkan seems to fit very nicely into the narrative flow. The preceding verse described Moshe's ascension to receive the Torah. There is a difference of opinion among various commentaries and *midrashim* as to whether the golden calf episode preceded or followed the instructions for building the Mishkan.

Rashi follows the opinion expressed in the Midrash that the Mishkan is commanded only after the golden calf debacle. Ramban, on the other hand, sees the Mishkan as directly following the Revelation at Sinai, as per the *Zohar* (see *Sheim MiShmuel, Terumah*).

An earlier verse apparently connects the giving of the Torah and the building of the Mishkan, independent of the golden calf. When Moshe speaks to God at the burning bush, Moshe questions his role in the redemption of the Jews. God responds,

> This shall be a sign to you that I sent you — when you take the people out of Egypt, you shall worship the Lord on this mountain.
>
> *(Shemot 3:12)*

Rabbi Soloveitchik, *zt"l*, once explained[1] that two things had to transpire in order for this Divine promise to be realized. First, the Jews needed to receive the Torah, and second, the Jews needed to build the Mishkan. Both are included in the phrase "worship the Lord on this mountain." Therefore, according to this understanding, once the Torah was given, the only thing left to do was to build the Mishkan. Consequently, our parashah follows the ascension of Moshe.

This explains the logical sequence of the verses, but the understanding of the Divine imperative to build the Mishkan seems elusive. There are numerous components to the Mishkan, but its central part was clearly the *Aron*, the Ark. On top of the *Aron* a pair of gold *Keruvim* were placed. These *Keruvim* were made of one block of gold. They had an angelic appearance, and they faced one another with their wings touching. It was from the space between the two *Keruvim* that God communicated with the Jewish people.

---

1 I believe he cited *Sefer HaChinuch,* but I was unable to locate the source.

> I will make Myself known to you there, and I will speak to you from above the *Kaporet*, from between the two *Keruvim* which are upon the *Aron* of Testimony, all that I command you regarding the Jewish people.
>
> *(Ibid. 25:22)*

The Divine Presence emanated from between the *Keruvim*, and communication flowed. This would serve as a further link between the Revelation on Sinai and the Mishkan — which would replace Sinai and become a conduit for further revelation. Ramban makes this observation, and explains:

> This is the mystery of the Mishkan. The glory of God which was manifest on Mount Sinai would now radiate [to Moshe] inside [the Mishkan].
>
> *(Ramban, Shemot 25:1)*

Nonetheless, it is somewhat strange that Judaism, which generally rejects representations of the human form and of the Divine form, as it were, should prescribe a pair of *Keruvim* in the holiest of places. After all, what is the difference between the *Keruvim* and the golden calf? Why should one serve as a place for communication, while the other is considered desecration?

Rashi alludes to an answer to this question in his comments on the verse following the Ten Commandments that describes the prohibition of constructing "gods of gold or silver" (*Shemot* 20:20). Rashi explains that even the slightest deviation from the Divine decree is tantamount to idolatry. *Keruvim* of silver instead of gold, the wrong number of *Keruvim*, or their incorrect placement would constitute a violation of the command. This teaches us that the *Keruvim* were allowed only because God commanded us to construct them. Conversely, the golden calf was considered idolatry because God did not command us to construct it. The word *mitzvah* means "command," while the phrase *avodah zarah* means "strange worship," that which was not commanded.

Therefore, on at least a procedural level we are able to distinguish between the golden calf and the *Keruvim*. However, on a substantive level there must be a difference as well. In order to fully grasp the meaning of this Divine imperative we must uncover the significance of the *Keruvim*.

There is some difference of opinion regarding the actual appearance of the *Keruvim*. The composite form was that of two young children (see *Rashi, Shemot* 25:18) with wings, without clothing. According to the Gemara the two *Keruvim* were embracing like two lovers (*Yoma* 54a–b). The *Zohar* clearly says that one was male and the other female.

> The word *equity* [*meisharim*, lit. *equities*] in the above quoted verse [*Tehillim* 99:4] indicates that the *Keruvim* were male and female.
>
> *(Zohar, Vayikra 59a)*

This image of naked, embracing innocents obviously could have been misunderstood. The Gemara relates that when the Babylonians captured the Temple and entered the Holy of Holies, they were shocked:

> When the gentiles entered the *Heichal*, they saw the *Keruvim* embracing one another. They took them out to the marketplace and said, "This [Nation of] Israel, whose blessings are blessings and curses are curses, are involved in such things!?" They immediately cheapened them, as the verse says, "All their valuables were cheapened, for they saw her nakedness" (*Eichah* 1:8).
>
> *(Yoma 54b)*

The invading forces were evidently quite surprised to see the representation of the human form in the midst of the Holy Temple. The Jews were not thought of as idolaters, and the uninitiated assumed that what they saw was not only prohibited in Jewish law, but objectively erotic. One can certainly understand how they arrived at that conclusion.

In order to find a deeper understanding of the meaning of the

Keruvim, we must investigate the other places that the *Keruvim* appear.

The first mention of *Keruvim* in the Torah is in the verse describing the eviction of man from Gan Eden:

> Man was evicted, and *Keruvim* were placed east of Gan Eden, and a revolving burning sword was placed in order to guard the path to the Tree of Life.
>
> *(Bereishit 3:24)*

As a result of man's sin, the *Keruvim* enter the world in order to protect the Tree of Life. We have noted the identification between the Tree of Life and the Torah.[1] It is interesting to note that in the Mishkan the *Keruvim* protect the *Aron*, which contains the Torah, and in Eden the *Keruvim* protected the path leading to the Tree of Life, symbolizing Torah.

Before the sin of Adam and Chavah, the *Keruvim* were unnecessary; they appear only as a result of the sin. This leads us to conclude that the *Keruvim* represent none other than Adam and Chavah themselves, young, innocent, and naked in Eden. Only as a result of their sin did they become aware of and embarrassed by their nakedness.

> The woman saw that the tree was good for eating, and it was desirable to the eyes, and the tree was pleasant to make one wise. She took of its fruit and ate, and she gave also to her husband with her, and he ate. The eyes of both of them were opened, and they knew that they were naked. They sewed fig leaves together, and made for themselves aprons.
>
> They heard the voice of God, the Lord, reverberate in the Garden in the spirit of the day; and the man and his wife hid from before God, the Lord, in the midst of the trees of the Garden.
>
> God, the Lord, called to Adam, and said to him, "Where are you?"

---

1 See my comments on *Shemot* and *Beshalach*.

> He said, "I heard your voice in the Garden, and I was afraid because I was naked; and I hid myself."
>
> He said, "Who told you that you were naked? Have you eaten of the tree which I commanded you not to eat from?"
>
> *(Bereishit 3:6–11)*

The new, "sophisticated" perspective of Adam and Chavah, born of partaking of the forbidden fruit, gave them a different, perhaps distorted view of the world. Now they knew that they were naked; now they needed to clothe themselves. Now they hid from God. It is fascinating that the Hebrew word for clothing is "*beged*" from the root בגד (*bagad*), treason or rebellion. The clothing which man wears is a memorial to rebellion and the resultant distancing from God.

Immediately after eating from the Tree of Knowledge, the Torah relates:

> They heard the voice of God, the Lord, reverberate in the Garden in the spirit of the day, and the man and his wife hid from before God, the Lord, in the midst of the trees of the Garden.

As a result of their sin, Adam and Chavah felt alienated from God. God, for His part, was accessible and willing to engage them in a dialogue, but Adam felt embarrassed, naked, seeing the world from a different perspective than he had previously. Man lost his innocence.

In the place of this jaded couple, pathetically attempting to hide from God, now stood an innocent-looking couple, representing Adam and Chavah before the sin, guarding the passage to the Tree of Life, the Torah.

How appropriate that in the Mishkan and later in the Temple itself, in the Holy of Holies, there was a symbol of man at his apex — before his sin, in a state of total innocence before God. Specifically from here would the word of God emerge and reverberate. How appropriate that in anticipation of the destruction of the Temple the *Keruvim* embrace, an act of innocence in the face of the corrupt, marauding legion of conquering warriors. Sin had again permeated the world, and the *Keruvim* were taken out and misunderstood, their "nakedness" uncovered.

Man's sense of abandonment in the wake of his sins is a universal feeling; it was part of the reassurance that God had to give Moshe, when Moshe sought forgiveness for the people for the sin of the golden calf:

> Rabbi Yochanan said: If it were not a verse then it would be impossible to say. We learn that God wrapped Himself [in a tallit] as a *shaliach tzibur* (leader of the congregation in prayer) and instructed Moshe as to the proper order of the prayers. He said, "Whenever Israel sin, perform this service before Me and I will forgive them.... I am God prior to man's sin, and I am God after man sins and repents."
>
> *(Rosh HaShanah 17b)*

While man feels the alienation caused by sin, God remains unchanged. The alienation leads to man's loss of innocence, and to hiding from God. God, for His part, insists that there is always a path of return. The *Keruvim*, the image of man's innocence, guard this path. They are armed with a revolving sword, to symbolize the shift which man must make in order to approach Torah.

The two *Keruvim* were made of one piece of gold, just as Adam and Chavah were initially joined together as one. The *Keruvim* symbolize the ultimate return to one's self.

> Adam and Chavah were created as a united pair, and since they were coupled together, God blessed them. For blessing does not reside except in a place where there are male and female.
>
> *(Zohar, Bereishit 165a)*

> "The man said, 'The woman whom You gave to be with me gave me of the tree and I ate' " (*Bereishit* 3:12). [Rabbi Shimon] said: The expression "with me" indicates that Adam and Chavah were created together, with one body.
>
> *(Zohar, Vayikra 83b)*

Throughout the generations, the *kohein gadol* would enter the Holy of Holies on the holiest day of the year — Yom Kippur, the day on which the Jews were forgiven for the sin of the golden calf. Yom Kippur more than any other day symbolizes rebirth, regained innocence. It is the day when the Divine Presence, the *Shechinah,* flows. The *kohein gadol,* attired in special clothing, would venture into the Holy of Holies. As he entered he saw before him this perpetual image of innocence, purity, and holiness: the *Keruvim,* symbolizing Adam and Chavah as they were meant to be. Standing before God, he prayed for cleansing, purity, and innocence for the entire nation.

> For on that day [the *kohein*] shall make an atonement for you, to purify you, that you may be purified from all your sins before God.
>
> *(Vayikra 16:30)*

The Mishkan was not designed to be a home for God, but a place where man could return home — to himself.

Parashat Tetzaveh

Where Is Moshe?

This week's parashah opens with a different type of dialogue than the kind we have grown accustomed to in the Torah:

> You command the Children of Israel: They shall bring to you pure olive oil, crushed for illumination, to burn continuously.
> *(Shemot 27:20)*

Instead of the familiar "God spoke to Moshe, saying," the Torah simply states, "You command." The classical commentaries have all but ignored this idiosyncrasy (with the exception of the Ba'al HaTurim, who quotes the *Zohar* without citing it), but the *Zohar*, in the *Midrash Ne'elam*, notes the different language employed and provides the theological rationale.

After the sin of the golden calf, God offered to create a new nation from Moshe's offspring:

> And now permit Me to allow My anger to burn against them. I will consume them, and I will make you into a great nation.
> *(Ibid. 32:10)*

Not only does Moshe reject the offer, but he is willing to sacrifice all in his valiant attempt to save his people:

> And now, if You will, forgive their sin; if not, erase me out from the book which You have written.
>
> *(Ibid. 32:32)*

The *Zohar*, looking at these verses, writes:

> "And now, if You will, forgive their sin; if not, erase me from the book which You have written." This is a conditional curse, and God overlooked Moshe's obligation. Nonetheless, Moshe was removed from one section of the Torah: the commandments regarding the Mishkan. Which parashah is this? *V'atah Tetzaveh*, which should have contained Moshe's name in each and every word and in each and every commandment. But his name was taken out of the entire parashah, which has no mention of him. This is an example of the curse of a sage [being fulfilled] even when it is conditional.
>
> *(Midrash Ne'elam, Shir HaShirim 4)*

The *Zohar* teaches that God took Moshe up, albeit only partially, on his "offer" to be taken out of the Torah. According to this approach, it would seem that our parashah follows the golden calf episode chronologically, although in the Torah the sequence is reversed. On the other hand, one could posit that this portion was written with Moshe's name, and the name was later removed as per Moshe's request. In either case, we must ask why it is specifically from this parashah that Moshe's name was expunged. This question is especially poignant in light of Moshe's unique connection with this parsha, stressed by the *Zohar* cited above:

> Which parashah is this? *V'atah Tetzaveh*, which should have contained Moshe's name in each and every word and in each and every commandment.

The main topic of the parashah is the selection of Aharon and his family as the *kohanim*. This choice is neither justified nor explained; the Torah merely states as fact that Aharon has been chosen to be *kohein*. Once again we return to the question of chronology: Does this section follow the episode of the golden calf or does it precede it? If the latter is the case, why would Aharon, who sinned in the golden calf, be rewarded with this most exalted appointment, and have virtually the entire parashah directed toward him and his sons, while Moshe, who desperately tried to save his people, has his name removed from the parashah? Indeed, why was Aharon chosen to be *kohein,* and not Moshe? Aharon's record should have disqualified him from this sacred role.

Again, why was Moshe "erased" from this section? Is it due to a deficiency in Moshe? Perhaps analyzing another more celebrated "deficiency" will shed light on the exclusion of Moshe.

The Torah tells us that Moshe suffered from some type of speech impediment. The Maharal questions whether Moshe's problem with speech actually implies some type of handicap or limitation. He goes on to analyze the power of speech itself. In *Gevurot Hashem* (p. 112), the Maharal explains that speech is a physical act which indicates that one is part of the human race. At creation, the Torah describes man becoming *"nefesh chayah,"* a living soul. The Targum translates *nefesh chayah* as *"ruach mimalila"* (spirit which speaks). The power of speech is perhaps the single defining attribute of humanity.

Moshe's inability to speak was not due to a limitation, but rather to an "excess" or abundance: Moshe was somehow more than a regular person. He was above the level of *ruach mimalila,* and therefore his speech was not on the same level as that of ordinary mortals. Along these lines, the Talmud and Midrash explain Moshe's preparation to ascend Mount Sinai as six days in which the food was purged from his body until Moshe became "like one of the angels of heaven" (*Avot D'Rabi Natan*). Here, too, we learn that Moshe existed on a different plane, removed from the spiritual and physical limitations which are the boundaries of our normal existence.

The Maharal (*Drush for Shabbat Shuvah* 82b) explains the passage in the Gemara which describes how an angel teaches every child the entire Torah in utero, and then touches the child's mouth at the moment of birth, causing him to forget it all (*Niddah* 30b). The child thereby undergoes the metamorphosis from spiritual existence to physical. He is born a complete, physical being, as evidenced by the power of speech. The purely spiritual experience which was his lot prior to birth cannot coexist with this physical being. The pure, spiritual roots of man are grounded in the complete knowledge of Torah before birth. At birth, when physical existence replaces this pure spiritual existence, speech becomes man's domain. As speech begins, Torah knowledge dissipates and disappears.

Moshe, however, existed on a different plane, not limited to the physical in the same way as other mortals. He transcended that level, and therefore did not have that indicator of physical existence. He could not speak; he was above speech. But he possessed the whole Torah as no other mortal ever could. Moshe had achieved the exalted status of a soul prior to birth, in its purest state.

Parashat Tetzaveh begins with the oil needed to light the Menorah and proceeds to the election of Aharon and the description of clothing and accouterments of *kohein* and *kohein gadol*. The end of the parashah describes the *ketoret*, a type of incense used in the Temple. The Talmud teaches that the purpose of the *ketoret* was to atone for the sin of slander and gossip (*lashon hara*):

> For what [sin] does the *ketoret* bring atonement? *Lashon hara*. Let something performed in secret atone for something done in secret.
>
> *(Yoma 44a)*

We now can understand why Moshe was not the *kohein gadol* bringing the *ketoret*, which related to slanderous talk: Moshe transcended speech. Furthermore, the Maharal explains that on Yom Kippur a special *ketoret* of the finest materials was offered. This fine *ketoret* paralleled the sin of *avak lashon hara* (literally, dust of *lashon hara*), a prohibition which virtually all humans transgress. On Yom

Kippur, when we endeavor to achieve the spiritual level of the angels, we are even concerned with *avak lashon hara*. This was clearly not the realm of Moshe. On Yom Kippur we do not eat or drink; we attempt to become angelic. Moshe was already on this level. He had lived for an extended period without food or drink. Moshe did not misuse his speech. He had achieved the spiritual level which others aspire to achieve on Yom Kippur. He did not require the process of spiritual elevation that all others undergo on Yom Kippur; but Aharon did.

Now we may return to our earlier query. Why didn't God simply wipe Aharon from the Torah, or at the very least from this role? Aharon's selection must surely be somehow interwoven with his behavior during the golden calf episode. The Gemara describes the scene:

> It is written, "When Aharon saw it, and he built an altar before it" (*Shemot* 32:5). What did he actually see? Rabbi Binyamin bar Yafet said, quoting Rabbi Elazar: He saw Chur lying slain before him and said [to himself], "If I do not obey them [the people], they will do to me as they did to Chur. Then [the fear of the prophet], 'Shall the *kohein* and the prophet be slain in the Sanctuary of God?' (*Eichah* 2:20), will be fulfilled, and they will never find forgiveness. Better let them worship the golden calf, for which they may yet find forgiveness through repentance."
>
> *(Sanhedrin 7a)*

Aharon viewed the frightening murder of his brother-in-law Chur, and immediately thought of the implications of a similar act being perpetrated upon him. His concern was not personal, for his own well-being, but for the spiritual future of his wayward flock. Aharon then decides to lead them in this worship.

The great chassidic master Rav Tzaddok HaKohen from Lublin expanded on this idea, with one crucial addition: Rav Tzaddok saw Aharon's proactive stance in the ritualistic rebellion as more enthusiastic than it needed to be. After Aharon witnessed the murder of

Chur, he quickly decided that it was preferable for him to sin than to have the entire people guilty of both killing him and subsequently worshipping the calf. Aharon decided that it would be far better for the Jewish people if he — individually — were guilty, rather than allow them to face collective guilt. Aharon was willing to sacrifice everything for his people, both in this world and the next.

The only problem with this tremendous act of heroism and self-sacrifice was the idolatry involved, good intentions notwithstanding. Aharon's intentions needed to be rechanneled. Aharon needed to express his great love of the people of Israel and God through Divine service within the Temple. Rav Tzaddok explained that Aharon became *kohein gadol*, not despite the golden calf, but because of it! (*Takanat HaShavim*, p. 20). This is an application of the Talmudic principle that *teshuvah* motivated by love of God will turn a sin into merit. For this reason, the entire parashah is concerned with Aharon and not with Moshe: Moshe was beyond the role of *kohein*. Moshe had become one with Torah. In the words of the *Zohar*, surely every word and every command should have been in Moshe's name. Certainly, Moshe was worthy to lead the people and serve as *kohein gadol*. But Moshe personally had no need for his soul to be perfected via this Divine service.

Moshe, like Aharon, also was willing to sacrifice himself for the sake of his beloved people. When Moshe challenged God to erase him from the Torah, the *Zohar* comments:

> Moshe was willing to sacrifice himself for his flock. What is the meaning of the verse, "And now, if You will, forgive their sin; if not, erase me from the book which You have written"? What does "erase me" mean? From this world and the next.
>
> *(Midrash Ne'elam, Bereishit)*

According to the *Zohar*, Moshe was prepared to sacrifice everything in order to save the people, just as Aharon was. The only difference was that Aharon had sinned and therefore needed personal forgiveness. Moshe did not sin; therefore his soul had no need to be a part of this parashah. Although every word and commandment should have borne Moshe's name, Moshe had simply transcended this parashah. By virtue of his self-sacrifice, Moshe needed no *kapparah* (atonement). Moshe was already angelic; he had become one with Torah and one with God. The role of *kohein* becomes the domain of Aharon, and here his great love of his people finds proper expression.

Only one who is willing to sacrifice for the people is worthy of leading the Jewish nation. Both Moshe and Aharon possessed this admirable trait. Both were prepared to be *moser nefesh* (sacrifice) in the most literal sense: to give up their soul for the sake of the people. That, as we have seen, is the litmus test of leadership. However, the method of Aharon's heroism left him in need of forgiveness and elevation. Aharon still needed to become angelic, like Moshe. Therefore, Moshe's name is absent from the parashah, while all the laws are directed toward Aharon and his children. They will be responsible for all aspects of Temple service for millennia. They will light the lights that will shine brightly over the generations, testimony to the Torah of Aharon who placed the people before himself, motivated by love of God and nation.

Parashat Ki Tisa

The Golden Calf

This week's parashah contains one of the great tragedies of Jewish history. The Jewish people, who had left Egypt miraculously, witnessed the great salvation at the sea, stood at Sinai, and experienced the Revelation, now awaited Moshe's descent from the mountain. Moshe was to bring with him the teachings of the Torah, the mandate given the Jews which was to change the course of world history. However, the wait became too difficult, and the people, perhaps searching for immediate gratification, made a calf of gold and worshipped it. Thousands of years later we are still shocked at how this generation, so privileged, could make so fundamental an error.

The *Zohar*, in almost the very first teaching, deals with this question via a discussion between Rabbi Shimon bar Yochai and his son Rabbi Eliezer regarding the meaning of the verse, "Lift your eyes to the heavens, and see who created these" (*Yeshayah* 40:26). The simple meaning of this verse is that contemplating the heavenly bodies leads to recognition of God's existence. Rabbi Shimon ben Yochai, however, was privileged to learn a deeper, mystical explanation to the verse from Eliyahu HaNavi.

> [Rabbi Shimon said:] "One day...Eliyahu [the Prophet] came and said to me, 'Master, what is the meaning of "*Mi bara eileh*

— Who created these"?' I said to him, "This refers to the heavens and their hosts, the works of the Holy One, blessed be He, works which lead man to bless [the Creator] when he contemplates them....'

"Then he said to me, 'Master, the Holy One, blessed be He, had a deep secret which He revealed at length to the Heavenly Academy. It is this: When the Most Mysterious wished to reveal Himself, He produced a single point, which was transmuted into a thought, and in this He executed innumerable designs and engraved innumerable engravings. He further engraved within the sacred and mystic lamp a mystic and most holy design, which was a wondrous edifice issuing from the midst of thought. This is called *Mi* (מי), and was the beginning of the edifice, existent and nonexistent, deep, buried, unknowable by name. It was only called *Mi* (who). It desired to be manifest and called by name. It therefore clothed itself in a refulgent and precious garment and created *Eileh* (אילה, these), and *Eileh* acquired a name. The letters of the two words intermingled, forming the complete name *Elokim* (א-לקים, Lord).

" 'When the Israelites sinned in making the golden calf they alluded to this mystery in saying, "These [*eileh*] are your Lords, Israel" (*Shemot* 32:4). And once *Mi* became combined with *Eileh*, the name remained for all time. Upon this secret, the world is built.'

"Eliyahu then flew away and vanished from my sight. And it is from him that I became possessed of this profound mystery."

Rabbi Eliezer and all the companions came and bowed down in front of him, weeping for joy. They said, "If we had come into this world only to hear this, we would have been content."

(Zohar, prologue 1b–2a)

Obviously, many of the philosophical issues in this passage are beyond the scope of this work, but we can reconstruct some basic teachings. The *Zohar* explains that the creation of the world is based on the combination of the *Mi* and *Eileh* which spell *Elokim* (by inverting the *yud* and *mem*). Therefore, the first verse in the Torah reads:

> In the beginning the Lord [*Elokim*] created the heaven and the earth.

The Name *Elokim*, which combines *Mi* and *Eileh*, is employed. The *Zohar*'s theological explanation is that the verse "*Mi bara eileh* — Who created these?" lies behind the first verse in the Torah, "In the beginning *Elokim* created...." It follows, then, that the question, "Who created these?" must always remain a question, a rhetorical, unanswerable question. The Jew understands that there are certain mysteries which are impenetrable. The essence of God is one such mystery. The transcendent, essential aspect of God remains elusive. This is expressed by the idea of *Elokim*, which contains the *Mi*, the "who," as a question. Man may contemplate Creation, but if we think the question is answered and attempt to point a finger at God, we run into trouble.

The Jews who stood at Mount Sinai pointed a finger at the golden calf, which they had formed, and declared, "These are your lords, Israel." They wished to understand and experience God on their own terms, to provide a concrete answer for this unanswerable question.

What was it that brought this response from these people? The people complained,

> The man Moshe who took us out of Egypt, we do not know what has become of him.
>
> *(Shemot 32:1)*

They believed they had the right to "know" that which was beyond them. But was it really knowledge that had eluded them?

Let us analyze the situation: The Jews are but moments before the descent of Moshe. They just need to be patient one more day and the precious Torah will be theirs. However, we know how the story ends: Instead of the *luchot*, the Tablets of Stone, coming into their hands, they were shattered at the foot of the mountain.

There is a fascinating parallel: At the dawn of history, man was told of two trees in Gan Eden which were distinct from all the others, the Tree of Life and the Tree of Knowledge of Good and Evil. Adam was permitted to eat of all the trees except the Tree of Knowledge. Again, we know how that story ended. Man ate from the wrong tree, death was brought into the world, and man was expelled from Eden.

The Sages note that there was no prohibition against partaking from the Tree of Life. In fact, we are taught that the original plan was for Adam to have eaten first from the Tree of Life and then from the Tree of Knowledge. Evidently, the sin of Adam was in eating from the trees in the improper sequence. In order for us to understand the significance of the order we must consider the nature of these two trees.

According to Rabbinic thought, the Tree of Life is identified with Torah:

> It [the Torah] is a Tree of Life to those who embrace it.
>
> *(Mishlei 3:18, Vayikra Rabbah 25:1)*

If the Tree of Life is identified with Torah, what is the meaning of the Tree of Knowledge? If anything, we would have a priori associated the Tree of Knowledge with Torah. Apparently, this knowledge has a very specific meaning. In the verses following the expulsion of man, the Torah says that Adam "knew his wife" (*Bereishit* 4:1). Here again the root "*yada*" (knew) is used, and here it is clear that this word does not refer to Torah, but rather implies experience.

This allows us to reinterpret the sin of Adam: The plan in Gan Eden was for man to eat from the Tree of Life — Torah, and only thereafter, with the onset of the first Shabbat, to eat from the Tree of Knowledge as well. The issue at hand is what should come first, Torah wisdom or experience? The advantage of Torah preceding experience is that the Torah, once internalized, will serve as a basis from which subsequent experience will be interpreted. Torah becomes a vantage-point from which experiences are viewed and understood. If, however, experiences are acquired first, they will serve as a basis for the interpretation given subsequently to the Torah. This latter sequence can lead to distortion of the Torah and misinterpretation based on the subjective experience of the individual. Torah must precede experience. Torah must be the benchmark by which Jews lead their lives and mold their views.

The tragedy of Eden was reexperienced at the foot Mount Sinai. The Jews were awaiting the descent of Moshe with the Torah, but they did not know where Moshe was (the word they use is *yadanu*, from the same root as the Tree of Knowledge in Eden). Here lies their difficulty: they wanted to "know" that which they could not. The episode ends with people arising in an orgiastic feast — experiencing god in their subjective manner, creating a graven image, instead of receiving the Torah from God via Moshe. Again, experience (the Tree of Knowledge) is chosen over Torah (the Tree of Life).

But why this particular response? Why a calf? The *Zohar* described the sin as the pointing with their fingers, saying, "Here [or *these*] are your lords, Israel," trying to know and experience that which they could not. In order to understand this, we must return to the previous time that the Jews pointed a finger and declared something about God. When the Jews passed through the sea, the Torah recounts that they declared:

> This is my God and I will cherish him.
>
> *(Shemot 15:2)*

Rashi, drawing from the Midrash, comments:

> They pointed Him out with a finger. We see that even a maidservant on the sea perceived more than the prophets.

Walking through the divided sea was an incredible religious experience, in which even the uninitiated perceived more than the prophets. Which prophets does Rashi have in mind? The source of

Rashi is the *Mechilta,* which writes "more than Yeshayah or Yechezkel." Ramban cites the *Mechilta* as making the comparison with Yechezkel. These two prophets both beheld the dazzling revelation known as the *Merkavah.*

> All that Yechezkel saw, Yeshayah saw. What does Yechezkel resemble? A villager who saw the king. And what does Yeshayah resemble? A townsperson who saw the king.
>
> *(Chagigah 13b)*

Can we learn from this comparison anything specific about the nature of the Jews' collective vision at the sea? What exactly did the people see?

The prophecy of Yechezkel is one of the most obscure sections in Tanach, the images and references transcending the understanding of the average reader. By the Kevar River, Yechezkel has "visions of God": he sees an image with "the leg of a calf" (*Yechezkel* 1:7). The image had the face of a person, a lion, a bull, and an eagle. In a later chapter, when Yechezkel repeats and expounds on his vision, he lists the four faces in greater detail:

> Every one had four faces: the first face was the face of a *keruv* [cherub], the second face was the face of a person, the third was the face of a lion, and the fourth was the face of an eagle.
>
> *(Yechezkel 10:14)*

The bull mentioned above is paralleled with the *keruv,* which will become the source of revelation in the Temple. If the sin of the golden calf took place after the order to build the Mishkan, we may be able to understand why the Jews built specifically a golden calf. They thought that this was part of the command to build the Mishkan. It reminded them of that glorious moment when they experienced God and thought that they understood Him. As they pointed a finger praising God, they also deluded themselves into thinking that they understood God. Such is the nature of experience. Knowledge of Torah would have corrected this error.

The Midrash also clearly connects the error of the golden calf with a misunderstanding of the *Merkavah*. When God speaks to Moshe from the burning bush, He states, "I have surely seen [*ra'o ra'iti*]...this nation" (*Shemot* 3:7). The Midrash explains why the verb *seen* is repeated.

> God said, "Moshe, you can only see one vision, but I see two visions. You see them [the people] coming to Sinai and receiving My law and so do I. This, however, is only one vision. I can also see the vision of the golden calf, as it says, 'I have seen this nation' (*Shemot* 32:9). When I come to Sinai to give them the Torah, I will come down in My chariot with four animals abreast. Yet though they will observe Me, they will unhitch one [of the four animals of My chariot] and provoke Me."
>
> *(Shemot Rabbah 3:2)*

The sin of the golden calf negated the great spiritual elevation which resulted from the Revelation at Sinai. By separating one of the animals from the *Merkavah*, the Jewish people reached a faulty, heretical conclusion about God.

> This is also what God said: "At Sinai, you prepared two cups — 'We will do' and 'we will hear.' By making the golden calf, you have shattered one — the [cup for] 'We will do.' Be very careful, therefore, with the second one — 'We will listen.' "
>
> *(Shemot Rabbah 27:9)*

After the debacle of the golden calf, the Jews needed to pay special attention to "the second cup," adhering to the word of God.

Rashi comments that the *parah adumah* (the red heifer whose ashes were used in the Mishkan and the Beit HaMikdash) is a *chok*, a command whose reason we do not understand. Yet, at a later point, Rashi cites a tradition that the *parah adumah* was a rectification for the sin of the golden calf (*Rashi, Bemidbar* 19:9). These two explanations of Rashi are not contradictory: The *parah adumah* brings about forgiveness for the golden calf, precisely because it is a commandment which we cannot understand. If the sin of the golden calf was indeed thinking that one can understand God, then forgiveness lies in performing a commandment despite this or perhaps because we do not understand its reason.

Death entered into the world when man ate from the Tree of Knowledge of Good and Evil, partaking of experience prior to acquiring Torah knowledge and attempting to understand that which is not given to our understanding.

> Had Israel waited for Moshe and not perpetrated that act, there would have been no exile, nor would the Angel of Death have had any power over them. And thus it says, "And the writing was the writing of God, engraved [*charut*] upon the tablets" (*Shemot* 32:16).
>
> What is the meaning of *charut* [which has the same root as the word *cheirut,* freedom]?... Rabbi Nechemyah says: [The Children of Israel were] free from the Angel of Death. When Israel exclaimed, "All that the Lord has spoken will we do and we will hear" (ibid. 24:7), the Holy One, blessed be He, said, "I gave only one commandment to Adam, so that he would fulfill it, and I made him equal to the ministering angels.... How much more so should those who practice and fulfill all the six hundred and thirteen commandments — not to mention their principles, details, and minutiae — be deserving of eternal life?" However, as soon as they said, "These are your lords, Israel," death came upon them. God said, "You have followed the course of Adam who did not withstand his trials for more than three hours, and at nine hours death was decreed upon him."
>
> *(Shemot Rabbah 32)*

The *parah adumah* is the antidote for death; it removes the spiritual stigma caused by death, because it is performed without understanding. It is performed simply because it is Torah. It is the ultimate acceptance of Torah, which eluded man at the dawn of history in Eden, and again at what should have been the apex, at Sinai.

Addendum:

On most years this parashah is read in close proximity to

Purim, and according to the *Tikunei Zohar* there exists an intrinsic relationship between Purim and *Yom Kippurim,* the day on which the Jews were forgiven for the sin of the golden calf. The Arizal explained this relationship: Purim is, in fact, a holier day, and *Yom Kippurim* should be translated as "a day like Purim." The *Talmud Yerushalmi* states that in the future none of the holidays will be observed except for Purim. We may describe the relationship as follows: Part of the sin of the golden calf was, as we said above, the choice of experience prior to Torah. On Yom Kippur Moshe descended from Mount Sinai with the second Tablets, and the Jews finally accepted the Torah. On this day we do not eat or drink, wash, or engage in sexual relations. This would serve as a *tikun* (rectification) for the sin of the golden calf and the festivities which accompanied it. Forgiveness on Yom Kippur is brought about by total abstention.

On the other hand, the Sages tell us that the Jewish people did not completely accept the Torah until the time of the Purim miracle, nearly a thousand years after the Torah was first given.

> They reaccepted it [the Torah] in the days of Achashveirosh, as it is written, "[The Jews] confirmed and accepted it" (*Esther* 9:27). [I.e.,] they confirmed what they had accepted long before.
>
> *(Shabbat 88a)*

The Gemara points out that Haman's name is hinted to in *Bereishit,* in a verse referring to Adam's sin: "Where is Haman hinted to in the Torah? In the verse "*Hamin ha'eitz hazeh* — Was it from this tree?" (*Chullin* 139b).

Haman is connected with the Tree of Knowledge, and we see that the problems in the time of the Purim story began in Shushan when the Jews partook of the King's party, an inappropriate action which echoes the festivities for the golden calf.

It was in Shushan so many years later that the Jews finally accepted the Torah completely. Only then could an attempt be made to elevate the eating and drinking into a holy context. This is why we are commanded to drink on Purim "until one cannot differentiate between 'Blessed is Mordechai' and 'Cursed is Haman' — *Ad d'lo yada.*" Again, the word *yada* is used. On Yom Kippur we abstain from eating and drinking, while on Purim we elevate eating and drinking. On Purim we attempt to elevate experiences into the context of Torah, which is accepted anew.

Parashat Vayakheil

Shabbat: Creation, Mishkan, and Infinity

The previous parashah, *Ki Tisa*, ended with Moshe coming down from the mountain, visibly changed by his experience of proximity to God. *Vayakheil*, as its name would indicate, begins with Moshe gathering the people, ostensibly to teach them the Torah which he received at Sinai. He begins with the laws of Shabbat. This should come as no surprise; we know that Shabbat is among the most "important" mitzvot, a cornerstone of Judaism. Some commentaries highlight the juxtaposition of this teaching with the sin of the golden calf.

The golden calf was idolatry on some level; Shabbat, as testimony to God's creation of the world in six days, serves as a spiritual antidote for idolatry in the future. Another connection between the sin of the golden calf and the choice of *hilchot Shabbat* as the first lesson lies in the very nature of the sin: If we say that the golden calf was an attempt to "know God," Shabbat is offered by Moshe as the correct method to achieve this goal. If you seek God and wish to know Him, observe Shabbat. This is the proper way to experience the Divine.

What is striking is that the Jews had already been commanded to keep Shabbat, and the idea of Shabbat was mentioned on four different occasions in *Shemot* (16:23, 20:7–10, 23:12, 31:13–17), aside from the teaching at Marah (15:25) where tradition teaches that the Jews were commanded to keep Shabbat (see *Sanhedrin* 56a). Why would it be necessary to teach it a fifth time? A closer look at the specific teachings in this section may be enlightening:

> Six days do work [*melachah*] and the seventh day shall be for you holy, a *Shabbat Shabbaton* for God; whoever does work shall be put to death. Do not burn fire in all your habitations on the Shabbat day.
>
> (*Shemot 35:2–3*)

We may reduce these verses to two central ideas: 1) a prohibition against *melachah*, and 2) a prohibition against the use of fire. But what is *melachah*, and why is fire excluded from the category of *melachah* and mentioned separately?

These questions are treated extensively in the Talmud in halachic discourse, and surely no laws of Shabbat may be understood without halachic definitions of work on the one hand, and the unique category of fire on the other. The general halachic framework of this section is built upon its context within the laws surrounding the building of the Mishkan.

The word *melachah* is the key to the section describing the work for the Mishkan (see, for example, *Shemot* 35:21, 31, 33, 35, and 36:1–8), as well as the key to our parashah, where Moshe teaches the laws of Shabbat observance. Our Sages therefore deduce that the types of work described in the instructions for building the Mishkan are the same types of work prohibited on the seventh day. In a word, the *melachah* prohibited on Shabbat is the very same *melachah* used in constructing the Mishkan.

That said, a more basic question now replaces our previous questions: Why are the laws of Shabbat derived from the section dealing with the building of the Mishkan? In a literal and literary sense, one might say that we have already answered this question: The same word, *melachah*, is utilized in both sections. But in a larger sense, this answer begs the question. Surely God could have provided a word play in any section of the Torah that He so chose. There could have been any number of alternative definitions for the key word *melachah*. Why specifically here, in the section which describes the building of the Mishkan, are the laws of Shabbat derived? There must be some intrinsic relationship between Shabbat and the Mishkan.

Of the two concepts, a priori, Mishkan seems more difficult for us to grasp. Why would God need an earthly "home"? This question was posed in the Midrash:

> When the Holy One, blessed be He, said to Moshe, "Make for Me a *mikdash*" (*Shemot* 25:8), Moshe said to Him, "Master of the Universe, the heavens and beyond cannot contain You, and You say, 'Make for Me a *mikdash*'!"
>
> The Holy One, blessed be He, said to him, "Moshe, you do not think I think. Rather, [build] twenty boards to the north and twenty boards to the south and eight to the west, and I will descend and contract My *Shechinah* (Divine presence) among you below."
>
> *(Pesikta D'Rav Kahana 2:10*[1]*)*

The need is evidently not God's, but man's. For God to allow His Presence to dwell in this *mikdash*, some type of contraction, as it were, is necessary on God's part. This same question may be posed about Shabbat. Why does God need a "day of rest"? In one sense we are comfortable with the idea of Shabbat; God created for six days, and rested on the seventh. But upon critical analysis it seems absurd — as absurd as God having a home.

Let us reconsider the idea of Creation. There was nothing, and then God created heaven and earth. This creation process continued for six days; at its completion God "rested." This description contains a number of deeply embedded athropomorphisms: God's "rest," as well as God's "creation." While our idea of work

---

1 Also see *Shemot Rabbah* 34:1, where the conclusion is "I will descend and contract My *Shechinah* in one *amah* by one *amah*."

(*melachah*) is to effect change in existing material, this is the perspective of a finite being utilizing creativity within a finite scheme. God, however, is infinite. The very notion of creation includes time, space, and matter, all concepts which God transcends. His creation is described as *yeish mei'ayin*, matter from nothingness, ex nihilo creation.

Kabbalistic writings offer an alternative understanding of creation as "*yeish mei'ayin,*" something from the *Ein Sof*, finite emerging from the Infinite. Consider the problem mathematically: Any value added to infinity necessarily yields a sum which is infinite. When God, who is infinite, creates a finite value — i.e., the world — the sum total of reality should remain infinite. How can finite be added to infinite? The Kabbalistic response to this question is a term known as "*tzimtzum*" — contraction. Creation is not the result of God adding something finite; rather, He "holds back" infinity, as it were.

We may now see Creation, and therefore Shabbat, from a different perspective. On the first day, God holds back infinity; likewise on the second through sixth days. Finally, at the end of the sixth day, the world is complete and God rests. In other words, God reverts back to a noncontraction mode, back to infinity. Shabbat is therefore the day which represents infinity, the one day which relates to and reflects God on His terms, not via the *tzimtzum*.

This concept of *tzimtzum* may give us further insight into Shabbat. As stated earlier, God exists outside of time; Creation marks the beginning of time. Shabbat alternatively represents the infinite. What time was it prior to Creation? It was a time of "infinity" or, in other words, it was Shabbat! In Jewish thought, creation takes place on "the first day," the day after Shabbat. Creation is in the evening: "It was evening, it was morning, one day." Therefore, it can be said that creation takes place the very moment that Shabbat is over. The moment prior to creation is infinity, or Shabbat, and the moment after the six days of creation is Shabbat, our own avenue to infinity. Both points indicate the same moment from God's perspective, though separated by a world of difference from our perspective.

We have noted that man has the opportunity to touch infinity by partaking of Shabbat. This observation may help us understand the exclusion of fire from the other *melachot*. When the Gemara takes up a question regarding certain details of Havdallah, a verse from *Bereishit* is brought as substantiation.

> One should not bless the candles until they give proper light. This was expounded by Rabbi Zeira the son of Rabbi Abahu: "God saw that the light was good" (*Bereishit* 1:4), and afterward it states, "God distinguished [*vayavdeil*] between light and darkness" (ibid.).
>
> *(Talmud Yerushalmi, Berachot 8:3, 126)*

When we appreciate that the first day is the moment after Shabbat, this teaching takes on more meaning. Our Havdallah mirrors this first, essential *havdallah* made by God with the act of creation. Rabbeinu Bechayei, commenting on this week's parashah, makes this connection very clear. He explains that fire is separated from the other *melachot* in Moshe's teaching because, just as God began the Creation with fire by saying, "Let there be light," so man begins the week with the fire of Havdallah.

Let us return to the laws of Shabbat, which are derived from the *melachot* of the Mishkan. Creativity is manifest when an object is improved in some way, but this type of work is fundamentally different from the work which God performed in Creation. God's work was "something from nothing," while our work is "something from something." Being that we are finite beings, our creation is necessarily different from God's. While God "held back" in order to create, man goes forward; while God goes into His "infinite mode" on Shabbat, transcending the *tzimtzum* He employed in creating the world, man must hold back his creative energies. What we have described is an inverse relationship, due to the fundamental difference between man and God.

One may describe the relationship in the following terms: Man is said to be in the image of God. We are, in fact, the mirror image of God. We are opposites. Therefore, on Shabbat we "hold back" while trying to be like God in the only way we can — by imitating the means of God's Creation, *tzimtzum*. Perhaps that is what we mean when we describe our rest on Shabbat as "a commemoration of the act of Creation": We do on Shabbat what God did in Creation.

We may now understand the intrinsic relationship between the laws of Shabbat and the building of the Mishkan. Both represent this idea of God "holding back." And just as God answered in the Midrash, "Moshe, you do not think I think. Rather, [build] twenty boards to the north and twenty boards to the south and eight to the west, and I will descend and contract My *Shechinah* [Divine presence] among you below," so, too, must God hold himself back in order to make possible the very creation of the world.

My rebbe, Rav Yosef Dov Soloveitchik, *zt"l*, explained these concepts as follows: For Jews, philosophical understanding leads to moral imperative. The Jew must emulate God and practice *tzimtzum* in various relationships. This is the idea of *gevurah* (strength), as in the *mishnah*,

> Who is strong? The person who controls his evil inclination.
> *(Avot 4:1)*

This idea arguably stands at the core of all Jewish ethics and marks a radical departure from the way man sees his responsibilities vis-à-vis his fellow man. It is noteworthy that the Torah begins with *"Bereishit bara Elokim,"* the Name *Elokim* being associated with the mystical realm of *gevurah*. God practices "self-control" by limiting the infinite in the process of Creation. Therefore, we may view Shabbat as a one-day adventure in self-control. Often we have to hold ourselves back from even the most mundane, arguably trivial activities, only because they are defined as creative activity, *melachah*. It is hoped that such self-control will spill over into the week, elevating all our actions and thoughts.

This idea may be illustrated by an apparent contradiction between the *Talmud Bavli* and *Yerushalmi*. The *Bavli* states:

> Rabbi Yochanan said in the name of Rabbi Shimon ben Yochai that if all the Jews were to observe just two Shabbatot properly, Redemption would come immediately.
>
> *(Shabbat 118b)*

The *Yerushalmi* states:

> If all the Jews were to observe just one Shabbat properly, [Mashiach] ben David would come.
>
> *(Yerushalmi, Ta'anit 1:1, 64a)*

We may say that the sources are not actually contradictory. In truth, we must observe only one Shabbat, as stated in the *Yerushalmi*, but the one we must observe is the second Shabbat, as stated in the *Bavli*. There is, after all, a significant difference between the first Shabbat and the second. A Shabbat observed in a spiritual vacuum would surely be spiritually uplifting, but this is not the type of Shabbat which would lead to Redemption. This first Shabbat should serve a different purpose, optimally influencing the ensuing week, affecting Sunday, Monday, and so on. The spiritual value of that first Shabbat observed gives a different hue to the rest of the week. The second Shabbat, approached after a week so influenced, is completely different. It marks a spiritual apex, not a spiritual island. This is the type of Shabbat whose observance will bring about Redemption. It is the Shabbat of a week, and a world, uplifted. (See the discussion in *Pri Tzaddik* by Rav Tzaddok HaKohen, vol. 4, 108–109.)

Both Shabbat and Mishkan are about God dwelling in this world. By virtue of our incorporating Godliness into our lives, we redeem the world. This was the great message imparted to the Jewish people by Moshe upon his descent from Sinai. This teaching gave them a channel to the Infinite God they sought.

Parashat Pekudei

Betzalel: Builder of the Mishkan

In his introduction to *Sefer Shemot,* Ramban calls *Shemot* the "Book of Redemption." This book begins with the slavery of the Jewish people, proceeds through their liberation and the triumphant moment at Mount Sinai, recounts the sin of the golden calf, and ends with the building of the Mishkan. The period of time which elapses from the Exodus until the end of *Sefer Shemot* is actually quite short; all of these events occurred in less than one year.

> God spoke to Moshe, saying, "On the first day of the first month [in the second year] erect the Mishkan, the Tent of Meeting."
>
> *(Shemot 40:1–2)*

The *sefer* ends as the Mishkan is enveloped by the cloud which would, from that point onward, indicate to the Jewish people the proper time to travel. The Glory of God fills the Holy of Holies, and the Mishkan is thereby completed.

The Mishkan is one of the major topics of *Sefer Shemot,* as is evidenced by the amount of space and detail devoted to the description of its construction. Minutely detailed instructions were given to Moshe, but implemented by a man named Betzalel. Who was this individual, Moshe's "right-hand man" in the project? The Torah states:

> God spoke to Moshe, saying, "See, I have called by name Betzalel son of Uri son of Chur, from the tribe of Yehudah. I will fill him with the spirit of God; with wisdom, understanding, and knowledge."
>
> *(Shemot 31:1–3)*

From this description, it does not sound as if Betzalel is endowed with the critical attributes as of yet. The verse says, "I will fill him with the spirit of God," using the future tense. If this is the case, what is the reason for his selection? Furthermore, the phrase "See, I have called by name Betzalel" implies that there is something special about his name. Our two main pieces of evidence seem contradictory: On the one hand, he does not yet possess the skills needed to perform the task, and on the other hand there is something about Betzalel which God has singled out, something which is indeed a part of his essence.

The Midrashim offer several accounts of the selection of Betzalel which together form a composite picture. First is a passage in the Talmud:

> The Holy One, blessed be He, said to Moshe, "Do you consider Betzalel suitable?"
>
> He [Moshe] replied, "Master of the Universe, if You find him suitable, surely I must also!"
>
> [God] said to him, "All the same, go and consult them [the nation]."
>
> He went and asked Israel, "Do you consider Betzalel suitable?"
>
> They replied, "If the Holy One, blessed be He, and you consider him suitable, surely we must!"
>
> *(Berachot 55a)*

This passage is strange. Why would Betzalel not be acceptable? Why was it necessary for Betzalel to be "accepted" by both Moshe and the nation? There are two factors which may contribute to the implied note of hesitation in the acceptance of Betzalel. The first was his age, and the second was his lineage.

> When Betzalel constructed the Mishkan, how old was he? Thirteen.
>
> *(Sanhedrin 69b)*

Why would a thirteen-year-old be chosen to build the Mishkan and its utensils? Surely there must have been more qualified artisans who could have performed this sacred task. Perhaps this was the reason that God "asked permission" to use such a young person for so important a task.

As far as his lineage, the Torah had told us that he was "son of Uri, son of Chur, from the tribe of Yehudah." Chur is a familiar, albeit somewhat mysterious character. When the Amaleikites waged war against the Jews almost immediately following the Exodus, it was Chur, together with Aharon, who supported Moshe's arms and assured victory (*Shemot* 17:10–12). Later, when Moshe prepared to go up to Heaven to receive the Torah, he tells the Elders that Chur and Aharon are in charge during his absence and should be consulted should any question arise. That, however, is the last we hear of Chur. The Midrash questions Chur's disappearance, and reports that Chur is killed when the Jews asked Aharon to construct a calf of gold.

> When the Israelites wished to do that deed, they said to Aharon, "Come and make for us a lord." Chur the son of Kaleiv arose and chastised them. They immediately arose and killed him.
>
> *(Tanchuma, Tetzaveh 10:10)*

If Chur was murdered as part of the golden calf episode, we can understand why employing his grandson to build the Mishkan may have been a sensitive issue. Obviously, Betzalel would serve as a constant reminder of the perfidy perpetrated by the people. On the other hand, having Chur's grandson represent them in this meaningful way may have served as an indication of complete forgiveness for their nefarious deed.

Another *midrash* spells out this relationship:

> "See, I have called by name Betzalel son of Uri son of Chur." Why was Chur mentioned in this context [building the Mishkan]? When Israel wished to commit idolatry, [Chur] offered his soul for the sake of God, and would not allow them [to sin]. They rose against him and killed him. God said to him, "By your life, I will repay you."
>
> *(Shemot Rabbah 48:3)*

This *midrash* teaches that there is a clear relationship between the death of Chur and the selection of Betzalel. Other *midrashim* note the strange phraseology: "See, I have called by name Betzalel son of Uri son of Chur, from the tribe of Yehudah." "I have called" is clearly past tense, and the word "see" is apparently superfluous. The Midrash explains:

> It does not say, "I have called by name Betzalel," but "See, I have called." You find that when Moshe went up to Heaven, God showed him all the vessels of the Mishkan and told him, "Thus and thus you shall do. You shall make a Menorah, a table, and an altar" — and so with all the work of the Mishkan.
>
> When Moshe was ready to descend [from Heaven], he was under the impression that he was to make them, but God called to him, "Moshe, I have made you a king; it does not befit a king to do anything [himself]. Rather, he gives orders and others do the thing for him. You, likewise, must not do anything yourself. Command others and let them do it."
>
> God did not, however, tell Moses whom he should appoint, so Moshe inquired, "To whom shall I speak?"
>
> God replied, "I will show you." What did the Holy One, blessed be He, do? He brought him the book of Adam and showed him all the generations that would arise from Creation to Resurrection, each generation and its kings, its leaders, and

> its prophets, saying to him, "I have appointed all these [for their destinies] from that time [Creation], and Betzalel, too, I have appointed from that time." This is why it says, "See, I have called by name Betzalel."
>
> *(Shemot Rabbah 40:2)*

Another *midrash* addresses the problematic tenses of the Biblical verse:

> "See, I have called by name Betzalel." This is the meaning of the verse, "That which was is called by name" (*Kohelet* 6:10). The Holy One, blessed be He, said, "He who was prepared from the beginning should make the Mishkan, for I have already called him by name".... While Adam was still a lifeless mass He [God] showed him each and every tzaddik who would descend from him.... He showed him Betzalel, hence the verse, "See, I have called by name Betzalel."
>
> *(Shemot Rabbah 40:3)*

These *midrashim* differ in focus. The first explains the word *see*, while the second examines the use of the past tense in the naming of Betzalel. Both *midrashim* agree that Betzalel was "prepared from the dawn of Creation" — before the murder of his grandfather Chur. Therefore, we must conclude that there is something special about Betzalel himself, apart from his lineage.

> See, I have called by name Betzalel son of Uri son of Chur, from the tribe of Yehudah.

The verse indicates that the name *Betzalel* was chosen by God, and it seems particularly appropriate for the man who built the Mishkan. The meaning of the name is "in the shadow of the Lord." The Midrash (*Shavuot* 15b and others) teaches us that on the day that Moshe completed the Mishkan, he recited the psalm which begins, "He who dwells in the secret place of the most High shall abide in the shadow of the Almighty..." (*Tehillim*, ch. 91).

The Mishkan itself may be considered the "shadow of the Almighty," for its purpose was to allow the "Shadow of God" into this world. It is our belief that a person's name reflects his inner self. In this case, the quality reflected in Betzalel's name is the very same quality possessed by the Mishkan itself. Perhaps this is the reason that he was chosen.

There is another aspect of Betzalel which has eluded us. The Torah records that Betzalel built the *Aron*, the ark (*Shemot* 37:1). Rashi explains why Betzalel's name is mentioned specifically in connection with the *Aron*, while in the case of all the other utensils, the text simply states that they were completed.

> Since he displayed more self-sacrifice than the other sages, the *Aron* was called by his name.

Rashi's source is a *midrash* which recounts a dialogue between Moshe and Betzalel:

> At the time that God told Moshe to make the Mishkan, he [Moshe] came and told Betzalel. [Betzalel] said, "What is the purpose of the Mishkan?"
>
> [Moshe] answered, "That God may allow His Presence to rest within it, and thereby teach Torah to Israel."
>
> Betzalel said to him, "Where will the Torah be placed?"
>
> He answered, "After we build the Mishkan, we will build the *Aron*."
>
> He said, "Moshe, our master, this is not honor for the Torah. Rather, first we should make the *Aron* and then make the Mishkan."
>
> Therefore, the *Aron* was called in his name.
>
> *(Shemot Rabbah 50:2)*

Betzalel's wisdom was such that he could question Moshe and ultimately understand the essence of the Mishkan. Although Betzalel was the builder of the entire Mishkan, the heart and soul of the Mishkan, the *Aron*, was attributed to him.

The *Aron* was built, in the words of the Midrash, to allow God's presence to dwell among the Jewish people, in order to teach them Torah. Ramban, explaining the idea of the Mishkan, writes:

> The secret of the Mishkan is that the glory which rested on Mount Sinai should rest on it secretly.
>
> *(Ramban, Shemot 25:2)*

To paraphrase Ramban, the purpose of the Mishkan was to allow the experience of Mount Sinai to accompany the Jews on all of their travels. This seems to be what Betzalel understood: The essential purpose of the Mishkan is to teach Torah to the Jewish people; consequently, the *Aron* must be built prior to the Mishkan. When the Cloud of Glory, last seen on Mount Sinai, entered into the Mishkan upon its completion, it was clear that the project was a success. God now dwelled among the people, or perhaps we can say that the people now dwelled in the shadow of God.

Let us take this one step further: Why Betzalel? We have already seen the answer to this question: because he was the grandson of Chur. Why was Chur chosen? Why was he one of a select group of two, entrusted by Moshe in the latter's absence? Why, out of the whole nation, was Chur holding up Moshe's arm in the midst of that first battle against the Amaleikites?

> See, I have called by name Betzalel son of Uri son of Chur, from the tribe of Yehudah.

The answer lies in the end of the sentence, "from the tribe of Yehudah." Yehudah represents kingship, as manifested by David and his dynasty, and Chur functioned in the capacity of future king both in the battle of Amaleik and at the golden calf. The other leader entrusted by Moshe was Aharon, the future *kohein gadol*. These were the two empowered by Moshe on the first occasion when Moshe had to establish the subsequent tier of leadership. Aharon and Chur are the two who would one day lead, each in a different sphere.

When the people made the calf, Chur heroically stood against them, but they rejected him and his teachings. In much the same way, his grandson Betzalel was concerned that the teachings of the Torah receive their proper place.

At Mount Sinai, all present had complete clarity that God is One. They felt God; they experienced God. At that moment sin and rebellion seemed foreign, impossible. But a short time later, the impossible became horrific reality: the calf was built. Chur tried to stop them, but he was prevented from doing so. The man who could have been king was dead. His grandson then set out to build the Mishkan in such a way that the teachings of the Torah would always be felt.

As Rashi stated, Betzalel was prepared for self-sacrifice in building the *Aron*, just as his grandfather had been, but with one important distinction: His grandfather gave up his life attempting to prevent sin. Betzalel tried to prevent sin preemptively, by making sure that God would always be felt and the Torah would constantly be taught. Betzalel achieved a clarity of vision, an understanding of his mission and of the power of Torah as the most direct connection of the Jewish people to God, which paralleled the clarity achieved at Sinai.

Many years later, a descendent of Chur named David would be king (see *Sotah* 11b). He would be endowed with special qualities which would allow him to establish kingship in Israel. His son Shlomo would follow, ascending the throne at the tender age of twelve. When God appeared to Shlomo in a dream and encouraged him to make a request, Shlomo responded:

> "I am but a young lad.... Therefore, give Your servant an understanding heart to judge Your nation, to discern between good and evil...."
>
> God said to him.... "Behold I have given you a wise and understanding heart...."
>
> *(Melachim I 3:7–12)*

Shlomo, the young king from the tribe of Yehudah, asks for wisdom and understanding; he asks for the attributes bestowed upon Betzalel. When Shlomo awakes from his dream, he travels to Yerushalayim:

> Shlomo awoke and behold it was a dream, and he came to Yerushalayim and stood in front of the *Aron* of the Covenant of the Lord....
>
> *(Ibid., 15)*

How appropriate that Shlomo asks for wisdom and comes to pray in front of the *Aron*, the same *Aron* that Betzalel was willing to sacrifice himself for, the *Aron* which represented Torah and understanding of God. It is Shlomo who proceeds to build the Temple in its proper place, just as Betzalel built the Mishkan, and both are endowed with the same gifts that allow them to complete their mission.

Many years later, the prophet Yeshayahu has a vision regarding the end of days:

> A rod shall come forth out of the stem of Yishai, and a branch shall grow out of his roots. The spirit of God shall rest upon him [Mashiach], the spirit of wisdom and understanding, the wisdom of counsel and might, the spirit of knowledge and fear of God.... The wolf shall dwell with lamb, and the leopard shall lie down with the kid, and the young lion and the fatling together, and a little child shall lead them.... They shall not hurt nor destroy on My holy mountain. For the earth shall be full of the knowledge of God, as the waters cover the sea.
>
> *(Yeshayah 11:1–9)*

The prophet sees a young, gifted child, endowed with a combination of the spiritual traits of all his ancestors — his "roots." This descendant of David will succeed in spreading the wisdom of Torah to all the inhabitants of the planet. This child will complete the work begun all those years ago in the desert, bringing the vision of Chur, Betzalel, and Shlomo to fruition. He will bring Sinai to the people, and sin, conflict, and pain will become a memory, a relic from the past. Now we understand why Betzalel's name was written in the book of Adam: a character so crucial in the end of days must be present in thought from the beginning of time.

Sefer Vayikra

Parashat Vayikra

To Elevate the Physical

One of the main topics of *Vayikra* is the *korbanot* (offerings). This concept may come as somewhat of a surprise, for if Judaism believes in an all-powerful, transcendent God, what is the purpose of the *korbanot*? After all, why would God, who creates and sustains all, need our offerings?

Clearly, the answer must be that God has no "need" for these offerings. If this is the case, why does the Torah command us to bring offerings, and in such detail? Ramban, in his Commentary to the Torah, deals with this question by first introducing and rejecting the rational approach offered by Rambam in his *Moreh Nevuchim*: The Jews, influenced by other cultures, had become accustomed to this type of ritualistic dependency. Allowing for their weakness, the Torah made some basic adjustments and called upon man to offer that which he desired. God, for His part, has no need for these offerings.

We should note that in his legal work, the *Mishneh Torah*, Rambam states that the *korbanot* are *chukim*, laws whose reasons we do not know. But, Rambam adds, it is certainly "one of the foundations of the world." Rav Chaim Soloveitchik's method of solving apparent contradictions among the writings of Rambam is illuminating in this case: Rav Chaim taught that when there is a contradiction between the position of Rambam is his legal work, *Mishneh Torah*, and his philosophical work, *Moreh Nevuchim*, the former is considered the more authoritative, especially when, as in the case of the reason for *korbanot*, a philosophical view is espoused in the *Mishneh Torah.*[1]

While Rambam's treatment of *korbanot* in the *Moreh Nevuchim* does solve at least the basic question, it leaves an unpleasant taste. For if *korbanot* were simply an accommodation to the relatively low level of the community at the time, why would the Torah deal with the issue in such detail? Furthermore, why would these laws continue into the Second Temple period, when the Jews were no longer effected by pagan influences, having long since left Egypt? Moreover, in the *Mishneh Torah,*[2] Rambam writes clearly that sacrifices will be a part of the service in the Third Temple. In short, while answering the main problem, Rambam causes new ones.

Ramban strongly attacks this approach, one of his main arguments being that sacrifice predates pagan influence — Kayin's offering being a perfect example. Furthermore, the *korbanot* are described as pleasant to God. If the *korbanot* are simply a concession to frail, spiritually challenged human nature, why would God be pleased by them? We might posit that God responds to the *korbanot* as man's way of seeking out a relationship with God and not to the *korbanot* per se, but this seems to contradict the verses dealing with *korbanot*, such as those referring to *"rei'ach nicho'ach laHashem* — a pleasant fragrance to God."[3]

Ramban's polemic against Rambam is reminiscent of his attack against commentaries associating the Mishkan with the golden calf, where he argues that something as profound as the Mishkan must have a better rationale than merely a response on God's part to the sinful behavior of the nation. Ironically, Ramban's attack against Rambam's position only served to publicize it, effectively

1 Heard from Rabbi Yosef Soloveitchik.

2 The *Mishneh Torah* includes the laws which will be practiced in the future.

3 See *Bereishit* 8:21; *Vayikra* 1:13,17; 2:2,9; 3:5; 6:8,14; and 23:13,18; and *Bemidbar* 15:3,7,10,13,14; 28:8, 13,24; 29:8,13,36.

broadening the sphere of influence of the very opinion he wished to discredit.

Ramban's own position is that the various actions involved in bringing a *korban* relate to different aspects of man's need for exoneration. The most descriptive aspect, the spilling of the blood, is intended to serve as a symbolic reminder that the man who has sinned has, in a sense, forfeited his own life.

The Chafetz Chaim stresses that any sin is tantamount to heresy — rejection of God. In order for a person to sin, he must believe that God does not really exist, or, at the moment of sin, he must believe that God is not aware of his action or does not care. Alternatively, a sinner may accept Divine existence and omniscience, but thinks he may be able to "bribe" God at a later point. For if a person considered that God is indeed always watching, always cares, will always respond to every rebellious action, and cannot be bribed, sin would be impossible. Thus we see that in order for man to sin he must espouse some type of heretical position, if only on a temporary basis.

Any sinful action is, therefore, separation from God, and indeed from life itself. It is the mercy of God which will allow a sinner to achieve forgiveness. In this approach, it is not God who "needs" the offering, but man who needs to be rehabilitated. The blood of the animal serves as a vivid reminder of man's vulnerability and mortality. This "near-death" experience is meant to be an impetus for spiritual growth, calling on man to sacrifice the animal within himself which allowed him to sin in the first place.

Bringing a *korban*, then, is a powerful cathartic experience, which takes man's psychological makeup into consideration. After giving this explanation, Ramban writes:

> But the true [Kabbalistic] path has an elusive mystical reason for *korbanot*.... The name of God used exclusively in regard [to the *korbanot*] is not *Keil* nor *Elokim*...but rather God [*Yud-kei-vav-kei*], the unique Name...so that no one should think that the *korban* is brought in order to feed God.
>
> *(Ramban, Vayikra 1:9)*

Ramban reminds us that the Name *Yud-kei-vav-kei* refers to the transcendent aspect of God; it is the Name that indicates that God is beyond man's understanding. Employing this name, to the exclusion of all other names of God, points up the incongruity of the idea of "God's needs." The Name *Elokim*, on the other hand, refers to God as Judge and Creator, concepts which humans can grasp. Had this Name of God been used in connection with *korbanot*, one might have been tempted to imagine that a "bribe" is possible. But, when we contemplate that the *korbanot* are commanded by God, who is *Yud-kei-vav-kei*, we realize that no bribes can be offered.

The following passage in the Gemara is the source of Ramban's teaching.

> Come and see what is written in the chapter of the sacrifices. Neither *Keil* nor *Elokim* is found there, but only God [*Yud-kei-vav-kei*], so as not to give sectarians any occasion to rebel.
>
> *(Menachot 110a)*

Additionally, the unique Name of God indicates the trait of existing outside of time. This may help us understand how forgiveness takes place: If a man sinned yesterday and repented today, how can his present attitude undo that which he did yesterday? If we understand that God exists outside of time — indeed, God creates time — and we try to reestablish a relationship with God, then time becomes less of a factor. When man connects with the Transcendent God, "yesterday" becomes a limited human perspective that no longer confines him.

This is the idea behind *teshuvah* and forgiveness. Man does *teshuvah*; he returns to God, and God forgives him. This explains why the word *korban* is derived from the root *karov* (to come close). The *korban* is the act that allows man to come close to God. *Teshuvah* is not only a return to God — it is also a return to oneself, to the potential within man, the image of God within each and every one of us. When man does *teshuvah*, he returns to the core of godliness within himself, that *tzelem Elokim* (image of God) which is his essence.

The importance of the *korbanot* lies in the rehabilitation of man, which is their intended result. Judaism is a religion that sees value in the life of animals. Animal sacrifice is not an expression of disregard for animals. Rather, it is a statement of the importance of human life: If the price to be paid for the rehabilitation of a person is the life of an animal, then it is not a high price. The key is in man's rehabilitation, in his finding the image of God within him.

As God is compassionate, so must man be compassionate. People, however, have a tendency toward paganism, and instead of undergoing real, profound change, man often prefers to "pay the price" financially, without effecting internal change. In the words of the prophet Hoshea,

> I desired *chesed* (kindness) and not sacrifice [*zevach*], and the knowledge of God more than burnt offerings.
>
> *(Hoshea 6:6)*

The term utilized by the prophet is *zevach* — "to slaughter." This is far afield from the exalted *korban* which, as we have seen, has its root in *karov*, which means to come close. When one kills an animal without an elevated purpose, one has performed "slaughter." This, the prophet tells us, is a far cry from the Divine imperative.

This point is clearly evidenced by a tragic story told in the Gemara of two *kohanim* who raced to perform the Divine service in the Temple.

> It once happened that two *kohanim* arrived [in the Temple] at the same time [to perform the service, which was performed on a "first come, first served" basis]. When one of them arrived first [literally, *within four cubits of the altar*], [the other] took a knife and thrust it into his heart.
>
> Rabbi Tzaddok stood on the steps of the Temple hall and said, "Our brethren of the house of Israel, hear ye.... On whose behalf shall we offer the heifer whose neck is to be broken [i.e., who is responsible for the deed], on behalf of the city or on be-

half of the Temple Courts?"

All the people burst out weeping.

The father of the young man [who had been stabbed] came and found him still in convulsions. He said, "May he be an atonement for you. My son is still in convulsions and the knife has not become impure."

This [remark] teaches you that the purity of their vessels was of greater concern to them even than the shedding of blood. Thus is it said, "Moreover Menasheh shed innocent blood very much, till he had filled Yerushalayim from one end to the other" (*Melachim* II 21:16).

(Yoma 23a)

When one *kohein* preceded his friend, the latter plunged a knife into his colleague's chest. He may as well have stabbed the Temple itself, for this story clearly describes misuse and total misunderstanding of religious life. The Temple was to serve as the symbol of religious life, not as a replacement for ethical life. In response to this type of behavior, the Temple came crashing down.

Because man strays from himself and from God the *korbanot* were necessary to refocus, to remind man of his mortality on the one hand and his mission on the other. The *korbanot* were intended as a means toward an end, a path toward finding one's own *tzelem Elokim*. The *korbanot* were meant to be the key which would allow faltering man to regain focus, in an attempt to mend the world, and not some sort of magical ritual needed to placate an angry God.

Judaism, with its universal concerns, called on *korbanot* as a way to take the profound religious experiences associated with the Temple into the lives of individuals. Judaism is holistic, with "religious" concerns, resonating in both the spiritual and secular domains. The experience of the *korban* in the Temple was intended to have a "spill-over" effect, impacting every aspect of our lives. At the point when people compartmentalized religious concerns, placing ritual above social and moral issues, the Temple became a hindrance rather than a place of salvation, and destruction was inevitable.

Parashat Tzav

Thoughts of Sin

In last week's parashah we discussed the spiritual and psychological dynamics of the sin offering (*chatat*). This week's parashah opens with the *olah*, an offering which is entirely consumed by fire. The Sages have a tradition that explains the purpose of this offering:

> Rabbi Shimon bar Yochai taught: The *olah* is brought for *hirhur haleiv* (contemplation of the heart).
>
> *(Vayikra Rabbah 7:3)*

This idea is further explained in *Talmud Yerushalmi*:

> The *olah* brings about *kapparah* (expiation) for thoughts of the heart.
>
> *(Yerushalmi, Yoma 8:7 45b)*

These two passages teach us that "sinful" thoughts of the heart necessitate forgiveness. At first glance this idea seems strange, especially from a contemporary Western perspective. After all, we live in a society that condones consensual behavior between adults. Since one's thoughts are private, no "sin" or harm takes place if one has mere thoughts, society says. In some circles, thoughts and fantasies are encouraged, and are seen as a part of a healthy, well-adjusted mind. Yet here we have the opposite teaching: mere thoughts can be sin, and therefore forgiveness is required.

The idea that thoughts must be controlled is a very basic one, found in the third chapter of the Shema:

> It shall be tzitzit for you, that you may look upon them and remember all the commandments of God and perform them, and so that you do not stray after your hearts and your eyes, which you are inclined to stray after.
>
> *(Bemidbar 15:39)*

The Gemara explains:

> Where do we find [warnings against] the opinions of the heretics and thoughts of immorality and idolatry? It has been taught: "After your hearts" refers to heresy.... "After your eyes" refers to thoughts of immorality.
>
> *(Berachot 12b*[1]*)*

What, then, is the connection between the *olah* and the thoughts for which it compensates? The Midrash explains:

> The *olah* is completely holy, because it was not brought for sins. The *asham* was brought for theft, but the *olah* was not brought for sin or theft, rather for thoughts of the heart.
>
> *(Tanchuma, Tzav 13:13)*

Here the *olah* is called "completely holy," referring to the fact that the *olah*, literally translated as "ascending," is completely consumed by the fire, and man derives no benefit from it. This is further explained by some commentaries to the verse:

> God said to Moshe, saying, "Command Aharon and his children saying, 'These are the instructions of the *olah*. It is an *olah* which shall burn on the *mizbei'ach* the entire night, until morning. The fire of the *mizbei'ach* shall be kept burning in it.' "
>
> *(Vayikra 6:1–2)*

The *olah* is an offering which brings about forgiveness for

1 See also *Bemidbar Rabbah* 17:6.

thoughts. Just as a person's passions burn at night, this sacrificed animal, which represents the physical side of the person, burns all night, until only spirit is left.[1] There is nothing "physical" left of the offering. This idea is illuminated by the *Zohar*:

> The essence of the offering is that it is analogous to the sin and that a man should offer to God his desires and passions, for this is more acceptable than all. Blessed are the righteous that they bring this offering every day [metaphorically]. However, the actual [physical] offering is better, because it brings blessing on all worlds.
>
> *(Zohar, Vayikra 9b)*

This relationship between the physical and spiritual worlds can be further elucidated by a passage in the Talmud:

> Thoughts of sin are *kasheh* (worse or more difficult) than sin.
>
> *(Yoma 29a)*

Rashi explains this passage,

> Sexual passion is more difficult to contain than the act itself.

According to Rashi, the term *kasheh* means "more difficult." Rashi understands this teaching to mean that it is easier for a person to control himself from doing a sin than to control his thoughts of sin. This explanation does not indicate which is more serious, or for that matter if thinking about sin is actually a sin in and of itself. Rashi only states that thoughts of this type are more difficult to control, a statement that we may understand on various levels.

As we have already noted, many people do not consider thoughts a religious or moral issue, and it is more difficult to control something that is not considered to be a problem in the first place. On the other hand, crimes of the heart are never known to others, and far less societal pressure to conform is brought to bear in such areas. As a general rule we may say that intrinsically,

---

1 See Rav Menachem Kasher in *Torah Sheleimah, Tzav* 9.

thoughts are more difficult to contain, and most people have greater success exercising control over their actions than over their thoughts.

Ironically, according to Rashi's analysis reward for controlling thoughts would be greater than the reward for avoiding an "actual" sin, following the principle taught in the Mishnah: "In accordance with the difficulty is the reward" (*Avot* 5:26). Even though a "real" sin in the world of action is worse, one would nonetheless receive a greater reward for avoiding thoughts of sin.

Rambam, in *Moreh Nevuchim*, has a radically different understanding:

> You already know the teaching "Thoughts of sin are *kasheh* (worse or more difficult) than sin" (*Yoma* 29a). I have a wonderful explanation [of this]: If a person sins it is generally due to circumstances which result of his being a physical creature, meaning that a person will sin due to the animal side of himself. But thoughts are a person's treasure, which result from his "form" [his image of God] and if a person sins with his thoughts, then he has sinned with his greatest asset.... The purpose of the mind is to cling to God, not to slip below [to the animal level].
>
> *(Moreh Nevuchim 3:8)*

Rambam explains that thoughts of the sin are *kasheh*, worse, than sin! A person is made up of two parts — the physical (animal) and the spiritual (intellectual). If a person sins with his body, it is understandable: The body is physical, and therefore has all sorts of physical urges and animal instincts. The mind, on the other hand, is the manifestation of our image of God. To sin with one's mind is thus a greater desecration than sinning with one's body. There is one caveat: Man is punished, in general, for action, not thought. Nonetheless, sinful thoughts may be more spiritually debilitating.[1]

The image of the *olah* now takes on new meaning. The person

1 Similarly, Rav Tzaddok HaKohen notes that the fantasy which accompanies masturbation is worse than the actual physical act. See *Takanat HaShavin* 64b–65a.

who has sinned with his mind has, in effect, turned his spiritual side into something animal. Therefore, the animal offering brought to make amends for such a sin must be completely consumed by fire, indicating that the mind must be completely dedicated to the spiritual. This idea may be illustrated by a second teaching of Rabbi Shimon bar Yochai, the authority who had taught that the *olah* is brought for forbidden thoughts:

> Rabbi Shimon bar Yochai said, in addition: Whoever puts the words of Torah on his heart [i.e., in his mind] is saved from thoughts of sin, thoughts [fear] of the sword, fear of tyranny, idle thoughts, thoughts of the evil inclination, thoughts of sexual licentiousness, thoughts of evil women, thoughts of idolatry, fear of being controlled by others, and obsessive thoughts....
>
> *(Tanna D'Vei Eliyahu Zuta 16)*

Here, Rabbi Shimon bar Yochai teaches that there is an antidote to sinful thoughts, namely, Torah. As we have seen, the mind represents the image of God and the spiritual side of man. This image is what enables us to have a relationship with God; therefore, the person whose mind is involved in words of Torah is spared the types of thoughts which haunt man.

The *Zohar* further explains this idea:

> "If his offering is a burnt offering..." (*Vayikra* 1:3). Rabbi Chiya cited here the verse: " 'For My thoughts are not your thoughts...' said God" (*Yeshayah* 55:8). "The Thought of God," he said, "is the fountainhead of all, and from that Thought spread forth ways and paths where the Holy Name can be found and fittingly established. From that Thought, too, issued the stream of Gan Eden to water all. On that Thought depend all beings above and below, and from that Thought come the Written and the Oral Torahs.
>
> "The thought of man is also the fountainhead of his life, and from it stretch ways and paths that can pervert his ways in

> this world and in the next. From that thought issues the defilement of the evil inclination to bring harm to him and to all, and from it come error, iniquity, presumptuous sin, idolatry, fornication, and bloodshed.... Hence it says, first of all, 'If his offering is a burnt-offering,' for the burnt-offering [*olah*] has reference to that which goes up [*olah*] on the heart, i.e., the thought, and therefore the first offering mentioned is the burnt-offering."
>
> *(Zohar, Vayikra 56–6a)*

This teaching reminds us of the passage in the Gemara, taught in the name of Rabbi Yishmael, that if the evil inclination takes control of a person the remedy is to be "pulled" into the study hall:

> Thus did the Holy One, blessed be He, say to Israel: "My children, I created the evil inclination, but I [also] created the Torah as its antidote. If you occupy yourselves with the Torah, you will not be delivered into its hand, as it says, 'If you do well, shall you not be exalted?' (*Bereishit* 4:7). But if you do not occupy yourselves with the Torah, you shall be delivered into his hand, as it says, 'Sin crouches at the door' (ibid.).
>
> "Moreover, it [the evil inclination] is altogether preoccupied with you [to make you sin], as it says, 'And to you shall be his desire' (ibid.). Yet if you want to, you can rule over him, as it says, 'And you shall rule over him' (ibid.)."
>
> Our Rabbis taught: The evil inclination is difficult [to withstand], since even its Creator called it evil, as it says, "For the inclination of man's heart is evil from his youth" (ibid. 8:21). Rabbi Yitzchak said: Man's evil inclination renews [its attack] against him dialy, as it says, "[The impulse of the thoughts of his heart] was only evil every day" (ibid. 6:51). Rabbi Shimon ben Levi said: Man's evil inclination gathers strength against him daily and seeks to slay him, as it says, "The wicked watches the righteous and seeks to slay him" (*Tehillim* 37:32). If the Holy One, blessed be He, did not help him [man], he would not be able to prevail against [the evil inclination], as it

says, "The Lord will not leave him in his hand" (ibid., 33).

The school of Rabbi Yishmael taught: My son, if this repulsive [wretch] assails you, lead him to the study hall.

(Kiddushin 30b)

There is a tension between the physical and spiritual aspects of man. Rabbi Yishmael's advice is to bring the battle onto your own turf. The Kotzker Rebbe once commented on this passage in Talmud: "Don't think for one second that the *yetzer hara* isn't waiting for you in the study hall as well!"[1] The only difference Rabbi Yishmael's advice will afford you is "home court advantage."

Man's role in this world is to elevate the physical. To facilitate this, man's mind, which is the core of his spirituality, and according to Rambam is his *tzelem Elokim* (image of God), must remain pure, focused, and spiritual. The insidiousness of thoughts or fantasies of sin is that the physical has attained dominion over the spiritual, and the battle is thus lost before it is begun.

The Temple, as we saw in last week's parashah, is a place where errant man is rehabilitated. The sin offering, with the powerful cathartic imagery we examined last week, helps man when he has actually performed a sin. The *olah,* which is described at the beginning of this week's parashah, is brought for the "sin" of forbidden thoughts. As the entire animal is consumed by the fire, man's thoughts should now be turned toward redirecting all his mental energies to God.

---

1 *Emet MiKotzk Titzmach* 630.

Parashat Shemini

Nadav and Avihu

The parashah begins with the eighth day of celebration of the consecration of the Mishkan. Aharon is called upon to offer a calf as a sin offering, ostensibly to atone for the sin of the golden calf. The community of Israel is called upon to offer a goat offering, which the commentaries point out was meant to bring about forgiveness for the sale of Yosef, where a goat's blood was used as camouflage for the brothers' treacherous treatment of Yosef (*Targum Yerushalmi, Vayikra* 9:3). If this is the case, the two major transgressions of the Jewish people are to be forgiven on this awesome day.

Moshe and Aharon left the Ohel Mo'ed and blessed the people and "the Glory of God appeared to the entire people" (*Vayikra* 9:23). We are then told that a fire came down from Heaven and consumed the altar. "The people saw, they broke out in song and fell on their faces" (ibid., 24). The response of the people is clear; God had responded to their prayers, and apparently full forgiveness for their rebellion was achieved. What happens next can only be described as tragic:

> The sons of Aharon, Nadav and Avihu, each took a pan, placed fire inside them, and put incense upon it [the fire]. They brought before God a strange fire which He had not commanded them to bring.

> A fire came out from before God and devoured them, and they died before God.
>
> Moshe said to Aharon, "This is what God referred to, 'I will be sanctified by those close to Me, and [thus] I will be glorified by the entire people.' " Aharon was silent.
>
> *(Ibid. 10:1–3)*

Many questions arise about this incident. What was wrong with the behavior of Nadav and Avihu? What motivated them in this action? How are we to understand Moshe's response?

There are many opinions regarding the actions of Nadav and Avihu, almost all agreeing that a sin was committed. As to the nature and cause of the sin, the Midrashim, and the commentaries based on those Midrashim, differ. According to one approach, the problem was that they entered the sanctuary drunk, evidenced by the section in the Torah which follows this episode: Aharon is warned against entering the Temple to perform service while intoxicated.

> God spoke to Aharon, saying, "Do not drink wine or strong drink, neither you nor your sons, when you enter the Ohel Mo'ed, lest you die."
>
> *(Ibid., 8–9)*

> We would not know why they [Nadav and Avihu] died, but for [God's] commanding Aharon: "Do not drink wine or strong drink." We know from this that they died precisely on account of the wine. For this reason God showed love to Aharon by directing the Divine Utterance to him alone.
>
> *(Vayikra Rabbah 12:1)*

Alternatively we may say that the problem was the offering of incense which was not called for, but it was the drunkenness which caused the error in judgment, resulting in the "strange fire" which was offered. Other opinions state that it was the fact that they were unmarried, and therefore childless, which led to their deaths:

> Rabbi Levi said that they were arrogant. Many women re-

> mained unmarried waiting for them. What did they say? "Our father's brother is a king, our mother's brother is a prince, our father is a high priest, and we are both deputy high priests. What woman is worthy of us?"
>
> *(Ibid. 20:10)*

This source gives a different picture of Nadav and Avihu. They sound quite self-absorbed, and it is difficult to imagine such men being spiritual leaders. Another source identifies their downfall with their deciding a Torah law in the presence of Moshe and Aharon, without asking the opinion of their teacher. This may be seen in the text itself:

> The sons of Aharon, Nadav and Avihu, each took a pan, placed fire inside them, and put incense upon it [the fire]. They brought before God a [strange] fire which He had not commanded them to bring.

Our first reading would have implied that God had not commanded them, but Seforno explains that "he had not commanded" refers to Moshe, implying that their sin was in not asking their teacher, Moshe. Some commentaries opine that in and of itself, their action was correct, but deciding a Torah law in the presence of Moshe was their sin:

> It was taught in the name of Rabbi Eliezer that the only reason that Nadav and Avihu died was that they decided halachah in the presence of Moshe Rabbeinu.
>
> *(Pesikta D'Rav Kahana 26:7)*

Perhaps most sinister of all the allegations raised against them is the following passage in the Gemara:

> Moshe and Aharon were walking along, with Nadav and Avihu were behind them, and all of Israel behind them. Nadav said to Avihu, "When these two elders die, you and I will lead this generation."
>
> God said to them, "Let's see who buries whom."
>
> *(Sanhedrin 52a)*

The picture which emerges from all of these sources is of a pair of individuals who allowed their position to get the best of them. The sources essentially agree about the personality but differ as to the specific fault.

When we return to the narrative in *Shemot*, we see how Nadav and Avihu are raised and separated from the people. These verses contain the origin of Nadav and Avihu's trespass. The Torah recounts God's instructions to Moshe at Mount Sinai, in preparation for the giving of the Torah:

> To Moshe [God] said, "Ascend to God, you and Aharon, and Nadav and Avihu, and the seventy elders of Israel, and prostrate yourselves from afar...."
>
> Moshe and Aharon, Nadav and Avihu, and the seventy elders arose. They saw the Lord of Israel and beneath His feet, a kind of paved work of a sapphire stone, like the very heaven for clearness [*livnat hasapir, u'ch'etzem hashamayim l'tohar*]. To the aristocracy of the Children of Israel, He did not lay His hand. They viewed the Lord, and they ate and drank.
>
> *(Shemot 24:1, 9–11)*

This enigmatic passage may hold the key to understanding the offense of Nadav and Avihu. They are separated from the rest of the nation, leading them to think of themselves as future leaders. They are invited to join Moshe, and they have a better vantage point than the rest of the nation. The purpose of the ascent is to bow from afar — "and prostrate yourselves from afar." Instead of this, however, they stood and stared.

The Midrash contrasts this behavior with that of Moshe, when he saw the burning bush:

> It is good that Moshe hid his face. The Holy One, blessed be He, said, "I wanted to reveal Myself to you, and you honored Me by covering your face. I swear that when you will be with Me on the mountain for forty days and nights without food or

> drink, you will take pleasure in the radiance of the *Shechinah*, as it says, 'Moshe did not know that his face glowed' (*Shemot* 34:29)."
>
> But Nadav and Avihu uncovered their faces and filled their eyes with radiance of the *Shechinah*, as it says, "To the aristocracy of the Children of Israel, He did not strike His hand. [They viewed the Lord, and they ate and drank]" (*Shemot* 24:11). They were not punished for what they did.
>
> *(Shemot Rabbah 3:1)*

The Midrash states that as a result of their exalted position, Nadav and Avihu misused the opportunity, and instead of prostrating themselves they viewed the Divinity, as it were. One cannot help but notice that Moshe, as a result of covering his face, becomes angelic, needing neither food nor drink. Nadav and Avihu, on the other hand, "viewed the Lord, and they ate and drank." Strangely, their reaction to the ecstatic religious experience is eating and drinking. Furthermore, the next time we find eating and drinking in the Torah is at the golden calf! It may be argued that the source for the destructive behavior manifested at the golden calf was modeled upon what was perceived as the ecstatic behavior of Nadav and Avihu, at Sinai.

How could they have allowed themselves to drink again at the dedication ceremony, and then offer the "strange fire"?

The *Zohar* explains the significance of this wine, revealing the motivation of Nadav and Avihu:

> There is a mystical allusion in this verse. When Noach began to probe into the sin of Adam, not for purpose of practicing it but in order to understand it and so warn the world against it, he pressed grapes in order to research that vineyard. But when he reached that point he was "drunken and uncovered" (*Bereishit* 8:21). He lost his [mental] balance and uncovered the breach of the world which hitherto had been closed up....
>
> The same explanation applies to the case of the sons of Aharon, who, we have been taught, were drunk from wine

> [when they sinned]. Who, then, gave them wine at that place to drink? And is it conceivable that they would dare to get drunk at such a time? But in reality the wine which made them drunk was this same wine of Noach, as it is written, "they offered before God a strange fire."
>
> *(Zohar, Bereishit 73b)*

The wine which was drunk by Nadav and Avihu was the wine which Noach drank, and indeed it was the wine which Adam and Chavah drank! This teaching follows the opinion that the "Tree of Knowledge" was actually a grapevine, and the sin of Adam and Chavah was partaking of this forbidden wine.

> What was the tree from which Adam and Chavah ate? Rabbi Meir said: It was wheat.... Rabbi Yehudah bar Ila'i said: It was grapes, for it says, "Their grapes are grapes of gall, they have clusters of bitterness" (*Devarim* 32:32). Those clusters brought bitterness [i.e., sorrow] into the world. Rabbi Abba of Acco said: It was the *etrog* [citron], as it says, "The woman saw that the tree was good for food" (*Bereishit* 3:6).... Which tree has wood which can be eaten just like its fruit? You find none but the *etrog*. Rabbi Yosi said: They were figs.
>
> *(Bereishit Rabbah 15:7)*

The *Leshem*, one of the greatest modern-day Kabbalah *sefarim* (written by Rav Shlomo Elyashiv, the grandfather of the famous *poseik* Rav Shalom Yosef Elyashiv), explains that Nadav and Avihu were great religious leaders, and they were trying to bring about forgiveness for the sin of Adam. This is the reason that they used "Adam's grapes"; they wished to rectify his sin. At Sinai, at the moment of revelation, and now on this eighth day, Nadav and Avihu attempted to achieve this rectification.[1]

1 This theme, of trying to rectify the sin of Adam, is one of the prevalent ideas in mystical literature. Others who made the same valiant attempt were the four sages who entered *Pardes* (the Rabbinic description of Paradise): "Four men entered the Pardes: Ben Azzai, Ben Zoma, Acher, and Rabbi Akiva.... Ben Azzai cast a look and died. Of him Scripture says: 'Precious in the eyes of God is the death of His devout ones' (*Tehillim* 116:16)" (*Chagigah* 14b).

According to Rashi, Ben Azzai died looking at the *Shechinah*. The Arizal (*Yalkutei*

This last explanation allows us to view Nadav and Avihu in a different light. Rather than selfish sinners, they were great spiritualists trying to mend the world. Let us reconsider their actions on the day of the dedication of the Mishkan. On this day, the eighth day, which represents the metaphysical (the number eight is one beyond the natural, which is represented by seven), their father is called upon to offer a calf and bring about forgiveness for the sin of the golden calf. The people will offer a goat and bring about forgiveness for the sale of Yosef. Perhaps the only major sin that still needed rectification was the sin of Adam and Chavah in Gan Eden. If that could be accomplished, a new, cleansed world would dawn.

Adam drank and hid from God:

> They heard the voice of the Lord God walking in the garden in the cool of the day; and Adam and his wife hid themselves from the presence of the Lord God among the trees of the garden.
>
> *(Bereishit 3:8)*

Nadav and Avihu, on the other hand, drank after staring at God's glory. When, in the dedication of the Mishkan, the fire came down and filled the area, the people hid their faces. Nadav and Avihu felt that this generation needed a new approach, one that should have been adopted in Gan Eden: Instead of hiding from God, they confronted God, as if to show that they were indeed prepared and ready to accept the revelations and teachings of God, without recoiling.

They offered the fire back to God, but God took them as well. This, then, may unify most of the opinions regarding their sin: They sought a new direction for this generation, which they referred to in their speculations about leading the nation. They were infused with the sense of an historic mission, which would set the

---

Torah, Bereishit) and the Leshem (*Sefer HaDeah* 2:4:49:6) explain the entire *Pardes* sojourn as an attempt to rectify the sin of Adam. Therefore, *Pardes* is identified with Eden. There are numerous parallels between Ben Azzai and Nadav and Avihu, a theme which I hope to explore at another time.

world on a new course, and they therefore had no time or energy to spare for wives or children.

The *Midrash Tanchuma* teaches:

> In four places the death of the sons of Aharon is mentioned and each time their sin is mentioned with it, in order to teach you that this was their only sin.
>
> *(Tanchuma, Acharei Mot 6:6)*

This *midrash* supports the opinion that they were not selfish, self-centered sinners. They committed one sin only. This approach enables us to understand the comment of Moshe to Aharon immediately following the deaths:

> Moshe said to Aharon, "This is what God referred to, 'I will be sanctified by those close to Me, and [thus] I will be honored by the entire people.' " Aharon was silent.

Moshe describes Nadav and Avihu as those who are close to God. In Rashi's understanding, the inference is to those who were closest to God. Moshe's "eulogy" is based on a verse in *Shemot*:

> I will reveal Myself there to the Children of Israel, and be sanctified in My honor.
>
> *(Shemot 29:43)*

There is a tradition that the text should read "Sanctified by those who honor Me," a reference to Nadav and Avihu. Moshe explains that he knew the dedication of the Mishkan would necessitate the death of a great person, one of the leaders. Moshe tells Aharon that he had thought that either he or Aharon would have to die in the establishment of the Mishkan but in the end it turned out to be Nadav and Avihu. Moshe says to Aharon, "Now I see that they were greater than you or I" (*Rashi*, based on the Midrash).

As it turned out, two of the leaders were taken. This is what the text means when it says that they died "before God."

The understanding that Nadav and Avihu were attempting to reach religious greatness allows us deeper understanding of other mystical traditions. At a later time in front of the Mishkan a terrible scene would unfold:

> Behold, one of the people of Israel came and brought to his brothers a Midianite woman, in the sight of Moshe and in the sight of all the congregation of the people of Israel, who were weeping before the door of the Tent of Meeting.
>
> When Pinchas, the son of Elazar, the son of Aharon the Kohein, saw it, he rose up from among the congregation and took a spear in his hand. He went after the man of Israel into the chamber, and thrust both of them through, the man of Israel and the woman through her belly. Then the plague ceased from the people of Israel.
>
> *(Bemidbar 25:6–8)*

Pinchas acted swiftly and heroically in order to prevent further desecration. From where did Pinchas get this spiritual strength and fortitude?

> "Elazar, Aharon's son, took one of the daughters of Putiel as a wife, and she bore him Pinchas: These are the heads of the fathers of the Levites according to their families" (*Shemot* 6:25). Why does it say "these are the heads" when the only one mentioned is Pinchas? The truth is that because he saved thousands in Israel from the plague [see *Bemidbar* 25:8], bringing atonement for the Children of Israel and their chiefs, they are all included in him and he is referred to as "these." This expression also suggests that he, in his own person, compensated for the loss of the heads of the Levites [Nadav and Avihu]. They sinned and were burned, but their souls found their abode in Pinchas. They separated the sign of the Covenant from its place [by leaving no issue], and he came and united it again. Therefore, the heritage and spirit of both of them were given to him.
>
> *(Zohar, Shemot 26b)*

Nadav and Avihu died in the proximity of God, in the

Mishkan. Their souls were nearly complete. There is a mystical teaching known as *sod ha'ibur*, the phenomenon of a soul entering another body in order to accomplish a great deed. The *Zohar* explains:

> As Rabbi Shimon was once studying this portion, his son, Rabbi Elazar, came and asked him, "What is the connection between Nadav and Avihu and Pinchas? If Pinchas had not yet been born when they died and had afterwards come into the world and taken their place, I could understand, but he was alive at the time, and his soul was already in its place?"
>
> He replied, "My son, there is a deep mystery here. When they [Nadav and Avihu] departed from the world, they were not sheltered under the wings of God because they had no children, and they were therefore not fitted for the high priesthood. When Pinchas rose up against the adulterers, when he saw all the hosts of the tribe of Shimon gathering around him, his soul fled from him. Then two souls which were flying about naked joined it, and they all became one and, thus united, entered him, so that he took the place of Nadav and Avihu to become high priest."
>
> *(Zohar, Bemidbar 217a)*

The *Zohar* teaches that Nadav and Avihu entered the body of Pinchas when he confronted Zimri (the leader of the tribe of Shimon, see above). What is the implication of this teaching? Nadav and Avihu sinned by not having children, but they had the purity and innocence necessary to counter the orgiastic scene unfolding in front of Pinchas within the shadow of the Mishkan itself. Their "naked," pure souls joined with Pinchas and empowered him to vanquish the spiritual obstacles facing him.

We saw above that one of the reasons listed for their demise was acting without conferring with Moshe. Pinchas, on the other hand, consults Moshe:

> "Moshe said to the judges of Israel, ['Slay every one of his men who has attached himself to Baal Peor']" (*Bemidbar* 25:5).

The tribe of Shimon [hearing this] went to Zimri ben Salu and said him, "Behold, capital punishment is being meted out, yet you sit silent [i.e., inactive]."

What did he do? He arose and assembled twenty-four thousand Israelites and went to Kozbi, and said to her, "Surrender yourself to me."

She replied, "I am a king's daughter, and my father has instructed me, 'Yield only to their greatest man.' "

He replied to her that he was the prince of a tribe; moreover, his [tribe] was greater than his [Moshe's], for [Zimri's] was second in birth, while [Moshe's] was third.

He then seized her by her coiffure and brought her before Moshe, [demanding,] "Son of Amram, is this woman forbidden or permitted? And should you say, 'She is forbidden,' who permitted you to marry Yitro's daughter?"

At that moment Moshe forgot the halachah [concerning intimacy with a heathen woman], and all the people burst into tears; hence it is written, "And they were weeping before the door of the Ohel Mo'ed" (ibid., 10).

It is also written, "Pinchas, the son of Elazar, the son of Aharon the Kohein, saw it." What did he see? Rav said: He saw what was happening and remembered the halachah, and said to [Moshe], "Great-uncle, did you not teach us this on your descent from Mount Sinai: 'He who cohabits with a heathen woman is punished by zealots'?"

He replied, "He who reads the letter, let him be the agent [to carry out its instructions]."

(Sanhedrin 82a)

Pinchas surely could have argued that Moshe had forgotten the halachah, and his role as leader was no longer appropriate. Yet Pinchas does the opposite; he respectfully asks Moshe the appropriate law. This serves as a rectification for Nadav and Avihu, who acted without seeking approval.

The identification between Pinchas and Nadav and Avihu allows us to forge ahead and understand one last identification: We are taught that Pinchas is Eliyahu; both shared a common soul.[1] The Arizal[2] draws out this connection by teaching that in the verse *"Ana Hashem hoshea na* — Please, God, save us now!" (*Tehillim* 118:25), the word *ana* (אנא) stands for Eliyahu (אליהו), Nadav (נדב), and Avihu (אביהוא).

When we analyze the behavior of Eliyahu we find some interesting parallels with Nadav and Avihu. Arguably, the most famous episode in Eliyahu's life was the confrontation with the false prophets on Mount Carmel.

After the false prophets have no success in demonstrating their god's prowess, Eliyahu brings his own *korban*.

> It was at the time of the *minchah* [afternoon] offering, and Eliyahu the Prophet stepped forward and said, "God, the Lord of Avraham, Yitzchak, and Yisrael, let it be known today that You are Lord in Israel, and that I am Your servant, and that I have done all these things at Your word. Answer me, O God, answer me, so this people will know that You are God, the Lord, and that You have turned their heart back again."
>
> Then the fire of God descended and consumed the *olah*, the wood pile, the stones, and the dust; and the water that was in the ditch it licked up. When all the people saw it, they fell on their faces and said, "God is the Lord, God is the Lord."...
>
> Eliyahu said to Achav, "Get up, eat, and drink; for there is a sound of the rumbling of the rain."
>
> *(Melachim I 18:36–41)*

Eliyahu brings an offering outside of the Temple, truly a "foreign offering," yet fire comes down from Heaven indicating his victory. The parallel with Nadav and Avihu and the fire descending from Heaven is fascinating, but incomplete: God Himself had called for Eliyahu's "foreign" offering. Immediately after the fire

1 *Zohar, Shemot* 190a, and *Pirkei D'Rabbi Eliezer* 46. See *Parashat Pinchas* for more on this identification.

2 *Shaar HaPesukim, Tehillim* 118.

descends on Eliyahu's offering, the masses cry out, "God is the Lord, God is the Lord," and Eliyahu commands Achav, the king, to "get up, eat, and drink."

Eliyahu later ascends to Heaven with fire, in a chariot of fire pulled by horses of fire.

> It was when God lifted Eliyahu to Heaven by a whirlwind. Eliyahu and Elisha went from Gilgal.... They were walking, talking on the way, and behold a chariot of fire and horses of fire [appeared] and separated them one from the other. Eliyahu went up to Heaven in the whirlwind. Elisha was watching and he cried, "My father, my father, the chariot of Israel and its horsemen." Then he no longer saw him, and he took hold of his clothes and tore them in two pieces.
>
> *(Melachim II 2:1, 11–12)*

According to Jewish tradition, Eliyahu became an angel at this point and visits our homes every Pesach. When he comes in and takes a sip of wine, he reminds us that redemption will yet come, and that in order to be redeemed we must be forgiven for the sin of Adam and Chavah, of drinking the wine from the forbidden grapes. He thus reminds us of the teaching of Nadav and Avihu.

God's original plan was for a partnership in creation with man. When Adam became intoxicated, his creative capacities were debilitated. Nadav and Avihu sought not only to atone for this sin, but to reestablish the partnership. They hoped to turn the clock back to a point before Adam's sin, actively engaging God and reclaiming the human position of power and creativity. This was Pinchas's position in "defending" God. He became active, independent, and a partner in God's will. Finally, on Mount Carmel, Eliyahu achieves the most perfect partnership with God and His Will, and, having completed his mission, the mission of Nadav, Avihu, and Pinchas, he ascends, complete, to Heaven. There Eliyahu waits, and occasionally he comes and visits this world. His final visitation is described in the last verse in Prophets:

Behold, I am sending you to Eliyah the Prophet before the coming of the great and terrible day of God. He shall turn the heart of the fathers to the children, and the heart of the children to their fathers....

(Malachi 3:23–24)

Parashat Tazria

Life and Death

> God said to Moshe, saying, "Speak to the Children of Israel, saying: When a woman conceives and gives birth to a male, she shall be *temei'ah* [impure] for seven days, as in the days of *niddah* [menstruation]. On the eighth day, circumcise the flesh of the [baby's] foreskin."
>
> *(Vayikra 12:1–3)*

The Torah begins to teach the laws of childbirth, the details of which include the *tumah* of ritual purity or "*tumah* and *taharah.*" The topic of purities and impurities was begun in the previous section, at the end of *Shemini*, where the laws of ritual purity in animals are discussed. The specific *tumah* discussed in this chapter is that of the new mother, who is compared to a *niddah*. The laws of *niddah*, however, are not mentioned in the Torah prior to this section. Therefore, the use of *niddah* as an explanatory comment is difficult to understand.

A second problem in the text concerns the response to childbirth which the Torah calls for:

> At the completion of her days of purification — whether she has a son or a daughter — she shall bring a...burnt offering and a...sin offering.
>
> *(Ibid., 6)*

The burnt offering is understandable, but why would the new mother be required to bring a sin offering? What sin did she commit? The Gemara explains that the pain of childbirth may have been so severe that she might have sworn not to be intimate with her husband again.

> Rabbi Shimon bar Yochai was asked by his disciples, "Why did the Torah ordain that a woman should bring a sacrifice after childbirth?"
>
> He replied, "When she kneels in bearing she swears impetuously that she will have no intercourse with her husband. The Torah, therefore, ordained that she should bring a sacrifice."
>
> *(Niddah 31b)*

The Baal HaTurim comments that the separation for seven days, which is like *niddah,* is comparable to the seven days of mourning.[1] This idea has its origin in the *Zohar,* and is understandable regarding *niddah*: The concept of mourning for seven days is man's response to death, and the period of mourning is one of separation from society. The essential gesture is one of *teshuvah*: the sackcloth and ashes, our most recognizable symbols of mourning, are seen twice in Tanach. The first time is by Mordechai and the second time by the people of Ninvei, both of whom used these symbols to awaken their people to *teshuvah.* When man confronts death, the response is mourning, which brings him to consider his own mortality, to mend his ways, and to mend the world. When we consider the time of *niddah* as a type of mourning, we realize that the menstrual blood is a very literal representative of a life which did not come to fruition, a missed opportunity to foster life. Therefore Judaism, with its supreme value for human life, goes so far as to call upon us to respond to the loss of potential life.

The *Zohar*'s teaching thus provides insight into the essence of

---

1 The Torah calls for seven days of separation, as evidenced by this verse. Current observance of the *niddah* laws follows Rabbinic injunction which calls for an additional five days.

the laws of *niddah*, where husband and wife separate and observe their private mourning for the child not born. But why would the Baal HaTurim introduce this concept at this juncture, in the case of an actual birth of a very real baby? Indeed, the question could be posed on the verse itself: Why would the separation called for after childbirth be paralleled with the *niddah* state at all?

In order to resolve these difficulties, let us consider Rashi's first comments on this parashah. Citing the Midrash, Rashi observes:

> Just as man's creation followed that of all of the animals...in the process of creation, so the laws of his [*tumah*] are detailed in the text following those of the animals.

There is evidently something about these laws which invites us to compare and contrast them with the days of creation. The reference to the number seven should alert us to a possible connection with the seven days of creation. On the sixth day, after all other creatures are created, man is created. Adam is commanded:

> God, the Lord, commanded Adam, saying, "Of all trees of the garden you shall eat. And from the Tree of Knowledge of Good and Evil you will not eat, for on the day you eat from it you will surely die."
>
> *(Bereishit 2:16–17)*

We are well acquainted with the tragic end of the story: Chavah and Adam eat from the tree, and although death is not the immediate result of their transgression, they become mortal. Apparently, the meaning of God's decree was that eating from the tree would bring death into the world. Thus, "On the day you eat from it you will surely die." God's specific reaction to Chavah's sin sheds light on our subject:

> To the woman He said, "I will greatly increase your sorrow and your pregnancy. In sorrow will you bear children."
>
> *(Ibid. 3:16)*

Instead of death, Chavah, and all of womankind, are told what awaits them in childbearing and childbirth. The Gemara examines the phrase "I will greatly increase your sorrow."

> Chavah was cursed with ten curses, as it is written, "To the woman He said, 'I will greatly increase,' " which refers to the two drops of blood, one being that of menstruation and the other that of virginity....
>
> *(Eiruvin 100b)*

The implication is that, if not for the sin of the forbidden fruit, women would not have a menstrual cycle at all. Rather, childbirth would be a painless, automatic, almost immediate result of physical intimacy. Rashi understands that Kayin and Hevel were conceived and born on the very same day, in Gan Eden, in a "presin" childbirth:

> Three wonders were performed on that day: On that very day they were created, on that very day they cohabited, and on that very day they produced offspring.
>
> *(Bereishit Rabbah 22:2)*

In a perfect, idyllic world, there is no pain and no mourning. Now, perhaps, we can understand the comments of the Baal HaTurim: Every childbirth reminds us of the sin and punishment of Chavah. We live in a world bounded by mortality, and we are forced to realize that the child who was born is destined to die. This explains the separation following childbirth which is compared to *niddah*. Both are results of the same sin. *Niddah* is a response to the potential life which was frustrated, while the separation after childbirth is mourning and *teshuvah* for the necessity of the process of childbirth and for the mortality of the child born of this process. The logic in requiring a sin offering now becomes apparent: The childbirth is so completely intertwined with the sin of Chavah, so totally identified with and resultant from it, that a sin offering at the conclusion of this process is completely natural.

We may now understand why the separation period following the birth of a daughter is twice as long as the seven-day period described thus far. After the birth of a girl, the mourning for our mortality and pain is that much greater, for the child born is not only the victim of mortality but also the transmitter, as it were. She, too, will die, but more poignantly, she will carry the results of sin into the next generation. She will be the next to suffer the unavoidable consequences of sin which have become part and parcel of human existence.

Let us return to the beginning of the parashah.

> God said to Moshe, saying, "Speak to the Children of Israel, saying: When a woman conceives and gives birth to a male, she shall be *temei'ah* for seven days, as in the days of *niddah*. On the eighth day, circumcise the flesh of the [baby's] foreskin."

The Torah commands us to circumcise the son born on the eighth day of his life. The number eight represents that which is beyond the physical, beyond the seven days of "nature." The idea of circumcision is that man controls his desires and transcends his own physical identity. In that sense, circumcision is a perfection of nature which elevates mankind. It was Adam and Chavah succumbing to their desires which set in motion the chain of mortality and pain, and the Torah here supplies us with a means of breaking the chain.

The laws of *niddah* detail the counting of seven "clean days" prior to immersion in the *mikvah*, which is referred to as "*mayim chayim*," literally, "living water" or "water of life." Another reference in the Torah to counting is in the days known as the "Omer," specifically the period between Pesach, the day of liberation, and Shavuot, the day the Torah was given at Sinai. The *Zohar* compares the counting of the seven clean days with this counting of the seven weeks of the Omer.

> "You shall count for yourselves from the day after the Sabbath" (*Vayikra* 23:15). Observe that when Israel were in Egypt they were under an alien domination and they were en-

> trenched in impurity like a woman in the days of her menstruation. When they were circumcised, they entered the holy portion which is called "covenant," and the impurity left them like the blood of menstruation leaves a woman. Just as a woman then has to count seven days, so now God bade the Israelites to count days for purity. They were to count "for themselves," so as to be purified with supernal holy waters, and then to be attached to the King and to receive the Torah. A woman must count seven days, the people seven weeks. Why seven weeks? So that they might be worthy to be cleansed by the waters of the stream which is called "living waters," and from which issue seven Sabbaths.
>
> When Israel drew near to Mount Sinai, the dew that descends from the supernal Point came down in its fullness and purified them so that their filth left them, and they became attached to the King and received the Torah.... Any man who does not count those seven complete weeks so as to qualify himself for purity is not called "pure" and does not qualify as "pure," nor is he worthy to have a portion in the Torah. But if a man has reached this day in purity and has not lost count, then it behooves him on this night to study the Torah and to preserve the special purity to which he has attained on this night.
>
> *(Zohar, Vayikra 97a–b)*

Just as a woman counts the time between *tumah* and *taharah*, so too Israel counted the period between their redemption from the impurity and suffering of Egypt and the culmination of this period at Sinai. When a woman emerges from the *mikvah*, what follows is a reunion with her husband and a chance for new life to enter the world. When the Jewish people rendezvoused with God at Sinai, they, too, formed a union which gave new life and hope. The imagery of Torah as a Tree of Life is one which has been repeated time after time, as are references to Torah as water.

At Sinai, the Jews received the Torah, the true elixir of life. Adhering to the Torah keeps man actively in union with God. When the time comes and all the world accepts God and His Torah, death will become a thing of the past, as it says,

> Death will be erased for all eternity, and God, the Lord, will wipe away all tears.
>
> *(Yeshayah 25:8)*

On that day there will be no death and no more sorrow.

Parashat Metzora

The Sanctity of Speech

One of the main topics of *Parashiyot Tazria* and *Metzora* is *tzara'at. Tzara'at* has been translated as leprosy, but virtually all our commentaries tell us that this is not the type of leprosy with which we are familiar today; the *tzara'at* discussed in the Torah is a disease of a spiritual nature. Consequently, the *kohein,* who deals with issues of spirit, and not a doctor, "treats" the victim. The spiritual implication of *tzara'at* is that the sufferer is guilty of slanderous speech, the term *metzora* (one afflicted with *tzara'at*) being connected with the term *"motzi sheim ra,"* which describes the classical case of slanderous talk.

> Anyone who bears evil tales will suffer from the plague of *tzara'at,* as it says, "He who slanders his neighbor in secret, him I will destroy [*atzmit*]" (*Tehillim* 101:5). And there it says, "*Letz'mitut* [in perpetuity]" (*Vayikra* 25:30), which we translate as "absolutely" [permanently]. And we learned: The *metzora* who is shut up differs from the *metzora* who is certified impure only in respect to unkempt hair and rent garments. Reish Lakish said: What is the meaning of "This is the law of the *metzora*" (ibid. 14:2)? This is the law of one who utters evil reports [*motzi sheim ra*].
>
> *(Erachin 15b)*

There are two sections of the Torah where we can see this association, the more prominent one being the section dealing with Miriam's slander of Moshe, where she is punished by *tzara'at*. After Miriam discusses Moshe's family behavior, the Torah relates:

> God descended in the pillar of the cloud and stood in the doorway of the Tent. He called Aharon and Miriam, and they both came forth. He said, "Hear now my words: If there is a prophet among you, I, God, will make Myself known to him in a vision and will speak to him in a dream. Not so with My servant Moshe, for he is the trusted one in all My house. With him I speak mouth to mouth, manifestly, and not in riddles; and he views the form of the Lord. Why then were you not afraid to speak against My servant Moshe?" The anger of the Lord was kindled against them, and He departed.
>
> The cloud departed from the Tent, and, behold, Miriam had been stricken with *tzara'at*, white as snow. Aharon turned to Miriam, and, behold, she was stricken with *tzara'at*.
>
> *(Bemidbar 12:5–10)*

The second incident which ties *tzara'at* to slander concerns Moshe himself: When he stands before the burning bush, he states that the people will not believe that God has sent him. God instructs Moshe to put his hand into his cloak; when he removes the hand it is stricken with *tzara'at*, ostensibly because of the slander said about the Jewish nation.

> Moshe answered, "But they will not believe me, and they won't listen to my voice. They will say, 'God has not appeared to you.' "
>
> God said to him, "What is that in your hand?"
>
> He said, "A staff."
>
> He said, "Throw it to the ground."
>
> He threw it to the ground, and it became a snake; and Moshe fled from it.
>
> God said to Moshe, "Put out your hand, and take it by the tail."

> He put out his hand and took it, and it became a staff in his hand....
>
> God spoke to him further, "Put your hand into your bosom."
>
> He put his hand into his bosom; and when he took it out, behold, his hand was stricken with *tzara'at*, white as snow.
>
> *(Shemot 4:1–6)*

We might ask why slander should have such a direct effect on its perpetrator. Perhaps if we go back to the origins of speech we will better appreciate this issue.

When man is created, the Torah describes him as being formed from the dust of the earth. When this body is combined with the spirit — or soul — which God breathes into him, the result is man becomes a *"nefesh chayah"* (*Bereishit* 2:7).

Targum translates this phrase as "a speaking spirit." According to this approach, the ability to speak is the result of the merger of the physical and the spiritual within man. Only man is endowed with the ability to speak, and this is either man's soul or the result of his having a soul.

Speech itself makes an earlier appearance in *Bereishit*; Creation itself is described as the result of God speaking. The Mishnah teaches that the world was created with ten sayings:

> With ten [Divine] utterances was the world created. What is this information [meant] to convey, for surely [God] could have created [the world] with one utterance? It is in order to exact punishment from the wicked, who destroy the world that was created with ten utterances, and to give a good reward to the righteous, who maintain the world that was created with ten utterances.
>
> *(Avot 5:1)*

Here we find God, the Creator, speaking and man, created in the image of God, endowed with the ability to speak. To take this analogy one step further, Adam speaks for the first time when he gives names to the animals. Yet man's creativity is unlike God's.

God creates something from nothing by virtue of speech, whereas man creates categories and names of animals by virtue of speech. Man's creative ability differs from God's, but we can gain an appreciation for speech based on the comparison: Man's speech is "Godly" activity.

The first time that speech is misused is in Gan Eden, with the sinister, seductive comments of the snake. The snake is therefore the archetype for evil in general, and misused speech in particular.

> He [the snake] began speaking slander about his Creator, saying, "Of this tree He ate and then He created the world. Therefore, He orders you not to eat from it, so that you will not create other worlds, for every craftsman hates his fellow craftsmen."
>
> *(Bereishit Rabbah 19:4)*

> The snake was the first to make a breach in the world's fence, and so he has become the executioner of all who make breaches in fences (i.e., those who violate Rabbinical law, which is "fence" to the Torah).
>
> The snake was asked: "Why do you bite? What do you gain from it? The lion tears his prey and eats it, but you simply bite and kill!"
>
> He answered, " 'Does the snake bite without a whisper?' (*Kohelet* 10:11). Is it conceivable that I should do anything unless instructions were given me from Heaven?"
>
> He was asked, "How is it that you bite into one limb and your poison travels to all the limbs?"
>
> He answered, "Do you say this to me? 'The master of the tongue has no advantage' (ibid.), for he can live in Rome and slay in Syria, or live in Syria and slay in Rome."
>
> Why is a slanderer called "third"? Because he kills three: the one who utters [the slander], the one who listens to it, and the one about whom it is spoken.
>
> *(Vayikra Rabbah 26:2)*

The response of God to man's sin may be better understood based on the holiness of speech. After eating from the tree, man feels alienated and hides from God. For His part, God tries to engage man in dialogue in order to give him the opportunity to admit his guilt: He called to Adam, "Where are you?" (*Bereishit* 3:9). Rashi comments that God certainly knew where Adam was, but He engaged him in dialogue so as not to catch him off guard.

Only when man fails to find the proper words and blames Chavah (or perhaps God for giving him his mate) is he expelled from the Garden.

The laws of *teshuvah* include the requirement to verbalize one's sins.[1] Given our present perspective, we understand that this requirement will enable man to reacquire his exalted status, his own "image of God."[2]

The Jewish people were guilty of many transgressions during the forty years in the desert. During the first months alone, the Jews rebelled on numerous occasions, but one transgression stands out from all the others: the sin of the spies. As a result of that sin the entire generation died in the desert and the nation's entrance to the Land of Israel was delayed for some forty years. The Mishnah teaches:

> Thus we see that he who speaks with his mouth suffers more than he who commits an act. Thus we also find that the judgment against our fathers in the wilderness was sealed [i.e., decided] only because of their evil speech, as it says, "Yet have put me to proof these ten times, etc." (*Bemidbar* 14:22).
>
> *(Erachin 15a)*

The *Zohar* explains:

> Had Israel entered the Land under the sign of the evil tongue [i.e., associated with evil speech], they would not have endured an instant. Observe how much evil was wrought by the evil speech [spoken by the spies sent to see the Land of Israel]:

1 See Rambam's *Hilchot Teshuvah*.
2 See my comments on *Bereishit*.

> It brought about the decree that our ancestors should not enter the Land, those who uttered [the evil report] died, and [a day of] weeping [the ninth of Av] was decreed for succeeding generations. Their slander of the Holy Land was, as it were, a slander of the Almighty, and therefore God was angry because of this. All Israel would have been destroyed had it not been for the prayer of Moshe.
>
> *(Zohar, Vayikra 161a)*

For the sin of the golden calf, the nation was forgiven; for complaining about God having taken them from Egypt, they were forgiven. But for speaking evil about the Land of Israel, the Jews are punished for millennia! The *Zohar* (ibid.,) explains that this sin of misusing words — evil speech — is the sin of the snake, and God will forgive all except the sin of *lashon hara*.

The *Zohar* added that the ninth of Av, the day the spies returned to the camp, became the saddest day in the calendar due to evil speech. Had the spies not said the terrible things they did, and had the people not believed them, the Jews would have entered into Israel immediately. However, there may be a deeper message in this passage. The Chafetz Chaim, in his monumental work on *lashon hara*, cites the passage from the Gemara that explains why the two Temples were destroyed:

> Why was the First Temple destroyed? Because of three [evil] things which prevailed there: idolatry, sexual immorality, bloodshed.... But during the period of the Second Temple, [the Jewish people] were occupied with Torah, mitzvos, and acts of kindness — why was it destroyed? Because groundless hatred prevailed there. This teaches you that groundless hatred is considered as grave as the three sins of idolatry, sexual immorality, and bloodshed together.
>
> *(Yoma 9b)*

In a separate discussion, the Gemara teaches:

> Whoever speaks slander increases his sins even up to [the degree

> of] the three [cardinal] sins: idolatry, sexual immorality, and bloodshed.
>
> *(Erachin 15b)*

The Chafetz Chaim therefore concludes that *lashon hara* is part and parcel of the sin of groundless hatred. The motivation for evil speech is groundless hatred. The connection made in the *Zohar* between the sin of the spies and the ninth of Av, the day of mourning for the Temple, becomes all the more poignant: *Lashon hara* is the common element, the core at the heart of these disasters. Therefore, the *Zohar* states, *lashon hara* caused the ninth of Av to be a day of crying throughout the millennia.

The Gemara discusses the possibility of a cure for *lashon hara*:

> If one is a scholar, let him occupy himself with Torah.... [If he is] a common person, let him humble himself.
>
> *(Ibid. 15b)*

A person who speaks *lashon hara* misuses his mouth and the words which were given to him for the purpose of speaking Torah; to correct the flaw, he is instructed to spend his energies on Torah. The simple, "common person" should endeavor to spend his time learning Torah as well, but until he becomes proficient, let him at least humble himself. How will humility help? The core of *lashon hara* is groundless hatred, and when a person practices humility he will avoid the jealousy which leads to hatred. This lesson may be learned from the very same snake in Gan Eden which introduced *lashon hara*. Our Sages teach that the snake was spurred by his jealousy of Adam; he envied Adam on account of Chavah, but had he been suitably humble he would not have thought himself worthy of such a helpmate.[1]

The sin of *lashon hara* is the tarnishing of the image of God within us. This image may be likened to the human mind:[2] The capacity to speak is the ability to bring the Divine into this world. Therefore, at the moment when the soul and body merge, speech is

---

1 See *Avot D'Rabbi Natan* 2.

2 See my comments on *Tzav*.

the result. Speech is the defining capacity of man. This is why misusing speech is so evil. Furthermore, to speak about another person in a negative manner is tantamount to rejecting the image of God in that person. Therefore we may say that evil speech is the misuse of our divinity in order to reject the Divinity of God. It is no wonder, then, that the Temple was destroyed because of *lashon hara.*

This awareness of the sanctity of speech will also give us an appreciation of another passage in the Torah. When the people complain about not having water, the Torah relates:

> God said to Moshe, "...Speak to the rock in front of them [the congregation] and it will yield its water...."
>
> Moshe lifted his hand and struck the rock with his staff twice. Much water came out, and the nation and its animals drank.
>
> God said to Moshe and Aharon, "Because you didn't believe in Me to sanctify Me in front of the Children of Israel, you will not bring this congregation to the land which I have given you."
>
> *(Bemidbar 20:7–12)*

What was the great offense which Moshe and Aharon committed? They were told to speak, to sanctify God by speech. This would have rectified the *lashon hara* uttered by the spies, by using speech in a positive manner, to cause a sanctification of God's Name and not a desecration. But by not using the power of speech, Moshe and Aharon lost the opportunity to enter the Land.

Perhaps now we understand why the *metzora* came to the *kohein.* The role of Aharon was to "Love peace and pursue it" (*Avot* 1:12). The blessing that a *kohein* makes before blessing the people reminds us of this task:

> Blessed are You, God our Lord, King of the Universe, who has sanctified us with the sanctity of Aharon and has commanded us to bless Your people, Israel, with love.

A person guilty of misusing speech was commanded to spend

time in the presence of a *kohein* in order to learn how to love. Furthermore, the sages explain that the various rites of purification of the *metzora,* including shaving the hair, washing the body and clothing, and finally ritual immersion, were designed to foster humility. We may also understand why *lashon hara* brings *tzara'at* to the perpetrator's home as well as to his body: *Lashon hara,* and the groundless hatred at its core, can spread beyond the individuals involved, affecting even God's House and bringing about the Temple's destruction.

Addendum:

Most years this parashah is read after Pesach, during the time of year known as *"Sefirah." Sefirah* is a time of mourning for the students of Rabbi Akiva who did not treat one another with respect.

> It was said that Rabbi Akiva had twelve thousand pairs of disciples, from Gabbat to Antipatris; and all of them died at the same time because they did not treat each other with respect.... All of [Rabbi Akiva's original students] died between Pesach and Shavuot.... All of them died a cruel death.
>
> *(Yevamot 62b)*

Perhaps this is the perfect time to think about the value of each person, the image of God in each person, and to use our words judiciously.

Parashat Acharei Mot

Twins

In this week's parashah we find the instructions given to Aharon regarding the service for Yom Kippur. The service is introduced by reminding us of the death of the two sons of Aharon, Nadav and Avihu, thus drawing a connection between the service performed and the fate of the two sons of Aharon. In order to understand the service of Yom Kippur, we must compare and contrast it with the actions of the sons of Aharon which led to their deaths.

The objective of Yom Kippur is to bring about forgiveness for the entire people:

> For on that day I will forgive you, to purify you from all your sins. In front of God you will become pure.
>
> *(Vayikra 16:30)*

Aside from the entire nation, special attention is given to the Temple and the *kohanim*:

> He shall make an atonement for the Holy Sanctuary, and he shall make an atonement for the Tent of Meeting and for the *Mizbei'ach*, and he shall make an atonement for the *kohanim* and for all the people of the congregation.
>
> *(Ibid., 33)*

Part of the service, then, deals with improper behavior on the part of the *kohanim*. We are told at the outset that Aharon himself should not enter the inner sanctum at all times, only at the proper time and in the proper sequence of worship (ibid., 2–3). While Nadav and Avihu entered the Temple and approached God in a moment of ecstasy, Aharon is given very specific instructions on the manner and conditions for service. The line between service of God and self-styled service may be a thin one, but that line may be the difference between life and death. Here, Aharon is being warned of the consequences of entering the Temple inappropriately:

> God said to Moshe, "Speak to Aharon, your brother. He should not come at all times to the holy [place] within the curtain...so he will not die."
>
> *(Ibid., 2)*

Sheim MiShmuel suggests that the sin of Nadav and Avihu resulted from unbridled passion and love of God; they tried to relate to God via this love. The Gemara teaches that this day was beloved for God as well.

> On that day there was as much joy in front of God as there was on the day of creation of heaven and earth.
>
> *(Megillah 10b)*

Sensing this joy, Nadav and Avihu seized the moment and tried to respond to God's great love of man. Their response was improper for it was not called for by God. The seriousness and somberness of Yom Kippur stands in stark comparison to the ecstasy of Nadav and Avihu. This is God's response to the behavior of Nadav and Avihu. Religious experience born of ecstasy can create a relationship which has an alien component, and it may result in the worship of an alien god. In order for the religious experience to be valid it must be objective; it must be part of the fulfillment of a directive from God. Otherwise, the experience is a subjective one and may cross the line between manifesting the image of God within ourselves and creating God in our image.

This does not mean that Judaism does not recognize the joyful, ecstatic relationship with God, but such a relationship may only be developed after "fear of God" is perfected. Only after the Yom Kippur service in which we follow God's detailed instructions may we find ourselves relating to God via love. In Temple times, the Yom Kippur service concluded in a great outpouring of joy:

> They [the nation] would then bring him [the *kohein gadol*] his own garments, and he put them on. They would accompany him to his house, and he would arrange a day of festivity for his friends whenever he had come out of the Holy of Holies in peace.
>
> *(Yoma 70a)*

> There were no days as joyful in Israel as the fifteenth of Av and Yom Kippur.
>
> *(Ta'anit 4:8)*

The Sages tell us that the streets of Yerushalayim were filled with well-wishers; the *kohein gadol,* making his way through the crowds, would arrive home hours after the service was completed. The greatest celebration, though, the *simchat beit hashoeivah,* would follow Yom Kippur by a week.

> Whoever never saw the *simchat beit hashoeivah* never saw joy in his life.
>
> *(Sukkah 5:1)*

The balance between fear of God and strict adherence to the details of observance, on the one hand, and joyous celebration of the love between God and man, on the other, is highlighted by this festival. Rambam in his *Mishneh Torah* (*Sukkah* 8:14) limits the active celebration in the *simchat beit hashoeivah* to great sages and scholars; all others attended as spectators.

The archetypical model of ecstatic expression in front of God was David HaMelech:

> David went and brought up the *Aron* of God from the house of Oveid Edom to the City of David in joy. And it was when those who carried the *Aron* of God had gone six paces, he sacrificed an ox and a fatling. David was dancing before God with all his might; and David was girded with a linen *eifod*. So David and all the House of Israel brought up the *Aron* of God with the blowing and the sound of the shofar.
>
> *(Shmuel II 6:12–15)*

But David also possessed a profound sense of fear of God, as the entire book of *Tehillim* bears witness.

As a response to the passion of Nadav and Avihu, we see the detailed, intricate, serious service of Yom Kippur. The incense which they offered is replaced by the incense which Aharon is commanded to offer, and one error in the performance of this task could be fatal. The food and drink of Nadav and Avihu is replaced by a day of complete abstinence from food and drink. Similarly, the details of the service of Yom Kippur service take on new meaning when contrasted with the actions of Nadav and Avihu.

The central worship of the day involved two goats, one offered in the Temple, the other sent to the desert. This practice would seem to be a response to the different types of worship we have been discussing: the first, in the Temple, for God, and the other which had no place — not in the Temple and not among the living at all, sent to a place of desolation. This second goat was destined for Azazel, the Satan. Upon consideration, this worship seems quite bizarre. Why would we take a goat, only to reject it and send it away? The law seems to teach us about the stark difference between service of God which is accepted and beloved to God and that which is rejected by God. What could be more different than service of God and *avodah zarah*? These are surely diametrical opposites.

Yet are they? The Mishnah provides some details about the goats.

> The two goats of Yom Kippur — the mitzvah is for them to be identical in appearance, size, and value, and they should be chosen together.
>
> *(Yoma 6:1)*

The Mishnah teaches that these two goats should look identical — like twins. This seems strange, considering that their fates and the ideas they represent are so different. Yet the theme of twins who are opposites is actually a familiar one in the Torah.

The most famous twins are Yaakov and Eisav. They were complete opposites, one good, the other evil. No one could ever confuse them. On the other hand, perhaps they did possess some similarities. Rashi (on *Bereishit* 25:27) tells us that until the age of thirteen they were indistinguishable, at least in behavior. In the words of the Midrash:

> Eisav was worthy to be called Yaakov, and Yaakov was worthy to be called Eisav.
>
> *(Midrash Zuta, Shir HaShirim 1:15)*

They were so similar that at times their similarity caused confusion. One brother dressed like or spoke like the other. It is strange that the Divine plan required twins, when perhaps just being siblings would have been enough. Evidently the Torah wanted these two, Yaakov and Eisav, to be almost the same. Perhaps their similarity represents the thin line between acceptable behavior and idolatry, between good and evil. Rav Yitzchak Hutner noted this parallel, and suggested that when things look alike from the exterior, it is a sign that one must look within, at the essence, in order to discern the difference (*Pachad Yitzchak, Purim* p. 43).

The idea of the two goats is intrinsically related to the personalities of Yaakov and Eisav, identical on the outside but so different in terms of their essence. The origin of the two goats themselves may very well be found in that famous episode when Yaakov is persuaded by his mother to dress up like his brother and receive the blessings from his father. Rivkah instructs him:

> Go now to the flock and bring me two good kid goats....
>
> *(Bereishit 27:9)*

The Midrash expands on this idea:

> How do we know that it was in the merit of Yaakov [that we take the two goats on Yom Kippur]? These are the goats that his mother referred to [when she said], "Go now to the flock and bring me two good kid goats...." Why are they called "good"? Rabbi Brechia said in the name of Rabbi Chelbo: They are good for you and good for your children. They will be good for you when you enter and take the blessings from your father, and they will be good for your children — when they soil themselves in sin all year round, they will bring these two goats, offer them, and be cleansed.
>
> *(Pesikta Rabbati 47)*

Yaakov's entrance to his father's room may be paralleled with the once-a-year entrance of the *kohein gadol* into the Holy of Holies on Yom Kippur. Yaakov prepared for this appearance with the two goats, as his descendants would in the future. The Yom Kippur offering of the goat to Azazel serves to atone for the recurring sin of "dressing up" like Eisav instead of behaving like the nation of Yaakov we are.[1]

While we may now understand the symbolism of the two goats, we have not gained any insight into Azazel.[2] Rabbi Menachem Azarya DeFano, in his work *Sefat Emet*, explains that the name *Azazel* is an acronym for "*Zeh le'umat zeh asa HaElokim*," a verse in *Kohelet*:

> On a day of prosperity be joyful, and on a day of adversity consider: The Lord has made the one as well as the other [*zeh le'umat zeh asa HaElokim*].
>
> *(Kohelet 7:14)*

---

1 Eisav, whose other name is Edom, which means "red," is the symbol of blood and strictness. It is interesting that the Gemara associates the forgiveness on Yom Kippur with the red string turning white.

2 In *Parashat Vayishlach*, I discussed the association between Azazel and the angel or spiritual power of Eisav.

According to Rabbi DeFano, the contrast between good and evil, with the recognition that both emanate from God, is encapsulated by the verse "the Lord has made one as well as the other," encoded in the word *Azazel*. The Midrash explains this idea:

> "The Lord has made one as well as the other" — God has made righteous men and evil men, as it is written, "Then his brother emerged [from the womb] and his hand grasped the heel of Eisav" (*Bereishit* 25:26).
>
> *(Pesikta D'Rav Kahana 28)*

It is fascinating that the example brought to illustrate that both righteousness and evil are from God is none other than the case of Yaakov and Eisav. We understand from this that, in a sense, good needs evil in order to exist, if for no other reason than to be rejected. It is the contrast with evil which allows good to shine. This idea is illustrated in the *Zohar*:

> "[You shall love God, your Lord,] with all your soul" (*Devarim* 6:5) — the "all" includes all the aspects of the soul, *nefesh, ruach,* and *neshamah*. As "with all your possessions" (ibid.) — these also have various aspects, each one different from the other. True love to the Holy One, blessed be He, consists of just this, that we give over to Him all our emotional, intellectual, and material faculties and possessions, and love Him.
>
> If it is asked, "How can a man love [God] with his evil inclination? Is not the evil inclination the seducer, preventing man from approaching the Holy One to serve him? How, then, can man use the evil inclination as an instrument of love to God?" The answer lies in this, that there can be no greater service done to the Holy One than to subdue the evil inclination by the power of love to the Holy One, blessed be He. When it is subdued and its power is broken by man in this way, then [man] becomes a true lover of the Holy One, since he has learned how to make the evil inclination itself serve the Holy One.

This is a mystery entrusted to the masters of esoteric lore. All that the Holy One has made, both above and below, is for the purpose of manifesting His glory and making all things serve Him. Would a master permit his servant to work against him, and to continually lay plans to counteract his will? It is the will of the Holy One that men should worship Him and walk in the way of truth, so that they will be rewarded with many benefits. How, then, can an evil servant come and counteract the will of his Master by tempting man to walk in an evil way, seducing him from the good way and causing him to disobey the will of his Lord?

But, indeed, the evil inclination also does the will of its Lord through this. It is like a king who had an only son whom he dearly loved. Because of this [love], he warned him not to be enticed by bad women, saying that anyone defiled could not enter his palace. The son promised his father to do his will in love.

Outside the palace, however, there lived a beautiful harlot. After a while the king thought, *I will see how devoted my son is to me.* He called to the woman and commanded her, saying, "Entice my son, for I wish to test his obedience to my will."

She used every blandishment to lure [the son] into her embraces. But the son, being good, obeyed the commandment of his father. He refused her allurements and thrust her from him.

Then the father rejoiced exceedingly, and brought [his son] into the innermost chamber of the palace, bestowed upon him gifts from his best treasures, and showed him every honor. And who was the cause of all this joy? The harlot! Is she to be praised or blamed for it? To be praised, surely, on all accounts, for she fulfilled the king's command and carried out his plans for him, and she also caused the son to receive all the good gifts and deepened the king's love to his son.

Therefore, it is written, "The Lord saw all that He had made,

> and behold it was very good" (*Bereishit* 1:31). The word *very* refers to the Angel of Death [i.e., the evil inclination]. Similarly, if it were not for this accuser, the righteous would not possess the supernal treasures in the World to Come. Happy, therefore, are they who come into conflict with the tempter and prevail against him, for through him they attain bliss and all the good and desirable possessions of the World to Come, about which it is written, "No eye has seen...what He will do for the one who waits for Him" (*Yeshayah* 64:3).
>
> *(Zohar, Shemot 163a)*

The problems arise when man adopts the ways of evil, identifying with them instead of rejecting them. This path is a rejection of God and the image of God within us, as is illustrated by another detail of the Yom Kippur service:

Lots are drawn to determine which of the two identical goats will be sacrificed in the Temple and which will be for Azazel. The idea of drawing lots is apparently a concession to the "random" element of human existence. The word *goral* (lots) itself can also be translated as "fate." When the Torah describes the attack of Amaleik (a grandson of Eisav) on the Jewish nation, it says:

> Remember what was done to you by Amaleik, on the way as you left Egypt. When they happened upon you....
>
> *(Devarim 25:17–18)*

Rashi explains "they happened" as "coincidence." In his brief comment, we can discern the philosophical difference between Judaism and "Amaleikism": We believe in a God who is involved in history, while for Amaleik, life is no more than a series of coincidences. Haman, one of the most famous descendants of Amaleik, used lots to determine the best day to attack and destroy the Jews. The Jews, for their part, turned to God and put their faith in His involvement in history, just as Moshe lifted his hands Heavenward in prayer while the battle against Amaleik raged around him, signaling to the Jews that faith in God is the only ammunition against Amaleik.

When the Jew has sinned and has begun to act like Eisav, worshipping the worthless ideas of "coincidence" and "fate" that are represented by Azazel, forgetting God who is constantly involved in history, God invites him to enter the Temple, represented by the *kohein gadol*. The lots drawn force us to examine our behavior and the underlying philosophy of chance and coincidence.

The breeding ground for sin is in this forgetfulness. Therefore, on Yom Kippur, every detail is important. Every detail is recognition of God's involvement in our lives. The day is filled with awe and fear, a fear which can only spring from the understanding that God is intimately involved in our lives. This fear, in turn, gives birth to the joy which can only spring from the understanding that this same God is a God of forgiveness and unlimited love.

The cathartic power of Yom Kippur lies in this: We are all guilty, at times, of dressing up like Eisav and deluding ourselves. On Yom Kippur we banish our "evil twin" to the empty desert, as we redouble our efforts to serve God. When we succeed, the result is celebration and joy.[1]

1 This also explains the "dressing up" on Purim, based on the idea of Yom Kippur being a "Yom Kippurim," a day like Purim.

Parashat Kedoshim

Holiness

> God spoke to Moshe, saying, "Speak to the entire Community of Israel, and say to them, 'You shall be holy for I, God your Lord, am Holy.' "
>
> *(Vayikra 19:1–2)*

For many people this serves as the introduction to the most important teachings in the Torah and, by extension, of Judaism. The central laws governing man's relationships with his fellow man are enumerated in the verses which follow: "Do not curse the deaf," "Do not put a stumbling block before the blind," "Do not stand idly on the 'blood' of your brother," and, arguably the most famous verse of all, "Love your neighbor as yourself." All these injunctions follow, one after the other, in rapid fire.

Despite the decidedly ethical emphasis of many of the commandments, the chapter does deal with ritual concerns as well. What is perhaps most striking about this section is the intertwining of laws which are man-oriented with commandments which are God-oriented. This is actually a trait of the entire Torah. Other ancient systems dealt with either ritual considerations or social considerations; the uniqueness of the Torah is the understanding that the ethical and the ritualistic are two parts of one organic whole. The Code of Hammurabi, for example, is a series of torts which

Rousseau would have labeled a "social contract," but its social concerns are not a function of a relationship with a deity. On the other hand, our parashah teaches:

> You shall fear your mother and father and guard my Sabbaths; I am God, your Lord.
>
> *(Ibid., 3)*

This one verse concerns itself both with an individual's relationship with his parents and with the Sabbath. The verse is "signed," "I am God," as if to say, "I am God who commanded you to observe both the ethical and the ritual." The conclusion we draw is that the individual who falls short in his responsibilities to his fellow man is, at the same time, transgressing against God as well. Even the verse "Love your neighbor as yourself" concludes with "I am God."

There is another, more subtle lesson to be learned from this textual juxtaposition: God is concerned, perhaps equally, with both the ethical and the ritual. Therefore, those who turn to the ethical teachings, as expressed by a few of the verses in this section, as their exclusive definition of Judaism, are misreading the intended message by ignoring the context of the verses.

The opening verses of the parashah are critical for an understanding of the Torah's message:

> God spoke to Moshe, saying, "Speak to the entire Community of Israel, and say to them, 'You shall be holy for I, God, your Lord, am Holy.' "

Why was it necessary to gather the entire community to teach this message? The Midrash answers:

> Why was this section taught in a gathering? Why does it not [merely] state, "Speak to the Children of Israel," as it does in the other sections of the Torah? Because all the [ten] commandments are included in it.
>
> *(Tanchuma, Kedoshim 3)*

The Midrash sees *Parashat Kedoshim* as a restatement of the Ten Commandments. Because of its importance it is appropriate that it be taught in front of the entire community. We should note that the Ten Commandments also combine the ritual with the ethical. The Gemara stresses this point in the following passage:

> When the Holy One, blessed be He, said, "I am [God, Your Lord]..." and "You shall have no other [gods before Me]..." (*Shemot* 20:2–3), the nations of the world said, "He is preaching for His own aggrandizement." But when He said, "Honor your father and mother" (ibid., 12), they [the nations of the world] praised the first commandments as well.... By the end of the commandments, they came to appreciate the truth in the first ones.
>
> *(Kiddushin 31a)*

According to this passage, the first commandments did not make a positive impression upon the nations of the world, perhaps because they were reminiscent of their own deities. But when God began to require man to behave ethically in interpersonal relationships as well, the nations understood that they must reevaluate the first commandments as well.

The command to be holy seems difficult to fulfill. How can finite, limited man be holy? Moreover, what is holiness? The commentaries teach that holiness translates as "separateness." Rashi, citing the Midrash, teaches that we must separate ourselves, specifically from elicit sexual relationships. With this reading, Rashi creates a logical flow of ideas from the previous parashah, *Acharei Mot*, which ended with a list of forbidden relations.

Ramban, on the other hand, sees this verse as a more general teaching to avoid excess. Ramban understands that we are to separate ourselves from things that are not explicitly forbidden, things that go against the spirit of Jewish law although they are within the letter of law. Ramban describes someone whom he calls a "*naval bi'reshut haTorah* — a slob or lecher with the permission of the Torah."

In either case, according to both Rashi and Ramban, we are called on to be holy — to be separate. The Torah gives a reason: "You shall be holy for I, God your Lord, am Holy."

If holiness is a trait of God, our question returns: How can man achieve "holiness"? The Kotzker Rebbe said, "How can man be holy? Only because 'I, God your Lord, am Holy' " (*Sheim MiShmuel, Vayikra,* p. 277).

The Sheim MiShmuel, a grandson of the Kotzker Rebbe, explained his grandfather's teaching as follows: Every Jew has within him a part of God's holiness, which enables him to achieve holiness. Man can become holy because man was created in the image of God. But since every person possesses a different soul, each person has a different holiness within him. A wonderful dichotomy emerges: This section was taught publicly in order to teach man how to become holy, and within the method of this teaching lies the essential message: Holiness is something that belongs to the collective Jewish community. If "holy" means separate, a person might be led to believe that in order to become holy he must withdraw from the community. Therefore, this section was taught publicly — to teach us that the holiness which we seek is found in the community.

New light is thus shed on the celebrated Gemara passage in which Hillel is asked by a potential convert to teach him the entire Torah while the man stood on one foot. Hillel responds:

> What is despised by you, do not do to your friend. This is the entire Torah. The rest is commentary; go learn!
>
> *(Shabbat 31a)*

Hillel's Aramaic paraphrase of the verse "Love your neighbor as yourself" is found in the *Targum Yonatan (Yerushalmi),* as the explanation of the verse. Rashi's comments on this passage are somewhat cryptic:

> "Your own friend and your father's friend do not forsake" (*Mishlei* 27:10). "Your friend" refers to the Holy One, blessed be He. Do not ignore His words for it is detestable when your friend ignores your words.

Rashi's explanation is based on the Midrash and is echoed in the *Zohar*:

> It is written, "Your own friend and your father's friend do not forsake and do not go into your brother's house in the day of your calamity".... "Your own friend" is the Holy One, blessed be He, for it says, "For my brothers and friends' sakes" (*Tehillim* 122:8).
>
> *(Shemot Rabbah 27:1)*

> Rabbi Chizkiyah interpreted the verse, "A friend loves at all times, and a brother is born for adversity" (*Mishlei* 17:17), as follows: "A friend" is the Holy One, of whom it is written, "Your own friend and your father's friend do not forsake," (ibid. 27:10).... Indeed, "you must not forsake your Friend," you must worship Him, cleave to Him, keep His commandments. But "withdraw your foot" (ibid. 25:17) from your evil inclination so that he should not become your master. Withdraw it from your house — namely, from the holy soul which your Friend has put into you. The true worship of the Holy One, blessed be He, consists of loving Him above all and in all, as it is written, "You shall love God, your Lord" (*Devarim* 6:5).
>
> *(Zohar, Shemot 55b)*

Rashi's cryptic comment now becomes clear: Hillel's assertion that this one solitary verse encapsulates the entire Torah becomes understandable only when we translate "friend" as "God." The friend which you should not mistreat is none other than God Himself! If that is the case, Hillel's choice of this verse is straightforward, as it truly encompasses all aspects of the Torah, both the ethical and ritual, interpersonal relationships as well as the human relationship with God. We now see that the line drawn between the two types of laws is not as broad as we might have thought: Loving my neighbor includes loving God; loving God includes loving my neighbor. I must be holy because God is holy. To be holy means to be separate; the way I will become holy is by loving my neighbor.

By loving my neighbor I display my love of God.

We now understand why Jewish law legislates that before a person may approach God in prayer, he must first accept the commandment of loving your neighbor as yourself (*Magen Avraham* 46:1, in the name of the Arizal).

Let us return to the text of the Torah. After the teaching of loving one's neighbor, what comes next? What can come next? How can any commandment top this beautiful teaching?

> Guard my statutes. Do not mate your animals with different species, do not plant your field with combine species, and a garment of wool and linen shall not come upon you.
>
> *(Vayikra 19:19)*

This verse seems anticlimactic. The shift is sudden and brutal: From loving one's neighbor, the height of ethical discipline, we find ourselves confronted with the most obscure ritual — the prohibition against mixing wool and linen in our clothing, which is a commandment without apparent rhyme or reason.

Deeper analysis reveals the connection: As we noted above, to be holy means to be separate. Keeping the species separate is a lesson in holiness. The topic has not shifted as drastically as we imagined. The Vilna Gaon explains the origin of the prohibition of *sha'atnez* (mixing wool and linen) from a mystical perspective:

> This is the mystical secret of *sha'atnez*. For the offering of Kayin was linen, and [the offering] of Hevel was wool.
>
> *(Vilna Gaon, Sifra D'Tzniuta, ch. 4, 51b)*

Hevel was a shepherd, while Kayin worked the land. The first person to be guilty of not loving his neighbor as himself was Kayin. His sin had far-reaching repercussions, resulting in a need for more holiness in the world, more separateness, more appreciation of the existence of different realms. Had Kayin fully understood that a unique aspect of God existed in Hevel, he never would have killed him. He failed to understand that the image of God within every person is unique, and that for mankind to achieve holiness all of these different parts of God need to be united. Consequently, a new type of separateness needed to be introduced to the world, in order to remind us of the terrible crime of Kayin. Thus, the fratricide of Kayin resulted in the prohibition against *sha'atnez*! The laws of separate species follow, naturally, logically, immediately after the commandment, "Love your neighbor as yourself."

Loving our neighbors brings Godliness into the world, as illustrated by the following *midrash*. (Note: This *midrash* is relatively long, and it exists in two sources, with slight variations. See *Otzar Midrashim*, p. 319, and *Yalkut Me'am Loez, Vayikra*, p. 210. Following is a paraphrase.)

> There once were two friends who were extremely close. Because of wars and various intrigues, the friends were separated for many years. Finally one heard where his friend was, so he traveled to visit him.
>
> Unfortunately, the countries where the two lived were at war with one another. Rumors began to spread regarding the mission of the stranger who had come to visit. Soon he was arrested and charged with espionage. He was found guilty and sentenced to death by the king himself.
>
> The man pleaded with the king to grant him one last the wish.
>
> The king asked, "What is your wish?"
>
> The man answered that he was a prominent businessman in his home country, and, since he was well known, he often did business on credit, by a handshake. The plain truth was that though he accumulated a small fortune, most of his money was lent out to people without contracts. He asked the king to allow him one last trip home to put his affairs in order and say goodbye to his family. If not, the king was not merely sentencing him to death but also his children to a life of poverty.
>
> The king was incredulous. "How am I to believe you that you will return? What can you possibly give me as a collateral?"

The man responded that he had a good friend who lived in the city and he was sure that the man would be willing to take his place on death row until he returned.

The friend was brought in. "Would you take your friend's place?" he was asked. "You understand that if he does not return it is your head that will roll."

The man agreed. "After all," he said, "what are friends for?"

The king was intrigued to see if the man would truly return, so he allowed him to leave, knowing that the execution would take place in thirty days.

The appointed time came, but the man had not returned. The king instructed his guards to take out the friend and decapitate him. They brought the man out and put his head on the block.

As the knife was about to come down, a loud murmur could be heard from the city. The executioner was told to wait; lo and behold, the [first] man had returned.

He walked bravely up to the executioner, grabbed the sword, and said, "I am here and prepared to meet my fate."

His friend stood up and grabbed the sword as well and said, "You are late. The deal was for you to be back by this morning. Since you did not arrive, I am the one to be killed."

The friend responded, "But it is I whom they accuse of treachery; it is I who was sentenced to die."

The king observed the argument and summoned both men. "Neither of you will be killed, on one condition."

They both looked at the king and asked, "What is the condition?"

The king answered, "That I can become your third friend."

Yalkut Me'am Loez uses this story to teach the meaning of the verse "Love your neighbor as yourself; I am God." The profound message of the story is that if man truly and wholeheartedly loves his neighbor, God promises to love both men and be our constant Partner, our third Friend. The commandments which are between man and his fellow man include God as well.

We now understand why "groundless hatred" caused the destruction of the Temple. When we act with love for our fellow man, we bring the *Shechinah* down into the world; hatred between men expels the *Shechinah* from the world. The holiness of God is reflected by the holiness of man; the uniqueness of God is manifested in the collective uniqueness of all men. The bonding of two people causes more Divinity to be revealed in this world. To be holy means to be separate: Each person must find the unique divinity within themselves and within their fellow man. This necessitates our "separateness" and our unity. The result is holiness.

Parashat Emor

Temimut

P*arashat Emor* begins with instructions given to Moshe which affect his brother, Aharon, and all of Aharon's descendants.

> God said to Moshe, "Speak to the *kohanim*, the sons of Aharon, and say to them, 'Do not defile yourselves to [with] the [dead] souls among your people.' "
>
> *(Vayikra 21:1)*

In this verse, one of the central characteristics of the priestly family, the *kohanim*, is introduced: A *kohein* is not permitted to come in contact with the dead. To those brought up within the Jewish tradition, this prohibition is familiar, almost obvious. Only when we consider this issue a priori does it seem strange: Why should a *kohein* not be permitted to be exposed to the dead or death? If such contact is fundamentally wrong, it should be inappropriate for all Jews. Is there something unique about being a *kohein* which makes contact with the dead unsuitable?

Insight into this question may be found in the verse immediately preceding this prohibition (the last verse of the previous parashah, *Kedoshim*):

> Any man or woman who is involved in the practices of *ov* or *yidoni* [mediums or oracles] shall be put to death....
>
> *(Ibid. 20:27)*

This is the third instance in *Parashat Kedoshim* in which this prohibition is reiterated, and here it serves as the conclusion of *Kedoshim*. We cannot help but contrast this finale with the opening verses of *Emor*, in which the *kohanim* in particular are instructed in such a closely related matter. The contrast becomes even sharper when we realize what the practices of *ov* and *yidoni* involved. In *Devarim*, the prohibitions are repeated yet again:

> When you come to the Land that God, your Lord, has given you, do not learn to do the revolting practices of those nations. The practice of *ov* or *yidoni* or the attempt to communicate with the dead should not be found in you.
>
> *(Devarim 18:9–11)*

From the context, we learn that *ov* and *yidoni* were types of witchcraft involving communication with the dead. The Gemara explains that a human skull was used in the rite of *ov*.

> *Ba'al ov* denotes both one who conjures up the dead by means of soothsaying and one who consults a skull.
>
> *(Sanhedrin 65b)*

Shaul HaMelech made use of this method in an attempt to communicate with Shmuel HaNavi, who had passed away:

> Shmuel died, and all of Israel eulogized him. They buried him in Ramah, in his city. Shaul eradicated the *ovot* and *yidonim* from the Land.
>
> *(Shmuel I 28:3)*

Next, the text tells us that the Philistines attacked Shaul, and he was frightened. With his prophet, Shmuel, no longer at his side, Shaul did not know where to turn for counsel. When his prayers went unanswered, he became frustrated:

> Shaul said to his servants, "Find for me a woman who mastered the practice of *ov* and I will go to her and seek [an answer] from her."

> His servants said to him, "There is a woman who is a medium in Ein Dor."
>
> Shaul disguised himself and put on other garments, and he went with two men. They came to the woman by night, and he said, "Please divine for me by a spirit [*ov*], and bring up for me whoever I shall name to you."
>
> The woman said to him, "Behold, you know what Shaul has done, how he has expelled those who practice *ov* and *yidoni* from the land. Why are you laying a trap for my life, to cause me to die?"
>
> Shaul swore to her by God, saying, "As God lives, you shall not be punished for this thing."
>
> She said, "Who should I bring up for you?"
>
> He said, "Shmuel...."
>
> Shmuel said to Shaul, "Why have you angered me and raised me up?... God will tear the kingdom from your hands and give it to your friend, David."
>
> *(Ibid., 7–17)*

In this most unusual passage, Shaul HaMelech utilized the forbidden services of a medium and communicated with the dead, clearly violating Jewish law.

The passage from *Devarim* quoted earlier concludes:

> When you come to the land that God, your Lord, has given you, do not learn to do the revolting practices of those nations.... The practice of *ov* or *yidoni* or the attempt to communicate with the dead should not be found in you. For all who do these things are an abomination to the Lord; and because of these abominations God, your Lord, is driving them out from before you. Be complete [*tamim*] with God, your Lord.
>
> *(Devarim 18:9–13)*

The opposite of these practices is to be *tamim*, complete, "one" with God. The word *tamim*, or its singular form *tam*, can have connotations of innocence, simpleness, or completeness. The first two definitions often carry with them a negative nuance. Here, God calls upon man to trust Him, and thus to be one with Him. This is the opposite of confusion, fear, and neurosis, which lead man to seek guidance and certainty in the occult, the archetype of such behavior is none other than Shaul HaMelech. When man is complete in his trust in God, on the other hand, he is spiritually uplifted as well as psychologically comforted.

Sheim MiShmuel observes that the first instance of lost *temimut*, lost innocence or oneness with God, was the fall of Adam and Chavah. In Eden, they were truly one with God, experiencing His presence in the Garden, but they exchanged that for a bite of fruit, which they hoped would give them knowledge of God. The result was the introduction of death into the world. Death is the opposite of *temimut*; once man separated himself from God, the power of *tumah* (impurity) gained a foothold. Death was born. In fact, the *Zohar* notes that the word *tam* (תם) is the reverse of the word dead, *meit* (מת). When man is no longer *tam*, having reversed and perverted his natural innocence, the result is inevitable, inexorable.

The mandate of the *kohein* is to reunite man with God through *korbanot*. The *kohein*'s function is to bring about *sheleimut* (oneness or wholeness), a return to the original state forfeited by Adam and Chavah. We now understand why the *kohein* is to avoid contact with death. The corpse represents the separation of the Divine from our physical existence, since the difference between a corpse and a living person is only the breath of God, the soul. Here is where the Jewish concept of spirituality diverges from the magical rites and incantations of the heathen: The *kohein* avoids death and seeks *temimut*, while the practices of *ov* and *yidoni* use death to gain understanding and security in this world.

The person most clearly identified as *tam* was Yaakov, who was described by the Torah as "a complete man, sitting in the tents" (*Bereishit* 25:27), as opposed to Eisav, the warrior, who gallivanted in the fields. Yaakov was *shaleim*, complete (*Bereishit* 33:18); Yaakov was one with God. All he needed could be found in the tents of study. Eisav sought adventure and conquest. It is no coincidence, then, that our Sages taught that Yaakov, the *ish tam*, was untouched by death:

> Thus said Rabbi Yochanan: "Yaakov our Patriarch is not dead."
>
> [Rabbi Nachman] said to him, "Was it then for nothing that he was eulogized and embalmed and buried?"
>
> The other replied, "I derive this from a scriptural verse, as it is says, ' "Therefore do not fear, Yaakov, My servant," said the Lord; "and do not be dismayed, Israel, for I will save you from afar and your seed from the land of their captivity" ' (*Yirmiyah* 30:10). The verse likens him [Yaakov] to his seed [Israel]; as his seed will then be alive, so too he will be alive.
>
> *(Ta'anit 5b)*

Yaakov was *tam* and *shaleim*.

The word *shaleim*, whole, is closely associated with the word *shalom*, peace. Another function of Aharon, the prototype of all *kohanim*, was to purvey peace among Jews:

> Hillel said: Be of the disciples of Aharon, loving peace and pursuing peace, loving mankind and bringing them closer to the Torah.
>
> *(Avot 1:12)*

Hillel emphasizes that Aharon's function was not only to bring about *sheleimut* between man and God, but also, and no less importantly, to bring about *shalom* between man and his fellow man. *Shalom* and *sheleimut* are intertwined; they are two sides of the same coin. The Maharal teaches that *shalom* is Godly; it emanates from God and is thus an aspect of God Himself.[1] For this reason, one of the Names of God is *Shalom*.

Avot D'Rabbi Natan describes Aharon's method of pursuing peace: If he heard of two people who had a falling out, he would tell each one individually that the other had expressed a strong desire to make amends.[2] This method, while certainly successful and well-

1 *Netivot Olam*, p. 215.
2 *Avot D'Rabbi Natan*, ch. 12.

intentioned, is disturbing. Was it truly necessary for Aharon to lie to have two people make peace?

Aharon's actions become less troubling when we familiarize ourselves with a teaching of Rambam: According to Jewish law, a *get* (writ of divorce) is only valid if given of free volition by the husband. Nonetheless, if a court of law decides that a man should grant his wife a divorce but he refuses to do so, the court may appoint emissaries to physically beat him until he says, "I agree" (*Mishneh Torah, Geirushin* 2:20).

This would appear to contradict the law that a *get* granted under duress is invalid. Rambam, however, explains that once the court rules that a man must divorce his wife, the husband truly wishes to comply rather than defy the decision of the court. The evil inclination is all that stands in his way. In the philosophy of Rambam, a Jew always wants to do the right thing; circumstances or ego may sway him, but they do not change his basic nature.

Aharon's understanding of the essence of the Jewish soul is echoed in this teaching of Rambam. He knew that two people at odds with one another always hope for reconciliation, although on the operative level they may allow extraneous considerations to sway them from the course of peace. Aharon pursued peace by bringing people in touch with themselves, their fellow man, and God. Only someone who is *tam*, complete, can bring out the completeness in others. Aharon was not guilty of naivete, assuming that all men are completely good. Rather, because of his positive view of man, he was able to see beyond the layers of narcissism and self-indulgence and discern the essence of man — the good in man. Aharon's function was therefore one: *sheleimut*, reuniting man with God and reuniting man with himself.

Moshe and Aharon represent two different aspects of leadership: Moshe was a teacher of Torah. He taught truth — direct, clear, unadulterated truth. Aharon sought peace. While the pursuit of peace may sometimes seem to compromise or pervert truth, peace emanates from God. Peace is neither a compromise nor a perversion of truth. It is an expression of Godliness; indeed, it is the very Name of God.

> Great is peace, for even the Holy One, blessed be He, modified a statement for its sake. At first it is written, "My lord [Avraham] is old" (*Bereishit* 18:12), and afterwards it is written, "I [Sarah] have grown old" (ibid., 13).
>
> *(Yevamot 65b)*

When Sarah heard God's promise that she would have a child at the age of ninety, she laughed at the idea — both she and her husband were old. When God reported her reaction to Avraham, however, He quoted her saying, "I have grown old," without mentioning her reference to Avraham's age. Why? Our Sages teach us this was for the sake of maintaining harmony, *shalom*, between Avraham and Sarah.

Truth is a means of approaching God, while peace is the destination. In reality, truth and peace work together, as we see from the verse in *Tehillim*:

> Kindness and truth met; righteousness and peace kissed.
>
> *(Tehillim 85:11)*

The Midrash associates kindness and peace with Aharon, and truth and righteousness with Moshe.

> When it says, "Kindness and truth met; righteousness and peace kissed," "kindness" refers to Aharon, of whom it is said: "Of Levi he said, 'Your *tumim* and your *urim* will be with Your man of kindness' " (*Devarim* 33:8), while "truth" refers to Moshe, of whom it says: "My servant Moshe is not so; he is trusted in all My house" (*Bemidbar* 12:7).... "Righteousness" refers to Moshe, of whom it is said, "He executed the righteousness of God" (*Devarim* 33:21), and "peace" refers to Aharon, of whom it says, "He walked with Me in peace and uprightness" (*Malachi* 2:6).
>
> *(Shemot Rabbah 5:10)*

It should come as no surprise that peace and kindness are attributes of Aharon, while truth and righteousness are attributes of Moshe. The verse, though, concludes that righteousness and peace can kiss, in expression of harmony, of oneness. Moshe teaches Torah, truth, and he represents righteousness. In this realm, reality cannot be bent or distorted. Aharon, on the other hand, operates on the level of purity, distanced from death, from *tumah,* from the distortions of sin. These two realms are not in conflict. They meet, they kiss, and they converge in their ultimate goal, which is *sheleimut* and *shalom.* Truth is a means of achieving the goal, of mending the world. Peace is the result.

Aharon, the archetypal *kohein,* represents this unity and completeness, as is expressed so beautifully in the priestly blessing he is instructed to bestow upon all Israel:

> May God bless you and safeguard you. May He make His face shine upon you and be gracious to you. May God lift up His countenance upon you and grant you peace.
>
> *(Bemidbar 6:24–26)*

The idea of *temimut* is discussed explicitly in the parashah itself:

> You shall count from the next day after the sabbath, from the day that you brought the sheaf offering, seven complete [*temimot*] weeks.
>
> *(Vayikra 23:15)*

Here, we are instructed to count seven complete weeks between Pesach and Shavuot. Unlike the counting of *shemittah* years, which is the obligation exclusively of the Sanhedrin (high court), the counting of these seven weeks applies to the entire nation. The entire nation was to be *tamim.* The entire nation was actually called *kohanim*:

> You shall be for Me a nation of priests, a holy nation.
>
> *(Shemot 19:6)*

Every person must prepare to receive the Torah on Shavuot. The way to prepare is to become *tamim*, complete. This is the meaning of "*na'aseh venishma* — we will do and we will listen." With this phrase, the Jewish people expressed their total trust in God, a trust which was lacking in Adam and Chavah and all doubters who followed.

> When the Israelites gave precedence to "we will do" over "we will listen," a Heavenly Voice went forth and said to them, "Who revealed this secret to My children? The ministering angels use it, as it is written, 'Bless God, His angels of his, you mighty ones who fulfill His word, to listen to the voice of His word' (*Tehillim* 103:20). First they fulfill and then they listen."
>
> *(Shabbat 88a)*

A prerequisite to receiving the Torah in the fullest sense is *temimut*, both in our relationship with God and in our relationship with our fellow man. The description of Yaakov as "*ish tam* [a complete man] sitting in tents," referring to the tents of Torah study, illustrates the connection between interpersonal and religious *temimut*. As we saw above, man sins when he ignores the good within him, when he ignores his essence. This completeness is a prerequisite for learning Torah. In the words of the Midrash,

> [The duty of] *derech eretz* preceded the Torah by twenty-six generations. This is [implied in] what is written, "To guard the way to the Tree of Life" (*Bereishit* 3:24). [First the verse mentions] "the way" [*derech*] which means *derech eretz*, and afterwards [it mentions] the "Tree of Life," which means the Torah.
>
> *(Vayikra Rabbah 9:3)*

Derech eretz kadmah laTorah — proper (interpersonal) behavior precedes Torah. The Kotzker Rebbe was fond of saying that "*derech eretz hakdamah laTorah*" — proper behavior is the introduction to Torah. Every book has an introduction, and the Torah's introduction is *derech eretz*. When the Torah describes the period of time to be counted, the term *temimot* is used in reference to this aspect of completeness in human relations. When the students of Rabbi Akiva, arguably the greatest Torah scholars of their generation, mistreated one another during the omer, the result was their deaths. Again, the opposite of *tam* is *meit* (death).

The key to being *tam* is rejecting the *yetzer hara*, which enslaves us and causes us to be incomplete, fragmenting our souls. The truly free person is the one who involves himself in Torah. He becomes unified in spirit, both *tam* and *nishlam*, and achieves oneness with man and God. This was the message of Aharon, who attempted to introduce people to the purity within them. When this message is finally fully understood and internalized, *sheleimut* will become a reality, between man and his fellow man and between man and God. The result will be *shalom* — true, everlasting peace.

Parashat Behar

A Sabbath for God

> God spoke to Moshe at Mount Sinai, saying, "Speak to the Children of Israel and say to them, 'When you enter the land which I am giving to you, the land shall rest, a Sabbath for God.' "
>
> *(Vayikra 25:1–2)*

The Torah proceeds to give detailed instructions regarding the laws of *shemittah* — the sabbatical year. There are two idiosyncrasies which concern the commentaries: First, why was it necessary for the Torah to stress that this law was given at Mount Sinai? Second, why is this law taught in such detail, while other basic concepts in Judaism are transmitted mainly through extensive comments in the oral tradition and only limited text, what the Talmud calls "mountains held by a thread" (*Chagigah* 10a)?[1]

Rashi cites the Midrash,

> What is the connection between *shemittah* and Mount Sinai? Were not all mitzvot taught at Sinai? Just as *shemittah* was

1 The Gemara quotes the following *mishnah*: "[The laws concerning] the dissolution of vows hover in the air and have nothing to rest on. The laws of Shabbos, festival offerings, and acts of trespass are as mountains hanging by a hair, for they have scant scriptural basis but many laws. [The laws concerning] civil cases, [Temple] services, levitical purity and impurity, and the forbidden relations have what to rest on, and it is they that are the essentials of the Torah."

> taught with general principles and detail at Sinai, so were all the mitzvot taught with general principles and detail at Sinai.

Rashi has noted in his explanation both peculiarities, but in a sense, his answer begs the question. Why was *shemittah* chosen as the archetypal commandment? Surely any of the 613 mitzvot would have been equally appropriate. There must something intrinsic to *shemittah* which caused it to be chosen.

Ramban makes reference on numerous occasions to a mystical tradition which contains within it a key to understanding the laws, and indeed the entire process, of *shemittah.*

> [The Sages] here have roused our attention to one of the great secrets of the Torah. Rabbi Avraham Ibn Ezra has already hinted to it when he wrote, "The meaning of a 'Sabbath for God' is like that of the Sabbath day. The secret of the years of the world is alluded to in this place." Bend your ear to understand that which I am permitted to inform you about, in the words that I will cause you to hear, and if you will be worthy, you will contemplate them [and understand them].
>
> *(Ramban, Vayikra 25:2)*

Ramban cites Rabbi Avraham Ibn Ezra, who alluded to what Ramban calls "one of the great secrets of the Torah." The explanation of Ibn Ezra is somewhat cryptic, but before we analyze his comments and Ramban's explanation, let us first see other instances where Ramban makes reference to this particular mystical tradition.

Commenting on the very first verse of the Torah, Ramban explains why the Torah had to begin with "In the beginning the Lord created heaven and earth." He states that belief in God, who created and sustains the universe, is the starting point and basis for all belief, and then adds:

> The process of creation is a deep mystery not to be understood from the verses, and it cannot truly be known except through the tradition going back to Moshe, our teacher, who received it

from the mouth of the Almighty, and those who know it are obligated to conceal it.

From Ramban's previous comments we know that *shemittah* is somehow connected to Shabbat, thus the verse "a Sabbath for God," referring to *shemittah*. Elsewhere, in a discussion of slavery, Ramban links the two topics once again: The question he raises considers why slavery is mentioned before all the other laws in *Parashat Mishpatim*:

> It contains a remembrance of the process of creation just as the Sabbath does, for the seventh year for a servant is a [time of] complete rest from the work of his master, just as the seventh day of the week is [a time of complete rest]. There is, in addition, a seventh among the years, which is *yovel* (the jubilee), for seven is the chosen of the days, of the years, and of the *shemittot* (the sabbatical years). They all point to one subject: the secret of the age of the world.... Therefore, this commandment deserved to be mentioned first, because of its extreme importance, alluding as it does to great things of Creation.
>
> *(Ramban, Shemot 21:2)*

Again Ramban uses the term "process of creation," but now he connects Creation with the age of the world. The implication is that speculation about the age of the earth would be included in the list of mystical topics which may not be taught publicly,[1] and therefore Ramban is cautious in his comments.

Ramban was one of the greatest Kabbalists of his time, and we can assume that he would have connected the idea of *shemittah* with mystical considerations without any assistance from Ibn Ezra. In fact, Ramban writes elsewhere:

> Rabbi Abraham Ibn Ezra already intimated it when he wrote,

1 The Mishnah teaches: "The [subject of] forbidden relations may not be expounded in the presence of three, Creation may not be in the presence of two, and the Chariot may not be in the presence of one, unless he is a sage and understands his own knowledge" (*Chagigah* 2:1).

> "The secret of the years of the world is alluded to in this place." Nowhere else in Ibn Ezra's works is there a statement better than this which indicates his good [understanding of] Kabbalah.
>
> *(Writings of Ramban [Chavel English edition], p. 117)*

Ramban refers here to a passage in Ibn Ezra's writings which concerns the age and the duration of the earth. Ramban was privy to a teaching which is reported in an ancient mystical treatise called *Sefer HaTemunah. Sefer HaTemunah* teaches that there is a cosmic *shemittah* cycle which effects the Creation and the world's duration of existence. The teaching itself is alluded to in a passage in the Gemara:

> Rabbi Katina said: Six thousand years shall the world exist, and one [thousand, the seventh,] it shall be desolate, as it says, "God alone shall be exalted on that day" (*Yeshayah* 2:11)....
>
> It has been taught in accordance with Rabbi Katina: Just as the seventh year is one year of release in seven, so the world is one thousand years of release out of seven, as it says, "God alone shall be exalted on that day," and it further says, "A psalm and a song for the Sabbath day" (*Tehillim* 92:1), meaning the day that is completely Sabbath. It also says, "For a thousand years in Your eyes are but as yesterday gone by" (ibid. 90:4).
>
> *(Sanhedrin 97a)*

The idea which is taught in this passage is quite well known; the world is destined to exist six thousand years, followed by the culmination of history. Rather than choosing the more familiar model of days of the week and Shabbat, the Gemara utilizes *shemittah* to illustrate this concept. We cannot help but notice, though, the major difference between Shabbat and *shemittah*: Shabbat is six days of work and one of rest; *shemittah* is six years of work and one of rest, but it is part of a greater system known as *yovel*. At the end of seven *shemittah* years there is a year of *yovel*, in which everything returns to its natural place. *Sefer HaTemunah* sees our existence within this larger framework of *shemittah* and *yovel.* While existence as we know it may come to an end in the year 6000, another cycle may be awaiting us.

Furthermore, as Ramban said, belief in a God who created and sustains the universe is basic to Judaism. There is a secret, unfathomable from the verses alone, regarding Creation — namely, that there may have been cycles before ours. "In the beginning, the Lord created heaven and earth" refers to the very beginning — arguably, in a previous cycle. The mystical commentaries have traditions and speculations regarding the question of which cycle we are in now:[1] A Kabbalistic tract entitled *Ma'arechet HaElokut* says, "We don't know in which cycle we exist.... However, it would seem that we are not in the first."[2] Rabbi David ben Rabbi Yehudah HaChassid, in *Livnat HaSapir,* held the opinion that the progression of the worlds are in an ascending order within the *Sefirot* and not a descending one, hence the first cycle, rather than the last, is *Malchut,* while the last would be *Chesed.* Others believe that we are in fact in the *Sefirah* of *Gevurah* (strict judgment). This would seem to be the accepted view.[3]

Rabbi Yaakov ben Sheshet of Gerona, a contemporary of Ramban,[4] believed that we are in the cycle of *Din.*[5] A student of Ramban, Rabbi Yitzchak of Acco, also felt this is the cycle of *Gevurah*:

> This world, the *shemittah* (cycle) which we are in, is the *Sefirah* of *Gevurah,* as we see all the punishments in this world are via fire.
>
> *(Yitzchak of Acco, Sefer Yetzirah)*[6]

Rav Yitzchak of Acco returns to the topic of cosmic jubilees in another treatise, where he states:

> I, the insignificant Yitzchak of Acco, have seen fit to write a great mystery that should be kept very well hidden. One of God's days is a thousand years, as it says, "For a thousand years

1 See Israel Wienstock, *BiMaglei HaNigla ViHanistar.* Mosad HaRav Kook (1969), p. 162–166.

2 The work is attributed to Rabbi Peretz. Mantoba: Mikor Chaim (1963), p.189b.

> in Your eyes are but as yesterday gone by." Since one of our years is 365¼ days, a year on High is 365,250 of our years.... This is to refute those who believe the duration of the world is only 49,000 years, which is seven jubilees.
>
> *(Otzar HaChaim, p. 86b–87b)*

The language which Rabbi Yitzchak employs is somewhat reminiscent of Ramban. He speaks of "a great secret which should remain very well hidden." He also gives a key to unlock the mystery. When we speak of time, inevitably we speak from a human perspective. Yet this vantage point seems unjustified, inappropriate, prior to the appearance of humanity.

The Jewish tradition, as we saw above, treats God's day as if it were a thousand human years. If we were to apply Rabbi Yitzchak's tradition, we would find that each cycle of 7,000 years is actually 2,556,750,000 years from man's perspective. We should also note that Rabbi Yitzchak was of the opinion that our history is not in the first cycle, but in the cycle of *Din*, which is normally understood as being the second cycle. If that is the case, our 5,760 years from Creation follow 2.5 billion years of prehistory, after which Adam initiated our cycle and our counting of time. (However, if *Din* is the sixth cycle, as per the opinion cited above, five cycles of 7,000 years or 35,000 years as seen from God's perspective — 12,783,750,000 years when seen from human perspective — transpired before Adam. We must note that aside from a desire to approximate the current scientific understanding, we would have no reason to assume that when Rabbi Yitzchak says *Din* he really means the sixth cycle. We should also note at this point that Rabbi Yitzchak is not dealing with the question of the age of the world, but rather with the duration of the world.[1])

---

3 See Wienstock, p. 163.

4 This view has been attributed to Ramban, see Wienstock idem. note 47 (who shows how Rabbi Yaakov cleverly hid his own name in the title).

5 See *Shemot Rabbah* 30:13: "With *din*, the world was created." The Name of God associated with *din*, *Elokim*, is used exclusively in the Creation story (*Kitvei Ramban*, vol. 2, p. 363).

6 Rabbi Yitzchak of Acco, commentary on *Sefer Yetzirah Kiryat Sefer* 31 (1957) p. 392.

There has been some misunderstanding on this point in recent years. Rabbi Arye Kaplan, who had intimate knowledge of both physics and Kabbalah, taught and wrote of this system in general and of the understanding of Rabbi Yitzchak in specific. Rabbi Kaplan, in a speech delivered to the Association of Orthodox Jewish Scientists in 1979 (Keynote Address, Midwinter Conference, February 18, 1979) asserted that the view of Rabbi Yitzchak is correct and we must multiply each day by 1,000. He further asserts that the most authoritative interpretation of *Sefer HaTemunah* is Livnat HaSapir, who believes that we are presently in the sixth cycle: "When Adam was created, the world was forty-two thousand years old" (See Rabbi Arye Kaplan, *Immortality, Resurrection and the Age of the Universe,* Ktav Publishing House, 1993). By multiplying 42,000 by 365,250, Rabbi Kaplan concludes that the universe is 15 billion years old according to this tradition.

There are a number of problems with this approach. Rabbi Yitzchak, whose system multiplies one day by 1,000 years, does not say we are in the sixth cycle, but rather that we are in *Din*, which would seem to be the second cycle. Livnat HaSapir, who says we are in the sixth cycle, does not multiply a day by 1,000 years. Furthermore, even if we are in the sixth cycle, five cycles of 7,000 years have passed, totaling 35,000 at the appearance of Adam and not 42,000.

Speculation was put to rest by the Arizal, who maintained that the cosmic jubilees referred to by *Sefer HaTemunah* refer to spiritual upheaval in the *Sefirot* and not to historical fact. Whether we adopt this view or the alternate view of Ramban, who contends that the age of the world is the subject of the Torah's detailed information about the *shemittah* cycles, the deep theological significance of this topic of *shemittah* is clear. This, then, would answer the first question we raised at the outset regarding the great lengths to which the text goes in explaining *shemittah.*

We then return to our second question: Why does the Torah

---

arrive, according to Rabbi Yitzchak — after 6,000 man years or 2.2 billion man years?

stress that this law was given at Mount Sinai? Rabbeinu Bechayei, commenting on Ramban, raises the following question: When the verse says that God spoke these details about *shemittah* and *yovel* at Sinai, is it referring to the first time Moshe ascended Mount Sinai or the second? Rabbeinu Bachayei says that it must be the second, because in *Parashat Mishpatim* there is only a brief reference to the laws of *shemittah*:

> For six years you shall plant your land and gather its fruits, but the seventh year you shall let it rest and lie fallow, so that the poor among you may eat, and what they leave the beast of the field shall eat. In the same manner you shall deal with your vineyard and your olive grove.
>
> *(Shemot 23:10–11)*

Here, the Torah briefly outlines the laws of *shemittah*, but with nowhere as much depth or detail as it does in *Parashat Behar*. Therefore, Rabbeinu Bachayei asserts that the first time Moshe ascended Mount Sinai he brought back all the laws as written in *Mishpatim*. The second time he came down, he brought detailed laws, as they appear in *Parashat Behar*. What is curious is that the laws as stated in *Mishpatim* make no reference to *yovel*. This may be a function of the general terseness of *Mishpatim*; all the laws in *Mishpatim* are more detailed than the text itself indicates.

Another possibility is that certain laws were not written because they were not applicable. This can be understood through a deeper look at the laws of *shemittah* and *yovel*. *Shemittah* parallels Shabbat, six years of work and one year of rest. This rest is significant for the land and the worker alike. *Yovel*, however, has no apparent parallel with Shabbat. It is a time when all land returns to its original owner. In a word, *shemittah* is a time of renewal while *yovel* is a time of complete return.

The Torah instructs that the shofar be blown in the *yovel* on Yom Kippur:

> You shall sound the shofar on the tenth day of the seventh

> month, on the Day of Atonement; you shall sound the shofar throughout the land.
>
> *(Vayikra 25:9)*

The verse seems quite clear, but for one question: If these details were taught when Moshe ascended the mountain the first time, the reference to Yom Kippur would be inappropriate. Yom Kippur came into existence when the people were forgiven for the sin of the golden calf. That sin was committed while Moshe was on Sinai the first time, and the people were granted forgiveness only when Moshe ascended the second time. This would support the position of Rabbeinu Bechayei that this section was taught when Moshe was on the mountain the second time.

We can see a parallel between *yovel* and Yom Kippur. Yom Kippur is known as "*Shabbat Shabbaton*" (the Sabbath of Sabbaths). *Yovel* is the time that comes after seven *shemittot* — also a "Sabbath of Sabbaths" of sorts. Moreover, had there not been a sin of the golden calf, there would not have been a Yom Kippur. Had there not been a sin of the golden calf, the punishment of exile would never have entered the lexicon of Judaism.

> Rabbi Eliezer said: What is the meaning of the verse, "Engraved upon the Tablets" (*Shemot* 32:16)? If the first Tablets had not been broken, the Torah would never have been forgotten by Israel.
>
> Rabbi Acha bar Yaakov said: No nation or tongue would have had any power over them [the Jewish people], for it says, "engraved" [*charut*]. Do not read "*charut*" but "*cheirut*" (freedom).
>
> *(Eruvin 54a)*

The sin of the golden calf took place due to a basic lack of trust in God. This breach of trust served as the negative spiritual precedent for future generations who sinned similarly and were exiled. Our Sages teach us that one of the reasons for the exile was laxity in the observance of *shemittah*.

> Exile comes to the world because of idolatry, sexual immoral-

> ity, bloodshed, and [not observing] the *shemittah* of the land.
> *(Avot 5:9)*

This idea is implicit in the verse in next week's parashah which describes the exile:

> Then the land will enjoy her Sabbaths, all the days that it is desolate and you are in the land of the enemies.
> *(Vayikra 26:34)*

Exile is the result of (among other things) the failure to observe *shemittah*. This idea is obvious when we consider that exile came into existence as a result of the golden calf, when the people displayed their lack of trust in God, while the observance of the laws of *shemittah* demonstrate one's trust in God. The Torah promises that God will supply our sustenance directly during the sabbatical year.

> If you shall say, "What shall we eat the seventh year? Behold, we shall not plant or gather in our produce," then I will command My blessing upon you in the sixth year, and it shall bring forth fruit for three years.
> *(Ibid. 25:20–21)*

In this sense, *shemittah* and its message of renewal reminds us of Adam prior to the sin, possessing no need to work, existing in the shadow of God.

> To Adam [God] said, "Because you listened to the voice of your wife and you ate from the tree, of which I commanded you, saying, 'You shall not eat of it,' cursed is the ground for your sake. In sorrow you shall eat of it all the days of your life. Thorns and thistles it shall bring forth for you; and you shall eat the grass of the field. By the sweat of your brow you shall eat bread, until you return to the ground; for out of it you were taken. You are [formed of] dust, and to the dust you shall return."
> *(Bereishit 3:17–19)*

The sin and its punishment in the generation of Moshe mirrored the sin of Adam and his exile from the Garden. The golden calf changed the course of history in its own way, just as the sin of Adam did. In the aftermath of the Revelation at Sinai, the Jewish people were to enter the Land of Israel immediately, with Moshe himself leading the victorious march. This would have resulted in the immediate building of the Temple in Yerushalayim, with Moshe as king and Aharon as *kohein gadol*. Such a Temple never would have been destroyed. The Word of God would have spread like wildfire throughout the world. Moshe would have been Mashiach. But this dream never materialized. It was shattered by the sin of the golden calf. A nation who did not trust in God sufficiently could not mend the world, even with the greatest leaders.

There would be exile. Lack of trust in God would, once again, bring exile. For this reason, of all the commandments, *shemittah* was repeated with explicit detail when Moshe came down from Sinai for the second time. The relationship with Mount Sinai is clear: *Shemittah*, as the essential mitzvah of trust in God, is a prototype, a "cure" for the lack of faith expressed in the sin of the golden calf. Had the Jews not been lacking in this area, there would not have been a need for Moshe to ascend the mountain a second time, and there would not have been any such thing as exile.[1] The very existence of the Jews in the Land depends on the observance of *shemittah*. Just as there was now a need for a Yom Kippur to forgive the Jews for the golden calf, there must now be a *yovel*, a time of complete return, a national return or renaissance. Trust in God, as indicated by observance of *shemittah*, is the path to our final destiny of a world perfected.

1 Furthermore, had there been no lack of faith and the resultant sin of the golden calf, the entire Torah would have been given in detail within the Ten Commandments. See my comments on *Parashiyot Yitro* and *Mishpatim*.

Parashat Bechukotai

To Serve with Joy

In this week's parashah we come to the end of *Sefer Vayikra*. The "style" of *Bechukotai* marks somewhat of a departure from the other sections of *Vayikra*, and indeed the entire Torah. In place of the narrative or legal stricture to which we have become accustomed, *Bechukotai* contains an extensive *tochechah* (rebuke). Here, man is called upon to follow the Torah in law and spirit and warned of the consequences of abandoning the Torah and God. This is one of two major *tochechot* in the Torah, the other coming at the end of *Sefer Devarim*.

The context of the *tochechah* at the end of *Devarim*, before the people enter the land, seems natural and understandable: As the Jewish people are about to face the responsibilities and challenges of their encounter with the peoples of the Promised Land, the Torah imparts extensive warning to follow the mandate of the Torah and not to stray from the word of God. On the other hand, the section of *tochechah* here in *Bechukotai* is not as readily placed in context, coming in the very middle of the Torah, with the books of *Bemidbar* and *Devarim* still to follow. However, we should recall that the Jews were not originally supposed to wander the desert for forty years; the decree that the sojourn would be lengthened did not come until after the episode of the spies, which had not occurred by this point in the narrative. At this point in the text, at the completion of *Vayikra,* the Jews should be preparing to enter the Holy Land. The *tochechah* here in *Bechukotai,* then, is similar in context to the *tochechah* which will appear at the end of *Devarim.*

While we now understand why these sections were taught to the people at these junctures in the desert, another question arises: Why were each of these sections recorded for posterity, especially when the Jews did not enter the land as per God's original plan? Ramban addresses this issue in his comments on *Bechukotai*: "Know that all of these curses refer to the destruction of the First Temple" (*Ramban, Bechukotai*).

The source of Ramban is actually a passage in the *Zohar*:

> It is said [we have a tradition] that the curses in *Torat Kohanim* [*Vayikra*] are referring to the destruction of the First Temple, while the curses listed in *Mishneh Torah* [*Devarim*] refer to the Second Temple. The curses in *Vayikra* contain guarantees and display the love which God has for man.... The curses in *Mishneh Torah* contain no such guarantees or comforting words [that one day redemption will come]...and no one knew how to answer this question.[1]
>
> *(Zohar Chadash, Ki Tavo 59c–60a)*

Our conclusion must be that, according to Ramban, a parallel exists between God's original plan to bring the people into Israel and the First Commonwealth that arose so many years later. Furthermore, a parallel is drawn between the Second Temple and the second, alternate plan described in *Devarim.* Despite the fact that these sections were related in a specific context to a specific audience, they are recorded in the Torah because they contain information which would be vital for future generations.

A number of sections in the Gemara record various reasons for the destruction of the two Temples and the subsequent exiles. Clearly, an event as momentous and devastating as the *Churban* could have multiple causes. The most famous teaching regarding

1 For more on this passage in the *Zohar,* see my comments in *Ki Tavo.*

the destructions is recorded in *Yoma* 9a–b, based on the *Tosefta* in *Menachot,* which I quote for reasons of clarity:

> Why was Shilo destroyed? Because of the degradation of the holy things in it. [What about the destruction of] Jerusalem? The First Temple, why was it destroyed? Because of idolatry, sexual immorality, and bloodshed which took place. However, the last [most recent Temple], we knew them: They were diligent in Torah study and were careful with tithes. Why were they exiled? Because they loved money and man hated his neighbor, which teaches us that when man hates his neighbor it is as difficult before God as idolatry, immorality, and bloodshed.
>
> *(Tosefta, Menachot 13:4)*

These reasons for the *Churban* have entered into the consciousness of the Jewish community, to the point that we would expect some reference to these imputed sins in the Biblical text which would prove Ramban's theory. Analysis of the *tochechah* in *Bechukotai* reveals one word, which is repeated time after time, to describe the type of behavior which would lead to destruction:

> If you walk after Me with *keri,* and not desire to listen to Me....
>
> *(Vayikra 26:21)*

The word *keri* is used no less than seven times within a short span of text in our parashah[1] and never mentioned again in the entire Torah. In this context, the word means "happenstance" or "nonchalance." The implication is that all the terrible curses listed will result if we take God for granted. The worldview which results from the attitude of *keri* is one in which God ceases to be an integral part of the individual's life. This is the beginning of a process that may lead to a far more dangerous conclusion: As God is forgotten, man deludes himself into thinking that life is merely a series of coincidences. He believes that there is no Divine hand guiding his personal existence or the unfolding of world history. The conclu-

1 Verses 21, 23, 24, 27, 28, 40, and 41.

sion of such an approach is atheism, and this is the view the Torah ascribes to Amaleik:

> Remember what Amaleik did to you: When you left Egypt, they "happened" [*korcha*] upon you on the road.
>
> *(Devarim 28:17–18)*

The word *korcha* (happened) is derived from the same root as *keri*. Rashi explains the term *korcha* as "a term of coincidence." We learn from this short comment that the spiritual power of Amaleik emanates from a worldview that all is coincidence, blind and meaningless fate, and that there is no higher or greater significance to life. When the Jews became bogged down in a spiritual quagmire, behaving like Amaleik, they were susceptible to the attack of the real Amaleik. The Jews in the desert failed to appreciate the Divine Presence that enveloped and protected them, and they became their own enemies; they became Amaleik. Therefore, the real Amaleik appeared and attacked. Their only recourse was to pray to God, an explicit expression of faith and cognizance of the existence of a Divine Being.

The Torah states that during the battle with Amaleik Moshe stood at the top of a mountain, holding his hands high. As long as Moshe's hands were raised, the Jewish people were successful in battle, but when he lowered his hands, Amaleik grew stronger (*Shemot* 17:11). The Mishnah comments on this:

> Do the hands of Moshe make war?... Rather, this teaches us that the whole time that the Jews looked heavenward and dedicated their hearts to their Father in Heaven, they were victorious; if not, they fell [in battle].
>
> *(Rosh HaShanah 3:8)*

The Mishnah stresses that it was not some magical intercession on the part of Moshe which brought victory in the war with Amaleik, but the prayer of the people. The people had failed to properly appreciate God; they took Him for granted. The opposite attitude, as expressed by prayer, mended the rift that had been formed between them and God.

Now, in the *tochechah* the people are warned not to lead a life based on this philosophy of coincidence, for this approach — seeing the world without God — is the first step toward an abandonment of all values. This idea is expressed in a *Tosefta* which asks, "Who is the most dangerous man?" (*Shavuot* 3:6). The *Tosefta*'s answer is that the atheist, even if he is a moral man, is most dangerous because there is no basis for his morality. In the eyes of the *Tosefta*, today's moral atheist may be tomorrow's murderer. The Jews who no longer felt a connection with God soon found themselves alienated from God to the extent that idolatry, sexual immorality, and bloodshed not only were no longer taboo, they had become the norm. The Gemara's expression of this phenomenon is fascinating:

> The Temple was destroyed...because they [the Jewish people] did not make a blessing before learning Torah.
>
> *(Nedarim 81a)*

This statement seems difficult to understand. If Jews of that time were actively engaged in Torah study but merely forgot to make the proper blessings, should the terrible *Churban* be the consequence? Clearly, we are not hearing about mere forgetfulness. Rather, the Gemara uses this concise language to point out a "secularization" of what should be holy: One who does not make a blessing prior to learning is making a statement about his learning. Torah learned in this fashion is something mundane; it may be intellectually stimulating, but it is not part of a dialogue with the Divine. A person who can learn and not feel the breath of eternity on his face, a hint of Heaven, holiness, is missing the essence of learning. Only those who have created the break in their minds between themselves and God's personal involvement in their lives can forget to make a blessing on learning. They transform a potential rendezvous with the Divine, Eternal God into a mere intellectual exercise.

We may now look back at the teaching of Ramban and the Talmudic tradition regarding the destruction of the First Temple. The connection between the happenstance attitude of *keri* and the total moral breakdown of Jewish society which led to the *Churban* becomes more clear. However, the destruction of the Second Temple raises a more serious challenge: our tradition teaches that the cause for the destruction was the groundless hatred which was prevalent at that time. Yet in the case of the second *tochechah*, the Torah gives us a clear reason for the calamities that have befallen on us:

> All these curses will come upon you, pursue you, and overtake you until you are destroyed, because you did not listen to the voice of God, your Lord.... Because you did not serve God with joy and with gladness of heart.
>
> *(Devarim 28:45–47)*

The Torah informs us, in clear, unequivocal terms, what spiritual deficiency would be cause for the *tochechah* to come to fruition. How is the failure to serve God with joy related to the groundless hatred which we are taught is the cause of the second *Churban*? I heard Rabbi Yochanan Zweig (principal of the Talmudic University of Florida) explain the connection, noting the one person in Tanach described as having the trait of "joy and gladness of heart":

> Haman went out that day joyful and with a glad heart.
>
> *(Esther 5:9)*

How strange that Haman, the most famous of Amaleik's descendants, should serve as a prototype for proper behavior! The fact of the matter is that Haman had every right to be happy: The queen herself had just invited him to a second private party, with only the king and queen in attendance. He saw himself as a success. Arguably there was not a richer, more powerful man in all the kingdom, and Haman knew it.

> When he came home, he called for his friends and for his wife, Zeresh, and Haman recounted for them the glory of his riches and his many children....
>
> *(Ibid., 10)*

Haman had everything going for him. Nonetheless, when he saw Mordechai, who refused to bow to him, Haman was filled with anger. After recounting to his loved ones all his good fortune, Haman says,

> But all this is meaningless to me when I see Mordechai the Jew sitting at the king's gate.
>
> *(Ibid., 13)*

Let us consider Haman's "plight": He is the most powerful man in the empire, save the king. He has a loving, supportive wife, many children, countless wealth. He has one minor problem: There is this one Jew who refuses to deify him. Haman plans to wreak his vengeance on Mordechai: Not only is Mordechai to die, but his entire extended family will die with him. Haman's demented mind called for a holocaust in response to being slighted by one man. But the knowledge that Mordechai and all the Jews would soon be dead was not enough to satiate the evil within Haman — he needed more. His hatred was so consuming that he displayed remarkable carelessness in his decision to execute Mordechai. Even a cursory glance at the king's records would have made Haman realize that targeting Mordechai as an individual was unwise. Yet Haman's anger seethed. He needed vengeance and he needed it immediately. This overwhelming anger caused Haman's downfall. He was unable to enjoy the gifts bestowed upon him because he was fixated on anger and hatred toward Mordechai.

It is interesting to note that Haman, a descendant of Amaleik, represents "Amaleikian" philosophy. He draws lots, leaving the life and death decisions to "chance," and then sets out to control the destiny of an entire nation. His philosophy begins with seeing the world without a God and leads to seeing himself as a deity. From this warped perspective, we can understand his anger toward Mordechai, who refused to bow down.

The sudden fall of Haman was precipitated by the hatred he harbored in his heart, an all-consuming hatred which obliterated his "joyful and glad heart." We can therefore conclude that there is, in fact, a connection between a joyful heart and groundless hatred: One can expel the other.

When we take the broader perspective, an interesting pattern emerges: When the Jews acted like Amaleik and took God for granted, they were exiled, and soon found themselves under the thumb of a crazed Amaleikian despot, as if to drive home to them a Divine message: "If you choose Amaleik and their worldview over Me, I will fulfill your wish." Divine justice was exact. The people who saw life as coincidence found themselves confronted by the leading representative of coincidence — Haman, who promptly drew lots to determine the proper time to destroy the Jewish nation. Just as their ancestors before them, when the Jews finally turn to their Father in Heaven, admit that they have erred, and fully accept the dominion of the Almighty, the power that Haman has over them dissipates.

The Jews are victorious. As a gift, God leaves the Jews with a phenomenal lesson in how not to behave as they are about to reenter the Land of Israel and rebuild the Temple. God reiterates, in *Megillas Esther*, His message that man must worship God with joy and appreciate all the good in his life. Otherwise, man runs the risk of turning his joy into hate and turning the Temple to rubble. Our meeting with Haman was the punishment for the sins that led to the destruction of the First Temple and a warning to stay clear of the type of sins that would destroy the Second Temple.

The parallels drawn by Ramban are indeed consonant with the Talmudic tradition. The lesson is simple but powerful: Idolatry, sexual immorality, and bloodshed have their roots in the lack of God-consciousness in our lives, and groundless hatred has at its core a lack of appreciation for what we are given. This was the lesson to be learned from Haman. Let us not repeat his mistake. Instead, let us turn to the teaching of the Sages:

> Who is wealthy? He who is happy with his share.
>
> *(Avot 4:1)*

It is this happiness which is the key to service of God; it was the lack of this happiness which destroyed the Temple. Relating to God with this type of attitude will surely contribute to the rebuilding of the Temple.

Let us return to the concluding teaching of the *Tosefta* in *Menachot*:

> [In the time of] the Third Temple, may it be built speedily in our days... "Many nations will gather and say, 'Let us go to the Mountain of God, to the House of the Lord of Yaakov.... Arise, let us go up to Tzion, to God, our Lord' " (*Yeshayah* 2:3).
>
> *(Tosefta, Menachot 13:4)*

When we cease to act like the nations of the world, and they begin to act like we are supposed to, history will reach its apex, and a wonderful new day will dawn. God's presence will emanate from Zion, and war will become a thing of the past. The world will become a joyful place, with no hatred, and all people will serve God with joyfulness and gladness of heart. May we all live to see and partake of the joy on that day. Amen!

Sefer Bemidbar

Parashat Bemidbar

Klal Yisrael

This week, we begin a new book, *Sefer Bemidbar*. The parashah and the *sefer* begin:

> God spoke to Moshe in the Sinai Desert in the Ohel Mo'ed [Tent of Meeting], on the first of the second month in the second year after leaving Egypt, saying....
>
> *(Bemidbar 1:1)*

The Jews are still in the desert, awaiting their glorious march to the Promised Land. Of course, we know how this book ends. The Jews endure various trials and tribulations and never do enter the Land of Israel, that privilege falling to their children in the following generation.

The Torah continues:

> Count the heads of all the community of the Children of Israel, according to their families, their fathers' households, by the number of names; count the males...from the age of twenty and above, all those who would go out for battle in Israel.
>
> *(Ibid., 2–3)*

The Divine imperative to count the people at this juncture must be understood. This is not the first time that the Jews have been counted since leaving Egypt. Rashi explains:

> Out of love for [the people, God] counts them at every point. When they left Egypt, He counted them. When they died in the [sin of] the golden calf, He counted them to know how many remained. When it was time for the *Shechinah* to envelop them, he counted them. On the first of Nissan, the Mishkan was erected, and on the first of Iyar He counted them.

Rashi deals with the motivation to count the Jews yet again, since this is the third time within a year that a census is taken. Rashi explains that God's love for the Jews is the reason why He counts us time and time again.

While not discounting this explanation, I believe the nearly identical results of each census point to another understanding of the phenomenon of counting. Each time the people are counted, the result is 600,000, more or less; in fact, the number 600,000 becomes a descriptive term for the totality of the Jewish people. Our question, then, should be obvious: Virtually every generation from the Exodus onward outnumbers 600,000, yet this number is still used to describe the totality of the nation. Even in the desert, there were more than 600,000 people; there, the number 600,000 refers to the number of men between the ages of twenty and sixty. All others were not included in the tally. Are we to assume that the others — men above or below the age limit, women, and children — were of no significance?

The Midrash applies the number 600,000 in a different way:

> God said [to Moshe], "By your life, I will go down and save them. One woman went to Egypt and on her account I went down and saved her." When was this? When Pharaoh took Sarah, as it says: "God plagued Pharaoh" (*Bereishit* 12:17). "If on account of one woman I came down, should I not come down for the sake of six hundred thousand men, six hundred thousand women, and six hundred thousand children?"
>
> *(Shemot Rabbah 15:14)*[1]

1 See also *Shemot Rabbah* 42:1.

On a mystical level, the number 600,000 is identified with the number of souls comprising the Jewish nation. The Gemara teaches that the arrival of Mashiach will transpire when all these souls are "complete."[1]

> [Mashiach] ben David will not come before all the souls in the body will be completed, since it is said, "For the spirit that unwrappeth itself is from Me..." (*Yeshayah* 57:16).
>
> *(Yevamot 62a)*

In fact, this source goes even further, implying that the Jewish nation is one body with 600,000 parts.

The *Zohar* carries this numeric parallel even further, stating that there are 600,000 letters in the Torah which are meant to parallel the 600,000 souls (*Zohar Chadash, Shir HaShirim* 74d). Another mystical source, the *Megaleh Amukot*, expands on this idea:

> Every one of Israel has for his soul one letter of the six hundred thousand letters of the Torah.... Yisrael (ישראל) is an acronym for "*Yeish shishim ribo otiyot laTorah* — there are six hundred thousand letters in the Torah" (יש שישים ריבוא אותיות לתורה).
>
> *(Megaleh Amukot, section 186)*

One difficulty which arises from these teachings is the fact that the letters of the Torah actually number only 304,805, slightly more than half the number we expected to find. One way of resolving this contradiction would be to cite another mystical tradition, found in Ramban's introduction to his Commentary to the Torah,[2] which refers to a primordial Torah which preceded the creation of the world, written in black and white fire. We may conclude that the letters that we see on the parchment represent the black fire, while the parchment itself, the background on which the words are written, or the spaces between the letters represent the white fire. Thus, we may account for the missing letters with these "white letters," which would fill in the count to 600,000.

---

1 See *Zohar, Bereishit* 119a.

2 For the source of Ramban, see *Yerushalmi Shekalim* 6:1.

Alternatively, others explain that many letters of the Torah are compounds of other letters — for example, an *alef* can be broken down to two *yuds* and a *vav.*[1] When we add these letters up, we get 600,000.

When we merge these teachings, we conclude that the Jewish people as a whole equal 600,000, with one letter of the Torah for each soul. There are 600,000 souls — even though there are more than 600,000 people. Several people can share the same "soul root." The people who parallel the letters in the Torah are actually greater in numbers, while the number of letters is actually fewer, teaching that it may take many people working together to accomplish a single aspect of the Torah.

The number 600,000, then, is an expression of the totality of the Jewish nation in its spiritual capacity, which in a sense mirrors the Torah. That being so, we can appreciate the need to count the nation. The first counting takes place after the nation leaves Egypt, at the moment the Jews become a nation. Yosef and the brothers entered Egypt as a family, a clan, perhaps a tribe, but it was a nation that eventually marched out. We have seen (in *Parashat Vayeitzei*) that part of the disagreement between Yaakov and his sons Shimon and Levi was this very question of personal versus national status: Yaakov saw his children as a family, or at most a tribe, while Shimon and Levi saw them as a nation, or at least as the forerunners of a nation, whose personal actions affect the collective consciousness of future generations of the nation. *Yalkut Shimoni* spells this out in clear terms, which have direct impact on our topic:

> Yaakov said to Shimon and Levi, "You have endangered me for I am small in number... There is a tradition among the Canaanites that in the future they will fall into the hands of my children."
>
> But God said to him, "Not until the Land is liberated and inherited by six hundred thousand."
>
> *(Yalkut Shimoni, Vayishlach 135)*

---

1 For a full discussion of this topic, see Rabbi Reuven Margoliot in *HaMikra VeHaMesorah*, ch. 12.

Not until the Jews are a bona fide nation — represented by 600,000 — will the Land of Israel be theirs. In the words of another passage in the *Yalkut,*

> Leaving Egypt was with 600,000. Entering the Land was with 600,000. In addition, the Messianic Age will consist of 600,000.
>
> *(Yalkut Shimoni, Hoshea 518)*

The spiritual identity of the Jewish people is made of 600,000 parts; therefore, until this identity had been achieved, the Exodus from Egypt was impossible. Furthermore, entering the Land of Israel in either biblical or eschatological times is only possible if the Jews number at least 600,000. [It is fascinating to note that in 1948 there were approximately 600,000 Jews in Israel, and it was not until almost 1967 that there were 600,000 males of fighting age, in accordance with a teaching in the *Zohar* that Yerushalayim will only be united when 600,000 males are in the Land.]

For this same reason, the Jews were counted after the sin of the golden calf. If 600,000 did not remain, those who survived would not be considered the nation of Israel until they once again numbered 600,000; the historical clock would have been put on hold. Being unable to take possession of the Land of Isael, the people would have been forced to wait in the desert until their numbers were replenished. In the words of the *Zohar*:

> No one is missing of the six hundred thousand which emerged by the power of the Name.... Therefore, whenever Israelites died on account of a national sin, the people were afterwards numbered, and it was found that the number of six hundred thousand had not been diminished even by one, so that the likeness to the supernal prototype was still complete; just as no one was missing above, so no one was missing here below.
>
> *(Zohar, Bereishit 2b)*

The requirement that there be no fewer than 600,000 in order to enter the Land of Israel is here coupled with the understanding that this number reflects an equally significant number in the higher realms. The 600,000 souls of Israel are a reflection of the various aspects of God revealed in the letters of the Torah.

But why were they counted at this particular juncture in the desert, "on the first of the second month in the second year after leaving Egypt"?

By this point in history, the Torah had been given, the Mishkan was built, and the *Shechinah* rested on the people via the Mishkan. They needed only to complete their march into the Holy Land.[1] Of course, that is not the way the story unfolds, but the further wanderings in the desert are not part of the original plan. They come only as a result of further intrigue which will take place in the desert.

Another teaching in this week's parashah provides insight: Chapter 2 of *Bemidbar* describes the formation in which the Jews are to encamp and march.

> God spoke to Moshe and to Aharon, saying, "Every man of the people of Israel shall camp by his own flag, with the ensign of his father's house; opposite and around the Ohel Mo'ed they shall camp. Those who camp on the east side shall be the flag of the camp of Yehudah according to their hosts. And the leader of the sons of Yehudah shall be Nachshon son of Aminadav."
>
> *(Bemidbar 2:1–3)*

According to the Midrash, the model for the formation is taken from the only other time that the people marched to Israel, following the death of Yaakov. On his deathbed Yaakov commands his children:

> Take heed that no stranger touches the bed [i.e., my casket] so that the *Shechinah* will not be expelled. Rather, in this particular order you are to carry me. Three in the north.... This is the

1 See the comments of Seforno (*Bemidbar* 1:2), who states that it was indeed time to enter the Land at this juncture. We will return to this theme in *Parashat Beha'alotcha*.

manner which you are destined to do in the desert, with the *Shechinah* in the center.

(Bereishit Rabbah 100:2)

The parallel between Yaakov's death scene and the formation in the desert is highly significant. On the basic level, this confirms that the time to march to Israel has indeed arrived, and the full circle of our history is evident. Furthermore, there is a fascinating parallel to be drawn between Yaakov and the *Aron* containing the Tablets. Yaakov is described as "one who dwells in the tents," a description understood to portray Yaakov as representing Torah. Now, even in death, Yaakov is compared to a Torah scroll, just as his coffin, his *aron*, is compared to the *Aron* of the Mishkan. In this Midrash, Yaakov represents the Torah in a very real sense.[1]

Yaakov's insistence that no stranger join the entourage seems unusual, but when we recall that this march in the time of Yaakov serves as the prototype for the march in the future of the 600,000 Jews, of all of Israel, the parallel becomes instructive. No strangers are to join the ranks, for this would cause the *Shechinah* to be expelled. This is all the more poignant when we look at the larger picture. The nation, which consists of 600,000 souls, is paralleled to the Torah, which has 600,000 letters. A Torah with too many or too few letters is invalid. If even one half of a letter is missing, the Torah is rendered unkosher. So too with the Jewish nation; with either one person missing or one person too many, the glorious march to Israel can not begin. One extra person can have severe mystical implications.

Happy are Israel in that God has chosen them above all peoples, and for the sake of His love has given them true laws, instilled in them the Tree of Life, and made His Divine Presence

1 Similarly, we find Yerusahalayim surrounded by the twelve tribes: "The 'daughters of Jerusalem' are the twelve tribes, as we have learned that Jerusalem is established on twelve rocks, three on each side.... These are called 'the daughters of Jerusalem,' and they testify to the king concerning the Community of Israel, as it is written: 'The tribes of God are a testimony to Israel, to give thanks to the Name of God' (*Tehillim* 122:4)" (*Zohar, Bereishit* 242a).

dwell with them. Why? Because [the people of] Israel are stamped with the holy impress on their flesh, and they are marked as being His and belonging to His Temple. Therefore all who are not stamped with the holy on their flesh [i.e., circumcision] are not His, and they are marked as coming from the side of impurity, and it is forbidden to associate with them or to converse with them on matters of the Holy One, blessed be He. It is also forbidden to impart to them knowledge of the Torah, because the Torah consists wholly of the Name of the Holy One, blessed be He, and every letter of it is bound up with that Name.

(Zohar, Vayikra 72b–73a)[1]

We are taught that a large number of Israelites perished in Egypt during the plague of darkness.[2] Only those whose souls paralleled one of the letters of the Torah left Egypt. Only those souls can enter Israel.

The traditional sources point out that there was an *eirev rav*, the mixed multitude or "hangers on," who did leave Egypt with the Jews.[3] Apparently, this is precisely what concerned Yaakov. The tragic consequences of the existence of the *eirev rav* are well known: The sin of the golden calf, as well as other indiscretions, are "credited" to them. Yaakov, who represents Torah, is concerned lest an extra letter find its way into the walking, breathing entity known as *am Yisrael* (the nation of Israel). One extra or missing letter, and the Divine plan may be altered, just as one letter or even part of one letter missing can invalidate a Divine book.

---

1 This is the source for the mystical saying, "[The nation of] Yisrael, the Torah, and God are all one." Also see *Zohar, Vayikra* 93b: "Similarly, the Holy One, blessed be He, and the Community of Israel are called one when together, but not when apart; and so now that the Community of Israel is in exile, it is, as it were, not called one, and will only be called one when Israel emerges from captivity."

2 Rashi cites this tradition in his commentary to *Shemot* 13:18: "One out of five left Egypt while four of five perished during the three days of darkness." The source of this teaching is *Mechilta,* ch. 18.

3 The Midrash specifically associates the sin of the golden calf with the *eirev rav* (*Shemot Rabbah* 42:6). Rashi follows this tradition. See his comments to *Shemot* 32:7.

The *eirev rav* did join and march with *am Yisrael*, and the Divine plan was changed, but that story is told in other *parashiyot*. Our lesson for this *parashah* is that many Jews are needed to realize the Divine plan; there are indeed far more that 600,000 Jews and all are vitally necessary for the creation of a whole entity. Indeed, there are 600,000 core souls, which represent the different aspects of the Divine Spirit contained in each of us uniquely.[1] Only a merger of these entities will allow the Jewish people to realize their divine mission. The Jewish people as a whole is a reflection of the Torah, which itself is composed of 600,000 individual, independent characters and in turn reflects that aspect of the mind of God which He reveals to us.[2]

1 The Arizal therefore writes of 600,000 different approaches to the Torah, each legitimate, each based on a different aspect of the Torah (*Shulchan Aruch of the Arizal*, p. 49).

2 For an expression of the connection between God, the Torah, and water, see *Zohar, Shemot* 60b.

Parashat Naso

Shefa Eloki

Parashat Naso begins with a continuation of the counting of the tribes, begun in *Bemidbar*. Here, the emphasis is on the tribe of Levi. The parashah goes on to introduce various laws, such as the *metzora* (one afflicted with *tzara'at*) leaving the camp, the consequences of thievery, the laws of the *sotah* (a woman suspected of unfaithfulness), and the laws of the *nazir*. The bulk of the parashah deals with the *korbanot* brought by the heads of the various tribes at the consecration of the Mishkan. Immediately preceding the list of the offerings is this instruction:

> God spoke to Moshe, saying, "Speak to Aharon and his sons, saying: 'So shall you bless the Children of Israel. Say to them: "May God bless you and guard you. May God's face shine on you, and may He find favor in you. May God lift His face toward you and grant you peace." ' They shall put My name on the Children of Israel and I shall bless them."
>
> *(Bemidbar 6:22–27)*

This blessing is known as *birchat kohanim* (the Priestly Blessing). It is the last injunction given prior to the completion of the consecration of the Mishkan, and clearly must have an intrinsic relationship with the section which follows. The next verse states:

> It was on the day that Moshe completed setting up the Mishkan....
>
> *(Ibid. 7:1)*

Before we look at the connection between *birchat kohanim* and the Mishkan, we must address a more fundamental question: What is the purpose of *birchat kohanim*? If God desires that the people be blessed, why not bless them Himself?

Ramban alludes to this issue when he states in his commentary,

> The true understanding [generally a euphemism for Kabbalistic doctrine] is that the blessing comes from above.
>
> *(Ramban, Bemidbar 6:24)*

The comments of Ramban seem obvious; of course this blessing, like all blessings, comes from above. Furthermore, if the blessing indeed comes from above why are Aharon and his sons commanded to bless the Jewish people? Ramban continues in his comments, citing a Midrash which describes a prayer uttered by God when He completed Creation:

> "May He find favor in you" — May you find favor in His eyes, as our (Rabbis) [explained God's response to the completion of Creation] said "My world, My world, if only I could find favor [grace] in you all the time (*Bereishit Rabbah* 9:4).[1]
>
> *(Ibid.)*

---

1 The Midrash reads: "Rabbi Chama bar Chanina and Rabbi Yonatan explained it as follows. Rabbi Chama bar Chanina said: Compare this to a king who built a palace. He saw it and it pleased him. 'Palace, palace,' he exclaimed, 'may you find favor in my eyes at all times just as you have found favor in my eyes at this moment!' Similarly, the Holy One, blessed be He, said to His world: 'My world, My world! May you find favor in My eyes at all times just as you have found favor before Me at this moment.'

"Rabbi Yonatan said: Imagine a king who gave his daughter in marriage and arranged a bridal chamber and a home for her, plastering, panelling, and painting it. He saw it and it pleased him. 'My daughter, my daughter!' he cried to her, 'may this bridal chamber find favor before me at all times just as it has found favor before me at this moment.' Similarly, the Holy One, blessed be He, said to His world, "My world, 'My world! May you find favor before Me at all times just as you have found favor before Me at this moment' " (*Bereishit Rabbah* 9:4).

This suggests an interesting parallel: Just as God prays when the world is completed and about to take its own course, He commands the *kohanim* to pray as the Mishkan is completed and the Jews are about to continue on their march toward their destiny. This further confirms an idea that we had seen in *Shemot* that the Jews leaving Egypt marked a reconstruction or rebirth of the world. Here, at the final step prior to the Mishkan's completion the *kohanim* are instructed to bless the people, as God blessed His Creation all those years before, at the dawn of history.

However, a larger question emerges: If God "prays," why is that not sufficient? What sense is there in man giving over God's blessing? This question is strengthened by Rashi's comments on the text of *birchat kohanim*:

> "May God lift His face toward you" — may He control his anger.
> *(Rashi, Bemidbar 6:26)*

The idea of God's face being turned toward us is the opposite of *hester panim*, when God hides His face from us — an expression of God's anger and the resultant distance between God and His people.[1] According to Rashi, the essence of this blessing is that we are praying for God to control His anger in His relationship with us. This, too, is connected with the idea of God praying, as indicated by the following passage in the Gemara:

> Rabbi Yochanan said in the name of Rabbi Yosi: How do we know that the Holy One, blessed be He, prays? Because it says, "I will bring them to My holy mountain, and I will cause them to be happy in *My* house of prayer" (*Yeshayah* 56:7). It does not say "their house of prayer," but "My house of prayer." From here we see that the Holy One, blessed be He, prays.
> *(Berachot 7a)*

The Gemara is willing to entertain the idea of God praying, and asks the obvious question:

1 See *Bereishit* 4:14, *Devarim* 31:18.

> What does He pray? Rav Zutra, son of Tuvia, said in the name of Rav: "Let it be My will that My mercy suppresses My anger, that My mercy prevail over My other attributes, that I deal with My children with the attribute of mercy, and that I deal with them beyond the letter of the law."
>
> *(Ibid.)*

Not only does the Gemara conclude that God Himself prays, but the essence of His prayer is that He control His anger. What, then, is the purpose of the *kohanim* blessing the people as well? Why would God command us to say a blessing which He has already said? Moreover, if this is the prayer that God says, how is it that at times God does hide His face from us and treat us with anger? These questions become even stronger when we see the continuation of the passage in the Gemara:

> Rabbi Yishmael the son of Elisha said, "I once entered into the innermost [part of the sanctuary] to offer incense, and I saw Akatriel Kah [a Name referring to the crown of God],[1] the Lord of Hosts, seated upon a high and exalted throne. He said to me, 'Yishmael, My son, bless Me!'
>
> "I said, 'May it be Your will that Your mercy suppresses Your anger, that Your mercy prevail over Your other attributes, that You deal with Your children with the attribute of mercy, and that You deal with them beyond the letter of the law.'
>
> "And He nodded to me with His head." [*Rashi*: "As if to say amen."]

In the conclusion of the passage, not only does God pray but He also asks Rabbi Yishmael ben Elisha for a blessing! If God Himself prays, why would He need or desire man to pray for Him? One of the most basic concepts in Judaism is the fact that God is infinite and therefore unchanging, God does not need our prayers, and they do not change God.[2]

---

1 There is some debate whether the Name *Akatriel* refers to God or to an angel, see *Malachei Elyon* by Rabbi Reuven Margoliot, p. 12, footnote 1.

This question becomes even stronger when we consider the context of this passage. Rabbi Yishmael ben Elisha was the *kohein gadol*. For that reason he was in the innermost part of the sanctuary — the *Kodesh HaKedashim* — offering the incense, the rite of Yom Kippur. The blessing that he offers is that God treat man with kindness and compassion, beyond the letter of the law, and God nods in approval. It would seem that the world was now guaranteed forgiveness and future success — in the words of Rashi, God said, "Amen!" Yet we find the following passage in the *Mechilta*:

> Rabbi Yishmael and Rabbi Shimon [ben Gamliel] were taken out to be executed. Rabbi Shimon said to Rabbi Yishmael, "Master, my heart is broken, for I do not know for what offense I am being executed."
>
> Rabbi Yishmael said to Rabbi Shimon, "Did it ever happen that someone came to you with a case to be adjudicated or with a [halachic] question, and you had him wait until you finished your glass [of drink], until you tied your shoe, or until you put on your cloak? The Torah says, '[Do not abuse the widow or orphan.] If you abuse them at all, [and they scream to Me, I will surely hear their cry. My anger shall be inflamed, and I will kill you by the sword. Your wives will become widowed and your children orphaned!]' (*Shemot* 22:21–23). [These verses are fulfilled because of] any abuse, be it large or small."
>
> He said to him, "Master, you have comforted me."
>
> *(Mechilta, Mishpatim, section 18)*

This amazing passage relates the final discussion between two of the ten martyred Sages, the most prominent scholars of their generation who were executed by the Romans for the crime of being rabbis. Rabbi Shimon asks the classic, almost unanswerable question on theodicy (belief in God despite the fact that evil oc-

2 These passages, with their anthropomorphic qualities, are among the most complex Aggadic sections in the Talmud. They received a great deal of attention by dissident Jewish groups in antiquity through modern times, and they also attracted the attention of other religions in the Middle Ages. See *Decoding the Rabbis* by Marc Saperstein (Harvard University Press, 1980), p. 1–21, for a historical survey.

curs), yet Rabbi Yishmael offers a response, suggesting a possible reason for their harsh fate. Rabbi Shimon accepts the rationale and they go to their deaths with dignity.

When we consider the explanation Rabbi Yishmael suggests, we understand that the Sages' deaths are the result of God treating them with the strictest possible judgment imaginable. This is a far cry from the blessing that the same Rabbi Yishmael[1] gave God — to treat man beyond the letter of the law, with compassion, controlling His anger! How ironic that the very same man received such strict justice and accepted it with such equanimity, even though He knew precisely what blessing to say to God. If God said "amen" and accepted the blessing, then why was it not effective? Our original questions return, with a vengeance.

Rabbi Chaim of Volozhin, in his masterpiece *Nefesh HaChaim*, discusses some of the spritual dynamics which relate to this question: God has a desire to give man all the blessing in the world — to cause the *shefa Eloki* (the Divine abundance) to rain down on man. But in order for this to transpire man must create a world which is deserving of such abundance.

This idea may be explained by an obscure comment of Rashi. The Gemara teaches:

> Anyone who enjoys this world without a blessing is like robbing the Holy One, blessed be He, and the community of Israel, as it says, "He who robs his father and mother and says it is no transgression is a destructive person's friend" (*Mishlei* 28:24). His father is none other but the Holy One, blessed be He, as it says, "Is He not your father who has acquired you?"

1 There were, in fact, two Sages named Yishmael ben Elisha. They were grandfather and grandson. I am assuming in this analysis that both passages are referring to the same person, although there is contradictory evidence regarding the identification of the martyred Rabbi Yishmael. The first passage (*Berachot* 7a) certainly refers to the grandfather, because the grandson never served as *kohein gadol*. The description of the martyred Rabbi Yishmael in the prayers of Yom Kippur seem to say that he was the one who served as *kohein gadol*. This identification is supported by Rav Sherira Gaon (*Iggeret Rav Sherira Gaon*, Lewin edition, p. 74). (However, see *Semachot* 8:8, which implies that the martyred Rabbi Yishmael is the grandson.)

> (*Devarim* 32:6), and his mother is none other than the community of Israel, as it says, "Listen, my son, to the instruction of your father, and do not forsake not the teaching of your mother" (*Mishlei* 1:8).
>
> *(Berachot 35b)*

The implication of this teaching is that if one does not say a blessing before eating he has no right to the food. Rashi explains, "Like robbing the Holy One, blessed be He, of His blessing."

Rashi does not give the obvious explanation, that the stolen article is the food consumed without a blessing, and maintains that it is God's blessing which is stolen. Within Rashi's brief comment is a profound idea. When a person eats without saying a blessing, God does not miss the food. God created this physical universe as a place where man can develop a relationship with Him, and when man does so, the *shefa Eloki* flows. When man leaves God, the result is that God becomes distanced from man and the *shefa Eloki* becomes scarce. Thus, Rashi comments that the person who eats without saying the blessing has stolen the blessing, and hence the opportunity for God to shower us with His blessing.[1]

Therefore we can posit that although blessing truly flows from above, as Ramban said (quoted at the outset), the amount of blessing which comes from above is dependent on man's actions below.

We saw above that despite the prayer of Rabbi Yishmael the Kohein Gadol, he was treated with strict Divine justice. This is now understood based on a passage in the Gemara:

> Rabbi Yochanan[2] taught: Yerushalayim was destroyed because the people judged with Torah law.
>
> *(Bava Metzia 30b)*

---

1 I believe that Rashi did not explain the passage with the more obvious explanation, that it is the food which was stolen, because the previous passage stated: "Anyone who enjoys anything of this world without a blessing is like making personal use of things consecrated to Heaven, as it says, 'God's is the earth its fullness' (*Tehillim* 24:1)...." This passage focuses on the food. Therefore the following teaching, in Rashi's opinion, must have a different focus.

2 Let us recall that the passage cited above, that God prays, was also taught by Rabbi Yochanan.

The Gemara finds this suggestion strange. Why should using Torah law be bad? What better alternative exists? It therefore concludes:

> They judged according to the law of the Torah, and never went beyond the letter of the law.

The terrible deed which caused the fall of Yerushalayim was that everyone stood up for his rights before the law, and the judicial system followed suit, meting out justice "strictly by the book." Consequently, God treated them likewise — according to the letter of the law — and Yerushalayim fell.

Rabbi Yishmael understood the symbiotic relationship between man's behavior and God's judgment. When God asked for a blessing, Rabbi Yishmael knew exactly what to say, and when he was taken out for execution he knew that his generation had failed, because the people had been so strict with one another. God, in turn, would mirror their own behavior and be just as strict with them and their leaders, who had the responsibility to set the example of an existence which transcends the letter of the law. Perhaps God nodded to Rabbi Yishmael as if to say, "It's up to you."

The Gemara, commenting on *birchat kohanim,* poses the following question:

> The ministering angels said to Holy One, blessed be He, "Master of the universe, it says in Your Torah, '[God] does not lift His face to anyone and does not take bribes' (*Devarim* 10:17). But You favor Israel, as it says, 'May God lift His face toward you and give you peace.' "
>
> He answered them, "I shouldn't favor Israel? I wrote in My Torah, 'You shall eat and be satiated, and then bless God, your Lord' (*Devarim* 8:10); yet they are careful [to bless] even after [eating] an amount of food [the size of] an olive or an egg."
>
> *(Berachot 20b)*

Although the Torah only commands us to recite *Birkat HaMazon* (Grace after Meals) if we have eaten to satiety, the Sages decreed that one should recite the blessing even if he has only eaten an anount of food the size of an olive (or an egg, in certain instances). In response to the Jewish people blessing God even for small amounts, God declares his special love for us. We see the same idea being expressed about *birchat kohanim*, the blessing which God gives us from above, which is directly related to the behavior of man below.

Rabbi Yishmael the Kohein Gadol would say *birchat kohanim* daily. He knew that all blessing comes from Heaven, but he also knew that the mandate to create an elevated world was given to man. The blessing of the people was given over to the *kohein* in the final preparation for the Mishkan. The Mishkan must become a place where the blessing flows; after all, the Mishkan is where the *Shechinah* rests. Only once the blessing was given over to Aharon and his sons could the Mishkan be complete.

To paraphrase the Kotzker Rebbe (*Emet MiKotzk Titzmach*, p. 76, section 232):[1]

> The *Shechinah* can only rest in a place where man allows it to rest. May we all help create a world where the Divine abundance flows as per God's true desire. May we create a world where God's mercy is allowed to prevail over His other attributes. May God bless you and guard you. May God's face shine on you, and may He find favor in you. May God lift His face toward you and grant you peace. Amen!

1 The Kotzker was once asked, "Where is God?" He replied, "Wherever man allows Him."

Parashat Beha'alotcha

The Unfinished Book[1]

The parashah of *Beha'alotcha* contains a unique idiosyncrasy: two verses enclosed, as if in brackets, by letters written upside down in every Torah scroll. The letters that are upside down are *nuns* and the impression that they leave is that these verses are written parenthetically.

> When the Ark traveled, Moshe said, "Arise, God! Scatter Your enemies, and let those who hate You flee before You." And when the Ark rested, he would say, "Return, God, the myriad of thousands of Israel!"
>
> *(Bemidbar 10:35–36)*

The Gemara and Midrash provide insight into this phenomenon:

> The Holy One, blessed be He, put signs above and below this section in order to say that this is not its proper place.
>
> *(Shabbat 115b–116a)*

According to the Gemara, these verses are indeed parenthetical,

1 Most of the ideas discussed in this week's section were taught by Rav Yosef Dov Soloveitchik, in a lecture given in honor of Rabbi Israel Klaven. I heard the *shiur* from my father, and later from an audiotape. As I returned to research the ideas articulated, I found that the Rav had used the Seforno as his basis. Indeed, it is overwhelming how two lines in the Seforno were transformed into a two-hour *shiur*. Nonetheless, I will cite the Seforno later as the source of the ideas. A number of times I have found that the Rav developed entire *shiurim* from "simple" comments of the Seforno.

inasmuch as they were extricated from their proper context and placed here. Generally, we find different opinions among the various commentators to the *Chumash* regarding the proper sequence of the events recorded in the Torah (or the more basic question of whether there is any sequence at all). Be that as it may, even according to the opinion that the Torah does not record events in sequence, it is curious that specifically in this instance the Torah itself would leave a mark in order to indicate the change.

The Gemara, however, goes even further, offering an opinion that flies in the face of one of the most widely held beliefs of Judaism, that there are five books of the Torah:

> Our Rabbis taught: The Holy One, blessed be He, put signs above and below this section in order to say that this is not its proper place. Rabbi said: [The signs] are not on that account, but because [this section] ranks as a separate book. The dictum of Rabbi Shmuel ben Nachmani, in Rabbi Yonatan's name, agrees: "[Wisdom] has hewn out her seven pillars" (*Mishlei* 9:1) — this refers to the seven books of the Torah.
>
> *(Ibid.)*

The seven "pillars of wisdom" in the book of *Mishlei* refer to the seven books of the Torah. This reference does present somewhat of a difficulty to those of us who know of only five books in the Torah (and hence the name *Chumash* — from the word *chameish*, five)!

The Midrash asks:

> Are there not five [books of the Torah]?... The reason for this statement is that Bar Kappara counted the portion of *Bemidbar* from the beginning until "When the Ark travelled" (*Bemidbar* 10:35) as one book; "When the Ark traveled..." and the following verse as another separate book; and from the end of that section until the end of that book [*Bemidbar*] another separate book.
>
> *(Bereishit Rabbah 64:8)*[1]

The *midrash* explains that there are, indeed, seven books:

1 This idea may also be found in *Vayikra Rabbah* 11:3.

Bereishit; Shemot; Vayikra; Bemidbar — up to but not including these two verses, these two verses; the rest of *Bemidbar*; and *Devarim*. To say that *Sefer Bemidbar* should be divided into two sections is understandable — even if we lose the familiar "five books" formula in the process. But how can two isolated verses be considered a "book" by themselves? We must point out that the approach that opines that these two verses form a separate book is not singular. The Mishnah in *Yadayim*, which discusses the ritual sanctity of Scripture, teaches:

> A scroll on which the writing has become erased and eighty-five letters remain on it, as many as are in the section beginning, "When the Ark traveled," renders the hands impure [i.e., is susceptible to *tumah* transmitted by touch]. A single sheet on which there are written eighty-five letters, as many as are in the section beginning, "When the Ark traveled," renders the hands impure.[1]
>
> *(Yadayim 3:5)*

The section from *Shabbat* cited above, which introduced the notion of seven books, was the continuation of a halachic question which the Gemara grappled with, namely the type of Scripture that may be saved in the event of a fire breaking out on Shabbat. In that case, as well as in the discussion of ritual sanctity of Scripture here, the conclusion is that the minimum requirement for a scroll to be considered a "book" is eighty-five letters.

We see, then, that these two verses are considered for some legal issues to be a book unto themselves. Our understanding that there are but "Five Books of Moshe" is somewhat shaken.

In order to understand this phenomenon, we must take a closer look at the context in which these verses appear. As we begin reading the parashah of *Beha'alotcha*, we sense that the Jewish people are nearing their goal, the Promised Land. The Torah has been received, the Mishkan has been completed and consecrated, all seems in place for the glorious march. But something tragic

1 Exactly the number in the demarcated section in *Beha'alotcha* has holiness, for a "book" remains.

happened on the way to Israel.

Let us consider the sections of the parashah: First, Aharon is commanded regarding the lighting of the candles. Aharon, of course, follows the Divine command:

> Aharon did that [which he was commanded], lighting the candles to illuminate the Menorah, as God had commanded Moshe.
>
> *(Bemidbar 8:3)*

Next comes the section of sanctifying the *Levi'im*:

> God spoke to Moshe, saying, "Take the Levites from the midst of the Children of Israel and sanctify them."
>
> *(Ibid., 5–6)*

What follows next are two sections which revolve around the celebration of the Exodus. Moshe is commanded to repeat the rites which were performed in Egypt on the eve of the Exodus. A whole year had passed, and the practices which were instituted in Egypt on that night will now be repeated. A problem arose, for there were those who were ritually impure and therefore could not partake of the *korban Pesach*. These individuals were told that they would have a second chance to bring the *korban*, in the following month. On the fourteenth day of the second month they would have their Pesach.

Let us consider the chronology of events: The Jews, as we know, left Egypt on the fifteenth of Nissan — year one. Fifty days later, they stood at Sinai. They sinned in the golden calf episode on the seventeenth day of the fourth month. Moshe prayed for the nation and was invited to ascend Mount Sinai for the second time on the first day of Elul, the sixth month. Forty days later, on Yom Kippur, the tenth day of Tishrei, Moshe came down from the mountain with the second Tablets and with the instructions to build the Mishkan. The people collected the materials and started to build the Mishkan. On the first day of Nissan in the second year the Mishkan was complete. The twelve tribes, represented by their leaders, offered *korbanot*, one each day, which brings us to the thirteenth day of Nissan in the second year. The Jews will now observe Pesach. Those who are unable to partake of the Pesach will have another opportunity on the fourteenth of the second month.

We are now up to date. The second Pesach was observed. How would the people know when it was time to march on? The Torah reports a Divine sign:

> On the day when the Mishkan was erected, a cloud enveloped the Mishkan...and in the evening what appeared to be fire [enveloped the Mishkan] until the morning. When the cloud would lift from the tent the people would travel, and in the place which the cloud would rest, there the people would camp.
>
> *(Ibid. 9:15–17)*

One last law was taught prior to the beginning of the journey from Sinai: The trumpets would be used in order to give commands regarding the march.

All was now in place. The march begins:

> In the second year, on the twentieth of the second month, the cloud arose from on the Tent of Meeting. The Children of Israel thus began their travels from the Sinai Desert [until] the cloud rested in the Paran Desert. This was the first journey; by the word of God, via Moshe.
>
> *(Ibid. 10:11–13)*

The march begins, but where are they going? Moshe provides the answer when he invites Chovav, his father-in-law (or, according to some, his brother-in-law) to join them:

> "We are traveling to the place of which God has said, 'I am giving to you.' Join us...."
>
> *(Ibid., 29)*

Moshe speaks in present tense, "We are traveling," rather than in the future tense. Moshe believes that the Jews are about to enter the Promised Land! He believes that the promises of God to our forefathers are about to come to fruition. The future is now. Let the trumpets blow — let the conquest begin! Chovav declines, and the Jews continue alone; the destiny of the Jews and other peoples of the world would not merge as of yet. Chovav will travel a different road; his path to Yerushalayim will have to wait for the End of Days. The Jews are headed directly for Israel.

It is at this point that the two "parenthetical" verses appear.

> When the Ark traveled, Moshe said, "Arise, God! Scatter Your enemies, and let those who hate You flee before You." And when the Ark rested, he would say, "Return, God the myriad of thousands of Israel!"
>
> *(Ibid., 35–36)*

As we know, the Jews do not enter the Land of Israel immediately. They travel their own circuitous route for the next forty years. The facts in this case go against the conceptual view of history. At this point, when all the prerequisites for conquest of the Promised Land have been fulfilled, Moshe's understanding is correct. The Jewish people should begin their march at exactly this point. Yet the linear view of history prevails. Moshe's vision is overtaken by more mundane concerns. The time has not arrived.

The pathos of Moshe's situation is palpable; before these two mysterious verses, Moshe was in a marching mood, inviting others to join him in the Promised Land. After these two verses, Moshe becomes, quite literally, suicidal. As shocking as this observation may be, the verses themselves attest to the radical change in Moshe:

> Moshe heard the nation weeping with its families, every man at the door of his tent. The anger of God was kindled greatly; and in Moshe's eyes it was bad.
>
> Moshe said to God, "Why have You afflicted Your servant? Why have I not found favor in Your eyes, that You lay the burden of this entire people upon me? Have I conceived all this

people? Have I fathered them, that You should say to me, 'Carry them in your bosom,' like a nursing parent carries the sucking child, to the land You swore to their fathers?

"From where should I have meat to give to this entire people? For they weep to me, saying, 'Give us meat, that we may eat.' I am not able to carry this entire people alone, because it is too heavy for me. And if You deal thus with me, kill me, I pray You, at once, if I have found favor in Your eyes; and let me not see my wretchedness."

(Ibid. 11:10–15)

What precipitated the drastic transformation in Moshe's outlook? Rabbi Soloveitchik explained that at the moment the people demanded immediate gratification of their needs, this desire for the physical served as more than a mere stumbling block on the path to Israel. At that point Moshe understood that the Land of Israel was more distant than he had ever imagined.

The shift in Moshe's response was almost brutal: A mere ten months earlier Moshe grappled with God to save his errant people from the death sentence God pronounced following the sin of the golden calf.[1] Now, Moshe prays for his own death. As Rabbi Soloveitchik explained, the difference lies in two different aspects of idolatry — form versus content. When the people were guilty of the golden calf, Moshe understood the offense as being the result of adopting Egyptian religious practices. The problem was one of form; the question was how to worship God. While this offense was considerable, Moshe felt that it was defendable. Once the Jews accept the Torah, he argued, they would naturally shift the form of their religious expression.

---

1 As a response to the golden calf, Moshe is prepared to go to any lengths to secure forgiveness for the people. The Gemara writes: " 'Now therefore let Me alone so that My wrath may wax hot against them and that I may consume them, and I will make of you a great nation' (*Shemot* 32:11). Rabbi Abahu said: Were it not explicitly written, it would be impossible to say such a thing. This teaches that Moshe took hold of the Holy One, blessed be He, like a man who seizes his fellow by his garment, and said before Him: 'Master of the universe, I will not let You go until You forgive and pardon them' " (*Berachot* 32a).

But now, upon seeing the people's hedonistic character, Moshe realizes that the problem is deep-seated within the collective consciousness of the community, and vast time and energy will have to be spent to cure the people of this malady. For the first time, Moshe realizes that he is not taking the first steps of the final march to Israel; the effects of two hundred years of slavery have made deep inroads into his people, and they are not as far away from Egypt as he had imagined and hoped. Moshe had a premonition that neither he nor his entire generation would cross the border into the Promised Land, and the weight of this realization was crushing. He understood, all at once, that he would never enter the Promised Land, that his mission would end prior to the conquest. He would not see the beauty of the Temple in Jerusalem. For Moshe, like so many Jews in history, the Promised Land would remain just that — a promise.

But what is it about these two verses, these eighty-five letters, which cause our Sages to call them an entire book? The answer is obvious: These verses represent the book that was never written, the book of the conquest spearheaded by Moshe, fought by God. These verses represent the book that was to have been, but was not. The key to understanding this teaching is a number of comments by the Seforno:

> "When the Ark traveled" — to enter the Land of Israel.
>
> "Arise, God! Scatter Your enemies" — had it not been for the spies, they would have entered [Israel] without battle, for the inhabitants of [the land] would have fled.
>
> *(Seforno, Bemidbar 10:35–36)*

Seforno explains that these verses are what Moshe said upon entering the Land. But Moshe never did enter the Land! This, then, is what he would have said had he entered, and the result would have been a peaceful conquest. When we read the first comments of Seforno to *Bemidbar*, we see this idea already developed:

> "Count the heads of all the community of the Children of Is-

rael" — to put them in order, so that they can enter the Land immediately.

The Jews were supposed to enter the Land of Israel at this juncture. However, due to their own failures and failings, this generation does not merit the Promised Land. With these two parenthesized verses, God leaves a sign, a reminder, of what could have been, or, more precisely, what should have been. Why, then, are a mere two verses called a "book"? There was supposed to be far more information in this book. The first verse was to contain the beginning of the redemption — "When the Ark traveled, Moshe said, 'Arise, God! Scatter Your enemies, and let those who hate You flee from before You.' " The second verse represents the last verse of this book — "And when the Ark rested, he would say, 'Return, God, the myriad of thousands of Israel!' " The end of the Redemption would mark the return of all Jews to the nation, to the Land of Israel, to the Torah; to God.

Indeed, these two verses represent a whole, incomplete book, the book of the destiny of the Jewish people. Even when we fail, God will not allow us to forget our mission. Even when we deviate from our destiny and stray from the proper path as we did in the desert, even as we wander through the desert, reaping the bitter fruit of our own sins, we are reminded of our mission. There is a portion of the Torah, an entire book, dedicated to telling the unfinished story and encouraging us to complete it.

> Rabbi Shimon ben Gamliel taught: In the future this section will be removed from here and written in its proper place.
>
> *(Shabbat 116a)*

Moshe was correct; this was the proper place for the conquest to begin, and he was ready to fulfill what he saw as his most important task. Tragically, however, the people were not ready to enter the Land. Moshe's dream was vanquished. In retrospect, but only in retrospect and in light of the shortcomings of the people, this is not the proper place for the story of redemption to be told. Rabbi

Shimon ben Gamliel[1] assures us that indeed this story will be completed, when the glorious march takes place and the myriad of lost Jews return, to link with the missing letters of this book which awaits completion.[2]

1 Rabbi Shimon ben Gamliel disagrees with the opinion that this constitutes a separate book, but he agrees that the section is out of context here:

"Who is the Tanna who disagrees with Rabbi? It is Rabbi Shimon ben Gamliel. For it was taught, Rabbi Shimon ben Gamliel said: This section is destined to be removed from here and written in its right place. And why is it written here? In order to provide a break between the first [account of] punishment and the second [account of] punishment. What is the second [account of] punishment? 'The people were as murmurers...' (*Bemidbar* 11:1) The first [account of] punishment? 'They moved away from the mountain of God' (ibid. 10:33) which Rabbi Chama bar Chanina expounded [as meaning] that they turned away from following God. And where is its [rightful] place?... In [the chapter on] the flags" (*Shabbat* 116a).

2 See my comments on *Parashat Bemidbar*, where I discuss the number of letters in the Torah and the interdependence with the number of souls of the Jewish people.

Parashat Shelach

The "Spies"

> God spoke to Moshe, saying, "Send for you men to tour the Land of Canaan, which I am giving to the Children of Israel."
>
> *(Bemidbar 13:1–2)*

In this week's parashah, Moshe is called upon to send a reconnaissance mission, ostensibly to assess the lay of the land in advance of the upcoming conquest. He is told to send one person from each tribe. The text attests to the greatness of this select group:

> All of them were leaders of the people.
>
> *(Ibid., 3)*

The mission ends in failure. The men return, but instead of planning a means of conquest, they conclude that entering the Land is an unattainable goal:

> [They said,] "However, the people of the land are strong and the cities are fortified...."
>
> *(Ibid., 28)*

Of course, the question, "What went wrong?" is immediately posed. After all, it seems to have been God's idea to send the spies, and Moshe handpicked the people. What accounted for the failure? We should note that this indiscretion had greater implications than the other episodes in the desert, such as the golden calf or the various incidents when the people demanded water or food. The *Zohar* takes up this question:

> "Moshe sent them" — they were all men, they were righteous prominent leaders of Israel, but their words caused terrible calamity. What made them do this? They said, "If Israel enters the Land, Moshe will cause us to be replaced, for we can only lead in the desert, but in the Land we will not lead."
>
> *(Zohar, Bemidbar 158a)*

The *Zohar* paints a picture of leaders who are more concerned with their own position of power than the good of their constituents. In a move that would have made Machiavelli proud, they guarantee their own standing by preventing the situation that would have caused their removal from power. It is hard to imagine that such people are the elite, the men handpicked by Moshe to lead the Chosen People. What could have caused such a myopic outlook, such a breakdown in leadership?

Of the twelve spies, two men — Yehoshua and Kaleiv — rejected the nefarious plot. Of the two, Yehoshua is more familiar to us; he was Moshe's "right-hand man" and the one who eventually took the reigns of leadership from Moshe. However, upon analysis of the text, we find, surprisingly, that Yehoshua remained silent when the other spies gave their report. It was Kaleiv, and Kaleiv alone, who spoke up:

> Kaleiv silenced the nation before Moshe and said, "We shall surely go up and inherit the Land, for we can indeed take it."
>
> The men who had gone up with him said, "We will not be able to go up against the nation [living there] for it is stronger than we are."
>
> *(Bemidbar 3:30–31)*

Kaleiv's heroism is striking. He stands up against the crowd, silences the rabble, and attempts to sway public opinion toward Moshe and away from the naysayers. Yehoshua's silence, on the other hand, is equally striking. Surely, when the verse refers to the other spies, Yehoshua is not included, despite the implications of a literal reading of the text. It is only later in the narrative that we hear Yehoshua's voice:

> The people said to one another, "Let us appoint a leader and return to Egypt."
>
> Moshe and Aharon prostrated themselves in front of the community.... Yehoshua bin Nun and Kaleiv ben Yefuneh, from those who had toured the Land, tore their clothes, and they said to the entire congregation of the Children of Israel, "The land which we traveled...is a wonderfully good land."
>
> *(Ibid. 14:5–7)*

Here, finally, Yehoshua speaks. He follows the lead of Moshe, Aharon, and Kaleiv. But the question remains: Why was Yehoshua silent up to this point? This question, as well as our earlier query regarding the breakdown of leadership among the spies, can both be answered by a comment of the Shelah HaKadosh (Rabbi Yeshayahu Horowitz). He explains that, indeed, all the spies were great men, but the consideration of the ten errant spies was that they wished to remain in the desert with their beloved leader Moshe. They did not reject the Land of Israel, but preferred to learn Torah from Moshe in exile. They appreciated that the Land was a Holy Land, a special land, but they believed that the Jews needed to earn their entry into the Land. They knew that the Land of Israel would "vomit out" any who were undeserving.[1]

This would explain the passage from the *Zohar* cited above: Their choice to remain in the desert was not a cynical misuse of power; rather, it was an earnest, thought-out strategy. They felt the people were simply unready to enter the Land, and that they needed the old generation of leadership, of the type represented by Moshe. The problem was that they had been instructed to find the facts; they were not asked to draw conclusions. Perhaps power, which is often intoxicating, clouded their judgment and brought them to the conclusion that the generation still needed them as leaders and Moshe as teacher.

---

1 See comments by Rav Tzaddok HaKohen in *Pri Tzaddik*.

This understanding of the spies' intent is entirely contingent on the knowledge that Moshe would not be entering the Land, that Moshe would not be leading the Jews across the Jordan River to Israel. But why would they have suspected that this would be the case? If we follow the chronology of the narrative, Moshe had not yet sinned by striking the rock, and it had not yet been decreed that he would die and be buried in the desert.

An enigmatic passage in last week's parashah provides the key to unraveling this mystery. We are told that Moshe gathered seventy elders and the Divine Spirit rested on them, and they began to prophesize. In the aftermath, we are told:

> Two men remained in the camp. One was named Eldad and the other was named Meidad. The Spirit rested upon them...and they prophesized in the camp....
>
> Yehoshua bin Nun, the servant of Moshe since his youth, said, "My master Moshe, stop them."
>
> Moshe said to him, "Are you jealous for me? Would that all the nation were prophets, that God would rest His Spirit upon them."
>
> *(Ibid. 11:26–29)*

Here, Yehoshua speaks. Moshe's honor is his foremost concern. But what was it that evinced such a strong response from Yehoshua? Seventy elders had just prophesized; what was it about these two prophets in the camp that so upset Yehoshua? Perhaps the content of their prophecy is what concerned him:

> What did they prophesize? They said, "Moshe dies, and Yehoshua leads to the Land."
>
> *(Sanhedrin 17a)*

Yehoshua's outburst is understandable. This terrible prophecy must be false, he thinks. He calls upon Moshe to silence them. Moshe's response is all the more poignant, for at this point Moshe understands that he is not to enter the Land.[1] Yet Moshe instructs Yehoshua not to be jealous on his account.

The *Zohar* explains:

> The Holy One, blessed be He, in effect said to him: "On every such occasion you wish to die, so 'I will take of the spirit which is upon you and put it upon them' (*Bemidbar* 11:17)."
>
> Observe that Moshe was here made to know that he would die [in the wilderness] and not enter into the Land, as, in fact, Eldad and Meidad announced. This is a lesson that in a time of wrath a man should not utter anything in the nature of a curse against himself, because ever so many malignant powers are standing by, ready to take up that utterance.
>
> On the other occasion when Moshe prayed for death to himself his request was not taken up, because Moshe meant it then all for the benefit of Israel. Here, on the other hand, Moshe only gave vent to his anger and anguish of heart; his words, therefore, were taken up, and Eldad and Meidad, who remained in the camp, announced, "Moshe will be 'gathered in' and Yehoshua will bring Israel into the Land." This made Yehoshua jealous for the sake of Moshe, and so he came to him and said, "My master Moshe, stop them," or, as we might also render, "withhold from them these words."
>
> But Moshe, regardless of his own glory, did not consent. Observe the meekness evinced in the reply of Moshe: "Are you jealous for me?" Happy is the portion of Moshe, who rose high above the highest prophets. Rabbi Yehudah remarked, "All the prophets were to Moshe like the moon to the sun."
>
> *(Zohar, Bemidbar 155b)*[1]

Our earlier questions are thus resolved: The spies were aware of the dreadful prophecy that Moshe would not lead the people into the Land of Israel. The "spies" knew that the path which would lead

1 "For Moshe already knew at this time that he was not to enter the Land, and since he wanted to know of it before he departed, he sent the spies. When they failed to bring him back a proper report, he did not send again, but waited until God showed him the Land" (*Zohar, Bemidbar* 157a).

1 For a discussion on the other occasions when Moshe wished to die see *Parashat Beha'alotcha* and *Parashat Titzaveh*.

to the Land would be one fraught with spiritual and physical perils, and they felt that the nation was not prepared enough to face the challenges ahead. They sought to "buy time," time in which the entire nation, and the leaders in particular, could benefit from Moshe's teaching and become ready for the tasks they would face. In a word, they felt the people were not ready to enter the Land, nor leave Moshe behind. Yehoshua was effectively placed in an impossible position. Had he spoken out and expressed any desire to enter the Land, he would have been accused of seeking power. Had he expressed faith, in the face of the other spies' message of despair, he would have been called treacherous, faithless, and megalomaniacal. Yehoshua had no choice but to remain silent.[1]

The other ten spies did not account for Kaleiv's bravery, but when we consider who Kaleiv was and where he came from, we can gain insight into his strength. The two dissident spies, Kaleiv and Yehoshua, were from the tribes of Yehudah and Yosef, respectively. These are the two tribes which will one day produce the two Mashiachs, son of David and son of Yosef. Yehoshua served as the prototype for Mashiach ben Yosef, whose role focuses on the physical deliverance of the Nation of Israel, just as Yosef himself was the great provider for his entire generation. Kaleiv, though, from the tribe of Yehudah, is an essential link in the chain leading to the Davidic dynasty, which culminates in Mashiach ben David.

While the other spies outmaneuvered Yehoshua, forcing him into silence, they did not anticipate the profundity of Kaleiv's spirit. Kaleiv, from the tribe of Yehudah, is the prototype of Davidic leadership which brought the Temple to fruition. Kaleiv's spirit is foreshadowed in the text, when we are told:

> They entered in the Negev, and he came up to Chevron.
>
> *(Bemidbar 13:22)*

Rashi notes the peculiarity in the text: The first half of the verse

1 See the comments of the Alshich HaKadosh, who offers two possible reasons for Yehoshua's silence. The first is as I suggested, and the second is in deference to his teacher, Moshe.

is plural, while the second half is singular. This leads Rashi to state, based on a Talmudic teaching, that Kaleiv went to Chevron alone, in order to pray over the graves of his ancestors. As a reward for Kaleiv's later actions, he is allotted Chevron as his inheritance (see *Devarim* 1:36 and *Shoftim* 1:20). There is another aspect of Chevron. Not only did Kaleiv pray at the graves of his ancestors, but he also effectively established the spiritual antecedents of the reign of King David:

> The years that David ruled over Israel were forty years. In Chevron, he ruled seven years, and in Yerushalayim thirty-three years.
>
> *(Melachim I 2:11)*

The beginning of David's monarchy is in Chevron, in the portion of Kaleiv. If the foundation of the Davidic dynasty lies in the greatness of Yehudah, the infrastructure for that dynasty lies in Kaleiv.[1] This was something the spies never anticipated.

The error of the spies, placing their devotion to Moshe (and their own jobs) over their love for the Land, was justified in their minds as "true dedication to Torah." This error is mirrored in another episode later in the parashah:

> The Children of Israel were in the desert, and they found a man gathering wood on the Sabbath.
>
> *(Bemidbar 15:32)*

Tosefot (to *Bava Batra* 119b) explains that this episode immediately follows the incident of the spies. The entire generation, with the exception of Yehoshua and Kaleiv, has just been sentenced to death in the desert. The man who gathered the wood on Shabbat felt the people may have given up on Jewish practice, feeling that their actions were no longer relevant. He deliberately desecrated the Sabbath in order to force the issue, to demonstrate that they would still be held responsible for their actions. In the words of Targum Yonatan (Yerushalmi), the wood-gatherer desecrated Shabbat in order to illustrate what the punishment for this sin would be.

The common denominator between these two explanations is that the wood-gatherer gives up his life for Torah. He certainly saw his own behavior as heroic; like the spies, he had placed Torah on a pedestal, in conflict with the word of God and the teachings of Moshe. The spies, and the wood-gatherer soon after, distorted Torah.

Moshe instructed the spies were sent to inspect the Land:

> Is it fat [i.e., fertile] or lean? Does it have a tree or not?
> *(Ibid. 13:20)*

Why would Moshe ask if the Land had "a tree"? Wouldn't that be an obvious assumption? According to the *Zohar*, Moshe is asking about a specific tree, the Tree of Life.

The first instruction that Moshe gave to the spies was to dis-

---

1 See *Zohar, Shemot* 31a:

" 'But My servant Kaleiv, because he had another spirit with him and has followed me fully...' (*Bemidbar* 14:24). 'Another spirit' signifies that Kaleiv separated himself from the other spies and went alone to Chevron in order to prostrate himself at Mearas HaMachpeilah before the graves of the patriarchs. Chevron was allotted to him as his inheritance, as it is written: 'To him will I give the land that he has trodden upon' (*Devarim* 1:36). Why was Chevron given to him? There is an esoteric reason for this, the same which also underlies David's connection with Chevron. For we find that when Shaul died and David inquired of God, 'Shall I go up into any of the cities of Yehudah?' the answer was that he should go up to Chevron (*Shmuel* II 2:1). Now, since Shaul was dead and David was already the rightful king, why did he not at once proclaim his rule over the whole land? Why was it necessary for him to go to Chevron and there become anointed as king over Yehudah only for seven years, not being declared monarch over the whole of Israel until after the death of Ish Boshet?

"Truly, the Holy One, blessed be His Name, had a deep purpose in this. The holy kingdom could not be fully established without first attaching itself to the patriarchs in Chevron. When that contact was established, the kingdom was firmly erected with support from the world above, whose symbol, in David's case, was 'seven years,' seven being the number of perfection, because it contains all. So when it is said of the Temple, 'He built it seven years' (*Melachim* I 6:38), the same perfection is suggested. David desired to build the perfect kingdom here below as a counterpart of the Kingdom above; but before he could achieve his desire he had to acquire power for the task by attaching himself to the patriarchs for seven years. Only thus was he enabled to establish his kingdom in perfection, in the fashion of the Kingdom of supernal light: a kingdom never to be shaken. And, guided by a similar inspiration, Kaleiv also went to Chevron."

cover whether there were trees in it or not. In fact, Moshe knew already, and what he really referred to was the Tree of Life, of which the proper place is the terrestrial Garden of Eden. He said, "If this tree is in it, I shall [be permitted to] enter, but if not, I shall not be able to enter. Observe that there are two Trees, one higher and one lower. In the one there is life and in the other death, and he who confuses them brings death upon himself in this world and has no portion in the World to Come." Rabbi Yitzchak said: Moshe took for himself the Tree of Life, and therefore he wished to know whether it was in the Land or not.

(Zohar, Bemidbar 157a)

The wood-gatherer, on the other hand, gathers the trees together, effectively confusing the Tree of Knowledge and the Tree of Life — causing death.

The Torah is compared to the Tree of Life; this is what Moshe is seeking. The spies' confusion begins when they do not find the Tree of Life and the Garden of Eden in Israel. They think that Moshe seeks life for himself at all costs. Their actions, despite their good intentions, had a disastrous effect on the community, which was quickly frightened and lost faith. The wood-gatherer confused the different types of trees, symbolically represented by his gathering the trees together, thereby allowing him to sacrifice his life in order to teach an idea.[1]

Both the spies and the wood-gatherer were well intentioned, but neither consulted with Moshe. Instead, they distorted the teachings of Torah, and the results were disastrous. The spies chose Torah in exile over inheriting the Land without Moshe; the wood-gatherer hoped to illustrate that there was no goal for the Jewish people other than Torah, in its narrowest application — which was suicidal. But both of these trends of thought are deviations. True

1 "Tzelafchad [the wood-gatherer] was one of the principal men of the sons of Yosef, but because he did not know the ways of the Torah sufficiently he did not become their leader" (*Zohar, Bemidbar* 205b).

Torah is a Tree of Life for all who embrace it, a way of life and a way of living in this world. Neither the spies nor the wood-gatherer understood that.

The parashah concludes with the instructions regarding tzitzit.

> God spoke to Moshe, saying, "Speak to the Children of Israel, and tell them that they should make for themselves fringes on the borders of their garments, throughout their generations. They should put upon the fringe of the borders a blue thread. It shall be for you a fringe, that you may look upon it and remember all the commandments of God, and do them; and that you do not seek after your heart and your eyes, which incline you to go astray. So that you may remember, and do all My commandments, and you will be holy to your God. I am God, your Lord, who brought you out of the land of Egypt, to be your God; I am God, your Lord."
>
> *(Bemidbar 15:37–41)*

The Torah uses the word *seek, taturu*. It is fascinating that this word has been used numerous times in the parashah describing the mandate of the spies. Tzitzit is a tool designed to remind us to adhere to all the commandments. This explains the linguistic parallel with the spies, who decompartmentalized their religious experience and allowed concern for their roles to seduce their thoughts and create a worldview based on a warped view of their task.

Man is often guilty of subjective thinking. Tzitzit work to keep the commandments together as an organic whole. The tool that reminds us of all the commandments is the tzitzit, which had both blue and white strings. The blue indicated the Heavenly, the Divine, and the white indicates the earthly, the logical. Only when the two are bound together can man make the proper choices and defeat the subjectivism inherent within himself.[1]

The spies were guilty of being too "logical," using a bit too

---

1 See my discussion in *Parashat Vayeitzei*, where I expand on the symbolism of blue and white. Also see "The Symbolism of Blue and White" in Besdin, *Man of Faith in the Modern World*, vol. 2, p. 25ff.

much "white." On the other hand, the wood-gatherer was guilty of using too much blue, sacrificing himself misguidedly for a greater goal. Had any of these people consulted with Moshe, all the mistakes in this parashah could have been avoided. For posterity, man is instructed, via the tzitzit, to recall all the commandments and to merge the logical with the metalogical, thereby creating a holistic relationship with God.

Parashat Korach

Rebellion

The breakdown in leadership recorded in last week's parashah is followed by a direct, full-scale rebellion against Moshe, Aharon, and God in *Parashat Korach*. The foreboding report of the spies, the very men entrusted with leadership, caused the masses to reevaluate continued allegiance to Moshe as leader. This misuse of power brought calamity upon the nation. In this week's parashah, Korach takes advantage of the undercurrents of discontent. The time is ripe — and he strikes. Who was Korach[1]? What motivated him? What was his agenda? A review of the episode will help us understand these issues.

First, let us consider Korach's strategy.

> Korach, son of Yitzhar, son of Kehat, son of Levi; and Datan and Aviram, sons of Eliav; and On, the son of Pelet, of the sons of Reuven, took men. They rose up before Moshe, with some of the people of Israel — two hundred and fifty princes of the assembly, regularly summoned to the congregation, men of renown.
>
> *(Bemidbar 16:1–2)*

1 It seems somewhat ominous that Eisav had a son by the same name — "Aholivamah bore Yeush, and Ya'alam, and Korach; these are the sons of Eisav, who were born to him in the land of Canaan" (*Bereishit* 36:5). There are a number of parallels between Korach and Haman, a famous descendant of Eisav — see below.

Korach's initial move was to galvanize the various segments of the population who felt disenfranchised, particularly from the tribe of Reuven: If anyone felt that his position had been compromised, he must have been from the tribe of Reuven. Reuven was, after all, the firstborn of Yaakov. Accordingly, the kingship, the priesthood, and the double inheritance should all have been within their purview.[1] Yet these privileges were stripped away by Yaakov, and handed over to Yehudah, Levi, and Yosef respectively.[2] Therefore, in his initial move Korach manipulates the leaders of Reuven to join his rebellion.

Next we see the argument which he uses:

> They gathered themselves together against Moshe and against Aharon, and said to them, "You take too much upon yourselves, for all the community is holy, and God is in their midst. Why do you raise yourselves above the community of God?"
>
> *(Ibid., 3)*

Rashi's comments on their complaint are instructive:

> "You take too much upon yourselves" — You have taken too much greatness for yourselves.
>
> "For all the community is holy" — All heard the sounds at Sinai emanating from Heaven.
>
> "Why do you raise yourselves above the community of God?" — If you [Moshe] took the kingship for yourself, you did not need to give your brother the priesthood....

What is Korach's agenda? On the one hand, he correctly points out that the entire nation stood at Sinai. This provides the basis for the claim that leadership can belong to any of the people. While this argument is certainly populist, and may perhaps bring him

1 See comments of Rabbeinu Bechayai on *Bereishit* 49:3.

2 Before his death, Yaakov spells out Reuven's inappropriateness for these roles. "Reuven, you are my firstborn, my might, and the beginning of my strength, the excellency of dignity, and the excellency of power. Unstable as water, you shall not excel; because you went up to your father's bed and then defiled it..." (*Bereishit* 49:3–4).

even greater "grass roots" support, it can lead to anarchy, for ultimately his argument leads to the conclusion that there is no need for any leadership at all: No individual should be placed on a pedestal over all others. Perhaps leadership should be based on rotation, creating "a nation of comrades — all for one and one for all." Despite the grand message, Rashi indicates that Korach himself does not believe the words that leave his lips, for in the next breath he says:

> "Why do you raise yourselves above the community of God?" — If you took the kingship for yourself, you did not need to give your brother the priesthood....

In the text, it is unclear whom Korach attacks: Is Moshe his nemesis, or Aharon?[1]

Here Korach slyly seems to say, "We can make this whole thing go away if you agree to share some of the wealth."

Korach wants power. He finds what he believes to be an expedient way to accomplish his goal: Attack Aharon. Aharon is the weak link, for Aharon alone was guilty in the golden calf tragedy.[2] Why should he be rewarded and become *kohein gadol*? Why not find a more appropriate leader to serve as *kohein gadol*, namely Korach?

In reality, this attack is against Moshe and, indeed, against God Himself.

> The reason why Korach refused to allow the quarrel to be settled by Moshe's intervention was that he had not entered

---

1 The Midrash implies that the high priesthood was his goal (*Bereishit Rabbah* 51:1).

2 Aharon himself sensed the inappropriateness of his being appointed *kohein gadol*. See *Bemidbar Rabbah* 18:9:

"Observe the piety of the righteous Aharon! When Moshe poured the anointing oil on his head, Aharon was filled with trepidation and dismay. He said to Moshe, 'My brother, perhaps I have been unworthy of being anointed with the anointing oil and have committed a trespass, thus incurring the penalty of excision, for the Holy One, blessed be He, said, "Upon the flesh of man it shall not be poured" (*Shemot* 30:32)?'

"Scripture therefore testifies concerning him by saying, 'Behold, how good and how pleasant it is for brothers to dwell together in unity! It is like the precious oil upon the head, coming down upon the beard; Aharon's beard...like the dew of Chermon' (*Tehillim* 133:1–3)."

> upon it for a truly religious motive, and that he had scant regard for the glory of God and refused to acknowledge His creative power. When Moshe perceived that he [Korach] had thus separated himself [from God and holiness], he "was very angry" (*Bemidbar* 16:15). He was "angry" because he was not able to settle the quarrel; he was "very angry" because they denied the creative power of God. Korach denied this power wholly, both in the higher and the lower sphere, as implied in the phrase, "When they incited against God" (ibid. 16:9).
>
> *(Zohar, Bereishit 17a–b)*

> Moshe said to the Levites, "If Aharon, my brother, had taken the priesthood on his own initiative, you would have been right in being indignant against him. Now, however, that it was given to him by the Holy One, blessed be He, to whom belongs greatness, might, and sovereignty, then anyone who rises against Aharon, does he not rise up against the Holy One, blessed be He?"
>
> Accordingly, it is written, "And as to Aharon, what is he that you complain against him?" (ibid. 16:11).
>
> *(Bemidbar Rabbah 18:9)*

It is God, not Moshe, who gives out appointments. Perhaps by stressing that the entire nation stood at Sinai (as per Rashi), Korach implies rejection of Moshe's leadership, for Moshe differed from the nation in that he did not merely stand at Sinai, he ascended the mountain and brought back the Torah with him.

Korach's tactics seem less than direct; perhaps he understood that a direct attack against Moshe would surely have failed. However, had Moshe bowed to Korach's demands for priesthood, Moshe's own position would have been irreparably compromised, and the path to his removal would have been paved.

What was it that corrupted Korach? What caused his rejection of God's authority? The Midrashic and Kabbalistic traditions abound with suggested explanations of Korach's failure. One explanation describes Korach as a wealthy man who, not unlike other men of great wealth, desired power as well:[1]

> You will find that there are riches that harm their possessors and other riches that stand [their possessors] in good stead. As an example of riches that do harm, take the case of Korach, who was richer than all Israel and of whom it is written, "So they and all that they owned went down alive into the pit" (*Bemidbar* 16:33).[2]
>
> *(Shemot Rabbah 31:3)*

Other sources indicate that Korach felt humiliated by Moshe for shaving his head (while preparing Korach for his service as Levite),[3] a suggestion which also explains the origin of the name *Korach*, which means bald.

> "Korach...took" implies that he took his cloak and went to take counsel with his wife. When the Holy One, blessed be He, said to Moshe, "Take the Levites from among the Children of Israel and purify them. Thus shall you do to them, to purify them...have them pass a razor over all their flesh" (*Bemidbar* 8:6–7), Moshe forthwith did so to Korach.
>
> The latter walked about among the Israelites and they did not recognize him. They said to him, "Who did this to you?"
>
> He said to them, "Moshe did it to me. Even more, he took hold of me by my hands and feet, and I was waved, and he told me, 'Behold, you are pure!' Then he brought his brother, Aharon, and decked him out like a bride and made him sit in the Ohel Mo'ed!"
>
> Instantly, Moshe's enemies began to incite Israel against him, saying, "Moshe is king, his brother Aharon is *kohein gadol*, and his [Aharon's] sons are deputy *kohanim gedolim*! The *kohein* gets *terumah*, the *kohein* gets tithes, the *kohein* gets twenty-four gifts!"
>
> *(Bemidbar Rabbah 18:4)*

In my notes on *Parashat Bereishit*, I cited the opinion of the

1 *Yerushalmi, Sanhedrin* 27d.
2 The *midrash* continues and compares Korach with Haman.
3 *Sefer Eitzot Yesharot.*

Arizal, who compares Korach and Kayin, noting the blind, self-destructive jealousy each exhibited against protagonists who were unwilling to do battle. In a sense, this first "argument" between Kayin and Hevel sets the spiritual stage for what is arguably the most famous of arguments in the *Chumash*, the argument between Korach and the establishment. I noted in that discussion the linguistic parallel of "the ground opening its mouth" (*Bereishit* 4:11) to swallow the blood of Hevel and the *middah keneged middah* (punishment in like measure) as the ground swallows Korach and his men (see *Devarim* 11:6). While this parallel needs to be studied and considered, other aspects of Korach's personality and tactics are also worthy subjects of study.

We have seen elements of vanity, megalomania, arrogance, and self-delusion in Korach's personality, and demagoguery and manipulation in his arguments.[1] Nonetheless, and not unlike the spies in the preceding parashah, Korach was not a marginal character. He was a leader of his tribe, entrusted with carrying the *Aron*:

> Korach was exceedingly wise, and he was among the carriers of the *Aron*.
>
> *(Bemidbar Rabbah 18:3)*

What was it, then, which led this man astray, and allowed so many negative traits to become manifest? Perhaps we can answer this question by noting a peculiarity about Korach. Despite his ability to gather support from various sections of the population, in his own home he was unsuccessful. The Torah reports in the next census:

> The sons of Korach did not die.
>
> *(Bemidbar 26:11)*

Apparently, the sons of Korach did not follow their father or his teachings. They carried the *Aron* with dignity. *Tehillim* chapters 42, 44–49, 84, 85, 87, and 88 are all attributed to the descendents of Korach.[2] The Midrash teaches that one of the most famous prophets, Shmuel, was a descendent of theirs.

---

1 *Bemidbar Rabbah* 18:2.

> He [Korach] should not say, "Since Shmuel is destined to descend from me, I shall be saved."
>
> *(Bemidbar Rabbah 18:15)*

In another section, the Midrash elaborates:

> Korach was a clever man — what reason did he have for such folly? His mind's eye misled him. He foresaw that a long and distinguished progeny would emanate from him, particularly Shmuel, whose importance would equal that of Moshe and Aharon, as may be inferred from the text, "Moshe and Aharon among His [God's] priests, and Shmuel among those that call His Name" (*Tehillim* 99:6). [He also foresaw] that from among his descendants there would be twenty-four levitical divisions, all of whom would prophesy under the influence of the Holy Spirit; as it says, "All these were the sons of Heiman" (*Divrei HaYamim* I 25:5). He argued, "Is it reasonable that, since such greatness is destined to emanate from me, I should keep silent?"
>
> He did not, however, foresee accurately. In actuality, his sons repented, and it was from them that the distinguished progeny was to emanate. Moshe, however, did foresee it.
>
> *(Bemidbar Rabbah 18:8)*

Korach believed in his superiority in the area of descendants, for he knew that great spiritual leaders were to descend from his line, whereas Moshe's line of descent is far less impressive. The Torah and Midrash speak infrequently about Moshe's progeny. Korach, on the other hand, thought himself worthy of a leadership role because of the descendants who would emerge from him. It is true that the sons of Korach were, in fact, superior individuals — as evidenced by their refusal to follow their father and their own view

2 See *Zohar, Vayikra* 5a: "Rabbi Abba discoursed here on the Psalm commencing, 'A song, a psalm of the sons of Korach' (*Tehillim* 48). 'This psalm,' he said, 'surpasses all the other hymns of praise, and it was sung by the sons of Korach, being hymn upon hymn, a hymn with two facets, song and psalm.... This is the song of the Holy One, blessed be He, which was sung by the sons of Korach, those who sat at the doorway of Gehinnom.'

of their holy mission of carrying the *Aron*.

This insight may allow us to appreciate the argument which Korach used, "For all the community is holy and God is in their midst." Rashi suggested that Korach was referring to the moment when the entire community stood at Sinai, but Rav Tzaddok HaKohen from Lublin suggests a different understanding of Rashi. While we generally understand that Rashi points to the past, Rav Tzaddok believes that Korach's reference is to the future. The Jews are truly a holy nation, and God is among us, but the holiness of the people and the manifestation of God in the community will grow exponentially when the Jews accomplish their collective mission. When Korach speaks of Mount Sinai and Revelation, he sees the community in idyllic terms. For Korach, the future is now; God is among all of us.

But this perspective had its pitfalls. Looking to the future, Korach saw that his descendants were clearly more distinguished than Moshe's. With this view, it seemed fitting that Korach, not Moshe or Aharon, lead the people. Korach's mistake, his misreading of the spiritual needs of the nation, was tragic. Instead of glory, Korach found despair and enmity.

According to the Midrash, Chanah, the mother of Shmuel, serves as the spiritual power who pulls Korach from the depths:

> So did the company of Korach sink and descend ever lower until Chanah arose and prayed for them: "God kills and brings to life; He brings down to the pit and brings up" (*Shmuel* I 2:6).
>
> *(Bereishit Rabbah 98:4)*

Ironically, Shmuel, the most notable descendent of Korach, supports the leadership in his generation. He is directly responsible for the anointment of the first two kings of Israel. He does not try to usurp kingship and attain power for himself; rather he is a faithful servant of God. Shaul, the first king of Israel, is anointed by Shmuel, and only Shaul's own sins cause him to lose his throne. Shmuel then initiates the Davidic dynasty with the anointment of David. Thus, while this week's haftarah contains many allusions to our parashah, the primary association is the line drawn between Shmuel and Korach, and the stark differences in their attitudes and behavior.

Korach's error was the belief that leadership is the result of intellect, wealth, and power. The Jewish idea of leadership is taking responsibility and serving as an agent of God. Shmuel understood that. Korach did not.

Korach claimed that God is among all the people. Of course, he was correct. The Kotzker Rebbe was once asked, "Where is God?" He responded, "Wherever we allow Him to be." God's presence is a question of man's spirit, not God's existence. The sons of Korach also understood this; in one of the most powerful prayers in *Tehillim*, they call out:

> To the chief Musician, a Maskil, by the sons of Korach: As the hart yearns for the water of the brook, so my soul yearns for You, Lord. My soul thirsts for the Lord, for the living God. When shall I come and appear before the Lord? My tears have been my bread day and night, while they say to me all day, "Where is your Lord?"
>
> *(Tehillim 42:1–4)*

In this profound passage, we understand why Korach had reason to be proud, but his descendants were quite different from him. They knew God was among them. They searched and longed to feel and experience God to greater and greater degrees. They were honored to sing in the Temple; perhaps they did not have starring roles — that role was reserved for the *kohein gadol* — but they were ecstatic with their supporting role, singing out powerful words, which, joined with stirring melodies, evoked moving images. Their words, which are the positive legacy of Korach, inspire us to this very day. Unlike Korach, who insisted that God is among all of us, his descendants sang songs describing how man must desire God, search for God, and be consumed with love of God.

> As the hart yearns for the water of the brook, so my soul yearns for You, Lord. My soul thirsts for the Lord, for the living God. When shall I come and appear before the Lord?

Parashat Chukat

Death

Parashat Chukat begins by teaching about the *parah adumah*, the red heifer, the rite that purifies those who come in contact with the dead. The *parah adumah* is one of the most obscure commandments, and serves as the prototypical example of *chok* — the type of commandment that transcends human understanding.[1] Not only is the response — the *parah adumah* — difficult for man to comprehend, but the cause — death — is also ultimately beyond human understanding.[2]

In a sense, death is the major theme of the parashah. Miriam and Aharon perish in this week's parashah and Moshe himself receives a death sentence. Reading between the lines of the text, the

---

1 See *Bemidbar Rabbah* 19:1: "When the dead body is in the house, the house is pure, but when it comes out it is impure. Who did this? Who commanded this? Who decreed this? Was it not the world's Only One? We have learned elsewhere: The people engaged in any part of the preparation of the red heifer from beginning to end defile garments, while the heifer itself makes garments ritually clean. The Holy One, blessed be He, says, 'I have laid down a statute; I have issued a decree! You cannot transgress My decree.' "

Also see *Bemidbar Rabbah* 19:3: "Shlomo meant: 'All these I have fully comprehended, but in regard to the section dealing with the red heifer, I have investigated and inquired and examined. "I said I will get wisdom, but it was far from me" (*Kohelet* 7:23).' "

2 The idea of death is most likely included within the topic of theodicy, Rabbi Meir opines that this was not revealed to Moshe, despite his request. See *Berachot* 7a.

deaths of many more people can be inferred, but before we explore what is between the lines let us consult the text itself:

> The Children of Israel, the entire congregation, arrived in the Tzin Desert in the first month. The nation settled in Kadeish. There Miriam died, and there she was buried. There was no water for the congregation, and they gathered around Moshe and Aharon.
>
> *(Bemidbar 20:1–2)*

The Gemara infers from this passage that the water the Jewish people drank in the desert came in the merit of Miriam, and with her demise the merit for water dissipated as well.

> Three good leaders arose for Israel, namely Moshe, Aharon, and Miriam, and for their sake three good gifts were conferred [upon Israel], namely, the well, the pillar of cloud, and the manna. The well was in the merit of Miriam; the pillar of cloud was in the merit of Aharon; the manna was in the merit of Moshe. When Miriam died the well disappeared, as it says, "There Miriam died," and immediately after it is written, "There was no water for the congregation." It returned in the merit of the [latter] two.
>
> *(Ta'anit 9a)*

The people were clearly concerned. This is not the first time that the nation approaches Moshe with a complaint about a shortage of supplies. It is not even the first time that a complaint was registered about a shortage of water. Here, however, there is a subtle difference. Let us return to the text:

> The people quarreled with Moshe, and spoke, saying, "If only we had died when our brothers died before God! Why have you brought up the congregation of God into this wilderness, that we and our cattle should die there? And why have you made us come out of Egypt, to bring us into this evil place? This is not a place of seed, figs, grapevines, or pomegranates, and there is no water to drink."
>
> *(Bemidbar 20:3–5)*

This litany of complaints has been heard before. Different words or images were employed, but the same message was conveyed: Egypt was superior to this. The people longed for their place of birth. The hardships of slavery were forgotten, and only nostalgia for the home of their youth remained.

Yet this description is somewhat imprecise, for this is a new generation. Most of these people never saw Egypt! Very quietly, with no fanfare, the forty years of wandering in the desert, promised in *Parashat Shelach*, have elapsed. This new generation, born in the desert, should have nothing to be nostalgic about. These people should not be suffering from a "slave mentality," for they were born free. Miriam's death occurs as the forty-year decree expires. Rashi alludes to this in his commentary:

> "The entire congregation" — the complete community, for those who were to die in the desert had perished, and these [the remainder] were separated for life.
>
> *(Rashi, Bemidbar 20:1)*

Miriam has died; Aharon and Moshe will soon follow. Moreover, the entire generation of Egyptian-born former slaves, anyone over the age of twenty when the nation left Egypt, had died.[1] The Torah did not mention the years that have elapsed, but the last date mentioned in the text was almost forty years prior to the events described in this passage. Perhaps this is why the parashah begins with the antidote to death: this is not a theoretical discussion, or a law that is occasionally applied. This is a situation that has arisen in virtually every home. An entire generation is now missing — dead.

And nonetheless, the children speak just as their parents did. Perhaps this should not surprise us; children often mimic their parents, even if their personal context has been altered. They question Moshe regarding the wisdom of the Exodus: "Why did you bring us from Egypt to this evil place?" While these people, on the whole, never saw Egypt, nor were they taken out, they had internalized their families' grievances.

1 See *Bemidbar* 14:27–35.

The observation that a new generation had emerged will help us understand the central episode of the parashah: The indiscretion of Moshe with the rock, the act that led to the death sentence of Moshe and Aharon.

Moshe and Aharon turn to God for guidance. God responds with the following instruction:

> God spoke to Moshe, saying, "Take the staff and gather the congregation, you and Aharon, your brother. Speak to the stone before the eyes of the people, and it will give its waters. Take from the stone's water, and give the congregation and their cattle to drink."
>
> Moshe took the staff from before God, as He commanded him. Then Moshe and Aharon gathered the people in front of the stone. [Moshe] said to them, "Listen now, you rebels, shall we extract water for you from this stone?"
>
> Moshe lifted his hand and struck the stone with his staff twice. An abundance of water came out, and they gave the people and cattle to drink.
>
> *(Bemidbar 20:7–11)*

A cursory reading does not produce anything exceptional. This is the type of event which had become commonplace in the desert. The people complain and Moshe turns to God, who in turn solves the problem but points out the people's shortcomings. Here, however, the conclusion contains a twist. Instead of pointing out the failure of the community, God responds:

> God said to Moshe and Aharon, "Because you did not believe in Me to sanctify Me in the eyes of the Children of Israel, therefore you will not lead this people to the land which I have given them. These are the waters of contention [*mei merivah*], for which the Children of Israel quarreled with God...."
>
> *(Ibid., 12–13)*

The response is stunning. Moshe and Aharon have failed their mission. Entering, conquering, and, most importantly, settling the

Land will take place without them. They will not cross the Jordan; Israel will remain a goal beyond their reach. But what was the sin? The Torah does not clearly state what they did; rather, the Torah seems to address the cause: "Because you did not believe in Me to sanctify Me in the eyes of the Children of Israel."

Similarly, the commentaries are not unified in their understanding of the actual offense committed by Moshe and Aharon. According to Rashi, the problem was striking the stone instead of speaking to it, but this "answer" raises a number of questions: First, if the problem was striking the stone with the staff, why was this procedure acceptable in a previous episode?[1]

> The people complained to Moshe and said, "Give us water that we may drink."
>
> Moshe said to them, "Why do you strive with me? Why do you tempt God?" The people thirsted there for water, and the people murmured against Moshe and said, "Why have you brought us up out of Egypt, to kill us and our children and our cattle with thirst?"
>
> Moshe cried to God, saying, "What shall I do to this people? They are almost ready to stone me."
>
> God said to Moshe, "Go before the people, and take with you of the Elders of Israel; and your rod, with which you struck the river, take in your hand, and go. Behold, I will stand before you there upon the rock in Choreiv; and you shall strike the rock, and water shall come out of it, that the people may drink." Moshe did so before the eyes of the Elders of Israel.
>
> *(Shemot 17:2–6)*

Immediately following the Exodus, the people demanded water; there, God called upon Moshe to bring his staff and strike the rock. In our present episode, God only told Moshe to bring the staff, and He did not say to strike the stone. One could attempt to

1 The Alshich explains the distinction as follows: Often a young child needs some type of corporal discipline, but as the child grows the parents should shift their methods and speak to the child. Similarly, the grown nation now needed to be spoken to, rather than shown force.

defend Moshe by saying that God's instructions were somewhat deceptive, commanding Moshe to bring the staff when it is not to be used, especially when the staff was, in fact, used on another, similar occasion. Yet this defense cannot stand in the face of God's instructions, which must be carried out exactly, with no deviation. Nonetheless, the resulting punishment seems excessive.

There is a second problem with this approach: Why was Aharon punished?[1] He did not strike the stone; only Moshe did so. "Moshe lifted his hand and struck the stone with his staff twice." Aharon ostensibly had no part in the actual sin; why should he share equally in the punishment?[2] Perhaps Moshe and Aharon discussed the issue and jointly concluded to strike the stone twice.[3]

Rambam opines that the sin was Moshe's anger in his response to the people.[4] A great man should not allow his anger to get the best of him in any circumstance. Again, Aharon's role seems questionable. According to Rambam, the phrase "Listen now, you rebels, shall we extract water for you from this stone?" was a display of anger. From the text itself, it is unclear whether Moshe or Aharon uttered these words. Perhaps here Moshe acts and Aharon speaks, as per the arrangement worked out at the burning bush. The only problem with this resolution is that Rambam explicitly states that it was Moshe who spoke. So, again, Aharon's role, and thus his responsibility, comes into question.

Likewise, Rashi in his commentary to the Gemara states:

> For the sin of saying, "Listen now, you rebels," he [Moshe] was

---

1 This question is posed in the Midrash; the answer, though, presupposes that the indiscretion was Moshe's anger. See *Bemidbar Rabbah* 19:9: "Why was Aharon made responsible, as it says, 'God said to Moshe and Aharon, "Because you did not believe in Me" '? This may be illustrated by a parable. A creditor came to take away a debtor's granary and took both that and the one belonging to his neighbor. Said the debtor to him: 'If I am guilty, what crime has my neighbor committed?' So also did Moshe our teacher say: 'I lost my temper, but what crime did Aharon commit?' "

2 See *Rashi* on *Devarim* 33:8.

3 See Rabbeinu Bechayei on the verse. The Ha'Amek Davar notes that Aharon's role was speaker for Moshe. By not speaking, Aharon was culpable.

4 See Rambam, *Shemoneh Perakim*, ch. 4.

punished and not permitted to enter the Land of Israel.

(Rashi, Sanhedrin 101b; see Rashi, Bemidbar 31:21)

According to this approach, Aharon's role in the sin, and therefore his punishment, seem elusive.

The more mystical commentaries, from Ramban and on, point at striking the stone twice as the sin: The stone should only have been struck once. The rationale was that the rock needed to be struck one time to bring water. The second time was to guarantee that the flow of water continued, an issue that arose only with the demise of Miriam. Moshe and Aharon were concerned that the water would run out; the second strike would assure that the water would be sustained.[1]

I would like to suggest a different resolution, based on several teachings of Rabbi Meir Simchah of Dvinsk in his commentary *Meshech Chochmah.*

Meshech Chochmah notes an apparent non sequitur in *Devarim.* Moshe delivers a soliloquy warning of the perils of idolatry, and he adds,

> God was angry with me because of you and swore that I will not be allowed to cross the Jordan [River] and not be allowed to enter the Land....

(Devarim 4:21)

After this Moshe returns to the topic at hand and continues to speak about idolatry.

> But I will die in this land, I will not pass over the Jordan; but you shall go over and possess this good land. Take heed to yourselves, lest you forget the covenant of God, your Lord, which He made with you, and make for yourselves an idol or the likeness of anything, which God, Your Lord, has forbidden you....

(Ibid., 22–25)

Meshech Chochmah suggests that Moshe's reference to the in-

1 See Levush, commentary to Rekanati.

cident of *mei merivah* and the resultant punishment are germane to the topic of idolatry.

> The higher wisdom was concerned lest when the people enter the Land they would treat him [Moshe] as a deity.
>
> *(Meshech Chochmah, Devarim 4:15)*

The reason that Moshe was not permitted to enter the Land was that this generation, raised in the desert and witness to miracles galore, ran the risk of seeing Moshe as something more than human. Perhaps they would think that miracles came from Moshe and not God. If we apply this approach to our passage, we find that after Moshe hits the rock, God pronounces:

> Because you did not believe in Me to sanctify Me in the eyes of the Children of Israel, therefore you will not lead this people to the land which I have given them.

The problem, as stated, is that Moshe and Aharon did not sanctify God sufficiently; rather, Moshe and Aharon gave the impression that the miracle came from them. Although this certainly was not their intention, it was the result of their actions. The purpose of Moshe bringing water from the rock was to show one and all that God is the source of all miracles. The damage was done; now, they would be unable to lead "this people," this particular generation, into the Promised Land.

If this is the case, Aharon was no different from Moshe. Their status in the eyes of the nation was similar. As a result of this display, neither Aharon nor Moshe could enter the Land.

Moshe, for his part, should have understood the inherent problem of perceived holiness in something other than God.[1] We recall that when Moshe came down from the mountain with the Tablets

---

1 In the description of the Midrash, it sounds as if Moshe acquiesced to the people's request because he had perceived an attack on his ability to perform miracles:

"In the present instance also, all Israel stood there and saw the numerous miracles in connection with the rock. They began saying, 'Moshe knows the natural properties of this particular rock! If he wishes [to prove his miraculous powers], let him bring out water for us from this other one!' " (*Bemidbar Rabbah* 19:9).

of Stone, the Word of God etched on stone by the "hand" of God, and saw the celebration around the golden calf, he destroyed the Tablets. According to the Gemara, God approved:

> How do we know that the Holy One, blessed be He, gave His approval? Because it says, "[The first tablets] which you have broken" (*Shemot* 34:1). Reish Lakish said: "Congratulations for breaking them."
>
> *(Shabbat 87a)*

Meshech Chochmah explains that just as the people had erred, thinking that through the golden calf they could forge a relationship with God, Moshe feared that they would transform the Tablets into something that contains divinity in and of itself, independent of God. In other words, if they had already worshipped a calf made of gold they would certainly end up worshipping the Tablets, which were made by God himself. This observation explains why Moshe is instructed to make the second Tablets himself, with his own hands, and not by the hand of God. God agreed with his analysis (see *Meshech Chochmah, Shemot* 32:19).

> God said to Moshe, "Cut for you two tablets of stone like the first; and write upon these tablets the words that were in the first tablets, which you broke."
>
> *(Shemot 34:1)*

This explanation is buttressed by a separate comment of Meshech Chochmah, in our passage in *Bemidbar*. Meshech Chochmah notes the interesting turn of phrase:

> God spoke to Moshe, saying, "Take the staff and gather the congregation, you and Aharon, your brother. Speak to the stone before the eyes of the people...."

What does it mean to "speak to the stone before the eyes of the people"? The implication is to speak so that the people can see, and not, as would be expected, in order for the people to hear. There was, of course, another instance when God spoke in order for the people to see: the Revelation at Sinai.

> All the people saw the sounds and the lightning, and the sound of the shofar, and the mountain smoking. The people saw it, and they trembled and stood far away. They said to Moshe, "Speak with us, and we will hear; but let the Lord not speak with us, lest we die."
>
> *(Shemot 20:15–16)*

This was a new generation, who had either not been present or had been too young to appreciate the Great Revelation. This new generation would soon enter the Land. God wanted to provide them with a new revelation,[1] but instead of a clear, visible revelation of God, Moshe and Aharon caused the people to see just one more miracle. Moshe and Aharon thus made themselves look more impressive, as we explained above, but deprived the generation that would enter the Land of Israel of their own revelation. In so doing, Moshe and Aharon had created a situation whereby they themselves could not enter the Land. Their "punishment" was not excessive; it was merely the result of their own actions.

What was Moshe's motivation in choosing this course of action? Rashi and Rambam pointed at anger as the cause. On the other hand, we may posit that when Moshe heard this generation complaining in much the same way as the previous generation, he began to consider the education these children received from their parents: If they had inherited the cynicism, the complaints, and the rebellious attitude, then they must have inherited some positive traits as well. Perhaps Moshe felt that the collective experience of Sinai had also been effectively communicated, and this generation did not need a new collective experience.

According to Meshech Chochmah, Moshe is barred from the Land of Israel, but not because his sin has made him unworthy;

---

1 This would explain why all the people needed to witness the event, as the Midrash says, " 'Moshe and Aharon gathered the congregation together before the rock' — this teaches that each individual Israelite felt himself standing before the rock" (*Bemidbar Rabbah* 19:9).

quite the opposite. Moshe was too great for this new generation. They were incapable of understanding the purity of spirit, the modesty, the greatness of Moshe. They were unaware that man could reach such a level. God desired that this generation be uplifted in order to merit leaders like Moshe and Aharon. Unfortunately, unwittingly, Moshe and Aharon thwarted that plan. They, too, would die in the desert, and this new generation would have to enter Israel without them. Yehoshua leads the nation into the Land. He is a great man, but he is not Moshe, and we are left with a haunting question: What would have been accomplished had Moshe joined them, had Moshe led them?

While such hypothetical questions may be tantalizing, we can say one thing with certainty: The theme of death, which permeates the parashah, would have been considerably limited had Moshe and Aharon acted differently, and had the people been worthy of them as leaders.

Parashat Balak

Bilam — The Man Without a Nation

The major figure in this week's parashah is a man named Bilam. He is described as a seer: Balak, King of Mo'av, sends him to attack the Jewish nation by means of a curse. Evidently, Bilam possessed unique capabilities, yet the plan to utilize his clairvoyance in an attack on the Jews was thwarted, and the Jewish people escaped unscathed.

The uniqueness of this parashah is that the story is told from the perspective of the other side, of the non-Jews. Here we have the opportunity to eavesdrop on conversations and learn about the type of plots which our enemies have planned for us. Bilam serves as a model for future generations of antisemites. However, we should note the Sages' observation that Bilam is not the only model, and that gentiles throughout the generations have acted in various cruel and brutal ways toward the Jews. In a fascinating passage, the Sages tell us of Pharaoh's three advisors, who are asked to advise regarding the "Jewish problem":

> Three were present during the consultation [of Pharaoh]: Bilam, Iyov, and Yitro. Bilam, who advised [to kill the Jews] was killed; Iyov, who was silent, was judged to suffer great pain; and Yitro, who ran away, was worthy to have

> [great] descendants....
>
> *(Sotah 11a)*

Yitro serves as the prototype for the moral, decent, caring non-Jew. He advocates sparing the Jewish people, but is forced to flee when his advice is sneered at. Iyov, in his silence, indicates that the outcome of the discussion will not affect him personally. The immense suffering which becomes his lot is the result of his own indifference to the suffering of others. Iyov apparently defines a good person as one who does no evil, in the most minimalist definition of "good." The suffering of others is not his concern. He will therefore be forced to experience personal pain until he is able to feel the pain of others.[1]

Bilam, on the other hand, is a sadistic misanthrope. He advocates the destruction of an entire people. Perhaps this position is intimated by his name, *Bilam* — *bilo am* — without a people.[2] He is an individual, a hired gun (or mouth, as the case may be) who is willing to advise and help implement a genocide if the price is right. Morality is of no concern. He is the ultimate self-centered individual. "Evil eye, arrogant spirit, and greedy soul" are his calling cards (*Avot* 5:19). There is no room in his worldview for others. The *Zohar* describes his individualism as the source of his destructive power.

> It is written of Bilam, "and he went *shefi* [to a bare height]" (*Bemidbar* 23:3). The word *shefi* signifies "alone," and it is also akin to the term *shefifon*, in the phrase "A horned snake [*shefifon*] in the path" (*Bereishit* 49:17). So Bilam went alone, like a snake that goes alone and lurks in by-paths and lanes, with the object of attracting to himself the impure spirit. For he who walks alone at certain periods, and in certain places, even in a town, attracts to himself the impure spirit. Hence one should never go on a lonely road, even in a city, but only where people are about. A man should also never go out in the

1 See Rabbi Joseph Soloveitchik, *Fate and Destiny* (translated from the Hebrew *Kol Dodi Dofeik*), where this idea is explored more fully.

2 *Sanhedrin* 105a.

> nighttime, when people are no longer about. It is for a similar reason that it is written, "His body shall not remain all night upon the tree" (*Devarim* 21:23), so as not to leave the dead body, which is alone, without spirit, above ground in the night. The wicked Bilam, however, for that very reason went alone, like the serpent.
>
> *(Zohar, Bereishit 170a)*

Nonetheless, Bilam remains a somewhat elusive character. The Sages, in various *midrashim*, offer different Jewish leaders as models for comparison in an attempt to better understand Bilam.[1] Textual and Mishnaic parallels are drawn between Bilam and Avraham. The Mishnah contrasts the descendants of Avraham with the descendants of Bilam, as if to say that Avraham became the forefather of a great nation based on these concerns while Bilam remained to himself. No nation, great or small, emerged from him.

> Whoever possesses these three things, he is of the disciples of Avraham Avinu; and [whoever possesses] three other things, he is of the disciples of Bilam the *rasha*. The disciples of

---

1 There is a tradition attributed to the Vilna Gaon that often when the Talmud refers to Bilam the Sages actually have a different erstwhile "prophet" of the non-Jews in mind — Jesus. Hereford, in *Christianity in the Talmud and Midrash*, utilizes this approach extensively. Consider the possible christialogical polemic in the following passage from *Sanhedrin* 106a–b (emphases added are my own):

"Bilam the son of Beor, the soothsayer, [the Children of Israel slayed by the sword]" (*Bemidbar* 31:8). A soothsayer? But he was a prophet! Rabbi Yochanan said: At first he was a prophet, but in the end [he was] a soothsayer. Rabbi Papa observed: This is what men say, "She who was the descendant of princes and governors *played the harlot with carpenters."*...

A certain apostate said to Rabbi Chanina, "Have you heard how old Bilam was?" He replied, "It is not actually stated, but since it is written, 'Men of blood and deceit shall not live out half their days,' [it follows that] *he was thirty-three or thirty-four years old.* He rejoined, "You have said correctly; I personally have seen *Bilam's Chronicle,* in which it is stated, 'Bilam the Lame was thirty years old when Pinchas the Robber killed him.' "

Mar, the son of Ravina, said to his sons, "In the case of all [those mentioned as having no portion in the future world] you should not take [the Biblical passages dealing with them] to expound them [to their discredit], except in the case of the wicked Bilam: whatever you find [written] about him, lecture upon it [to his disadvantage]."

Avraham Avinu [possess] a good eye, a humble spirit, and a lowly soul. The disciples of Bilam the *rasha* [possess] an evil eye, a haughty spirit, and an overambitious soul. What is [the difference] between the disciples of Avraham Avinu and the disciples of Bilam the *rasha*?

The disciples of Avraham Avinu enjoy [their share] in this world and inherit the World to Come, as it says, "To cause those who love Me to inherit substance, and that will fill their storehouses" (*Mishlei* 8:21). But the disciples of Bilam the *rasha* inherit Gehinnom and descend into the nethermost pit, as it says, "You, Lord, will bring them down to the nethermost pit. Men of blood and deceit shall not live out half their days. But as for me, I will trust in You" (*Tehillim* 55:24).

(Avot 5:19)

The verses describing Avraham and Bilam, as each one embarked on his mission, raise various issues as well. Both arise early and mount their donkeys:

> Avraham rose early in the morning, saddled his donkey, and took his two young men and Yitzchak, his son, with him. He split the wood for the offering, rose, and went to the place which God had told him.
>
> *(Bereishit 22:3)*

> Bilam rose in the morning, saddled his donkey, and went with the officers of Mo'av.
>
> *(Bemidbar 22:21)*

There is a subtle difference which may only be discerned in the Hebrew text: Avraham's form of locomotion is a *chamor*, while Bilam's is an *aton*. Avraham is the type of individual who transcends and harnesses the *chomer* (the physical, material), while Bilam simply rides on a donkey.[1] In a sense, the Torah tells us, Bilam was no

---

1 See my notes on *Vayeira* and *Chayei Sarah*, where the theme of controlling the *chomer* is explained. Only three people in the Torah ride a *chamor* — Avraham, Moshe, and Mashiach. This idea is based on the *Zohar*, and *Maharal*. See sources cited in *Vayeira*.

better than his donkey, and therefore his donkey speaks to him.

> For here was this donkey, the most stupid of all beasts, and there was the wisest of all wise men, yet as soon as she opened her mouth he [Bilam] could not stand his ground against her!
>
> *(Devarim Rabbah 20:15)*

And,

> All these [sins] were found in the wicked Bilam: Fornication and idolatry, as it is written, "Behold these [women] caused the Children of Israel to trespass against God through the counsel of Bilam in the matter of Peor" (*Bemidbar* 31:16). False witness, as it is written, '[So says] Bilam the son of Beor...who knows the knowledge of the Most High" (ibid. 24:15–16), while he did not know even the knowledge of his donkey. He perverted judgment, as it is written, "Come and I will advise you" (ibid., 14). He encroached on a domain which did not belong to him, as it is written, "I offered oxen and rams on the altar," and also, "The seven altars I have prepared" (ibid. 23:4). He fomented discord between brothers, between Israel and their Father in Heaven. As for slander, there was no other to equal him. And so with the rest.
>
> *(Zohar, Bemidbar 206b)*

The Sages accuse Bilam of almost every indecency, including bestiality with his donkey (see below).[1]

On the other hand, we find a comparison between Moshe and Bilam. When the Torah tells us that there was never a prophet among the Jews like Moshe, the Sages stress that among the non-Jews there was: Bilam.

> It was taught, "There has not arisen another prophet like Moshe in Israel" (*Devarim* 34:10). "In Israel" there had not arisen one like him, but there has arisen one like him among the nations of the world. This was so that the nations of the world would have no excuse for saying, "Had we possessed a prophet like Moshe we would have worshipped the Holy One,

1 *Sanhedrin* 105a.

> blessed be He." What prophet did they have who was like Moshe? Bilam the son of Beor.[1]
>
> *(Bemidbar Rabbah 14:20)*[2]

There is also room to compare Bilam with Yaakov: Both have visions regarding the End of Days, but Yaakov loses his vision.[3]

> Yaakov called to his sons, and said, "Gather yourselves together, that I may tell you that which shall befall you in the last days."
>
> *(Bereishit 49:1)*

---

1 The *midrash* continues and notes the distinction between Moshe and Bilam: "There was a difference, however, between the prophecy of Moshe and that of Bilam. There were three features of the prophecy of Moshe which were absent from that of Bilam. When He [God] spoke with Moshe, the latter stood on his feet, as it says, 'But as for you, stand here by Me, and I will speak to you...' (*Devarim* 5:28). With Bilam, however, He only spoke while the latter lay prone on the ground; as it says, 'Fallen down, and his eyes are opened' (*Bemidbar* 24:4). With Moshe He spoke mouth to mouth, as it says, 'With him do I speak mouth to mouth' (ibid. 12:8), while of Bilam it says, 'The saying of he who hears the words of God' (ibid. 24:4), which teaches that He did not speak with him mouth to mouth. With Moshe He spoke face to face; as it says, 'And God spoke to Moshe face to face' (*Shemot* 33:11), but with Bilam He spoke only in parables; as is confirmed by the quotation, 'He lifted up his parable, and said...' (*Bemidbar* 23:7). There were three features possessed by the prophecy of Bilam that were absent from that of Moshe. Moshe did not know who was speaking with him, [he did not know whether God or an angel spoke to him], while Bilam knew who was speaking with him, as it says, 'The saying of him who hears the words of God, who sees the vision of the Almighty' (ibid. 24:4). Moshe did not know when the Holy One, blessed be He, would speak with him, while Bilam knew, as it says, 'And knows the knowledge of the Most High' (ibid., 16). Bilam spoke with Him whenever he pleased, for it says, 'Fallen down, and his eyes are opened,' which signifies that he used to prostrate himself on his face and straightaway his eyes were opened to anything that he inquired about. Moshe, however, did not speak with Him whenever he wished. Rabbi Shimon says that Moshe also received communications from Him whenever he pleased, for it says, 'When Moshe went into the Tent of Meeting, that he might speak with Him, then — immediately — he heard the voice speaking to him' " (*Bemidbar Rabbah* 14:20).

2 See also *Sifri, Zot HaBerachah* 16. Generally, Bilam was considered to have possessed superior potential: "There have never arisen such great philosophers in the world as Bilam the son of Beor and Abnomos of Gadara" (*Bereishit Rabbah* 65:20). See also *Bereishit Rabbah* 93:10.

3 See my notes to *Vayechi*, where I cite the sources that note that Yaakov does not deliver on his promise to reveal the End of Days; at the moment he is to do so, Yaakov suddenly loses his ability to see the future.

> [Bilam said,] "I see it, but not now. I behold it, but it is not near. A star shall come out of Yaakov...."
>
> *(Bemidbar 24:17)*

This vision is generally understood as referring to the coming of Mashiach. Bilam sees that which eludes Yaakov.

There is another, less-obvious comparison of Bilam which receives great attention in Kabbalistic literature. Bilam is described as a descendant or even a reincarnation of Lavan. Targum Yonatan (Yerushalmi) in the beginning of the parashah (on *Bemidbar* 22:5) makes the identification, and Rashi (*Sanhedrin* 105a) also makes reference to this tradition. The *Zohar* details the connection:

> Lavan the Aramean was famous throughout the world as a master magician and sorcerer whose spell no man could escape. He was, in fact, the father of Beor, who was the father of Bilam, mentioned in Scripture as "Bilam the son of Beor, the sorceror" (*Yehoshua* 13:22). But for all Lavan's skill and preeminence in sorcery and magic, he could not prevail over Yaakov, though he employed all his arts to destroy him, as it says: "An Aramean designed to destroy my father" (*Devarim* 26:5).
>
> Rabbi Abba said: All the world knew that Lavan was the greatest of wizards and sorcerers and magicians, and that no one whom he wished to destroy could escape from him, and that it was from him that Bilam learned all his skill — Bilam, of whom it is written, "For I know that he whom you bless is blessed, and he whom you curse is cursed" (*Bemidbar* 22:6).
>
> *(Zohar, Bereishit 166b)*

What is it about Lavan which would cause the Sages to link him with Bilam? The Midrash notes at least one connection when it observes that God spoke to both in the evening.

> "The Lord came to Lavan the Aramean in a dream of the night" (*Bereishit* 31:24) What is the difference between the prophets of Israel and those of other nations? Rabbi Chama

> bar Chanina said: The Holy One, blessed be He, reveals Himself to heathen prophets with half speech only, as it says, "God happened upon [*vayikar*] Bilam" (*Bemidbar* 23:4).
>
> *(Bereishit Rabbah 74:7)*

The fact that God even spoke with either of these characters should be noted, but the Midrash points out that the language of the Torah is also similar. This similarity, while noteworthy, is not the full extent of the parallel. Both Lavan and Bilam misuse their words. Lavan is known for lies and deception, and Bilam for his desire to curse the Jewish people. But the comparison runs yet deeper. We are told in the Haggadah that Lavan wanted "to uproot everything," a statement for which we are hard-pressed to find evidence in the Torah. Such an accusation leveled against Eisav or Amaleik would be easily proven by the verses. But where is substantiation of Lavan's guilt?

Lavan's plan was simple, his reasoning straightforward: He wanted Yaakov to stay with him, because Lavan's own fortunes had so improved since the day that Yaakov arrived. Lavan did not want Yaakov to leave and he claimed that Yaakov's children were also his own. Where is the evil in such a magnanimous statement? Lavan was not in favor of Yaakov's independence. He wanted Yaakov and his children — Lavan's grandchildren — to stay. Yet had Yaakov stayed, the nation of Israel would never have emerged; it would have been subsumed within the nation of Lavan. By not allowing the nation to become a nation, the Haggadah says, "Lavan wanted to uproot everything."

This insight allows us to see how Bilam is the "new and improved" model of Lavan. He also wanted to destroy the nation of Israel, not by Lavan's assimilation technique, but rather by eradication. Only later, when Bilam senses that he will be unable to destroy the nation using his original tactics does he resort to plan B, assimilation.

We have seen that Bilam remains an individual, without confederates. The Jews are a nation, a nation with national pride on a mission, on their way to a collective rendezvous with destiny. This is what strikes Bilam as he observes the Jewish people and their elevated sense of community. We can imagine his twisted self-justification, that man cannot exist in a community, that a community drains the resources of the elite. Bilam had no need for a nation; such needs were for others, for the weak. He was Bilam — *belo am*, without a nation. When he observed the encampment of the Israelites, he realized that they managed to coexist without strife, as Rashi says:

> He saw that the openings of their tents did not face one another.
>
> *(Rashi, Bemidbar 24:5; based on Bava Batra 60a)*

He saw a sincere concern for morality, balanced with a strong sense of community. He saw individuals living together in harmony, forming a community without losing their sense of individuality.

Ultimately, Bilam arrived at a new plan, as is indicated at the end of the parashah.[1] Bilam advised that the women of Mo'av come down to the camp of Israel and attempt to wreak havoc from within, creating a sort of fifth estate. He realized that when united against an external threat, the Jews are invincible; the way to bring them to their knees is to break down the most basic relationships, between husband and wife. The destruction of the rest of the com-

---

1 The *Zohar* cites a tradition that the strategy to seduce the Jewish people originated in Midyan: "All the nefarious plan of Peor was from Midyan. On their advice they hired Bilam, and when they saw that Bilam could not prevail, they adopted another plan and prostituted their daughters and wives more than Mo'av. They planned with their prince that he should prostitute his daughter, thinking to catch Moshe in their net. They invested her with all kinds of magic in order to catch their chief, but God 'turns the wise backwards.' They foresaw that a chief of the Israelites would be caught in their net, but they did not understand what they foresaw. They enjoined her not to unite herself with any man save Moshe. She said to them, 'How shall I know him?' They said, 'Join the man before whom you see all others rise, but no other.' When Zimri, son of Salu, came, fifty-nine thousand of the tribe of Shimon rose before him, as he was their prince. She thought he was Moshe and joined him. When all the rest saw this they did likewise, with the consequences that we know. Thus all was from Midyan, and therefore Midyan was punished" (*Zohar, Bemidbar* 190a).

munity would surely follow.[1]

Bilam's strategy is outlined in stages in the text:

> Israel settled in Shittim, and the nation began to commit harlotry with the daughters of Mo'av. They [the daughters of Mo'av] called the nation to the sacrifices of their gods. The nation ate and bowed down to their gods. Israel became attached to Baal Peor; and the anger of the God was kindled against Israel.
>
> *(Bemidbar 25:1–3)*

He calls upon the women of Mo'av to seduce the men of Israel, both sexually and religiously. "Start with their bodies, but do not stop until you have their minds as well," Bilam instructs.

> The daughters of Mo'av followed Bilam's counsel, as is borne out by the text, "Behold, these caused the Children of Israel, through the counsel of Bilam, to revolt so as to break faith with the Lord in the matter of Peor" (*Bemidbar* 31:16). They made booths for themselves and placed in them harlots in whose hands were all types of desirable objects. An old woman would sit outside and keep watch for the girl who was inside the shop. When the Israelites passed by to purchase an article in the bazaar, the old woman would say to him: "Young man! Would you not like some linen clothing that comes from Beit She'an?" She would show it to him and say, "Go inside and you will see some lovely articles!"
>
> The old woman would ask him for a higher price and the girl for a lower. After this the girl would say to him, "You are now like one of the family. Sit down and choose whatever you desire for yourself!"
>
> A flask of wine stood by her, and as yet the wine of heathens had not been forbidden. A young woman would come out adorned and perfumed and would entice him, saying, "Why is

1 According to the Midrash, the people of Moav were open to this type of plan due to their lineage. See *Bemidbar Rabbah* 20:23.

it that though we love you, you hate us? Take this item for nothing! Are we not all the children of one man? The children of Terach, the father of Avraham? If you do not wish to eat of our sacrifices and of our cooking, behold, we have calves and cocks. Slaughter them in accordance with your own precepts and eat!"

Thereupon she would make him drink the wine, and the Satan would burn within him and he would be led astray after her; for it says, "Harlotry, wine, and new wine take away the heart" (*Hoshea* 4:11).

According to some authorities Bilam commanded them not to make them drink wine, so that they might not be judged as drunkards but as deliberate sinners. Once the Israelite solicited [the girl], she would say to him, "I will not listen to you until you slaughter this animal to Peor and bow down to the idol."

He would object, "I will not bow down to idols!"

She would answer him, "You will only appear as though you are uncovering yourself."

And so he would be led astray after her and do as he was bidden. This explains why the Sages have said that if a man uncovers himself before Baal Peor, by that act he worships it; for it says, "And bowed down to [i.e., worshipped] their gods."

"Israel became attached [*vayitzamed*] to Baal Peor" — At first they entered unobtrusively, but in the end they came in jointly [*tzemidim*], in pairs, like a yoke [*tzemed*] of oxen.

(Bemidbar Rabbah 20:23)

Bilam's philosophy embraced Baal Peor, whose worship included scatological behavior which seems bizarre from a modern perspective. The specific worship included defecating in front of the idol. While this seems to defy logic, in reality Baal Peor was only one step beyond pantheism. The worshipers of Baal Peor believed that all of nature and the natural processes are holy. Therefore, even defecating became an acceptable mode of worship. This also explains the public sexual display of Zimri at the conclusion of the parashah. If one considers all of nature holy, then all behavior can be justified, even the bestiality of which Bilam was accused. By spreading the word of Baal Peor, the holiness of the Jewish community was placed in mortal danger. This was Bilam's new plan: Cause the destruction of the community through assimilation and unholy behavior.

It is interesting that the individuals who eventually take Bilam's life are Pinchas and Yehoshua.[1]

> God spoke to Moshe, saying, "Avenge the Children of Israel from the Midyanites; afterwards you shall be gathered to your people."
>
> Moshe spoke to the nation, saying, "Arm some of yourselves for war, and let them go against the Midyanites, and execute God's vengeance in Midyan. A thousand from every tribe, of all the tribes of Israel, shall you send to the war."
>
> A thousand out of every tribe were delivered from the thousands of Israel, twelve thousand armed for war. Moshe sent them to the war, a thousand of every tribe, them and Pinchas, son of Elazar the Kohein, to the war, with holy instruments and trumpets to blow, in his hand. They warred against the Midyanites, as God commanded Moshe, and they killed all the males. They killed the kings of Midyan, beside the rest of the slain ones; that is, Evi, Rekem, Tzur, Chur, and Reva, five kings of Midyan. And Bilam, son of Beor, they also killed by the sword.
>
> *(Bemidbar 31:1–8)*

Pinchas goes to battle, but his role seems purely spiritual; presumably the military leader is Yehoshua. Yehoshua is from the tribe of Yosef. It was Yosef, perhaps more than any other figure in our history, who knew how to withstand the very temptations Bilam used to ensnare the Jewish people. (Interestingly, it was immediately following the birth of Yosef that Yaakov informs his family that it is time for them to return to Israel, time for the nation of Is-

1 The *Zohar* credits Pinchas with the vengeance on Bil'am. See *Zohar, Bemidbar 194a.*

rael to emerge![1]) The Gemara tells us that one of the considerations of Pinchas going to battle was the opportunity to avenge the misdeeds perpetrated upon Yosef by the Midyanites. Although the connection between Pinchas and Yosef seems obscure, the Gemara explains that Pinchas was descended from Yosef on his maternal side.[2]

It is also fascinating that it is Rachel, mother of Yosef, who tries to steal her father's idols. She fears neither Lavan nor the power of his gods. How appropriate, then, that Yehoshua is her descendant, and he will lead the battle to kill Bilam, "the magician." Yehoshua fears neither Bilam nor his magic.

Perhaps this explains the association between Bilam and Lavan: Neither of them were interested in the existence of the nation of Israel. Lavan tried to prevent the emergence of a nation via assimilation. Bilam was willing to curse and kill the entire nation. Only when that would not work was he willing to "settle" for assimilation. The sad part of the story is that there were thousands among the Jewish people who were enticed and fell into the trap laid by Bilam and his henchmen. Perhaps this is the darker side of the parashah's message: Throughout history there have been those who plotted the destruction of the Jewish people, yet time and time

1 "It says of Bilam that 'he lifted up his eyes and saw Israel dwelling according to their tribes' (*Bemidbar* 24:2). The tribe of Yosef and the tribe of Binyamin were there: the tribe of Yosef, over whom the evil eye has no power, and the tribe of Binyamin, who also has no fear of the evil eye. Bilam had said, 'I will cross this line which is of no account and look well at them.' Rachel was there, and when she saw that his eye was sharpened to do them hurt, she went forth and spread her wings over them and covered her sons. Hence it says, 'The spirit of the Lord came upon him' (ibid.) — to wit, upon Israel, whom He was protecting, and straightway Bilam retired. So at first the son protected the mother and later the mother protected the sons; for so God had said at the time when [Yosef] saved his mother from the eye of the wicked Eisav" (*Zohar, Bemidbar* 203a).

It is interesting to note that both Yosef and his mother are described as "*yefei einayim*" (beautiful of eye). This serves as an antidote to Bilam, the purveyor of *ayin hara*, evil eye (*Avot* 5:19). See my comments on *Mikeitz*, where I pointed out that the *yefei einayim* was manifested by self-sacrifice for others. This attribute is surely foreign to Bilam, the ultimate individualist.

2 Other facets of Pinchas's lineage will be considered in *Parashat Pinchas*. For the identification between Yosef and Pinchas, see *Sotah* 43a.

again God frustrated their plans. When we remain a unified nation, all working toward a common goal without sacrificing our individuality and our holiness, we know that no nation, no magic, and no curses can harm us.

> How good are your tents, Yaakov, and your tabernacles, Israel.
> *(Ibid. 24:5)*

Parashat Pinchas

Pinchas and Zimri

At the conclusion of last week's parashah, we read about the act of Zimri[1] and the response of Pinchas. The episode is described as follows:

> A man from the Children of Israel brought the Midyanite woman in front of his brethren, in sight of Moshe and the entire community, [and they engaged in sexual intercourse (*Sanhedrin* 82b)] in front of the Ohel Mo'ed. Pinchas the son of Elazar, son of Aharon the Kohein, saw them. He arose from the community and took a spear in his hand. He approached the man of Israel by the Tent and he pierced them both by the Tent.... The plague of the Children of Israel was stopped.
>
> *(Bemidbar 25:6–8)*

While the story was told last week, in *Balak*, certain elements of the episode are held in abeyance until this week's parashah, *Pinchas*. This parashah, named for the protagonist of the episode,

1 The Midrash cites a number of names for Zimri: "Zimri had six names: Zimri, Ben Salu, Shaul, Ben HaKena'anit, Shelumiel, Ben Tzurishadai. He was called 'Zimri' because he became, on account of the Midyanite woman, like a rotten [*muzeret*] egg; 'Ben Salu' because he was a son [*ben*] who outweighed [*silla*] in sin the rest of his family; 'Shaul' because he lent [*hish'il*] himself to transgression; 'Ben HaKena'anit' because he acted in accordance with the practice of Canaan [Kena'an]. And what was his real name? Shelumiel" (*Bemidbar Rabbah* 21:3).

informs us of the lineage of the perpetrators of the deed:

> The name of the man of Israel who was killed — together with the Midyanite woman — was Zimri son of Salu, the leader of the tribe of Shimon. And the name of the Midyanite woman killed was Kozbi daughter of Tzur — the head of a house of Midyan.
> *(Ibid. 25:14–15)*

These were not simple people; both were aristocrats, from leading families of their respective tribes. Rashi points to this fact as an indication of the Midyanites' burning hatred for the Jewish people. They were willing to send their own daughters into the fray. Targum Yonatan identifies Tzur with none other than Balak himself! His hatred was so profound that he was willing to prostitute his own daughter for the chance to corrupt the Jews in the process.

Pinchas, upon viewing this scene, acts in what the Torah describes as a "zealous" rage, and kills them both in order to put an end to the desecration. The act of Pinchas is the archetypical zealous act; others in the future who acted in a similar manner have been associated with Pinchas. Most notably, Eliyahu the Prophet is identified by the Sages as Pinchas himself, if not literally, then at least in the mystical sense; these two are said to share a common soul (see *Targum Yonatan* [Yerushalmi], *Shemot* 6:18).[1]

1 The source for Pinchas being identified with Eliyahu is somewhat elusive, though it seems to be assumed in a number of Talmudic and Midrashic sources. See *Bava Metzia* 114a–b: "Rabbah bar Abuha met Eliyahu standing in a non-Jewish cemetery.... He [Rabbah] said to him, 'Are you not a *kohein*? Why, then, do you stand in a cemetery?' " Only the assumption that Eliyahu is Pinchas the Kohein could lie at the basis of this and other similar discussions.

Medieval scholars treat the tradition as one which is subject to debate, and the question of Eliyahu being a *kohein* is the practical difference which would decide this debate. See *Rashbam, Ramban, Rosh,* and *Rashba* in *Bava Batra* 121b; and *Tosafot HaRosh, Kiddushin* 70a. For the specific identification, see *Zohar, Shemot* 190a; *Zohar Chadash, Rut, Maamar* "Mi Hu Eliyahu;" *Batei Midrashot* 1; and *Midrash Shocher Tov* (in manuscript), *Mizmor* 63.

But see the following Midrash, where Eliyahu himself settles the issue! "The Rabbis debated: To which tribe did Eliyahu belong? Rabbi Elazar said: To Binyamin, for it is written, 'And Yaareshiyah and Eliyah and Zichri were the sons of Yerocham.... All these were the sons of Binyamin' (*Divrei HaYamim* I 8:27, 40). ... On one occasion our Rabbis were debating about him [Eliyahu], some maintaining

However, it is possible to view this episode as more than a zealous act by Pinchas. Let us consider the motivation of the perpetrators, Kozbi and Zimri. These people were both leaders in their own right, each in their respective communities. Their "performance" followed the invasion of the idolatry of Baal Peor into the Israelite camp. Once this foreign cultic practice made inroads, what followed was the orgiastic, public display of behavior which in Jewish life is considered private and holy.

As we noted last week, one of the cultic rites in the worship of Baal Peor was defecating in the presence of the idol, reflecting the exalted, "holy" status of nature in the philosophy of Baal Peor worship. Behavior indicating a reverence of nature and all things natural were accepted practices. Once this "philosophy" is understood, the act of Kozbi and Zimri, from their perspective, was not a "crime of passion" as it were, but the culmination of worship of Baal Peor. Zimri was trying to make an ideological point; thus, the text stresses that he performed his act in front of the Ohel Mo'ed.

> ...in front of the Ohel Mo'ed. Pinchas the son of Elazar, son of Aharon the Kohein, saw them. He arose from the community and took a spear in his hand. He approached the man of Israel by the Tent and he pierced them both by the Tent.

Had this been an act of passion, surely the two of them could have slipped away, out of sight. But this was a public display, an act of rebellion, an act dictated by ideology — an act of fanaticism. They therefore chose the Ohel Mo'ed as the location for their tryst. The act of Zimri and Kozbi was premeditated. As leaders, they apparently had a well-thought-out plan of how to deliver the Jewish

---

that he belonged to the tribe of Gad, others, to the tribe of Binyamin. Whereupon he came and stood before them and said, 'Sirs, why do you debate about me? I am a descendant of Rachel [from Binyamin]' " (*Bereishit Rabbah* 71:9).

Perhaps, just as Pinchas was not born a *kohein*, and achieves the *kehunah* at a later stage, Eliyahu also achieves the status of a *kohein* at a later stage because he has the soul of Pinchas.

people from the holiness of the teachings of Moshe into the depravity of Baal Peor.

> "And the name of the Midyanite woman killed was Kozbi daughter of Tzur — the head of a house of Midyan." This serves to inform you to what extent the Midyanites had sacrificed themselves! They had actually made a king's daughter available to harlotry; as it says, "They killed the kings of Midyan beside the rest of the slain ones; that is, Evi, Rekem, Tzur..." (*Bemidbar* 31:8). If Tzur, the greatest of them all, though a king, made his daughter available, who would not make his available also? In consequence of his having degraded himself and made his daughter disgrace herself in public, Scripture reduced him to an inferior position and mentioned him third. In truth, however, he was king over them all.
>
> *(Bemidbar Rabbah 21:3)*

In a sense, Zimri is no less a fanatic than Pinchas, although they reflect different sides, very different directions. The fanaticism of Pinchas, and of Zimri, should come as no surprise, as it has its antecedent in *Bereishit*. In order to appreciate this connection we should recall the teachings at the beginning of this week's parashah: Pinchas was "the son of Elazar, son of Aharon the Kohein." He was from the tribe of Levi. Zimri was the "son of Salu, the leader of the tribe of Shimon." Shimon and Levi, together again, as in the past:

> Shimon and Levi are brothers.
>
> *(Bereishit 49:5)*

They are united, joined by their rage and zealousness. Yaakov, on his deathbed, curses this rage:

> Let their rage be cursed for it is powerful, and their wrath for it is harsh....
>
> *(Bereishit 49:7)*

What was it that Shimon and Levi did to evoke this response from their aged father? What was it that caused Yaakov to leave his sons with this legacy? To answer these questions we must return to their youth.

Our forefather Yaakov had a difficult life. He had a brother who was pining to kill him and a father-in-law who abused him. Upon his return to the Land of Israel after twenty-two years away from his parents, his daughter, Dinah, ventured away from her home to see how the other half lived. There she was ensnared in a "relationship" with Shechem the son of Chamor, who was smitten by her and took her against her will.

Shechem's father approached Yaakov in an attempt to work things out. The children of Yaakov surreptitiously approached Chamor and advised him to circumcise his entire tribe, which he did. When they were at the apex of their pain, Shimon and Levi entered the town and annihilated it. Yaakov, upset at this drastic move, rebuked his sons for putting him in such a precarious situation. By attacking such a large tribe, when Yaakov and his children were so small in number, Shimon and Levi had placed the entire Jewish nation in danger — other neighboring tribes might seek retribution. Shimon and Levi answer: "Will our sister be made into a prostitute?" (*Bereishit* 34:31). Yaakov leaves that question hanging, without response, until his deathbed, when he curses their rage.

The episode of Dinah and Shechem serves as an interesting parallel to the story of Zimri and Kozbi.[1] Shechem is the son of the head of a tribe, and Dinah is the daughter of Yaakov, also the leader of a people.[2] There, Shimon and Levi interpret the violation in national terms and attack the perpetrator of this atrocity. Their attack is ideological, yet motivated by anger, and may therefore be labeled an act of zealousness. Yaakov, for his part, is far more pragmatic and sees the situation in practical terms. Consequently, Yaakov

1 According to the Arizal, Zimri and Kozbi are reincarnations of Shechem and Dinah respectively. Cited by Rav Tzaddok HaKohen in *Pri Tzaddik, Parashat Pinchas; Machshevet Charutz*, ch. 7; *Dover Tzedek*, section 2; and *Divrei Sofrim*, section 34.

2 See my comments to *Vayeitzei*, where this issue is discussed in depth.

curses their anger, but he doesn't stop there:

> Shimon and Levi are brothers; instruments of cruelty are their swords. May my soul not come into their council, and may my honor not be united to their assembly; for in their anger they killed a man, and in their wanton will they lamed an ox. Let their rage be cursed for it is powerful, and their wrath for it is harsh. I will divide them in Yaakov and disperse them in Israel.
>
> *(Bereishit 49:5–7)*

Yaakov declares that these two sons, and their descendants, will be divided, for when they are united, their rage becomes obsessive and debilitating. The conspiracy against Yosef was instigated by Shimon and Levi (*Rashi, Bereishit* 49:6). Yaakov therefore prays for their division, for the danger lies in their unification.

The Midrash identifies this theme when it notes the inappropriateness of Zimri's behavior.

> "Zimri, the son of Salu" — Scripture states this about him with astonishment. It says, "Whoever breaks through a fence, a serpent shall bite him" (*Kohelet* 10:8). His ancestor was the first to display jealousy in regard to harlotry, as it says, "Two of the sons of Yaakov, Shimon and Levi...took each man his sword...and killed all the males" (*Bereishit* 34:25). Yet this man broke through the fence which his father had made!
>
> *(Bereishit Rabbah 21:3)*

Over the years, the descendants of Shimon and Levi take different directions. Levi's descendants become the elite of the Jewish people. On a personal level, when Moshe, a descendant of Levi, sees an Egyptian beating a Jewish slave, he rises up to defend the Jew and kills the Egyptian. Later, when the people worship the golden calf, Moshe calls out:

> "Whoever sides with God join me!" — and the entire tribe of Levi gathered about.
>
> *(Shemot 32:26)*

Here we see a zealousness on the part of Levi directed toward God against those who had rebelled. In this instance, Shimon is silent. Later on in history, other descendants of Levi, the Maccabees, lead a rebellion against the Greek Empire. We can trace the strain of zealousness in the tribe of Levi, but we must notice how differently this zealousness manifests itself in the tribe of Shimon.

In the case of Zimri, why should the entire tribe of Shimon be attacked for the indiscretion of one of its members? Clearly, the rebellion led by Zimri was not the act of one man. *Parashat Balak* concludes with the plague that took twenty-four thousand lives.[1] In this week's parashah, the census numbers the tribe of Shimon at 22,200 (*Bemidbar* 26:14). At the previous census, they numbered 59,300 (ibid. 1:23). We see that the largest negative differential in any tribe was in the tribe of Shimon; apparently, most or all of the dead were from that tribe. Likewise, Rashi concludes:

> From the number of people missing from the tribe compared to the previous counting in the Sinai Desert, it seems that all twenty-four thousand died from the tribe of Shimon.
>
> *(Rashi, Bemidbar 26:13)*

We may thus conclude that Zimri had supporters among the rank and file of his tribe. In other words, this was a rebellion against Moshe and God, spearheaded by Zimri but followed by great numbers of the tribe of Shimon. A stark and powerful contrast may be drawn: The entire tribe of Levi stands by Moshe's side in the aftermath of the golden calf, ready to do all for God, while the entire tribe of Shimon stands at the side of Zimri. The Gemara describes how the tribe of Shimon supported Zimri:

> "Moshe said to the judges of Israel[, 'Each man should kill his men that are attached to Baal Peor'] (*Bemidbar* 25:5). Thereupon the tribe of Shimon went to Zimri son of Salu and said to him, "Capital punishment is being meted out, yet you sit si-

1 Mystical sources connect these twenty-four thousand with the deaths of Rabbi Akiva's twenty-four thousand students.

lent [i.e., inactive]?"

What did he do? He arose and assembled twenty-four thousand Israelites and went to Kozbi, and said to her, "Surrender yourself to me."

She replied, "I am a king's daughter, and thus has my father instructed me, 'You shall yield only to their greatest man.' "

"I too," he replied, "am the prince of a tribe; moreover, my tribe is greater than his [Moshe's], for mine is second in birth, while his is third." He then seized her by her coiffure and brought her before Moshe. "Son of Amram," exclaimed he, "is this woman forbidden or permitted? And should you say, 'She is forbidden,' who permitted Yitro's daughter to you?"

At that moment Moshe forgot the halachah [concerning intimacy with a heathen woman], and all the people burst into tears; hence it is written, "And they were weeping before the door of the Ohel Mo'ed." And it is also written, "Pinchas, the son of Elazar, the son of Aharon the Kohein, saw it." What did he see? Rav said: He saw what was happening and remembered the halachah, and said to him, "Great-uncle! Did you not teach us this on your descent from Mount Sinai: He who cohabits with a heathen woman is punished by zealots?"

He replied, "He who reads the letter, let him be the agent [to carry out its instructions]."

Shmuel said: He saw that "There is no wisdom, no understanding, and no counsel against God" (*Mishlei* 21:30). Whenever the Divine Name is being profaned, honor must not be paid to one's teacher.

Rabbi Yitzchak said in Rabbi Elazar's name: He saw the angel wreaking destruction among the people. "He arose from the community and took a spear in his hand"; hence one may not enter the house of learning with weapons. He removed its point and placed it in his undergarment, and walked leaning upon the stock [of the spear, into which the pointed blade is inserted]. As soon as he reached the tribe of Shimon, he ex-

> claimed, "Where do we find that the tribe of Levi is greater than that of Shimon? [i.e., I too wish to indulge.]"
>
> They said, "Let him enter. He too enters to satisfy his lust. These abstainers have now declared the matter permissible."
>
> *(Sanhedrin 82a–b)*

The description of the Gemara is of a broad-based rebellion, not the act of one man.

When Pinchas took action against Zimri, there were those who attacked him, calling his behavior unacceptable, "un-Jewish." They claimed that Pinchas must have inherited some foreign traits from his maternal grandfather, Yitro. The Midrash explains that our parashah introduces Pinchas as a descendant of Aharon, as if to attribute Pinchas's response to Aharon's behavior, and not to an alien, pagan source.

> What reason had the Holy One, blessed be He, for stating the lineage of Pinchas after this particular incident?... You find that when Zimri was stabbed the tribe rose up against Pinchas and said, "Have you ever seen such a thing? This son of Putiel [Yitro], whose maternal grandfather fattened calves for idol-worship, has killed a leader of Israel!" Consequently Scripture comes and declares his lineage, by stating, "Pinchas, the son of Eliezer, the son of Aharon the Kohein."
>
> *(Bemidbar Rabbah 21:3)*

Aharon, too, was from the tribe of Levi. Perhaps the masses saw Aharon only as a lover of peace, and not as a passionate defender of truth. Aharon was a very sympathetic figure, and the people must have seen Pinchas's behavior as a radical departure from Aharon's. Moreover, the people must have reasoned that if Moshe did not respond as Pinchas did, Pinchas's behavior must have been off the mark: How could someone be more "religious" than Moshe?

On his deathbed, Yaakov attacked Shimon and Levi's anger; arguably, there is place for the behavior, but not when it is motivated by anger. So, too, there is an appropriate time and place for action of the sort that Pinchas took. Yaakov warned specifically against the merger of the two problematic tribes. While there may be a place for an individual's extralegal response, when such action becomes the fusing point of two tribes, the danger of anger for its own sake and of the resultant zealousness is too great. Once the tribes were divided, the descendants of Levi become the prototypical servants of God, the *kohanim* and *Levi'im*, who would between them perform the Temple service. Shimon, on the other hand, never succeeds in using anger in a positive manner.

Anger is a particularly dangerous trait. The Sages compare it to idolatry, for when a person feels anger he loses control and is no longer serving God. Levi was able to control the anger, retaining a single-minded, extreme relationship with God. This complete dedication to the Divine is what allowed members of this tribe to be *kohanim*. At times this intensity of purpose manifested itself in the Temple, and at times it manifested itself on the battlefield, as with the Maccabees.[1] The crucial point is the single-minded dedication to God. This trait, while being the domain of Levi, can be adopted by any Jew. Rambam, in a celebrated passage, comments:

> Not only the tribe of Levi, but any man of the entire world whose spirit moves him, and causes him to separate and stand in front of God to serve Him and worship Him, in order to know God, and walks along a straight path as God has made him and rejects the numerous calculations which occupy most men, this person becomes sanctified, a Holy of Holies, and God will be his lot, his portion forever and ever....
>
> *(Hilchot Shemittah V'Yovel 13:12)*

Any Jew can become a "Holy of Holies." What is needed is single-minded dedication to God, as was manifested by Pinchas. His love of God required his extreme response. The fanatical behavior of Zimri, which was followed by his tribe of Shimon, had to be

1 The main antagonists of the Maccabees were the Hellenists, who were also predominantly *kohanim*. In the following generation, the Sadducees were also from the tribe of Levi. Rambam, in his commentary to *Avot*, draws a connection between the Hellenists and the Sadducees. Likewise, the rebellion of Korach was lead by a member of Levi.

stopped. But to be holy one cannot have a personal agenda, as Zimri did. Perhaps Zimri deluded himself into believing that he was following the example of his great-grandfather Shimon. Pinchas, on the other hand, stood to gain nothing personally. Quite the contrary, his action was ridiculed by the other leaders.[1]

Pinchas was motivated by a profound love of God, which would not give in to public opinion or political expediency. For this reason he was rewarded with the Covenant of Peace. The mandate of the *kohanim* is to bring peace to the world. Sometimes it is accomplished by speaking words of peace, but at other times it is accomplished by force.[2] The reward which Pinchas receives gives us insight into his motivation: He desperately wanted peace, but the obscenity unfolding before his eyes left him no choice.

We are reminded of Hillel's teaching in the *mishnah* in *Avot*:

> Be like the students of Aharon: love peace and pursue peace.
> *(Avot 1:12)*

Occasionally the pursuit requires an unconventional display of love. The *kohanim* were imbued with love — love for God and their fellow man. The anger which Yaakov cursed had been replaced by love. Therefore, the tribe of Levi excelled. On the other hand, the tribe of Shimon represented the greatest failure during the years spent in the desert. Witness to this is borne by Moshe's final blessings to the tribes at the conclusion of *Devarim*. The conceptual and linguistic similarities to Yaakov's blessings are numerous, but the most striking difference between the blessings lies in Moshe's final words to Shimon and Levi. Whereas Yaakov gave harsh rebuke, Levi now receives a beautiful blessing:

---

1 *Rashi, Bemidbar* 25:11, based on *Sanhedrin* 82b.

2 The law is that a *kohein* who kills is disqualified from serving in the Temple. Ironically, by killing Pinchas became worthy of being a *kohein*. "It is a rule that a *kohein* who kills a human being becomes disqualified for the priesthood, and therefore by rights Pinchas should have been disqualified. But because he was zealous for the Holy One, blessed be He, the priesthood was assigned to him and to his descendants in perpetuity" (*Zohar, Bemidbar* 214a). The Sefat Emet explains that this is why Pinchas was not a *kohein* until this point. Had he been a *kohein*, he would have been unfit. Now, by virtue of his action, he becomes fit to serve.

> Of Levi he said, "Let Your *tumim* and Your *urim* be with Your pious one, whom You did test at Massah, and with whom You fought at the waters of Merivah. [He] said of his father and of his mother, 'I have not seen him'; nor did he acknowledge his brothers, nor knew his own children; for they have observed Your word and kept Your covenant. They shall teach Yaakov Your judgments, and Israel Your Torah; they shall put incense before You, and whole burnt sacrifice upon Your altar. God, bless his substance, and accept the work of his hands; strike through the loins of those who rise against him, and of those who hate him, so that they do not rise again."
>
> *(Devarim 33:8–11)*

The tribe of Levi is now called the "pious ones." The members of the tribe will be the intellectual and spiritual vanguard entrusted with the role of teaching Torah to the other tribes. Shimon, on the other hand, stands out as the only tribe to receive no blessing, no comment, from Moshe — only silence. And it is a silence which speaks volumes. This tribe's potential for greatness was not realized. Yaakov called for the separation of the tribes, and, indeed, they were separated, following two different paths to two different destinies.

The conflict of Zimri and Pinchas serves as a microcosm of this larger issue, of two tribes traveling in two different directions, one toward greatness, and the other toward infamy. Levi founded its unique path to God, but Shimon did not. We see in this week's parashah that two people, and indeed two tribes, can have the same makeup, the same characteristics, but not reach the same goal. Achieving greatness is less a function of inborn traits than a function of the use we make of those traits.

Parashiyot Matot and Massai

Reuven and Gad

The sequence of events in *Parashat Matot* is not immediately understood. The parashah begins with a discourse on the laws of oaths. The heads of the community, *rashei matot,* were gathered together to receive these laws, hence the parashah's name.

Next, the Torah calls for vengeance against the Midyanites, for their crime against the Jewish people. The Torah goes on to describe the ensuing battle and the spoils of war with which the victorious army returns. The subsequent section tells about the tribes of Reuven and Gad, who request that they be allotted the grazing land outside of Israel, on the east bank of the Jordan River, in order to accommodate their very large herds. Moshe chastises them for this request, and an arrangement is reached whereby these tribes will aid their brethren in the conquest, and only afterwards return to their lands across the River. The Torah adds that half of the tribe of Menasheh, son of Yosef, will join them. The connection with the laws of oaths, brought at the beginning of this parashah, is not immediately clear.

A closer reading of the text reveals that there is, in fact, a common thread connecting the various topics in *Matot*: the power of words. The parashah began with the laws of oaths, which demonstrate clearly the power of words to effect change and to create new reality. The next section of text recounts the vengeance against Midyan. The wrath of Israel is centered on Bilam, who attempted to curse the Jewish people:

> Bilam the son of Beor was killed by the sword.
>
> *(Bemidbar 31:8)*

Finally, the parashah ends with the "deal" which the tribes of Reuven and Gad reached with Moshe. Many details of the laws of conditions are derived from this deal, seen in the halachic literature as the archetypical condition.

> Any stipulation which is not like that of the children of Gad and the children of Reuven is not a [valid] stipulation, [because] it is written, "[Moshe] said to them, 'If the children of Gad and the children of Reuven will pass with you over the Jordan [...then you shall give them the land of Gil'ad for a possession]' " (*Bemidbar* 32:29). And it is also written, " 'But if they will not pass over with you armed, then they shall have possessions among you in the land of Canaan' " (ibid., 30).
>
> *(Kiddushin 61a)*

This last episode, involving the tribes of Reuven and Gad, deserves further attention. It seems quite strange that two tribes are willing to form an allegiance and avoid entering the Land of Israel. Yet these tribes have a number of things in common. First, they are both firstborn to their respective mothers, Leah and Zilpah. Furthermore, they have a common marching formation: the two were in the same group, and when they marched they surrounded the tribe of Shimon.[1] According to the Midrash, these two tribes were exceptionally wealthy and therefore preferred the greener pastures outside the Land of Israel.

> Likewise, in the case of the children of Gad and the children of Reuven, you find that they were rich, possessing large num-

1 The plan was for them to positively influence the tribe of Shimon (*Bemidbar Rabbah* 2:10).

> bers of cattle, but they loved their money and settled outside the Land of Israel. Consequently, they were the first of all the tribes to go into exile, as is borne out by the text, "And he [the King of Ashur] carried them away, the Reuvenites, the Gadites, the half-tribe of Menasheh" (*Divrei HaYamim* I 5:26). What brought it on them? The fact that they separated themselves from their brethren because of their possessions. Where can we infer this from? From what is written in the Torah — "The children of Reuven...had a very great multitude of cattle" (*Bemidbar* 32:1).
>
> *(Bemidbar Rabbah 22:7)*

The Midrash also sees the section dealing with the spoils of war as directed against these two tribes, as if to say, "If it is money which you seek, God has many ways of providing."

> Know that when He [God] wished the sons of Reuven and Gad to become wealthy, He sent the Midyanites before them. What is written before this? "The Children of Israel took captive the women of Midyan, their small children, and all their cattle" (*Bemidbar* 31:9). And afterward it says, "The children of Reuven and the children of Gad had a very great multitude of cattle" (ibid. 32:1).
>
> *(Bemidbar Rabbah 22:8)*

The Midrash goes to great lengths to point out the warped value system of these tribes. When they approach Moshe to argue their case and make their request, they mention their cattle before their children:

> We will build sheepfolds for our cattle and cities for our young children.
>
> *(Bemidbar 32:16)*

When Moshe responds, he places the children before the cattle:

> Build cities for your young children and sheepfolds for your cattle.
>
> *(Ibid., 24)*

The Midrash explains the shift in order:

> The expression "A wise man's understanding is at his right hand" (*Kohelet* 10:2) applies to Moshe, while "A fool's understanding is at his left" (ibid.) applies to the children of Reuven and the children of Gad, who made the main thing the subordinate and put the subordinate thing first. For they cherished their property more than human life, saying to Moshe: "We will build sheepfolds for our cattle and cities for our young children." Moshe said to them, "That is not right! Rather, do the more important things first. Build cities for your young children and [afterward] sheepfolds for your children."...
>
> The Holy One, blessed be He, said to them, "Since you have shown greater love for your cattle than for human souls, by your life, there will be no blessing in it." Of them it says, "An estate may be gotten hastily at the beginning, but its end shall not be blessed" (*Mishlei* 20:21). In the same strain, it says, "Do not toil to be rich; cease from your own wisdom" (ibid. 23:4). Who is rich? He who is contented with his lot, as it says, "When you eat [the fruits] of the labor of your hands, you shall be happy, and it shall be good for you" (*Tehillim* 128:2).
>
> *(Bemidbar Rabbah 22:9)*

The message is subtle but clear: Owning cattle is fine, but do not, even for one second, place material wealth above your children. We can only wonder at the confusion of values which the text brings into focus. This same confusion may be discerned in another, related teaching: The Torah speaks of the cities built as refuge for those who killed accidentally. Three cities were built in Israel proper, while another three were built in the territory across the Jordan settled by Reuven, Gad, and Menasheh. Rashi, drawing from the Gemara, points out this obvious inequity, the division so disproportionate to the relative populations (*Rashi, Bemidbar* 35:14). Why would two and a half tribes require the same number of cities of refuge as nine and a half tribes? The Gemara explains that there was a disproportionate frequency of bloodshed in this small territory.

> Moshe set apart three cities in Transjordan, and corresponding to them Yehoshua set apart [others] in the Land of Canaan. They corresponded on opposite sides like a double row [of trees] in a vineyard: Chevron in Yehudah corresponding to Betzer in the desert; Shechem in Mount Efrayim corresponding to Ramot in Gil'ad; Kadesh in Mount Naftali corresponding to Golan in Bashan. "You shall divide [the border of the Land] into three parts" (*Devarim* 19:3) means that they shall form triads, [namely,] that the distance from the southern boundary to Chevron should be similar to that from Chevron to Shechem; and that from Chevron to Shechem similar to that from Shechem to Kadesh; and that from Shechem to Kadesh similar to that from Kadesh to the northern [boundary].
>
> Were three cities [necessary] in Transjordan, [the same as] three cities for the [whole] Land of Israel? Abaye said: Because manslaughter was rife in Gil'ad.
>
> *(Makkot 9b)*

The obvious implication is that there was some sort of moral breakdown in that society. Something was wrong with the educational setup if people did not know how to take precautions which could save lives. This is a further indication of the bizarre value system, which favored possessions over children. By the time the fighters from these tribes returned after the years of conquest and division of the land, an entire generation had been raised in their absence, without the benefit of paternal guidance.[1] No wonder basic safety precautions were not taken. No wonder human life lost its

1 "When Israel were engaged in conquering and dividing the country, the tribes of Reuven and Gad were with them. They had left their children young: he who had left a child ten years old found him twenty-four years old; he who had left a son twenty years old found him now thirty-four" (*Bereishit Rabbah* 98:15).

value. The time and expense such precautions require might have cut into profits, and profits, not human life, were of prime importance.

We can see how the moral breakdown echoed in the request of the two and a half tribes affected the future, but what was its origin? In *Bereishit* we see Reuven standing out on a number of occasions. One such instance is at the sale of Yosef, where he heroically jumps into the fray and attempts to save Yosef from his tormentors. At that particular point in the text, Reuven's motivation escapes us. Only later, when Yosef was sold by the others without Reuven's knowlege, he "ripped his clothing [as a sign of mourning]...and said, 'The boy is gone and what will be with me?' " (*Bereishit* 37:29–30).

What may have seemed like a noble gesture turned out to be merely an expression of Reuven's responsibility as the eldest son. If something happened to Yosef, he felt that he would surely pay the price.

Later, as the story unfolds and the Egyptian "despot" demands to see Binyamin before providing more food, Reuven offers that his own sons be killed in the event that Binyamin is not returned unscathed to Yaakov.[1] Needless to say, Yaakov rejects this bizarre offer, but one cannot help but wonder what type of effect this had on these children, knowing that their father was willing to exchange them. Perhaps we can take this question one step further: What motivated Reuven's offer? Perhaps he suspected that because of his various indiscretions, he stood to lose the double portion of the firstborn, and this offer was a gamble which could win that double portion back. He was willing to place his own children on the table as "markers" in this game of "high-risk poker." Whether or not this is the case, the fact remains that Reuven does not seem to have

1 "Yaakov their father said to them, 'You have bereaved me of my children — Yosef is not, and Shimon is not, and you will take Binyamin away. All these things have come upon me." Reuven said to his father, saying, "Kill my two sons, if I do not bring him [Binyamin] to you. Deliver him into my hand, and I will bring him to you again' " (*Bereishit* 42:36–37).

placed a very high value on the lives of his children. We should not be overly surprised when Reuven's descendants prioritize in a similar fashion, i.e., possessions before children.

Perhaps Gad, as a firstborn, identified with Reuven's plight, feeling that the double portion should rightfully be his. This may also give us insight into the selection of Menasheh, the third tribe to join them. Why does Moshe choose Menasheh? Perhaps he hoped that they, as children of Yosef, would know how to survive in a foreign environment, having been raised in Egypt. Yosef himself serves as the prototype of the righteous individual who retains his values despite the temptations of the surrounding culture. On the other hand, it is fascinating that Menasheh was also a firstborn, and he, too, was displaced in favor of his younger, more successful brother (see *Bereishit* 48:19). It may be that these three, once united, commiserated on the inequity of losing the rights associated with being the older brother. Perhaps their pact was solidified around the decision to remain outside of the land which should have been theirs, more than anyone else's.

There is another, more elevated approach which may provide us with further insight into the motivation of the tribes of Reuven and Gad, as well as the connections between the various sections of the parashah. When God calls Moshe to ascend Mount Avarim and see the Land, *Sifri* explains:

> When Moshe entered the portion of the children of Gad and the children of Reuven, he rejoiced and said, "It seems to me that my vow [the vow of God regarding Moshe] has been lifted!"
>
> *(Sifri, Pinchas 23; cited in Rashi, Bemidbar 27:12)*

After striking the rock, Moshe knew that he could not enter the Land of Israel; this was the will of God, the word of God. But even so, could this vow not be broken?!

The idea expressed in this *Sifri* has been explained and expanded in other Midrashic and chassidic sources. The *Sefat Emet* cites Rav Simchah Bunim from Peshischa, that the phrase "*mikneh rav*" (vast herds) could be translated alternately as "an acquisition with their *rav*," their master. In other words, these two tribes were so dedicated to Moshe that they refused to part with him. In the *Piskei Teshuvah*, a chassidic halachah compendium authored by Avraham Petrakovsky, the same teaching is quoted in the name of the Chiddushei HaRim, also following a teaching of Rav Simchah Bunim from Peshischa,[1] with the following explanation:

> Their intention was for Moshe to enter the Land of Israel, by virtue of this.... Once their end of the bargain is kept [capturing the land with the other tribes], their portion will achieve the status of Israel.... Therefore, retroactively, when Moshe stands in their portion, he is standing in Israel, and the vow is broken, and he can then enter Israel proper. This was the intention of the children of Gad and Reuven, but in truth, prior to the capture and settling of the Land, this portion was not part of the Land of Israel at all.
>
> *(Piskei Teshuvah, vol. 2, section 249, fn.)*

This teaching is based on technical knowledge of the laws of oaths. Suffice it to say that this is a loophole, a technicality. Simply put, God swore that Moshe would not enter the Land; the portion of Gad and Reuven was not yet part of the Land, but one day it would be. Therefore, if they asked to stay on the eastern side of the Jordan, where Moshe was permitted to enter, and went on to fulfill their side of the deal, then their portion would achieve the same status as the rest of the Land of Israel, and effectively God's vow would be nullified.[2]

In this light, the parashah and its various parts becomes a more cohesive whole. Moshe teaches the laws and intricacies of oaths.

---

1 The teaching is cited in the name of Rav Simchah Bunim in the name of someone else, but the second name was expunged from the book. Perhaps the author is Kotzker Rebbe, as the teaching is cited in his name in *Emet MiKotzk Titzmach* 709.

2 This would create a parallel with the transgression of the spies as explained in *Parashat Shelach*, namely, the error which they committed was motivated by dedication to Moshe. This would explain why Moshe made reference to the spies in his response to Gad and Reuven.

One important part of these laws is that oaths can be challenged and rescinded. Once the tribes of Reuven and Gad hear this, they devise a plan for Moshe to join them in Israel. Perhaps they imagine that if the vow precluding Moshe's entrance to Israel could be reversed, then perhaps the loss of the double portion of Reuven could be reversed as well.

Moshe, for his part, does not seem interested in subterfuge. He continues his mission as the man of halachah he is. This may be evidenced by the middle of the parashah, the vengeance against Midyan. Moshe immediately sets a plan in motion to fulfill the Divine imperative. But did he have to? The Midrash makes the following comment:

> "Avenge the vengeance of the Children of Israel on the Midyanites; afterward you shall be gathered to your people" (*Bemidbar* 31:2). Rabbi Yehudah said: If Moshe had wanted to live many more years he could have lived, for the Holy One, blessed be He, told him, "Avenge and afterward you shall be gathered," making his death dependent on the punishment of Midyan. But the text apprises you of the greatness of Moshe. He thought, *Shall Israel's vengeance be delayed merely that I may live*? Immediately, "Moshe spoke to the people, saying, 'Arm men from among you for the war' " (ibid., 3).
>
> *(Bemidbar Rabbah 22:2)*

Delaying the battle and, as a result, his own demise, would have caused the Children of Israel to linger in the desert. Instead, Moshe sets off on his final mission, even though its completion will draw his own death nearer. Even one unnecessary day in the desert was too high a price to be paid; the welfare of his followers, his students, came before personal considerations, and Moshe immediately, heroically, sends Yehoshua to battle the Midyanites.

Another *midrash* offers some details of the events on the last day of Moshe's life, some of which are germane to this discussion.

> A heavenly voice came out and said, "You have but three hours in this world."

> Moshe said, "Master of the universe, let me remain with the children of Gad and the children of Reuven...and Yehoshua will rule and bring the Children of Israel into the Land of Israel."
>
> *(Otzar Midrashim, Eisenstein, p. 356)*

According to this *midrash*, Moshe himself makes the suggestion that he remain in the portion of Gad and Reuven.[1] God explains that such an arrangement is impossible. If Moshe were alive and remained in Jordan, who would go to Israel, when they could be with Moshe? A person like Moshe cannot simply retire and slip out of the public eye. God explains that ultimately such an arrangement would destroy the Torah. Moshe surely does not want to be party to anything that would have a negative effect on the people or the Torah. The events described in this *midrash* as occurring between the fourth and third hours before Moshe's death are striking: Moshe offers various suggestions whereby he can surreptitiously enter the Land — by air, by sea, even cut into pieces. Each time, God responds that an oath is an oath, and it cannot be broken. Here, the *midrash* introduces the motif we have traced throughout, the oath. Once he accepts the oath as irreversible, Moshe moves on to the next suggestion, that he remain with Gad and Reuven.

Moshe's approach differs from that of Gad and Reuven in that Moshe does not seek to harm the integrity of the Torah, or the Jewish people, whereas Reuven and Gad's suggestion ultimately harmed their own children. The earlier indiscretion of Reuven himself, when he intimated that his children were expendable, reemerges to harm his descendants. Whether motivated by their love of money or by their twisted love for Moshe, the result of par-

1 In another *midrash*, Moshe makes this suggestion in order to save his brother, Aharon: " 'Aharon shall be gathered' (*Bemidbar* 20:24). Moshe said to Him, 'Sovereign! Allow him to remain with the children of Reuven and the children of Gad!' He [God] to him, 'He shall not enter the land which I have given to the Children of Israel' (ibid.), implying: The delay in his death is holding back the giving of the Land. Do you wish that he should not die and that Israel shall not enter the Land? This is the reason why it says, 'Which I have given to the Children of Israel' " (*Bemidbar Rabbah* 19:17).

ents letting their children know that they are not their most valued possession proved disastrous for these tribes. Children inevitably learn from the actions and values of their parents. Therefore, the eastern bank of the Jordan River ultimately became a place prone to violence and bloodshed, and the children of these tribes were the first to be exiled.

Sefer Devarim

Parashat Devarim

The Words of Moshe

Both ancient and modern readers of *Sefer Devarim* have discerned a change in style from the other four books of the Torah. The book begins:

> These are the words of Moshe which he spoke to the Children of Israel on the other side of the Jordan.
>
> *(Devarim 1:1)*

After this introduction, the text switches to a monologue delivered by Moshe in the first person. This type of a syntax dominates *Sefer Devarim*, and is clearly a departure from the other books of the Torah, where the more familiar, "God spoke to Moshe, saying, 'Speak to the Children of Israel...' " is prevalent.

While modern secular scholars have quite comfortably suggested a different "source" or author for this book,[1] traditional opinion, both ancient and modern, insists that the entire Torah is the word of God. Even the suggestion that the Torah contains alien teachings is beyond the pale of traditional thought. The Gemara states that if a person denies the Divinity of even one word in the

---

1 There is a certain tautology in their argument. *Devarim* is clearly primarily a speech by Moshe; therefore, the style is different. Had the style been the same, the secular scholars would have argued that surely Moshe authored the other four *sefarim* as well!

Torah, he is guilty of heresy.

> "Because he has despised the word of God" — this refers to one who maintains that the Torah is not from Heaven. And even if he asserts that the whole Torah is from Heaven, except for a particular verse, which [he maintains] was not uttered by God but by Moshe himself, he is included in "because he has despised the word of God." And even if he admits that the whole Torah is from Heaven, except for a single point, a *kal vachomer* [*a fortiori*] deduction, or a certain *gezeirah shavah*, he is still included in "because he has despised the word of God."
>
> *(Sanhedrin 99a)*

This opinion has been codified by Rambam (*Hilchot Teshuvah* 3:8) and reflects normative Jewish law. Therefore, for the believing Jew, the flippant suggestion of different authorship of *Devarim* is not an option.

There is, however, another passage in the Gemara which is somewhat difficult to understand, given these limitations. While discussing details of public reading of the *Zohar,* the Gemara states that in *Vayikra,* in the portion of the *tochechah* (rebuke), the reader should not stop in the middle of the description of the calamities. In *Devarim,* on the other hand, the Gemara states that it is permissible to stop in the middle and divide the reading into two.

> This was only taught regarding the rebuke in *Torat Kohanim* [*Vayikra*], but in the rebuke in *Mishneh Torah* [*Devarim*] you may stop. These [the rebuke in *Vayikra*] were written in the plural, by Moshe from the mouth of the Almighty, while those were written in the singular, by Moshe, from his own mouth.
>
> *(Megillah 31b)*

This teaching seems to present tremendous difficulties. How can the Gemara suggest that even a portion of the Torah was authored by anyone other than God, even Moshe? At first glance our two Gemara sources seem contradictory. This passage has sent commentaries to both *Chumash* and Gemara scurrying in various directions in order to resolve the inconsistency. The *Zohar* deals with this issue in a number of places:

> Come and see, the verse says Moshe spoke and God responded in a loud voice. It was taught, what does it mean "with a...voice"? With the voice of Moshe, for Moshe achieved a level beyond all the prophets.... The voice was the *Shechinah* [the Divine Presence]. Rav Shimon said: We were taught that the rebuke in *Vayikra* was [written by] Moshe in the name of the Divinity, and in *Mishneh Torah*, it was Moshe from his own mouth. Do you think that Moshe said even one small letter by himself? No, it is written with precision. It doesn't say that Moshe said it by himself, but that it came out of Moshe's mouth. This was the voice which "possessed" Moshe.
>
> *(Zohar, Devarim 265a)*

In this passage, the *Zohar* poses the same question. How can we even consider that part of the Torah is not directly from God? The answer the *Zohar* offers is elegant: Of course, the entire Torah is Divine, but not all the Torah was communicated in the same manner. The *Zohar* thus introduces a concept which has become known as "the *Shechinah* speaking from the throat of Moshe." This phrase, which apparently does not have a source in Talmudic or Rabbinic literature,[1] became quite popular and can be found in the great works of the eighteenth to twentieth centuries.[2] The idea itself is clearly stated in the *Zohar*: at times Moshe, who rose to such a pro-

---

1 The encyclopedic *Michlol HaMa'amarim V'Hapitgamim* states conclusively that the precise phrase is not found in Rabbinic literature. Tiferes Yisrael (to *Yoma* 6:20) uses this idea to explain the *kohein gadol*'s ability to bless the people with the ineffable name.

2 The list reads like a virtual "who's who," from the Ba'al HaTanya (*Tanya* 1:34) to Rav Chaim of Volozhin (*Nefesh HaChaim* 3:14), from Rav Levi Yitzchak of Berditchiv (*Kedushat Levi, Toldot, Tetzaveh, Ve'etchanan*) to the *Meshech Chochmah* (*Bemidbar* 20:11, 32:31, *Devarim* 4:36), from Rav Tzaddok HaKohen (*Tzidkat HaTzaddik* 183, and numerous other citations) to the *Mishnah Berurah* (428:18). It is interesting that the Alshich HaKadosh does not use the phrase, even though he describes the concept in his commentary *Torat Moshe* to *Bemidbar* 12:8.

found level of prophecy, literally had the *Shechinah* speak from his throat.

The idea of Moshe possessing Divine diction is based on a number of verses. The first recounts Moshe's hesitation to represent the people due to his limited ability to speak.

> Moshe said to God, "Please, my Lord, I am not an eloquent man, not yesterday nor the day before, nor since You have spoken to Your servant. I am slow of speech and of a slow tongue."
>
> God said to him, "Who has made man's mouth? Who makes the mute, or the deaf, or the seeing, or the blind? Is it not I, God? Now therefore go, and I will be with your mouth, and I will teach you what you shall say."
>
> *(Shemot 4:10–12)*

Here God reminds Moshe that all voice comes from God and assures him that God's voice will "accompany" him. The second verse is a description of the Revelation at Sinai:

> Mount Sinai smoked in every part because God descended upon it in fire. Its smoke ascended like the smoke of a furnace, and the whole mountain trembled greatly. When the voice of the shofar sounded long, and became louder and louder, Moshe spoke, and God answered him by a voice.
>
> *(Ibid. 19:18–19)*

Moshe's voice at Sinai invites a response from Heaven, and a Divine duet rings forth. At the next stage we are told that when God speaks, the people prefer Moshe's speech:

> All the people saw the thunderings, the lightnings, the sound of the shofar, and the mountain smoking; and when the people saw it, they were shaken and stood far away. They said to Moshe, "Speak with us and we will hear, but let the Lord not speak with us, lest we die."
>
> Moshe said to the people, "Fear not; for the Lord has come to test you, and that His fear may be before your faces, so that you do not sin." The people stood far away, and Moshe drew

near to the thick darkness where the Lord was.

God said to Moshe, "Thus you shall say to the Children of Israel...."

(Ibid. 20:15–19)

This idea of Moshe being the mouthpiece for God is stressed in another episode, when Moshe's uniqueness as a prophet is questioned. God chastises Miriam and Aharon:

> God said suddenly to Moshe, to Aharon, and to Miriam, "Come out, you three, to the Ohel Mo'ed." The three of them went out. God came down in the pillar of cloud, stood in the door of the Tent, and called Aharon and Miriam; and they both went out. He said, "Listen now to My words. If there is a prophet among you, I, God, will make Myself known to him in a vision, and I will speak to him in a dream. Not so with My servant Moshe, for he is the trusted one in all My house. With him I speak mouth to mouth, manifestly, and not in dark speech; and he beholds the form of God. Why then were you not afraid to speak against My servant Moshe?"
>
> *(Bemidbar 12:4–8)*

Moshe's prophecy is described as "mouth to mouth" — from the mouth of God to the mouth of Moshe.

The *Zohar* further explains this phenomenon:

> "Moshe spoke and God answered him by a voice" (*Shemot* 19:19). This voice, as has been elsewhere explained, is the voice of Moshe, the Voice to which Moshe attached himself. It may be asked, does it not say further on that "the Lord spoke" (ibid. 20:1), and not Moshe? Some explain that the reason was because the people said to Moshe: "Speak with us and we will hear, but let the Lord not speak with us" (ibid. 19:15). But, in fact, there is no word in the Torah which Moshe spoke on his own authority. Hence it says, "Moshe spoke" with his own voice, "and God answered him with that mighty Voice," con-

firming what he said.

(Zohar, Vayikra 7a)

The *Zohar* explains that these verses represent a metamorphosis which transpired in Moshe:[1]

> "Moshe spoke before God, saying, 'Behold, the Children of Israel have not listenend to me. How then shall Pharaoh listen to me, when I am of uncircumcised lips?' " (*Shemot* 6:12). How did Moshe dare say this? Had not the Holy One already promised him, when he said that he was not eloquent, that He would be "with his mouth" (ibid. 9:10–12)? Or did the Holy One not keep His promise?
>
> However, there is here an inner meaning. Moshe was then in the grade of "sound," and the grade of "word" was then in exile. Hence he said, "How shall Pharaoh listen to me, seeing that my 'word' is in bondage to him, I being only 'said' and lacking 'word.' " Therefore, God joined Aharon, who was "word" without "sound," to him. When Moshe came, the voice appeared, but it was "a sound without speech." This lasted until Israel approached Mount Sinai to receive the Torah. Then the sound was united with the word, and the word was spoken, as it says, "and the Lord spoke all these words" (ibid. 20:1). Then Moshe was in full possession of the word, sound and word being united. That was the cause of Moshe's complaint (ibid. 5:23), that he lacked the word save at the time when it broke forth in complaint and "The Lord spoke to Moshe" (ibid. 6:2). On this occasion the word began to function, but it ceased again, as the time was not yet ripe; hence the verse continues, "and said to him, 'I am the Lord.' " Only at the giving of the Torah Moshe was, as it were, healed of his impediment, when the sound and the word were united in him as their organ. Before that event the power which is

---

1 Similarly, the Midrash observes: "For see, of Moshe before he was privileged to receive the Torah writes, 'I am not a man of words' (*Shemot* 4:10); but after he had proved himself worthy of the Torah his tongue became cured and he began to speak words. Where do we know this from? From what we have read in the passage under comment, 'These are the words which Moshe spoke' " (*Devarim Rabbah* 1:1).

> word guided Israel in the desert, but without expressing itself until they came to Sinai.
>
> *(Zohar, Shemot 25b)*

We now understand that the idea of the Divine presence emanating from Moshe's throat teaches that Moshe did not "author" this section of the Torah. Rather, it emanated from his mouth, for the *Shechinah* occupied his throat. The "problematic" passage in the Gemara never said that Moshe invented or authored the text of *Devarim*. Rather, it was Moshe *"mipi atzmo,"* from his own mouth; but in his mouth was the *Shechinah*, God's presence.

This idea helps us reconcile the problem of these two specific passages, namely the halachic differences between the *tochechah* in *Vayikra* and the *tochechah* in *Devarim*. But it does not seem to help for the larger issue, namely the "style" of the rest of *Devarim*.

In a second passage, the *Zohar* opens the door for more sections which emanated from the mouth of Moshe:

> Even though the entire Torah is the word of God, some is from the words of Moshe as well. Which part? For example, the rebuke in *Mishneh Torah* [*Devarim*]. Afterwards the[se words] were included in the Divine [*mipi hagevurah*], as the verse indicates: "Moshe spoke, and God answered him by a voice" (*Shemot* 19:19).
>
> *(Zohar, Vayikra 7a)*

Here we see that the section of rebuke is merely an example of this phenomenon — "For example, the rebuke in *Mishneh Torah*." The *Zohar* implies that there are other sections which were "produced" in a similar manner.

In another section of the *Zohar* we find,

> That which is called *Mishneh Torah*, Moshe said it [all] from his own mouth....
>
> *(Zohar, Devarim 261a)*

Here we see that the *Zohar* is willing to make a much broader assertion: the entire *Sefer Devarim* was communicated via the mouth of Moshe, with the *Shechinah* in his throat. The implication is that the stylistic differences in *Devarim* are of Divine origin. Most of the Torah comes from God, as dictated to Moshe, while *Devarim* is spoken by God via the mouth of Moshe. Why, then, did the Gemara only mention the section of the rebuke? Arguably, because that was the section under discussion. Thus, when explaining the difference between the sections, the Gemara introduces this principle which, according to the *Zohar*, applies equally for the entire *sefer*. Furthermore, according to this approach, when the *Shechinah* speaks, it speaks in the first person, as if it were Moshe, for Moshe's essence as been inextricably linked with the *Shechinah*.[1]

While a technical answer has been set forth, in a sense the major question has been avoided: Why is the style of this book different? Why, specifically at this juncture, do we find a shift in the Divine modus operandi? As stated at the outset, the question of the authorship of *Devarim* occupied many of the early sages and many answers have been offered. Abarbanel, in his introduction to *Devarim*, expands a teaching of Ramban in the following manner:

Sefer Devarim is referred to as "*Mishneh Torah*," which means the repetition of the Torah or of the law (in English, "Deuteronomy," which means, quite literally, "repetition of the law"). In this *sefer*, many laws are restated. On what basis did Moshe repeat these laws? Abarbanel answers very simply that the Oral Torah is what Moshe taught at this later opportunity. We know that God's com-

---

1 The Dubno Maggid, in *Ohel Yaakov MiDubna, Parashat Devarim,* cites in the name of the Vilna Gaon that the first four books where written by Moshe as the *Shechinah* emanated from Moshe's mouth, in an instantaneous fashion, while *Devarim* was revealed to Moshe and afterwards conveyed to the people, in a speech based on the revelation, in a manner similar to other prophets.

The *Or Gedalyahu* (*Parashat Devarim*) cites a different teaching of the Vilna Gaon, based on the *Aderet Eliyahu* (*Balak*; fourth edition): There are fifty levels of understanding, and Moshe at Sinai achieved the forty-ninth. The fiftieth, which remains the Divine realm, was revealed when God said, "I am God," in the first of the Ten Commandments. When Moshe repeated the Ten Commandments in *Devarim*, it was Moshe "from his own mouth," Moshe speaking from this forty-ninth level, which was beyond the level of other forty-eight prophets, who achieved only the forty-eighth level.

munication with Moshe on Sinai was much more in-depth than what is indicated in the written text of the Torah. At Sinai, all of Judaism was taught by God to Moshe. Not everything that God taught Moshe at that juncture became part of the Written Torah. Certain ideas remained unwritten, verbal.

According to Rambam, Moshe wrote down many of these teachings, but kept them private, for his own use and as a teaching tool. These notes were not meant to be passed on, at least not in the written form (Rambam, Introduction to the *Mishneh Torah*).

We may draw the following conclusion: The essential difference between the Written Torah and the Oral Torah was not that one was written and the other not written. Rather, one was meant to be passed on in written form, and the other was meant to be passed on verbally. Furthermore, the text of the Written Torah is sacrosanct, while in the Oral Torah, it is the ideas which are holy.[1]

Let us return to Abarbanel. Moshe, now in the last days of his life, will soon take leave of his beloved nation. Therefore, he teaches them the laws of the Torah yet again. What does he use as the basis for his lectures? The answer is simple — the Oral Torah which was taught to him by God at Sinai. According to this approach, the *Mishneh Torah, Sefer Devarim*, is in actuality the oldest source of Oral Torah extant. At the conclusion of Moshe's lecture, God asks him to write down his words.[2] At that point they become part of the Written Torah as well. Therefore, *Sefer Devarim* has the status of both the Oral Torah and the Written To-

---

1 Rashi in *Gittin* 60b has a different understanding of this concept, which has enjoyed much more popularity than Rambam's concept, outlined above. Rashi understands that there was a prohibition to write the Oral Law. These two approaches, of Rambam and Rashi, may mirror different versions of the Letter of Rav Sherira Gaon, which circulated in Sfarad and Ashkenaz respectively.

2 This may be alluded to in the verse, "Now write this song for yourselves and teach it to the Children of Israel. Put it in their mouths, so that this poem may be a witness for me with the Children of Israel" (*Devarim* 31:19). This verse refers to the *tochechah,* which we referred to earlier, but according to some approaches refers to the entire *sefer*.

rah.[1] The words are arguably the words of Moshe, based on the teachings that he heard from God.

Again, we must recall that the holiness of the Oral Torah is the concepts. Therefore, Moshe would have been expected to teach these ideas using his own words. Only after they are written, based on word-by-word, letter-by-letter dictation by God, do they achieve the status of Written Torah as well. This means that the books of *Bereishit* through *Bemidbar* were dictated by God to Moshe, and are, literally, the Word of God — the syntax, the words, the letters, and the spelling. *Devarim* is based on the teachings Moshe learned from God at Sinai, but the words are Moshe's. However, after Moshe addressed the people, God dictated to Moshe the text that became the fifth book — the very words that Moshe had already used! God's dictation of these words gives them equal status with the preceding books of the Torah, making them part and parcel of the Written Torah as well.[2]

Perhaps this teaching of Abarbanel, which is based on Ramban and echoed by many authorities, including the Vilna Gaon and Malbim,[3] is actually referred to in the *Zohar* cited above:

> Even though the entire Torah is the word of God, some is the words of Moshe as well. Which part? For example, the rebuke in *Mishneh Torah* [*Devarim*]. Afterwards the[se words] were included in the Divine [*mipi hagevurah*]....
>
> *(Zohar, Vayikra 7a)*

1 When Rabbi Soloveitchik taught these ideas, he explained that the Gemara utilizes different methodology in *Devarim* for this very reason. See *Berachot* 21b: "Should you say that Rabbi Yehudah does not derive lessons from the juxtaposition of texts, [this does not matter] since Rabbi Yosef has said: Even those who do not derive lessons from the juxtaposition of texts in all the rest of the Torah do so in *Devarim*; for Rabbi Yehudah does not derive such lessons in all the rest of the Torah, and in *Devarim* he does."

2 The Chatam Sofer describes the process. "Moshe intended to give a speech using his own words, as it appears.... When he spoke the *Shechinah* occupied his throat and spoke, without changing a word from Moshe's formulation" (*Chatam Sofer*, Stern edition, year 5590).

3 See Malbim, beginning of *Devarim*. Rav Tzaddok HaKohen echoes this idea when he describes *Devarim* as the root of the Oral Law (*Pri Tzaddik,* vol. 2, p. 39–40).

Here the *Zohar* states that the section in question is both by Moshe and God, first stated by Moshe, then repeated by God. In other words, the "*Shechinah* speaking from the mouth of Moshe" may be understood as follows: The words Moshe used indeed came from God. They are based on what Moshe heard at Sinai, when Moshe stood in proximity to the *Shechinah*. They are the words of the Oral Torah, oral in the sense that they are received through the mouth of Moshe! Later, when these words are written — based on clear, unequivocal instructions by God — they become part and parcel of the Written Torah, having the same authority as any other words in the five books. *Sefer Devarim* is quite special, as it comes from the mouth of God to the mouth of Moshe, to the quill of Moshe by the word of God.

Parashat Va'etchanan

Moshe's Prayer

The parashah of *Va'etchanan* contains some of the most important teachings of Judaism. Here the Ten Commandments are repeated, taught for the second time. Here we find the Shema, the declaration of monotheism. These ideas, together with lengthy instructions from Moshe, make for a parashah outstanding in its concentration of spiritual teachings and content.

The parashah begins with Moshe recounting for the people his dialogue with God.

> I pleaded with God at that time, saying, "God, O Lord, You have begun to show Your servant Your greatness and Your mighty hand; for who is almighty in heaven or in earth who can do as Your works and as Your might? I beg You, let me pass over and see the good land that is beyond the Jordan, that good mountain region and the Levanon."
>
> *(Devarim 3:23–25)*

Moshe had asked God to rescind the decree and to allow him to cross the Jordan with the people. God rejects this request:

> But God was angry with me because of you and would not hear

me. God said to me, "It is enough for you, speak no more to Me on this matter."

(Ibid., 26)

Moshe's plea was rejected, and he was told that he should not even attempt to continue his prayers, for the matter was sealed. Rather, Moshe should take solace in God's offer to see the Land from afar:

> Go on top of the [mountain] peak and lift up your eyes, westward, northward, southward, and eastward, and look with your eyes, for you will not cross this Jordan.
>
> *(Ibid., 27)*

Moshe's prayer was rejected. He would not enter with the people. The Sages have taught that it was not a solitary prayer — Moshe had offered 515 different prayers, but one and all were rejected.

> From where do we know that Moshe prayed at this juncture five hundred and fifteen times? For it says, "I pleaded [*va'etchanan*] with God at that time, saying..." (*Devarim* 3:23). The numerical value of *va'etchanan* is this number.
>
> *(Devarim Rabbah 11:10)*

This concept of Moshe having his prayers rejected is not an easy one for us to understand. How can it be that Moshe, the father of all prophets, could not have his prayers answered? Furthermore, if Moshe could not repent effectively and have his decree rescinded, then what does that say for those who have not reached — and cannot even imagine reaching — the exalted level of a man like Moshe?

There are various approaches to this issue in Talmudic and Midrashic literature. The Gemara understands that Moshe's prayers did have an effect:

> Prayer is greater than good deeds, for there was no one greater in deeds than Moshe our Master. Nonetheless, Moshe was only answered as a result of his prayer, for it says, "It is enough for

> you, speak no more to Me on this matter," and right afterward it says, "Go on top of the peak...."
>
> *(Berachot 32b)*

The Gemara clearly understands that Moshe's prayers were effective, albeit not as effective or in the manner which Moshe desired. The implication is clear — had Moshe not prayed, he would not have climbed the mountain and seen the Land. This notwithstanding, our questions remain: Moshe's prayers may have been answered, but the answer was not what Moshe had sought. Furthermore, why could Moshe not achieve complete rehabilitation for his "indiscretion"?

One approach, which may resolve our problem, regards prayer as effective only until the final judgment has been decreed; beyond that point, prayer cannot cancel the decree. This is based on a passage in the Gemara which explains why at times prayers are effective and at other times they do not seem effective.

> On the question of the final sentence of an individual, there is a difference between *Tannaim*, as it has been taught: Rabbi Meir used to say, Two men take to their beds, suffering equally from the same disease, or two men stand before a criminal court to be judged for the same offense. Yet one gets up and the other does not get up, one escapes death and the other does not escape death. Why does one get up and the other not? Why does one escape death and the other not? Because one prayed and was answered, and the other prayed and was not answered. Why was one answered and the other not? One prayed with his whole heart and was therefore answered, the other did not pray with his whole heart and was not answered. Rabbi Elazar, however, said: [One man was praying] before his final sentence had been pronounced [in Heaven], the other after his final sentence had been pronounced.
>
> *(Rosh HaShanah 18a)*

Sefer Chasidim (section 612, citing Rav Saadya Gaon) uses this principle to explain why Moshe's prayers were rejected: His judgment had been finalized. This idea dovetails with a number of the Sages' teachings which indicate that once this judgment was final, Moshe could say nothing more.

> "It is enough for you, speak no more to Me on this matter." What does this mean? The decree has been decreed and the judgment sealed.
>
> *(Avot D'Rabbi Natan, addition 2 to ch. 4)*

It seems, then, that there is a point where *teshuvah* is no longer effective. The *Zohar*, however, states that "true *teshuvah*" can always be of benefit.[1]

> Most assuredly the Holy One accepts every sinner who turns to Him. Such a one is set upon the path of life, and, notwithstanding his former stain, everything is put right and restored to its former position. Even when the Holy One has decreed most solemnly against a person, He forgives entirely where there is a perfect repentance. Thus we find it written concerning Yehoyachin: " 'As I live,' says God, 'if you, Koniyahu son of Yehoyakim were the signet upon My right hand, I tear you off.... Write this man childless...' " (*Yirmiyah* 22:24, 30). Yet when he repented and turned again to the Lord, we read: "The sons of Yechoniyah: Assir..." (*Divrei HaYamim* I 3:17), showing that, after all, he was not childless. This proves that repentance annuls all decrees and judgements and breaks many an iron chain, and there is nothing that can stand against it.
>
> *(Zohar, Shemot 106a)*

If this is the case, why would God have told Moshe that he need not pray? Rashi in his comments to the Torah addresses this

1 Rabbi Reuven Margoliot, in his notes to *Sefer Chasidim*, cites a teaching from the *Zohar* that *teshuvah* cannot always affect one's status in this world, but is always effective in terms of the World to Come (*Zohar, Shemot* 106a). My own reading of this passage differs from that of Rabbi Margoliot, and as I understand, the *Zohar* teaches that even in this world *teshuvah* is effective. Rabbi Margoliot's comments seem aimed at the assumption (*havah amina*) of the text, but not the conclusion.

point: When God says "It is enough for you [*rav lach*]," Rashi utilitzes the literal explanation of the words ("a lot is awaiting you") and explains, "A greater good awaits you in the next world; therefore you no longer need pray for your share]."[1]

Sifri[2] offers a completely different approach, according to which Moshe did not heed God's request and continued to pray.

> With regard to Moshe, whom God instructed, "It is enough for you, speak no more to Me on this matter," [Moshe] did not follow God's instructions and did not desist from asking mercy from the Holy One, blessed be He. Other people should certainly never [give up and stop praying].... Even if a sharp blade is on a person's neck, he should not cease to ask for mercy.
>
> *(Sifri, Devarim, piska 29)*

According to this approach, our previous questions resurface: Why did Moshe's prayers go unanswered, and why would God discourage Moshe from further prayer?

In order to answer these questions, we must reevaluate prayer and its spiritual dynamics.

When a person is ill, God forbid, he turns to God in prayer. If the prayer is accepted by God, the person recovers. Superficially, it seems as if God changed His mind, as if God can be sweet-talked into backing down from a previously stated position. Further, it seems as if God waits in Heaven for our words of supplication, and in the event that they do not arrive He wreaks His vengeance.

However, we are aware that God is an Infinite Being, and, by definition, unchanging. If this is the case, how can God "change His mind"? The answer is subtle, yet simple: God does not change,

---

1 In another passage the *Zohar* implies that prayer may have its limits, but tears do not. "When one prays and weeps and cries so intensely that he is unable to find words to express his sorrow, his prayer is prayer in the truest sense, for it is in the heart, and shall never return to him unanswered. Rabbi Yehudah said: Great is such crying in that it can effect a change in the Divine sentence of judgment. Rabbi Yitzchak said: Great is such crying in that it dominates the supernal attribute of justice" (*Zohar, Shemot* 20a).

2 The previous comments of Rashi are also based on the *Sifri*.

man does. The man who fell ill was relatively alienated from God; the man who prays is a man who is close to God, no longer the same man who fell ill.[1] He has forged a new relationship with God. God, for His part, remains unchanged. Man often believes that he prays because he is ill; he does not understand that the reason he is ill is because he has not prayed — or searched for a complete relationship with God. Now that he has prayed, he no longer needs to be ill.

Let us consider Moshe: was his angst due to some type of spiritual deficiency? Surely not! Moshe reached the most exalted status which man can ever dream of. He was not spiritually lacking, his prayers were no longer necessary. This idea is conveyed in the *Zohar*:

> "It is enough for you, speak no more to Me on this matter." Rav Chiya said: God said to Moshe, "It is enough that you have been united with the *Shechinah*. You can advance no further."
>
> *(Zohar, Devarim 260b)*

Moshe was unlike other people. There was nothing lacking in his spiritual makeup, and so nothing needed to be healed. Moshe did not need to pray. Even his share in the World to Come was assured, as we saw in the *Rashi* quoted above. If we take this idea one step further, we will gain great insight in the rest of the parashah.

Seforno comments:

> "God was angry with me because of you" — For I desired to keep you there [in Israel], so that you would never be exiled. But He [God] had already lifted up His arm to disperse you among the nations.
>
> *(Seforno, Devarim 3:26)*

---

1 Perhaps we can see this concept when the very first sin is performed: "They [Adam and Chavah] heard the voice of God, the Lord, walking in the garden in the cool of the day; and Adam and his wife hid themselves from the presence of God, the Lord, among the trees of the garden. God, the Lord, called to Adam, and said to him, 'Where are you?' " (*Bereishit* 3:8). God remains the same, but man changes by virtue of sin, and it is man who causes the distancing between himself and God. Part of the rehabilitation for man is seeking God.

According to Seforno, the object of Moshe's prayer was not his own spiritual well-being, it was the future of the community. Moshe was motivated by a profound concern for his people. This leads us to an astounding conclusion: Moshe's remaining in exile was not due to a lack in him. It was caused by the relatively low spiritual level of his people. We have seen on other occasions that had Moshe entered the Land of Israel, the Temple never would have been destroyed. Moshe would have been Mashiach. The only problem was that the people were unworthy.

Seforno insists that this decree had already been made: "He [God] had already lifted up His arm to disperse you among the nations." The obvious question which then emerges is, when did this decree come into existence? One possibility is, during the golden calf debacle. The Gemara teaches:

> Had the tablets not been broken, no nation nor language would have controlled them.
>
> *(Eiruvin 54a)*

The reason the Tablets were shattered was, of course, the sin of the golden calf. Once the Tablets were shattered, the spiritual ability of the nation was handicapped. Things had changed, and the people had become distanced from God, from the *Shechinah*.

With this insight we may now understand Moshe's plan of action. After his prayers prove unable to cancel the decree, he emphasizes the Revelation.

> Only take heed to yourself, and keep your soul diligently, lest you forget the things which your eyes have seen, and lest they depart from your heart all the days of your life. Teach them to your children and to your grandchildren — the day when you stood before God, your Lord, in Choreiv, when God said to me, "Gather the people together, and I will make them hear My words, that they may learn to fear Me all the days that they live on the earth and that they may teach their children."
>
> You came near and stood under the mountain; and the

> mountain burned with fire to the heart of heaven, with darkness, clouds, and thick darkness. Then God spoke to you out of the midst of the fire; you heard the sound of the words, but you saw no form, only a voice. He declared to you His covenant, which He commanded you to perform, Ten Commandments; and He wrote them upon two tablets of stone.
>
> *(Devarim 4:9–13)*

Moshe tries to recreate the Revelation at Sinai, intellectually, emotionally, and spiritually. Moshe reminds them what it was like to see the Heavens open and see the word of God.

> God talked with you face to face in the mountain out of the midst of the fire.
>
> *(Ibid. 5:4)*

Moshe now repeats the Ten Commandments.

Now we can understand why the Ten Commandments are taught again in this week's parashah. Moshe wishes to turn back the clock and take the nation to the spiritual strata which they enjoyed while standing at Sinai — prior to the sin of the golden calf.

On a deeper level, perhaps the deficiency which allowed the golden calf was the people's refusal to listen to the Ten Commandments directly from God. As Moshe introduces the Ten Commandments, he says:

> I stood between God and you at that time, to tell you the word of God (for you were afraid because of the fire and did not go up onto the mountain), saying: "I am God, your Lord, who brought you out of the land of Egypt, from the house of slavery. You shall have no other gods before Me...."
>
> *(Ibid., 5–7)*

The *Zohar* explains the implication of this fear:

> Israel were terrified and drew back, and therefore they said, "Please, you speak to us; we do not desire to be spoken to by the mighty Power from on high."...

> Moshe said to them, "You have weakened my power, and also another power." For had Israel not drawn back and had they listened to the remaining words as to the first, the world would never have been laid waste later, and they would have lasted for generations upon generations.
>
> *(Zohar, Devarim 261a–b)*

Because the people did not receive the Torah directly from God, the result was the golden calf. Now we can also understand why Shema is taught in this week's parashah. What better way to connect to God than via Shema, the ultimate statement of acceptance of God[1] and the ultimate vehicle to draw the *Shechinah*'s proximity?[2]

> If one dreams that he is reciting the Shema, he is worthy that the Divine presence should rest upon him, only his generation is not deserving enough.
>
> *(Berachot 57a)*

In order for Moshe to enter Israel, he did not need to fix anything in his relationship with God. His prayers were not necessary. For Moshe to enter, and, more importantly, for the people to stay, the people needed to change, to grow closer to the *Shechinah*. Therefore, Moshe is told by God to cease his prayers, and instead Moshe takes up what he does best — teach.

Moshe gives a phenomenal *shiur*, in the hope that this will lead his students, his followers, back to God. Moshe attempted to fix that which had been broken.[3]

1 Maharal, in his commentary to *Aggadot, Sotah* 17, explains that the reason that the section on tzitzit is said together with the Shema is that tzitzit are meant to be a vehicle to visualize the *Shechinah*, via the blue-colored strings. See my comments on *Parashat Vayeitzei*.

2 Ramchal authored a book on the 515 prayers, *Sefer Tav Kuf Tet Vav Tefillot*. In section 284 he writes that the primary manner to bring the *Shechinah* down is by saying the Shema. This idea was explored in my comments on *Parashat Vayechi*, where I cited the teaching that Yaakov's response to the return of his *ruach hakodesh* was the recital of the Shema (which is said there for the first time). Later, on Yaakov's deathbed, when Yaakov's *ruach hakodesh* eludes him, his children recite Shema to assure him of their devotion. According to one version of the Midrash, the *Shechinah* returns as a response to the Shema.

In the end, Moshe's efforts fell short, but the *shiur* which he left us remains. The Jewish people simply have to read this week's parashah in order to know how to reunite with God and to become one with the *Shechinah*, just like our teacher, Moshe.

3 According to the Midrash, Moshe had to remain in the desert in order to bring his generation, those who left Egypt and died in the desert, into the Land in the eschatological fulfillment of his mission.

Parashat Eikev

Reward and Punishment

In this week's parashah, one of the most seminal ideas of Judaism is articulated: the concept of reward and punishment. The term *punishment* may be a misnomer; the word *consequences* may be a more apt description of this spiritual dynamic.[1] This is not the first or the only time that this idea is mentioned, but the idea is dealt with more thoroughly here than in any other parashah.

Particular attention is paid to the people's long-anticipated entrance to the Land, where they must follow the Divine word with even more vigilance or run the risk of exile. The context of the instructions is clarified in the following verse:

> Hear, O Israel; you are crossing over the Jordan today, to go and to possess nations greater and mightier than yourself, great cities, fortified up to heaven.
>
> *(Devarim 9:1)*

It sounds as if "today" is the day when entrance to the Land will finally take place, and one of the great dreams and aspirations of the Jewish people will come to fruition. Some sources indicate

1 This may be indicated by the choice of words utilized to indicate God's response to man's infidelity — chastise, not punish: "You shall know in your heart that as a man chastises his son, so God, your Lord, chastises you. Therefore, you shall keep the commandments of God, your Lord, to walk in His ways and to fear Him" (*Devarim* 8:5–6).

that the verse is not intended to be understood literally, and the term *today* is being used in a metaphoric manner.[1] Be that as it may, the conquest is imminent, and the final preparations must begin. Thus Moshe warns of the dangers of straying from God's path; now, at the border, on the eastern bank of the Jordan, this message is more significant than ever.

This context, the particular moment in Jewish history captured by these verses on the verge of the entrance to Israel, will give us insight to other issues in this parashah.

In last week's parashah, the first chapter of Shema was taught. This week's parashah contains the second chapter, "*V'hayah im shamoa*" (ibid. 11:13). Superficially, the two sections are quite similar, with many themes introduced in one section and repeated in the other. Love of God and care in performing mitzvot are two of the basic teachings which are repeated. The Mishnah stresses the fundamental difference between the two, and teaches that awareness and cognition of this difference is part and parcel of the fulfillment of the commandments, performed by the recitation of the two sections respectively.

> Why was the section of Shema placed before that of "*V'hayah im shamoa*"? So that one should first accept upon himself the yoke of the Kingdom of Heaven and then take upon himself the yoke of the commandments.
>
> *(Berachot 13a)*

The *mishnah* teaches that the primary purpose of the Shema is the acceptance of the "yoke of Heaven," while the focus of the second chapter, "*V'hayah,*" is the acceptance of the commandments. Tradition has familiarized us with this distinction, yet a straightforward reading of the text does not necessarily yield a similar understanding. The first chapter also speaks of the commandments, while the second chapter also delineates our relationship with God. The simple opening sentence, "Hear, Israel, God is our Lord, God is one," reverberates with the conviction of monotheism. The rest of

1 The *Chizkuni,* however, writes that the period of conquest has begun.

the first section seems similar to the second chapter.[1]

The second chapter details the consequences of adherence to the commandments and, alternatively, the results of rebellion.

> It will be if you continually follow My commandments which I command you today — to love God, your Lord, and to serve Him with all your hearts and with all your souls — I will provide rain for your land in its proper time...and you will eat and be satiated. But take heed, lest your hearts become seduced and you deviate, and serve other gods and prostrate to them. Then God will be exceedingly angry with you, and He will restrain the heavens so that there will be no rain, and the ground will not yield its produce. You will be quickly exiled from the good land which God has given you.
>
> *(Devarim 11:13–17)*

Here the Torah describes a direct cause and effect for people's actions. This description is quite instructive. Often people question the relation between man's actions and God's knowledge, on the one hand, and man's freedom of choice on the other.[2] If God indeed knows all that was, is, and will be, then apparently man does not possess freedom of choice. However, life without freedom of choice is a theological nightmare. What is the purpose of existence if God sits in the Heavens pulling strings while we dance below like marionettes?

God's knowledge is beyond human understanding, but if we were to posit that God exists outside of time, then the problem would be solved. Judaism has taught for millennia that God transcends time. Time itself is a created entity and therefore God, as Creator, is outside time. "God knows yesterday what you did to-

---

1 Incidentally, the amount of text which must be recited according to the Biblical requirement of saying Shema is not that simple. There are *Rishonim* who opine that it requires only the first line. Others say the first chapter must be recited; yet others say the first two chapters.

2 Rav Meir Simchah of Dvinsk wrote an exhaustive essay on this topic. It may be found as an addendum to his commentary on the Rambam, *Or Sameiach*, after the laws of repentance.

morrow" is both theologically and gramatically correct. God's knowledge simply transcends time.

This still leaves us with the question of predeterminism, God pulling all the strings. I once saw this idea described in the following manner:[1] The idea of monotheism — one all-powerful God — suggests God's control over all. Therefore, the description of puppets on string would be appropriate. Rambam, with his passion and logic, cut down the strings and insisted on man's freedom of choice. No strings pull man; man has choice, and therefore life has meaning. Man controls his own destiny. The Kabbalists insisted that in truth, there are strings between man and God, and from afar, it seems as if God is pulling the strings. However, the reality is quite different. It is not God pulling the strings, but man. In a sense, existence is a cosmic puppet theater. It was certainly God who built the stage, connected the strings, and has the ability to pull them at will. But it is our actions which cause the reaction from God.[2]

This idea should not sound radical; it is the major message of the second chapter of Shema. As we have seen, if man performs God's commandments, a relationship is forged, and God will provide man with all his needs. Alternatively, when man rebels, God responds by withholding His Divine blessing. This description requires more explanation. Shouldn't this direct causal relationship be more obvious? Why do we not witness this relationship in action, daily and on individual basis?

To understand this, we must return to the comparison between the first two chapters of Shema. There is a fundamental but subtle distinction between the chapters. The first chapter is written in the singular, while the second chapter is written in the plural. (This is not always felt in English translations, where the distinction between singular and plural is often blurred.)[3]

The second chapter, which speaks to the community, speaks of

---

1 In Professor Shalom Rosenberg's pamphlet, *Good and Evil in Jewish Thought.*

2 For a fuller discussion on this relationship, see my comments to *Parashat Naso.*

cause and effect. It is here that we are told that our rebellious behavior will result in lack of rain and eventually exile. One cannot imagine a situation where it rains for one man but not for his neighbor. Certain punishments are communal. Exile is one such type of punishment, especially when we realize that the traditional understanding of exile is not a description of merely a geographical change, but refers to the exile of the *Shechinah* as well. This is obviously a response to communal behavior; either God's presence is among us, as best manifest by the Temple, or we suffer, as a community, the pain of alienation from God and His presence.

Now we can better understand the verse which immediately precedes the second chapter of Shema. The Land of Israel is described as "a land which God, your Lord, cares for; the eyes of God, your Lord, are always upon it, from the beginning of the year to the end of the year" (ibid., 12). This description seems obscure. What does it mean that God looks at this land all year round?

The previous verses contrast Israel with the land of Egypt.

> So that you may prolong your days in the land that God swore to your fathers to give to them and to their seed, a land that flows with milk and honey. For the land that you are entering to inherit is not like the land of Egypt, from where you came out, where you sowed your seed and watered it with your foot, like a garden of vegetables. The land that you are crossing into

---

3 This analysis helps us resolve a number of difficult halachic rulings. For example, we know that there is a Jewish ethic that "he who saves a life is as if he has saved an entire world." Elsewhere, we are taught that, for reasons of *tikun olam* (practical social concerns), a community should not spend exorbitant sums to free captives (see Rambam, *Matanot Aniyim* 8:10,12). Why should a limit be placed on the amount to be spent by a community? Or, in other words, how can a value be put on something of limitless value? The first chapter of Shema calls upon man to love God with all his heart, all his soul, and all his possessions, while the second chapter teaches us to love God "with all your hearts and with all your souls." The second chapter, which speaks to the community, never mentions all the community's possessions. Apparently, the community, as a community, possesses different responsibilities than the individual (Rav Chaim of Volozhin, *Nefesh HaChaim* 1:8. This idea has also been reported in the name of the Sefat Emet, but the exact citation has eluded me).

> to inherit is a land of hills and valleys, and from the rain of the skies you will drink water.
>
> *(Ibid., 9–11)*

The special status of the Land of Israel is manifested in the eyes of God observing the Land. It is a land that needs rain, a land of dry climate. If the rain is not forthcoming, man must turn to God and pray for it. It is a land that brings man in touch with the idea of the *Shechinah*, forcing him to have a relationship with the Almighty. It is not a place where water can be carried from the Nile. It is a land where the symbiotic relationship between man and God is felt. Now we understand why this is the introduction to the second chapter of Shema: If man behaves properly, the *Shechinah* will be felt amongst us. If man ignores God, exile will follow. Israel is a land whose very air makes us wise, because it is a land which demands of us a relationship with the Divine.[1] God, of course, rewards and punishes all men in accordance with their actions, and the purity of their deeds and minds. Nevertheless, the ultimate issues of reward and punishment are on a communal level.

Now we may gain insight into the nature of the community of Israel. We are taught in many sources and contexts that all Jews are responsible for one another.

> This serves to teach you that the great are exhorted concerning the small and are punished on their account if they fail to reprove them. In the same strain it says, "They shall stumble, a man through his brother" (*Vayikra* 26:37), meaning, one for the iniquity of another. This teaches that all Israel are responsible for each other.
>
> *(Bemidbar Rabbah 10:5)*

> For all transgressions in the Torah he alone is punished, but here he and the whole world. And for all transgressions of the Torah is not the whole world punished? It is written, "They

1 See *Bava Batra* 158b: "Rabbi Zeira said: From this one may deduce that the climate [or air] of the Land of Israel makes one wise." Also see *Zohar, Pinchas* 245b, and *Tikunei Zohar* 64a.

> shall stumble one upon another" (*Vayikra* 26:37) — one because of the iniquity of the other. This teaches us that all Israel are responsible one for another.
>
> *(Shavuot 39a)*

This principle of mutual responsibility teaches us that one Jew is responsible if another Jew sins. The negative actions of one person can affect the spiritual level of one's neighbor, and even of the entire community. The paradigmatic example of this principle is the embezzlement perpetrated by Achan.

> The Children of Israel committed a trespass in regard to the consecrated property, for Achan, the son of Karmi, the son of Zavdi, the son of Zerach, of the tribe of Yehudah, took of the consecrated things. The anger of God was kindled against the Children of Israel....
>
> God said to Yehoshua, "Israel has sinned, and they have also transgressed My covenant which I commanded them. They have taken of the consecrated things, and also stolen, and also lied, and also put it among their own possessions. Therefore, the Children of Israel could not stand before their enemies; they turned their backs before their enemies, because they were accursed. I will not be with you anymore if you do not destroy the accursed from among you. Arise, sanctify the people, and say, 'Sanctify yourselves for tomorrow; for so said God, the Lord of Israel: "There is consecrated property in your midst, Israel. You will not be able to stand before your enemies, until you remove the consecrated objects from among you." ' "
>
> *(Yehoshua 7:1–13)*

One man sins and the entire community feels the consequences. Moreover, the verse states that "Israel has sinned," which implies that the entire nation bears responsibility.

This idea is conveyed in *Tanna D'Vei Eliyahu* as follows: The Jewish people are compared to a boat. If there is even one hole, the entire boat is in jeopardy, not only the section with the hole (*Tanna*

D'Vei Eliyahu 11:2). A number of *Rishonim* go even further. The principle of mutual responsibility also teaches us that if one Jew makes a blessing, his friend can answer "amen" and be considered to have said the actual *berachah*. This principle applies when two people are eating and when two are about to perform a mitzvah. If one Jew made Kiddush, and his friend did not hear Kiddush as of yet, the first, who has already fulfilled his own obligation, may say Kiddush again.

The normative explanation for this is that aside from an individual obligation to fulfill commandments, there is also an obligation to insure that others fulfill the commandments as well. However, the Ran explains the idea as follows: As long as the second Jew has not fulfilled his obligation, the first has also not completed his. In a sense, each Jew's obligation to say Kiddush is multiplied by the number of Jews in the world. Therefore, the spiritual state of one Jew affects the spiritual reality of the entire community.[1] Similarly, when Achan sinned, all of Israel was responsible.

The Gemara stresses that this was not the first instance where Achan committed a trespass:

> "Achan answered Yehoshua and said, 'In truth, I have sinned against God, the Lord of Israel, and thus and thus have I done' " (*Yehoshua* 7:20). Rabbi Assi said in Rabbi Chanina's name: This teaches that Achan violated the ban three times, twice in the days of Moshe and once in the days of Yehoshua, for it is written, "I have sinned, and thus and thus have I done."
>
> Rabbi Yochanan said on the authority of Rabbi Elazar bar Shimon: He did so five times, four times in the days of Moshe, and once in the days of Yehoshua, for it is written, "I have sinned and thus and thus have I done." And why were they [the Israelites] not punished until this occasion? Rabbi Yochanan answered on the authority of Rabbi Elazar bar

1 Ran in his commentary at the end of the third chapter of *Rosh HaShanah* (29a).

Shimon: Because [God] did not punish for secret transgressions until the Israelites had crossed the Jordan.

This point is disputed by *Tannaim*: "The hidden [sins] belong to God, our Lord, but the revealed [sins] belong to us and to our children forever" (*Devarim* 29:28). Why are the words "to us and to our children" [*lanu u'lebaneinu*] and the *ayin* of the word "forever" [*ad*] dotted? To teach that God did not punish for transgressions committed in secret until the Israelites had crossed the Jordan.

(Sanhedrin 43b)

This passage refers to a verse at the end of *Devarim*:

God became angry at that land, to bring upon it all the curses that are written in this book. God rooted them out of their land in anger, in wrath, and in great indignation, and He sent them to another land, as it is this day. The hidden [sins] belong to God, our Lord, but the revealed [sins] belong to us and to our children forever, to fulfill all the words of this Torah.

(Devarim 29:26–28)

Rashi explains that we are not responsible for the secret sins perpetrated by others, but we bear responsibility to chastise people who perpetrate sins that we know about and eradicate these sins from our midst. Rashi qualifies the injunction, saying that it only began after the Jews crossed the Jordan. When they made the oaths on Mount Gerizim and Mount Eival, the Jewish people became responsible for one another.[1]

Though the Torah was given at Sinai and the Jews became a nation as they left Egypt, mutual responsibility begins as the people cross the Jordan. It is solidified as they stand on Mount Gerizim and Mount Eival. This is because mutual responsibility is inextricably related to national identity, of which inhabiting the Land is an

1 *Rashi, Devarim* 29:28. Rashi refers to separate actions, one crossing the Jordan, and the second standing on the respective mountains and making the vows. According to the story line in *Yehoshua*, the episode of Achan transpired prior to standing on Mounts Grizim and Eival. However, the sequence of events is debated in the Talmudic sources, see *Sotah* 37.

essential component. Only when the Israelites entered the Land was this aspect of nationhood complete. Now they were bidden to stand on Mount Gerizim and Eival and reaffirm their commitment to follow the Torah given at Sinai. At that moment mutual responsibility became a reality.

> "These are the words of the covenant which God commanded Moshe..." (*Devarim* 28:69), and it is written: "Keep the words of this covenant..." (ibid. 29:8). There were forty-eight covenants in connection with each commandment. Rabbi Shimon excludes [the occasion of] Mount Gerizim and Mount Eival and includes that of the Ohel Mo'ed in the desert. The difference of opinion here is the same as that of the teachers in the following: Rabbi Yishmael says: General laws were taught at Sinai and particular laws in the Ohel Mo'ed. Rabbi Akiva says: Both general and particular laws were taught at Sinai, repeated in the Ohel Mo'ed, and [taught] for the third time in the plains of Mo'av. Consequently, there is not a single commandment written in the Torah which did not have forty-eight covenants made over it.
>
> Rabbi Shimon bar Yehudah of K'far Akko said in the name of Rabbi Shimon: There is not a single commandment written in the Torah which did not have forty-eight times 603,550 covenants made over it. Rabbi said: According to the reasoning of Rabbi Shimon bar Yehudah of K'far Akko...it follows that for each Israelite there are 603,550 commandments. What is the issue between them? Rabbi Mesharshiya said: The point between them is that of personal responsibility and responsibility for others.
>
> *(Sotah 37b)*

The principle of mutual responsibility was taught as the Jews crossed the Jordan. In our parashah, as the Jews stood on the other side of the Jordan, issues of communal responsibility needed to be examined and understood. The Land has so much more than milk and honey; it has a spiritual capacity to bring us close to God, to make us wise. When communal responsibility is ignored, our existence in the Land is jeopardized. Spiritual havoc results, and the results for the nation and each individual comprising the nation are disastrous.

The Gemara, in an amazing passage, tells us of the destruction of Yerushalayim. The destruction befalls not only the wicked who rebelled, but also the "righteous," who did not attempt to influence the wicked.

> A favorable word never left the mouth of the Holy One, blessed be He, which was later retracted for evil, except for this, where it is written, "God said to him, 'Go through the midst of the city, through the midst of Yerushalayim, and set a mark upon the foreheads of the men who sigh and cry for all the abominations that are done in their midst' " (*Yechezkel* 9:4).
>
> The Holy One, blessed be He, said to [the angel] Gavriel, "Go and set a mark of ink upon the foreheads of the righteous, so that the destroying angels will have no power over them, and a mark of blood upon the foreheads of the wicked, that the destroying angels will have power over them."
>
> The Attribute of Justice said to the Holy One, blessed be He, "Master of the universe, how are these different from those?"
>
> He told it, "These are completely righteous men, while these are completely wicked."
>
> It said, "Master of the universe, they had the power to protest but did not."
>
> God said, "It was fully known to them that had they protested they would not have been heeded."
>
> It said, "Master of the universe, if it was revealed to You, was it revealed to them?"
>
> Thus it is written, "[Kill] the old man, the young man, and the maiden, the little children and the women; but do not come near any man upon whom is the mark; and begin at My Sanctuary" (ibid., 6). Then they began at the elders who stood before the Temple.[1]
>
> *(Shabbat 55a)*

The behavior of the nation as a whole is observed from Heaven, and even though the righteous are perhaps not personally deserving of punishment, nevertheless, they cannot escape it. This passage teaches us that the righteous are primarily responsible for the spiritual environment which was created. Why did the wicked feel that to fulfill their life's ambitions they would be better off abandoning Torah and embracing a different system of thought and a foreign mode of behavior? For this the righteous have to give an accounting. After all, if we were to observe those around us digging holes under themselves in a boat on which we were standing, wouldn't we respond quickly? Especially when those digging might not fully comprehend the ramifications of their actions? If the boat does sink, are not the "enlightened" responsible?

As the people stood on the banks of the Jordan River, poised to meet their destiny, they received a lesson in metaphysics. It was the type of lesson that, if learned, understood, and internalized, would have made our stay in Israel an eternal glorious stay. It is a lesson we still need to review today.

1 A number of *Rishonim* rule that this passage reflects the law that rebuke applies even if a person will not listen. See *Smag* 11, *Yerayim* 223.

Parashat Re'ei

A Blessing and a Curse

> See, I give you today [a choice of] a blessing and a curse: the blessing when you listen to the commandments of God, your Lord, which I command you today, and the curse, if you do not listen to the commandments of God, your Lord, and you deviate from the path which I command you today, in order to follow other gods which you did not know.
>
> *(Devarim 11:26–28)*

The parashah begins with Moshe placing before the people two choices — a blessing or a curse, the results of following the word of God or abandoning it and embarking on a path which will lead to idolatry. These verses encapsulate the entire parashah, which goes on to spell out the choices. In a sense, much of the parashah is a polemic against idolatry, but in order to understand this we first need to better understand the choice, the difference between the blessing and the curse.

Obviously, the blessing and curse are results of these two different paths which man may take — embracing the word of God or abandoning it. Later on in this soliloquy, Moshe describes the inevitable, catastrophic results of deviation from the teachings of God:

> God became angry at that land, to bring upon it all the curses written in this book.... It will be when all these things befall

> you, the blessing and the curse which I placed before you....
>
> *(Ibid. 29:26, 30:1)*

The same blessing and curse which our parashah introduced are now spelled out in detail. There the text continues:

> See, I have placed before you today life and good, and death and evil.... I call heaven and earth as witnesses against you. Life and death I have placed in front of you, the blessing and the curse. Choose life, so that you and your children can live.
>
> *(Ibid. 30:15, 19)*

This text bears remarkable similarity to the beginning of our parashah, where the same formula is used: "See, I have placed before you...." Here the text identifies the blessing with life and the curse with death. This is the real choice for man: life or death. It is hard to imagine a more stark distinction than that between life and death. They stand at the opposite poles of human experience. Why would anyone choose death over life? The choice seems illogical. Certainly, there are people for whom life becomes too painful, and they choose to avoid their pain. Some choose drugs, while others go one step further and choose death. But this is the description of a maladjusted individual. Why would the Torah have to speak at such great length about psychological maladies?

The choice between life and death has a famous parallel which was presented to man at the very dawn of existence:

> God, the Lord, caused every tree pleasant to the sight and good to eat to grow from the ground, as well as the Tree of Life in the Garden and the Tree of Knowledge of good and evil.... God, the Lord, took Man and placed him in the Garden of Eden, to work it and to guard it. God, the Lord, commanded Man, saying, "From every tree in the garden you shall eat. But from the Tree of Knowledge of good and evil, do not eat from it, for on the day that you eat from it you shall surely die."
>
> *(Bereishit 2:9, 16–17)*

One tree is associated with life, the other with death. Clearly, no sane person would choose death over life, unless, of course, there is a snake whispering seductive thoughts in his ear, leading him to self-destruction.

This description is a paradigm for all man. We have all been placed in a Gan Eden, life and death presented before us, and we are told by God to choose life. But alas, we continue to listen to the devious snakes, real or imagined, who encourage us to partake of the tree of death, despite the manifold curses which accompany that choice.

The world, from its very inception, was created with choices. Ultimately, these choices are between life and death, but rarely do people see their choices in such terms. The possibility for evil or pain is part of the process of creation, or, perhaps, is a result of Creation:

> "Behold, it was very good" (*Bereishit* 1:31). "Behold, it was good" alludes to the creation of Man and the good inclination; "very" alludes to the evil inclination. Is, then, the evil inclination "very good"? It is in truth to teach you that were it not for the evil inclination, no one would build a house, marry, or beget children.
>
> *(Kohelet Rabbah 3:15)*

The very Creation includes the evil inclination, and without it we cannot speak of the world being "very good." The possibility of evil is an essential part of the Creation.

This idea is expressed most clearly in a passage in *Yeshayah*:

> I am God, and there is no one else. There is no God beside Me. I girded you, and you have not known Me. So that they may know from the rising of the sun and from the west that there is none beside Me. I am God, and there is no one else. I form light and create darkness; I make peace and create evil; I, God, do all these things.
>
> *(Yeshayah 45:5–7)*

Here, in unequivocal terms, God proclaims that He creates for all phenomena, good and evil. To ascribe these things to any other power would necessarily impinge on the basis of monotheism. All things come from God. But why would God create a world with these things? Furthermore, how can the Midrash label these things as "very good"? How can a God who is all good, who defines good, cause evil?

On the one hand, we can appreciate that if all things come from Heaven, including pain and punishment, all of these things are motivated by God's absolute love for us. As a parent must discipline a child, so does God treat us.[1] If a parent responds to a child's antisocial behavior with rewards, the child will most likely become a sociopath. Likewise, if God responds to the antisocial behavior of the masses with rewards and gifts, an entire generation or nation of sociopaths would result.

However, the verse from *Yeshayah* cited above deserves a second reading.[2] Close inspection of the text offers a fascinating insight. Light is formed, while darkness is created; peace is made, while evil is created. What is the difference between formation and creation? Formation indicates an appearance of "something from something," while creation indicates ex nihilo — something from nothing. We may learn from careful examination of *Yeshayah*'s words that light, or good, is derived from a primordial source — from God — while evil is created. Despite the fact that evil was created by God, it does not emanate from Him. Light is refracted from the supernal good, while a separate act of creation results in the ap-

1 "You shall also consider in your heart that as a man chastises his son, so God, your Lord, chastises you. Therefore, you shall keep the commandments of God, your Lord, to walk in His ways, and to fear Him" (*Devarim* 8:5–6).

2 We are familiar with the more popular paraphrase of this verse which is incorporated in our daily prayers, concluding with "creates everything" instead of "creates evil." The Gemara observes that this language is a bit more palatable: "What benedictions does one say [in the morning]? Rabbi Yaakov said in the name of Rabbi Oshaya: '[Blessed are You] who forms light and creates darkness.' Should one rather say, 'Who forms light and creates brightness'? [No,] we keep the language of the Scripture. If that is so, [what of the next words in the text,] 'Who makes peace and creates evil' — do we repeat them as they are written? [No.] It is written 'evil' and we say 'all things' as a euphemism" (*Berachot* 11a–b).

pearance of something new, not part of God, called evil. The mystics described this process as *tzimtzum*, divine contraction. This process of creation allows the appearance of something other than God, which needed to be created because it did not exist in God's sphere. The Midrash alludes to this idea:

> "I form light and create darkness; I make peace." Having created them, He makes peace between them. "God called the light 'day' " (*Bereishit* 1:5). Rabbi Elazar said: The Holy One, blessed be He, does not link His name with evil, but only with good. Thus it is not written here, "God called the light 'day,' and God called the darkness 'night,' " but "The darkness called He 'night' " (ibid.).
>
> *(Bereishit Rabbah 3:6)*

This concept is encapsulated in a one-line phrase in the Midrash:

> No evil descends from Heaven.
>
> *(Yalkut Shimoni, Va'eira 186)*

The author of the *midrash* is clearly aware of the verse in *Yeshayah* cited above, but simply assumes, as we do, that creation differs from formation. Therefore, evil does not emanate from Heaven. Rather, it is a by-product of Creation.

Likewise, commenting on our parashah, Rabbi Chaim of Allepo (a student of Rabbi Chaim Vital), noted:

> "See, I give you today [lit., *I place before you*] a blessing and a curse" — "Before you" and not "on you," for no evil descends from Heaven. Rather, it is placed before you; the choice is yours.
>
> *(Torat Chacham 419:3)*

In a certain sense, this may sound like theological double-talk. If God causes evil, how can God remain completely good?[1] In a

1 The mainstream Christian response to this question is a combination of avoiding this verse on the one hand, and deifying the devil on the other hand. The devil thus becomes an adversary for God, instead of an adversary for man. This position clearly

lengthy passage, the *Zohar* addresses this question:

> True love to the Holy One, blessed be He, consists of just this, that we give over to Him all our emotional, intellectual, and material faculties and possessions, and love Him.
>
> If it is asked, "How can a man love [God] with his evil inclination? Is not the evil inclination the seducer, preventing man from approaching the Holy One to serve Him? How, then, can man use the evil inclination as an instrument of love to God?" The answer lies in this, that there can be no greater service done to the Holy One than to subdue the evil inclination by the power of love of the Holy One, blessed be He. When it is subdued and its power is broken by man in this way, then [man] becomes a true lover of the Holy One, since he has learned how to make the evil inclination itself serve the Holy One.
>
> This is a mystery entrusted to the masters of esoteric lore. All that the Holy One has made, both above and below, is for the purpose of manifesting His glory and making all things serve Him. Would a master permit his servant to work against him, and to continually lay plans to counteract his will? It is the will of the Holy One that men should worship Him and walk in the way of truth, so that they will be rewarded with many benefits. How, then, can an evil servant come and counteract the will of his Master by tempting man to walk in an evil way, seducing him from the good way and causing him to disobey the will of his Lord?
>
> But, indeed, the evil inclination also does the will of its Lord through this. It is like a king who had an only son whom he

undermines monotheism and is therefore untenable from a Jewish perspective. Ironically, the Jews, who believe in an all-powerful Deity who "creates evil," have been accused of "devil worship" — a conclusion which results from twisted, circular, tautological reasoning. Interestingly enough, most Jewish scholars who have attacked Christianity as being an affront to monotheism have based their attacks on the doctrine of the Trinity, and not on the exalted status reserved in Christianity for the devil — the "fallen angel."

dearly loved. Because of this [love], he warned him not to be enticed by bad women, saying that anyone defiled could not enter his palace. The son promised his father to do his will in love.

Outside the palace, however, there lived a beautiful harlot. After a while the king thought, *I will see how devoted my son is to me.* He called to the woman and commanded[1] her, saying, "Entice my son, for I wish to test his obedience to my will."

She used every blandishment to lure [the son] into her embraces. But the son, being good, obeyed the commandment of his father. He refused her allurements and thrust her from him.

Then the father rejoiced exceedingly, brought [his son] into the innermost chamber of the palace, bestowed upon him gifts from his best treasures, and showed him every honor. And who was the cause of all this joy? The harlot! Is she to be praised or blamed for it? To be praised, surely, on all accounts, for she fulfilled the king's command and carried out his plans for him, and she also caused the son to receive all the good gifts and deepened the king's love to his son.

Therefore, it is written, "The Lord saw all that He had made, and behold it was very good" (*Bereishit* 1:31). The word *very* refers to the Angel of Death [i.e., the evil inclination]. Similarly, if it were not for this accuser, the righteous would not possess the supernal treasures in the World to Come. Happy, therefore, are they who come into conflict with the tempter and prevail against him, for through him they attain bliss and all the good and desirable possessions of the World to Come.

(Zohar, Shemot 163b)

The *Zohar*, in this remarkable passage, describes in the clearest of terms how it is possible for the "king" — a metaphor for God — to allow this scenario to unfold outside the palace. The impetus for

1 It is important to note that in the *Zohar*'s typology, the devil must adhere to the command of the king — God.

evil is the king's will. The king wishes for evil to be rejected, but this is not possible within the palace walls. Likewise, man prior to Creation possesses a soul, but no free choice. He lives in the palace. Outside the palace, in this world, temptation exists — in order to be rejected.[1] Ultimately, all temptation is sent by God in order to be rejected. Therefore, evil may be seen as good "incognito." Despite the allure of desire at the moment of passion, the sinner will one day come to realize that what he embraced is merely an emissary of the King — God — which was meant to be rejected. This is the meaning of the *midrash*, "No evil descends from Heaven."

Likewise, we can now understand how the term "very good" applies to the evil inclination. By rejecting the evil inclination, man is enabled to reach a spiritual level unattainable in Heaven, where only good is a reality. The Gemara adds that this is the desire of the Satan:

> Rabbi Levi said: Both Satan and Peninah had a pious purpose [in acting as adversaries]. Satan, when he saw God inclined to favor Iyov, said, "Far be it that God should forget the love of Avraham." Of Peninah it is written, "Her rival provoked her [Chanah] sorely to make her fret" (*Shmuel* I 1:6). When Rabbi Acha bar Yaakov gave this exposition in Papunia, Satan came and kissed his feet.
>
> *(Bava Batra 16a)*

We further understand that our view of the world is somewhat skewed. We see evil as a reality, thus failing to realize that it is actually a servant of the King "dressed up." Evil, by virtue of being a cre-

---

1 Perhaps the Talmudic adage "It would have been better for man not to have been created" (*Eiruvin* 13b) would be better understood with a literal translation: "Man would have been more comfortable had he not been created." Life in the palace is certainly more comfortable, but less meaningful. "For two and a half years Beit Shammai and Beit Hillel were in dispute, the former asserting that it were better for man not to have been created than to have been created, and the latter maintaining that it is better for man to have been created than not to have been created. They finally took a vote and decided that it were better for man not to have been created than to have been created, but now that he has been created, let him investigate his past deeds or, as others say, let him examine his future actions" (ibid.).

ation, does not really exist in the palace of God. Rather, it is the result of an act of creation and will one day dissipate.

But what is the evil inclination? The Gemara identifies it with other known adversaries:

> Satan, the evil inclination, and the Angel of Death are all one.
>
> *(Ibid.)*

These three forces are instilled in the world as part of a cosmic balancing act, in order to give man free choice. The verse which we began with, "See, I give you today [a choice of] a blessing and a curse," is only relevant if man has free choice. Man's evil inclination does not necessarily work by calling upon man to perform objectively evil deeds. Rather, any action which distances man from God is sought out by the evil inclination. Furthermore, at times the choices with which man is faced are both positive, but one will bring man closer to God than the other. In such cases, the evil inclination is particularly insidious, for man himself may be unsure which choice represents the good inclination and which the evil. The litmus test must always be which of these choices will bring the individual closer to God. The Gemara expresses this succinctly:

> God created the evil inclination; He created the Torah as its antidote.
>
> *(Ibid.)*

The Torah is the only objective source that we possess which forces man to follow the good inclination. Following its rules, laws, morals, and systems of prioritizing is what enables man to define right and wrong and therefore to choose right from wrong. There are often situations which seem to fall in the "gray area." It is precisely in such cases that we must remind ourselves that the Torah defines right and wrong.

Now we can return to this week's parashah. One of the major attractions of idolatry was the possibility for local worship "under every leafy tree."

> You shall completely destroy all the places where the nations which you are inheriting [from] served their gods — upon the high mountains, upon the hills, and under every leafy tree.
>
> *(Devarim 12:2)*

The motivation of such worship was immediate gratification, which resulted from man worshipping his own desires and not God. We can appreciate how individuals who followed idolatrous practices could have deceived themselves into thinking that it was God that they were serving, here and now. But the Torah calls upon man to practice a centralized religion with its spiritual capital in a chosen place.

> But to the place which God, your Lord, will choose out of all your tribes to put His name there, to His habitation shall you seek, and there you shall come.
>
> *(Ibid., 5)*

This would force man to objectify his religious practice and take it out of the realm of instinct. How was the individual who felt within himself a burning need to reach out to God to know if his desire emanated from a place of holiness or from self-destruction? The only possible answer is to follow the rules set out in the Torah.

The parashah speaks of the false prophet:

> If there arises among you a prophet or a dreamer of dreams, and he gives you a sign or a wonder, and the sign or the wonder comes to pass, of which he spoke to you, saying, "Let us go after other gods which you have not known and let us serve them," you shall not listen to the words of that prophet or that dreamer of dreams; for God, your Lord, tests you, to know whether you love God, your Lord, with all your heart and with all your soul. You shall walk after God, your Lord. Fear Him, keep His commandments, and obey His voice. You shall serve Him and attach yourselves to Him.
>
> *(Ibid. 13:2–5)*

How can we, as individuals, know if an apparently holy person is the "real thing" or a charlatan? Again, the objective system is Torah: If the "prophet" encourages practices alien to the Torah, he is to be executed. At times, though, such issues are not as black and white as we would like. Once we realize that the evil inclination entices with arguments and experiences which are not intrinsically, objectively evil but are simply not the best way to relate to God, we are armed for this spiritual combat.

Ultimately, the evil inclination leads to self-deception and destruction. The choice between life and death is the result of the battle, but far more often than not, the battle is waged in more innocuous settings. The people entering the Land would only be spiritually armed for the ensuing battles if they were made aware that a spiritual battleground awaited them. They were armed with the ability to be victorious:

> See, I have placed before you today life and good, and death and evil.... I call heaven and earth as witnesses against you. Life and death I have placed in front of you, the blessing and the curse. Choose life, so that you and your children can live.

Indeed, let us choose life, the Tree of Life — the words of the living God.

Parashat Shoftim

"Justice, Justice"

> Judges and officers you shall appoint in all your gates, which God, your Lord, gives you, throughout your tribes; and they shall judge the people with just judgment. Do not pervert judgment; do not play favorites; and do not take bribes, for bribery blinds the eyes of the wise and perverts the words of the righteous. Justice, justice you shall pursue, so that you may live and inherit the land which God, your Lord, gives you.
>
> *(Devarim 16:18–20)*

The parashah begins with broad social concerns, namely the establishment of justice. In a sense, one may view these concerns as transcending the "religious" realm, but clearly a nation who will live in their own land requires what Rousseau called a "social contract." As we have seen in other instances, the Torah's weltanshaaung is exceedingly broad; consequently, the Torah does not limit its legislation to "religious" issues. Torts and damages make up a significant part of the legal sections of the Torah. Now, as the Jewish people find themselves at the threshold of the Land of Israel, and social ideals will hopefully be translated into a utopian society on earth, Moshe returns to the principles laid out in other sections of the Torah.

When it comes time to translate the theory into practice,

judges will be needed to apply the law and police will be needed to enforce the law. The Torah, in the verses quoted above, exhorts the people to refine social justice to unprecedented levels. Justice must not be perverted, as such behavior would circumvent the entire judicial system. There is one verse, though, that is most challenging:

> Justice, justice shall you pursue, so that you may live and inherit the land which God, your Lord, gives you.

Why is the term *justice* repeated? One may posit that the repetition is a literary device employed for emphasis. Such usage is common. For example, see this week's haftarah[1] for four examples of such usage. However, the word *pursue* implies an ongoing endeavor, a striving to succeed. If we already have this strong term, why is the repetition of "justice" necessary?

The Gemara addresses both parts of the phrase:

> "Justice, justice you shall pursue" means you shall follow an eminent *beit din*. For example, [go] after Rabbi Eliezer [ben Hyrkanus] to Lod or Rabbi Yochanan ben Zakkai to Beror Chayil.
>
> *(Sanhedrin 32b)*

The word which the Talmud is focusing on is *pursue*. How does one pursue justice? By finding a superior tribunal. The Gemara adds a proactive prescription:

> "Justice, justice you shall pursue" means you shall follow the scholars to their academies. [For example, go] after Rabbi Eliezer to Lod, Rabbi Yochanan ben Zakkai to Beror Chayil, Rabbi Yehoshua to Peki'in, Rabban Gamliel to Yavneh, Rabbi Akiva to Bnei Brak, Rabbi Mattiya to Rome, Rabbi Chananya ben Teradyon to Sikni, Rabbi Yosi [ben Chalafta] to Tzippori, Rabbi Yehudah ben Beteirah to Netzivin, Rabbi Yehoshua to the Diaspora, Rebbi to Beit She'arim, or the Sages to the Lishkat HaGazit.
>
> *(Ibid.)*

1 *Yeshayah* 51:12–17, 52:1–11.

We are told here that the best way to avoid the necessity for justice to be meted out by the courts is to obtain a quality education. Both of these Talmudic comments expound on the word *pursue*. This tradition is mirrored in the words of Rashi (based on *Sifri*):

> Go after a good court.
>
> *(Rashi, Devarim 16:20)*

However, we are still mystified regarding the meaning of the doubling of the word *justice*. The explanations that we have seen up to this point would still apply had the verse read "Justice you shall pursue" or "Pursue justice."

On the same page, the Gemara cites another teaching, which directly addresses this point:

> It is written, "Judge your neighbor with justice" (*Vayikra* 19:15), and it is written "Justice, justice you shall pursue".... One refers to a decision based on strict law, the other to a compromise. As it has been taught: "Justice, justice you shall pursue"; the first [mention of justice] refers to a decision based on strict law; the second, to a compromise.

Here we find the Gemara directly discussing the two "justices." The suggestion of the Gemara is fascinating: There are, in fact, two types of justice, strict law and compromise. The Gemara further illustrates the principle with the following example:

> How so? Two boats sailing on a river meet. If both attempt to pass simultaneously, both will sink, whereas if one makes way for the other, both can pass [without mishap]. Likewise, two camels on the ascent to Beit Choron meet. If they both ascend [at the same time], both may tumble down [into the valley]; but if [they ascend] one after another, both can go up [safely]. How then should they act? If one is laden and the other unladen, the unladen one should give way to the laden one. If one is closer [to its destination] than the other, the closer one should give way to the farther one. If both are [equally] closer

> to or farther from [their destinations], make a compromise between them. The one [which is to go forward] should compensate the other [which has to give way].

The "justice" described here is situational, subjective. The locale is not the pristine courts of law but the mundane rivers and streets. Here, too, justice must be pursued. Finding equitable solutions to complex practical situations is part and parcel of the pursuit of justice.[1]

We have seen the opinion that the two "justices" point to different types of justice, strict law and compromise. There is an alternative approach to the two types of justice, found in the writings of Rabbeinu Nissim of Gerondi. In order to understand his position, let us consider a passage of Gemara he cites:

> Rabbi Eliezer ben Yaakov said, "I have heard that the *beit din* may [when necessary] impose flagellation and pronounce [capital] sentences even where not [warranted] by the Torah — not with the intention of disregarding the Torah but [on the contrary] in order to safeguard it.
>
> *(Sanhedrin 46a)*

This teaching is most surprising. How can the court punish in a manner contrary to its own rules? The mandate of the court is to judge according to the rules laid down in the Torah, and there can be no extenuating considerations for a court, which must uphold the law. On the other hand, could there be?

There was, according to Rabbeinu Nissim,[2] a second, parallel

1 An interesting aside: When the modern State of Israel was established, the first prime minister, David Ben Gurion, asked various rabbis, "How does a modern secular state coexist with the religious community, which bases its existence on different values and laws?"

The Chazon Ish, who can be called the most eminent rabbi of his age, responded that points of conflict could be resolved based on the passage cited above. "When two camels meet at a narrow ledge, we must look which of the two has been traveling longer and bearing a greater burden." The Chazon Ish concluded that this analogy certainly applies to the religious community and that the State should therefore "step aside" and respect those values carried for millennia. There are various versions of the response or lack of response of the prime minister.

system, a system of checks and balances, as it were; namely, the system revolving around the king. The monarch in ancient Israel had a mandate to impose sentences outside of the normal legal establishment. The reason for empowering the king in this way was to safeguard the spirit of the law and prevent it from being trampled by strict adherence to the letter of the law. The mandate of the courts was to uphold the letter of the law, while the mandate of the king was to uphold the spirit of the law. This dichotomy created a wonderful, balanced whole. When the courts functioned as an autonomous arm of the legal system, adhering to and enforcing every law, the danger still existed that things might "fall between the cracks." In such cases, the king would act, guaranteeing that the spirit of the law remained intact.

This system, though, has a built-in danger. By definition, the role of the king was to reject the socially established morality. What prevented the king from abusing this awesome power? Rabbeinu Nissim presents a beautiful image in answer to this question. We know that there is a law that the king must carry a Torah scroll with him at all times. Rabbeinu Nissim explains that the very person empowered to break the law must hold the Torah near and dear. The kings of Israel were therefore commanded to hold the Torah with them at all times, as a reminder of what was at stake.

This analysis, interesting as it may be, does not seem to provide any insight into the passage cited above in the name of Rabbi Eliezer ben Yaakov concerning unusual measures taken by the courts. Rabbenu Nissim explains that the *gemara* is describing the situation that existed after the abolishment of the monarchy. In the absence of the king, the role of the king reverted to the courts. They became both the upholders of the letter of the law and the safeguarders of the spirit of the law. When a case ended according to the normative, prescribed process, the judges had to ask themselves a new question: "Was justice served?" If the answer was negative, the judges assumed the role of the king and sought out the

2 *Drashot HaRan*, section 11.

spirit of the law. Again, the people entrusted with this task were those with the greatest affinity for the Torah and its values.[1]

There are times where the law must be set aside in order to upkeep the law:

> It is time to act for God; they have made void Your Torah.
>
> *(Tehillim 119:26)*

The Gemara uses this verse as scriptural license to adjudicate and legislate against explicit Torah laws in order to uphold the Torah.

> "It is time to act for God; they have made void Your Torah." Rava said: The first clause of this verse can be taken as explaining the second, and the second can be taken as explaining the first. The first clause may be taken as explaining the second thus: "It is time to act for God." Why? Because "they have made void Your Torah." The second clause may be taken as explaining the first thus: "They have made void Your Torah." Why? Because "it is time to act for God."
>
> *(Berachot 63a)*

The upkeep of the law, where justice thrives, is one of the goals of Torah. The Gemara goes so far as to declare that

> Every judge who judges a true judgment according to its truth even for a single hour, Scipture considers him like a partner to the Holy One, blessed be He, in the Creation.
>
> *(Shabbat 10a)*

Utilizing the Torah and bringing its lofty ideas into this world makes one a partner with God. Nevertheless, this will only be the case when the law is judged according to truth. Using the proper tools but arriving at the wrong conclusion is not "a true judgment according to its truth."

The strict letter of the law arrived at via the judicial process may

1 Rabbi Reuven Margoliot, in his comments in *Margoliot HaYam* on the aforementioned passage in *Sanhedrin*, cites numerous examples from the Middle Ages where this theoretical power was employed.

be lacking. The Shelah similarly explains:

> "Justice, justice you shall pursue." It says "justice" twice. The first is directed to the judges who judge in accordance with Torah law. There is a second "justice" for compromise or emergency decrees, which are done occasionally by a prophet or king, in order for the world to exist. Therefore the verse concludes, "so that you may live and inherit the land which God, your Lord, gives you." As the Sages said, "Yerushalayim was destroyed only because [its judges] gave judgments within it according to Biblical law" (*Bava Metzia* 30b).
>
> *(Shnei Luchot HaBrit, Shoftim 101a)*

The first part of the teaching is the same as the idea we saw expressed by Rabbeinu Nissim. The concluding remarks are based on a passage in the Gemara:

> Yerushalayim was destroyed only because [its judges] gave judgments within it according to Biblical law. Should they then have judged according to untrained arbitrators? [No.] But say thus: [The city was destroyed] because [its judges] based their judgments [strictly] upon Biblical law and did not go beyond the letter of the law.
>
> *(Bava Metzia 30b)*

Strict adherence to law can be destructive. Yerushalayim, the center of the Torah world, the place from which Torah is to flow forth, was destroyed because the Torah, as it was lived there, did not bring about a merger with God. Somehow, the partnership had deteriorated, and Yerushalayim became rubble.

Ramban's understanding of the verse is that one "justice" refers to earthly courts, while the other "justice" refers to the Heavenly Tribunal. If man does not succeed in bringing about a just world, real judgment awaits him above. Ramban bases his teaching on *Sefer Bahir*, one of the most obscure mystical tracts:

> The first justice is literal justice. This is the Divine presence....

> The second justice frightens the righteous.
>
> *(Bahir, section 75)*

If man succeeds in attaining justice, the *Shechinah* flows. On the other hand, if man does not create a just world, Divine Judgment is applied.

Justice must be strived for, not only on a national level but on an individual level as well, for there is a Divine reaction to man's handiwork also on the individual level. And just as a nation may lose focus of the spirit of the law, so may the individual. This may be illustrated by the following passage:

> The halachah is always in agreement with Beit Hillel, but he who wishes to act in agreement with the ruling of Beit Shammai may do so, and he who wishes to act according to the view of Beit Hillel may do so. [However, he who adopts] the more lenient rulings of Beit Shammai and the more lenient rulings of Beit Hillel is a wicked man, [while of the one who adopts] the stringencies of Beit Shammai and the stringencies of Beit Hillel, Scripture said, "The fool walks in darkness" (*Kohelet* 2:14). A man should rather act either in agreement with Beit Shammai both in their lenient and stringent rulings or in agreement with Beit Hillel in both their lenient and stringent rulings.
>
> *(Eiruvin 6b)*

We can understand why the person who religiously adheres to the lenient opinion is considered wicked. By performing the minimum required of him, he consistently avoids developing his relationship with God. However, wherein lies the foolishness of the person who picks the strict opinion of each side? Should he not be applauded for his zeal? The answer is subtle yet profound: This person is no longer using law in order to relate to God. Rather, he is worshiping the law itself. The letter of the law becomes his god. Technically, he has done no harm, yet he is foolish inasmuch as his sensibilities have caused him to obscure his relationship with God, which becomes dysfunctional. The individual must seek truth, whether it is lenient or strict, and those who are unable to do so on their own should find a spiritual guide, and follow him consistently.[1]

The Imrei Emet from the Gur dynasty brings down a teaching which relates this idea back to our parashah:

> "Distance yourself from a false matter" (*Shemot* 23:7).... We [generally] do not find the Torah legislating distancing from prohibitions, for all the fences and limitations are Rabbinic. Only regarding falsehood is the distancing a Torah law. The Sefat Emet explained that the same idea is found regarding truth; pursing truth is a Torah law [mitzvah]. "Go after a good court" is in actuality the mitzvah to seek truth.... Searching for the truth is dependent on the individual, and he will receive assistance from Heaven.
>
> *(Imrei Emet, Shemot 5688)*

When man seeks truth, help comes from Heaven, but the search must be sincere: "Justice, justice you shall pursue." When we succeed, we become partners with God, for we have found truth, which is God's seal.

> Kindness and truth met together; righteousness and peace kissed each other. Truth shall sprout from the earth, and righteousness shall look down from Heaven. Also, God shall give that which is good, and our land shall yield her produce.
>
> *(Tehillim 85:11–13)*

When man seeks truth here on earth, God's righteousness flows from Heaven. The Sages explained these verses in a celebrated passage of Midrash:

> Rabbi Shimon said: When the Holy One, blessed be He, came

1 This idea has been observed by numerous scholars. The Kotzker Rebbe was quoted lamenting that the Jews can turn anything into idolatry — even Torah. Recently, Professor Haym Soloveitchik made a similar sociological observation, in his article in *Tradition*, "Rupture and Reconstruction."

> to create Adam, the ministering angels formed themselves into groups and parties, some of them saying, "Let him be created," while others urged, "Let him not be created." Thus it is written, "Kindness and truth fought together, righteousness and peace combatted each other" (*Tehillim* 85:11). Kindness said, "Let him be created, because he will dispense acts of kindness." Truth said, "Let him not be created, because he is compounded of falsehood." Righteousness said, "Let him be created, because he will perform righteous deeds." Peace said, "Let him not be created, because he is full of strife."
>
> What did the Lord do? He took truth and cast it to the ground. The ministering angels said to the Holy One, blessed be He, "Master of the universe, why do You despise Your seal? Let truth arise from the earth!" Hence it is written, "Truth shall sprout from the earth".... Rabbi Huna the Elder of Tzippori said: While the ministering angels were arguing with each other and disputing with each other, the Holy One, blessed be He, created him [Adam]. He said to them, "What can you avail? Man has already been made!"
>
> *(Bereishit Rabbah 8:5)*

Man seeks truth in his own domain, which is not always a simple task. But when he succeeds, he becomes a partner with God, which is something that even escapes the understanding of the angels.

The pursuit of justice is the pursuit of truth. Both the individual and the society must seek justice and truth, for when we succeed the *Shechinah* dwells among us, and we become partners with God. When we seek truth, we are aided from Heaven. However, the *midrash* in this week's parashah teaches that there is even more at stake:

> God said to Israel, "My children, by your life, as a result of your respecting justice, I am exalted." From where do we know this? As it is said, "God, the Lord of Hosts, is exalted through justice" (*Yeshayah* 5:16). "And because you exalt Me through jus-

> tice I too will act righteously and will cause My holiness to dwell among you." From where do we know this? As it is said, "The Holy God is sanctified through righteousness" (ibid.). "And if you will respect both righteousness and justice I will immediately redeem you with a complete redemption." From where do we know this? As it is said, "So said God: Keep justice and do righteousness, for My salvation is near to come and My favor to be revealed" (ibid. 56:1).
>
> *(Devarim Rabbah 5:7)*

In order to bring redemption we must adhere to the law — both the letter of the law and the spirit of the law. We must find the balance between justice and righteousness. Only someone who has a profound knowledge of law can dare overstep the letter of the law in pursuit of righteousness. Unapologetic, rigorous pursuit of truth, which will be aided from Heaven, will allow us to create a society which is just and righteous. Such a society will surely be redeemed.

Parashat Ki Teizei

Going to War

The parashah opens with the continuation of a topic raised in last week's parashah — going to war. We learned last week that before battle, a *kohein* would speak to the soldiers and call on the inappropriate recruits to return behind the lines, to the safety of their homes. In this week's parashah we are told:

> When you go out to war against your enemies and God, your Lord, delivers them into your hands, and you take them captive, and you see among the captives a beautiful woman and desire her, and you take her for yourself as a wife. Bring her home to your house, and she shall shave her head and pare her nails. She shall remove the garment of her captivity, remain in your house, and bewail her father and her mother a full month. After that you shall go to her and be her husband, and she shall be your wife. It will be, if you do not desire her, then you shall send her to go where she will. Do not sell her for money [and] do not treat her as a slave, because you have humbled her.
>
> *(Devarim 21:10–14)*

The law is both surprising and perplexing. How can the Torah allow this type of behavior? Later in the parashah a number of cases are presented which give us a glimpse of the higher moral standard which the Torah expects of man.

> Do not watch your brother's ox or his sheep straying and hide yourself from them. Return them to your brother. If your brother is not near you, and you do not know him, bring it to your own house, and it shall be with you until your brother seeks it, and you shall return it to him. So shall you do with his donkey, and so shall you do with his garment, and so shall you do with every lost item of your brother's which he loses and you find; you may not hide yourself. Do not watch your brother's donkey or his ox falling on the way and hide yourself from them; help him lift them up again.
>
> *(Ibid. 22:1–4)*

> If you chance upon a bird's nest on the way, in any tree or on the ground, whether [it contains] chicks or eggs, and the mother is sitting upon the chicks or upon the eggs, you shall not take the mother with the young. Send the mother away and take the young to you, so that it will be good for you and you will live long.
>
> *(Ibid., 6–7)*

How can the same system which is apparently concerned with the feelings of the mother bird, attempting to sensitize man to his exalted station, be insensitive to the feelings of the captive woman, taken from her people in war?

In a sense, the question is compounded when we consult a passage in the Gemara, which attempts to explain the propriety of this behavior:

> "A beautiful [woman]" — the Torah only provided a concession to the evil inclination, [because] it is better for Israel to eat the flesh of [animals] about to die but [ritually] slaughtered, than the flesh of dying animals which have perished.
>
> *(Kiddushin 21b–22a)*

We see that the Gemara frowns upon this type of behavior; the taking of such a war captive is considered wrong, and the Torah law represents a concession to human nature. The warrior, on the battlefield, is swept up in primordial, base feelings which he has never felt before. The terrible ordeal involved in the taking of another human life leaves the soldier which such ambivalent feelings about the value of love, dignity, and life itself that he feels that he must vanquish this captured woman here and now. The Torah nowhere condones the behavior. In fact, the Sages felt that, based on the context, a negative message was being communicated by the text of this law:

> Ben Azzai said: Mitzvah [draws] mitzvah in its train, and transgression [draws] transgression. How [is this to be explained]? As it is written, "When you go out to war...and you see among the captives...." God said, "Although I have permitted her [the captive woman] to you, I commanded you, 'She shall shave her head and pare her nails' so that she will not find favor in your eyes and you will send her away." But if you do not send her away, Scripture continues, "If a man has a stubborn and rebellious son" (*Devarim* 21:18), and the result will be, "If a man has committed a sin worthy of death" (ibid., 22). Thus, transgression draws transgression in its train.
>
> *(Devarim Rabbah 6:4)*

By framing this behavior as a "concession," the Torah is agreeing that fundamentally it is wrong, and while the Torah certainly does not encourage this behavior, it also does not legislate against it. So much of Torah and its laws and mores are an attempt to bring man to a higher spiritual plane. Why in this specific instance do we find a concession to the evil inclination? Why not allow pork chops once a month as a "concession"? Furthermore, if this woman is an incidental victim of this concession, how can we ignore her plight?

One could theorize that despite the allowance in the Torah, this is merely a ploy to calm the person in the heat of passion. Psychologically, the strategy is wonderful. This soldier wants the woman and he wants her now. The Torah says, "No problem, but there is one condition — she becomes your wife with all due privileges of that status." Perhaps this will help defeat the momentary passion, which is indeed a moral lapse.

On a deeper psychological level, we may posit that this "allowance" is merely a psychological ploy employed in the hope of manipulating the raging passion within. We find this idea expressed in the Gemara's discussion regarding the *kohein* who would bring the scapegoat to the desert on Yom Kippur. The *kohein* on this divine mission was permitted to eat and offered food at various intervals:

> At every booth they would say to him, "Here is food and here is water." A Tanna taught: Never did anyone [who carried the goat away] need [the food or water], but [this provision is provided because] you cannot compare one who has bread in his basket with one who has no bread in his basket.
>
> *(Yoma 67a)*

The very allowance of the food is what gives the *kohein* the strength to reject it. A certain moral fortitude emerges from the concession. Perhaps this is the meaning of the words "*keneged yetzer hara,*" which translate literally as "against the evil inclination," and not as we translated it above, as "a concession to the evil inclination."

While this explanation certainly gives insight into the psychological dynamic, the question posed earlier about the plight of the captured woman remains. Moreover, deeper understanding of the entire scenario will present yet more difficulties: The section of the captive woman applies only to nonobligatory battles, but in cases of *milchemet mitzvah* (obligatory battles) no such laws exist. Rashi comments on the very first verse of the parashah:

> "When you go out to war against your enemies" — the verse refers to an optional battle.

In reference to optional battles, we are told that not all eligible males are expected to participate. In last week's parashah we saw an entire list of those who receive dispensations, among them the individual who is afraid.

> The officers shall say to the nation, "Which man is there who has built a new house and has not dedicated it? Let him go and return to his house, lest he die in the battle and another man dedicate it. And which man is there who has planted a vineyard and has not yet eaten of it? Let him go and return to his house, lest he die in the battle and another man eat of it. And which man is there who has betrothed a wife and has not taken her? Let him go and return to his house, lest he die in the battle and another man take her." The officers shall speak further to the people, and they shall say, "Which man is there who is fearful and fainthearted? Let him go and return to his house, so that he does not make his brothers fainthearted like himself."
>
> *(Devarim 20:5–8)*

The Mishnah presents various opinions regarding the source of this person's fear:

> Rabbi Akiva says: "Fearful and fainthearted" is to be understood literally — he is unable to stand in the conflict or battle and see a drawn sword. Rabbi Yosi HaGelili says: ... [It] alludes to one who is afraid because of the transgressions he committed.... Rabbi Yosi says: A high priest who married a widow, an ordinary priest who married a divorcee or a *chalutzah*, a lay Israelite who married an illegitimate or a *netinah*, and the daughter of an Israelite who married an illegitimate or a *natin*....
>
> *(Mishnah, Sotah 44a)*

The Gemara explains the difference between the opinions of Rabbi Yosi and Rabbi Yosi HaGelili as follows:

> What is the difference between Rabbi Yosi and Rabbi Yosi HaGelili? The issue between them is the transgression of a Rabbinical ordinance. With whom does the following teaching accord: He who speaks between [donning] one phylactery and

> the other has committed a transgression and returns home under the war regulations. With whom [does it accord]? With Rabbi Yosi HaGelili.
>
> *(Sotah 44b)*

The transgression of speaking between donning one phylactery and the other seems quite minor. If individuals who had committed such minor transgressions did not participate in battle, those who remained in the ranks and actually went to war must have been on a very high spiritual level. And these are the people who may succumb to their evil inclinations in battle! The Gemara's statement, which sets such high moral standards for soldiers, deserves a closer look. The point of the passage was to illustrate a violation of Rabbinic law, but why was this particular example chosen above all others? In fact, why was any illustration of the point necessary, if the abstract form — "he who violates Rabbinic law" — is so clear?

The individual who speaks between donning the tefillin on the arm and the tefillin on the head essentially creates a separation between two things which should be unified: the arm, symbolizing physical strength, and the head, the intellect. To knowingly engage in battle required personal merit, but more importantly, it required a unified worldview. A person who separates the two aspects of human nature and sees his strength and mind working toward independent goals could not be a soldier in this army.[1] What Rabbi Yosi HaGelili was looking for were soldiers possessing of a very specific moral character.[2]

If this is the case, we should be more than a little surprised that any concession to the evil inclination was necessary for such people. Additionally, our question regarding the plight of the captive woman remains unanswered. A third question revolves around the teaching cited above which connects a war captive wife to the re-

1 This philosophy is encapsulated in the verse, "And you say in your heart, 'My power and the might of my hand has gotten me this wealth' " (*Devarim* 8:17).

2 A similar reaching is reported in the name of Rav Yitzchak Breuer (among others) in his explanation of *Avot* 3:9.

bellious son. If such results from the union between a soldier and a captive were foreseeable, why would the Torah condone the union?

The association with the rebellious son may be the key to a deeper understanding of the teaching regarding the captive woman. We are told that a rebellious son is to be executed, not for what he has done but for what he will do.

> Mishnah. A stubborn and rebellious son is tried on account of his ultimate destiny: let him die innocent and let him not die guilty.
>
> *(Sanhedrin 71b)*

> Mishnah. [The thief] who burrows his way in is judged on account of its probable outcome.
>
> *(Sanhedrin 72a)*

> Mishnah. The following must be saved [from sinning] even at the cost of their lives: he who pursues his friend to kill him....
>
> *(Sanhedrin 73a)*

These three laws, of which the rebellious son is the archetype, all have a common moral argument: We are to consider the outcome and take action with an eye toward the future.

If this is so, our quandary is resolved. We are told that taking a captive woman could lead to having a rebellious son. This idea is logical; taking a woman with alien values into one's home would certainly have an adverse effect. The child of such a woman will be a child raised by a mother who adheres to a radically different belief system. The child's rebelliousness against Judaism is understandable, predictable. This child was reared with intellectual dissonance, by virtue of being taught different ideas from his mother and father. It is easy to see how such an upbringing would produce a confused child, who suffers from spiritual angst.

There is, of course, a second possibility. What if this woman actually comes to reject her pagan past and accepts the tenets of Judaism? The Torah commands that she be given thirty days in order to separate herself from her father and mother, as is explained in the Gemara (*Yevamot* 48b).

This woman receives a crash course in Judaism. During the prescribed thirty days she is to separate from her idolatrous past. Again, this "experiment" could possibly meet with success, and the Torah makes allowances for that possibility.

Rav Elchanan Wasserman, in his *Kovetz Maamarim* (p. 11), raises an intriguing question which is related to our present query: How can the Torah expect a twelve-year-old girl or thirteen-year-old boy to be capable of belief in or knowledge of God, when some of the greatest philosophers in the world, who possessed keen, trained minds, have stumbled terribly in pursuit of intellectual truth? Reb Elchanan answered quite simply that knowledge of God is not as difficult as we might think: Were it not for the evil inclination, all mankind would be able to clearly see and understand truth. It is not the belief in God per se which people find difficult. Rather, the implications of this belief are what make it difficult. If the ramifications of belief were removed or disconnected from belief itself, belief would indeed be attainable by all those who seek truth, even the twelve-year-old.

The captive woman was raised in the pagan world, a world filled with fear and superstition, a world which worshipped power. When this woman sees that the soldiers of her people were vanquished and her gods therefore proven impotent, a startling discovery may occur to her: The pagan worldview is false. She will then be open to learn about the Jewish idea of God. If this happens, this woman may become a great believer, perhaps even something of a fanatic, a response which is often characteristic of those who change belief systems.

We may now view this law's creation as an antidote to the evil inclination in a new light: It is structured to weed out the evil inclination in both the conquerors and the conquered, the man and the woman! If the captive woman undergoes this metamorphosis, we may say that the logic is the same as in the case of the rebellious son. We are expected to look to the future, anticipating the results before setting the chain of events into action. Arguably, the strongest supporter of such a policy would be the changed woman herself, no longer a victim, but rather a newly enlightened person who has emerged from the dark pagan world. In the event that a rebellious son results, we know that the experiment failed, the woman was not open to change, and there is no need to wait any longer to take action.

This idea may be implied in the *Zohar*:

> "A beautiful woman" — a beautiful soul.
>
> *(Zohar Chadash, Ki Teitzei)*

The woman who successfully makes the transition possesses a beautiful soul, but needs some help in order to liberate herself from the psychological chains of paganism. Now we may understand why only the individual with an integrated worldview, one who does not create artificial barriers between the physical and the spiritual, may go to battle. When he sees this beautiful woman, he sees a beautiful soul. The question must be asked: Is it his evil inclination or his good inclination which has deemed her beautiful? The integrated person sees the woman's outward beauty but knows that it is the soul which is really important. However, he may be led astray by his own tendency not to distinguish between the physical and spiritual; he may actually be guilty of self-deception, hence the possibility of a rebellious son.

The Or HaChaim explains the idea of the captive woman in the following way:

> The foundation of the idea and its mystical secret is as follows: Our Sages have taught us that by virtue of the sin of Adam some precious souls were captured by the "other side" and these are the souls of converts. Go and see how many great people have come from other nations — Ruth...Shemaya and Avtalyon, Onkelos, and many others.
>
> *(Or HaChaim, Devarim 21:11)*

In a sense, there is poetic justice in his words: These souls were captured by the "other side" [a euphemism for the evil inclination] as a result of the apostasy of Adam. Now, in battle, we are given permission to bring these souls back, in defiance of the evil inclination. Such a battle is not simple. Success or failure will have severe ramifications. A family life either elevated or destroyed hangs in the balance. Only brave, holy soldiers may take part in this battle, those without sin, spiritually integrated, spiritually elevated.

Parashat Ki Tavo

First Fruits — A Time for Joy

As the Jews make their final preparations for the imminent conquest, Moshe instructs the people:

> It will be, when you come to the Land which God, your Lord, gives you for an inheritance and possess it and live in it, you shall take of the first of all the fruit of the earth, which you shall bring from your land that God, your Lord, gives you. Put it in a basket and go to the place which God, your Lord, shall choose to place His Name there.
>
> *(Devarim 26:1–2)*

The Jews are instructed here to fulfill the commandment of *bikurim*, the first fruits. The law itself is quite interesting. When the Jews finally settle and work the land, they are encouraged not to forget the trials and tribulations endured by their ancestors in order to allow them to see the fruits of their labor. The Torah thus fosters what may be called "historical consciousness."[1] Here Moshe encourages the people to look into the future and imagine the beautiful tranquillity of living in their own land, nomads no more. At that point, each man is commanded to look back and declare:

> A wandering Aramean was my father. He went down to Egypt

1 Rav Soloveitchik makes use of this term in *Kol Dodi Dofek*.

> and sojourned there with a few. He became there a great, mighty, and populous nation. The Egyptians did bad to us, afflicted us, and placed us under hard labor. We cried out to God, the Lord of our fathers, and God heard our voice and saw our affliction, our toil, and our oppression. God brought us out of Egypt with a mighty hand, with an outstretched arm, with great awesomeness, with signs, and with wonders. He has brought us to this place and has given us this land, a land that flows with milk and honey. And now, behold, I have brought the first fruits of the land which You, God, have given me.
>
> *(Ibid., 5–10)*

Our success is not to be viewed as a spiritual or historical vacuum. We must recognize not only where we came from, but also the Divine Hand that constantly guides us. At the conclusion of this ceremony the Torah further instructs:

> Rejoice with all the good that God, your Lord, has given you and your house, you and the *Levi* and the stranger who is among you.
>
> *(Ibid., 11)*

It is not sufficient to see the chain of events in a spiritual context. The result of such an analysis must be joy, the joy of standing in front of God, and thanking Him for all the gifts which have been showered upon us. The individual who sees his success in a myopic, self-aggrandized sense suffers from a spiritual malevolence with far-reaching consequences. In order to understand these issues we must forge ahead in the parashah. The latter part of the parashah contains a section of rebuke, *tochechah*, a litany of curses and warnings which will be the inevitable result if man does not adhere to the word of God.[1] The horrific behavior of the Jews, which will cause this outcome, is described as follows:

> All these curses shall come upon you, pursue you, and overtake you, until you are destroyed; because you did not listen to

1 See my comments to *Bechukotai*.

> the voice of the God, your Lord, to keep His commandments and His statutes which He commanded you. They shall be upon you for a sign and a wonder, and upon your seed forever. Because you did not serve God, Your Lord, with joyfulness and with gladness of heart, when you had an abundance of all.
>
> *(Ibid. 28:45–47)*

The terrible curses are brought about due to a lack of "joyfulness and...gladness of heart." We would not have imagined that this would be the core problem which would lead to a two-thousand-year exile, yet that is exactly what we learn. One often imagines that the emphasis on joy and happiness is some later, anachronistic chassidic idea, yet no one would claim that these verses are an interpolation dating to the eighteenth century. Therefore, the verse at the outset of the parashah must be understood in the same light: Bringing the first fruits was to be joyful occasion, an impetus to bring joy into the world. When joy is lacking, the results are catastrophic.

This analysis will aid us in understanding a *midrash* on this week's parashah:

> Moshe used his Divine vision and saw that the Temple would one day be destroyed and, therefore, the rite of *bikurim* would cease. He therefore initiated prayer three times a day.
>
> *(Tanchuma, Ki Tavo 1)*

This *midrash* seems somewhat obscure. Why, of all the rites and practices in the Temple, was *bikurim* singled out as the one which Moshe was concerned about? Secondly, what correlation exists between prayer and *bikurim*? Perhaps we can reverse the logic and say that it was the lack of observance of *bikurim*, with its stress on joy, which led to the destruction, thus the connection. This would support our understanding that the lack of joy described at the end of the parashah is connected with the joy described in the beginning.

The connection which we made in passing above, between the present exile and this week's parashah, is based on a teaching made famous by Ramban, in his commentary to *Vayikra*. Ramban's source is actually a passage in the *Zohar* which begins by telling us that when Rabbi Shimon bar Yochai and his son Rabbi Eliezer were hiding from the Romans, Eliyahu the Prophet would visit daily and teach them the mysteries of the Torah. One day during their absence a question arose in the study hall:

> It is said [we have a tradition] that the curses in *Torat Kohanim* [*Vayikra*] are referring to the destruction of the First Temple, while the curses listed in *Mishneh Torah* [*Devarim*] refer to the Second Temple. The curses in *Vayikra* contain guarantees and display the love which God has for man.... The curses in *Mishneh Torah* contain no such guarantees or comforting words [that one day redemption will come].... And no one knew how to answer this question [i.e., why there were no words of comfort for the curses in the *Mishneh Torah*]. Rabbi Yehudah bar Ila'i arose and said, "Woe to us for we miss Rabbi Shimon, and we do not know where he is."
>
> *(Zohar Chadash, Ki Tavo 59c)*

We must keep in mind that the time lapse between the destruction of the First Temple and the building of the Second Temple was but seventy years. Roughly seventy years after the destruction of the second Temple the Bar Kochba rebellion failed, and the Hadrionic persecution violently squashed the nascent messianic aspirations. Rabbi Akiva was dead, and the great Rabbi Shimon was in hiding. Instead of giving up hope, the remaining Sages were confident that there was a good explanation for the lack of guarantees and comforting words in the passages which described the exile they were enduring.

The passage in the *Zohar* continues,

> Rabbi Yosi bar Yehudah arose one morning and saw many birds flying about. Alone in the back of the group was one solitary dove. He stood on his feet and said, "Dove, faithful dove, since the days of the flood [of Noach] symbol of our holy peo-

ple...go and be my emissary to Bar Yochai, wherever he may be."

The dove, symbol of hope and peace from time immemorial, serves as a prototype for the behavior of the Jewish people because of its reputation for fidelity and monogamy.[1] Seeing the dove inspired Rabbi Yosi and gave him hope.

> The dove circled above while Rabbi Yosi wrote a letter.... [Then] the dove took the letter to Rabbi Shimon.... When Rabbi Shimon saw the letter he began to weep, he and Rabbi Eliezer, his son. He said, "I am crying because I am separated from my companions, and I cry for that which is not revealed to them. What will future generations do if they see this?"
>
> Eliyahu then arrived, and he saw that [Rabbi Shimon] was crying. [Eliyahu] said, "I was on a different mission, but God sent me to relieve [dry] your tears."

The *Zohar* then describes the End of Days. Eliyahu reveals to Rabbi Shimon that in reality all the punishment and curses emanated from God who, as a loving Father, must sometimes enforce discipline. At the very end of the passage, Eliyahu explains:

> "All this will take place at the end of days, and all is dependent on *teshuvah*, but it is hidden.... He who has a heart will look and return to his Master...."
>
> Rabbi Shimon wrote these things in a letter and sent it back with the dove to Rabbi Yosi who was still waiting....
>
> *(Zohar Chadash, Ki Tavo 59c–60a)*

The point of origin in the *Zohar* is the understanding that the two sections of rebuke in the Torah, in *Vayikra* and *Devarim*, refer to the First and Second Temples respectively. The main concern in the *Zohar* was how to explain the lack of guarantees on God's part. The conclusion of the *Zohar* is instructive: Man's repentance has the capacity to heal.

1 *Berachot* 53b; *Shabbat* 49a and130a; *Rashi, Sotah* 11b; *Shir HaShirim Rabbah* 1:2 and 4:2; *Rashi, Tehillim* 74:19; *Radak, Hoshea* 7:11.

In order to understand why the first destruction had guarantees while the second destruction is dependent on man's repentance, we must introduce a new concept: There are two ways to heal the rift in the relationship between man and God. One type is the "movement" of God toward man. This is described in Kabbalistic literature as an "awakening from above." The second type is the movement of man toward God, or an "awakening from below." The guarantees described in *Vayikra* indicate that the healing necessary at that juncture in history, after the destruction of the First Temple, was based on movement by God. On the other hand, the second exile will not come to an end until man reaches out toward God.

This idea is the essence of this week's parashah. Upon seeing the fruit of one's labor, an appreciation of God must be part of the experience. The rejection of God, or the absence of God from man's experience at the completion of the conquest, indicates man's failure to appreciate God's role in the human achievements of settling the land and normalization of life. This perspective results in a profound spiritual vacuum.

Man is supposed to sense God in all his endeavors. Through the variety of experience and permeating the vicissitudes of the human condition, God's role is to be recognized as dominant. Certainly at the moment of success, when the covenant formed with our forefathers comes to fruition, man was to recognize that the grace and love of God allowed all this. This was the objective of the *bikurim* ceremony. After all, what better symbol exists for the fulfillment of the covenant than the bringing of the fruits of the Land of Israel — living in our own land, supported by our own labor, independent of foreign powers or resources?

The trip to Yerushalayim is described in the Torah:

> You shall set it before God, your Lord, and bow down before God, your Lord.
>
> *(Devarim 26:10)*

This realization was to bring a person "before God." This is both a physical and a spiritual state. Standing before God, produce in hand, should lead man to feelings bordering on ecstasy. If man does not feel joy at the point when evidence of the fulfillment of God's promises are literally in hand, it is an indication that man has moved away from God despite all the blessing he received.

> Because you did serve God, your Lord, with joyfulness and with gladness of heart, when you had an abundance of all.
>
> *(Ibid. 28:47)*

When man has moved away from the Divine, the only rectification is for man to move back toward God. Therefore, the *Zohar* concludes that *teshuvah* is the only way to heal the rift which caused the destruction of the Second Temple. This would also explain the *midrash* cited at the outset: Moshe knew that without the Temple, destroyed because of man's movement away from God, a vehicle to facilitate man's movement toward God would be necessary. Therefore, Moshe established thrice-daily prayer as a constant reminder that in all his experiences man must not forget God. Rather, man should seize every opportunity to stand before God.

Prayer is described as "*avodah shebaleiv*" (service of the heart). The *Zohar* quoted above was very specific: "He who has a heart will look and return to his Master." Evidently the heart, the emotions, are crucial for this return.

Teshuvah itself may be divided into two types: There is repentance which is the result of man's fears and sense of mortality, and repentance which emerges from a profound sense of love toward God. This second type of *teshuvah* represents man's appreciation of all the gifts which God constantly provides. This type of *teshuvah* has healing qualities, both for individuals and for the entire creation. When the Jewish people succeed in relating to God via love, Eliyahu will return to dry our tears and the exile will come to end.

> Behold, I will send you Eliyah the Prophet before the coming of the great and terrible day of God. He shall turn the heart of the fathers to the children, and the heart of the children to

their fathers, lest I come and strike the land with a curse.
(Malachi 3:23–24)

The End of Days, then, will be a time when Eliyahu returns and fathers and sons will be united; the historical consciousness fostered by the *bikurim* ceremony, described at the beginning of this parashah, will be the order of the day. At that time we will be united with our Father in Heaven as well, and a joy the likes of which we have never known will spread throughout the earth. Yet it is joy which will cause this cosmic reunion. The impetus must come from below, the response will be from above.

Returning to the passage in the *Zohar*, Rabbi Yosi and the other scholars were comforted. Just as the raging waters of the flood were dried in Biblical times, the tears of Rabbi Shimon were dried. In another passage, the *Zohar* declares:

> Observe that from the time when the Temple was destroyed no day has passed without its curses. For as long as the Temple was in existence, Israel performed Divine service, offering up burnt-offerings and other offerings, while the *Shechinah* in the Temple hovered over them like a mother hovering over her children. All faces were lit up, and all found blessing both above and here below, and no day passed without its blessings and its joys. Then Israel dwelt securely in their land and all the world was provisioned through them.
>
> But now that the Temple is destroyed and the *Shechinah* is in exile with Israel, there is not a day that does not bring its curses, and the world is under a curse, and joylessness reigns on high and below. Nevertheless, the Holy One, blessed be He, will, in due time, raise Israel from the dust and suffuse the world with joy.
>
> Thus Scripture says: "I will bring them to My holy mountain, and make them joyful in My house of prayer..." (*Yeshayah* 56:7). And just as they went into exile with tears, as it is written, "She cries hard in the night, and her tears are on her cheeks" (*Eichah* 1:2), so shall they return with tears, as it is

> written, "They shall come with weeping, and with supplications will I [God] lead them" (*Yirmiyah* 31:9).
>
> *(Zohar, Bereishit 203a)*

Prayer is the classic example of man reaching from below, up to our Father in Heaven. Prayer is designed to bring the *Shechinah* down to earth. Moshe hoped to prevent the separation between man and God; therefore, he established our prayers. But the *Zohar* insists that *teshuvah*, coming from the heart, full of love and joy, is needed to return the Jews to the level which should have been reached via the *bikurim*. When this happens joy will become a reality — everlasting, complete joy.

Parashiyot Nitzavim and Vayeilech

The Sun and the Moon

> You stand today, all of you, before God, your Lord — your heads of your tribes, your elders, and your officers, with all the men of Israel; your little ones, your wives, and your stranger who is in your camp; from the hewer of your wood to the drawer of your water — that you should enter into a covenant with God, your Lord, and into the oath which God, your Lord, makes with you today. That He may establish you today as a people to Himself, and that He may be to you a God, as He has said to you, and as He has sworn to your fathers, to Avraham, to Yitzchak, and to Yaakov. And not with you alone do I make this covenant and this oath, but with whoever is present here with us standing, today before God, our Lord, and also with whoever is not here with us today.
>
> *(Devarim 29:9–14)*

Moshe addresses the people on the banks of the Jordan River; the context of this address is obviously of great importance, as is evidenced by the frequent repetition of the word *today*. Rashi makes note of this peculiarity in his comments and explains that this was indeed a day of monumental importance:

> This teaches that Moshe gathered them before God on the day of his death, in order to have them enter the covenant.
>
> *(Rashi, Devarim 29:9)*

Moshe, who had been the leader from the very beginning of the Exodus, was now to leave his charges on the threshold of the Holy Land. On this unforgettable day, the reins of leadership would be passed on to Yehoshua. When noting the significance of the day, Rashi adds that with Moshe gone, a new covenant will need to be established. This second point is not immediately clear. Why would Moshe's demise, tragic as it may be, require a new covenant? Leaders come and go; why was it necessary to reestablish a covenant at this juncture?

Later in the text, Rashi returns to comment on this first verse, this time explaining it according to what he calls the "Aggadah." The opening words, "*Atem nitzavim*," generally translated as "You stand," are rendered by Rashi in the more literal sense, from the word *matzeivah*, "monument" or "altar."[1]

> Israel was leaving from one leader to the next leader, from Moshe to Yehoshua. Therefore, he made them as a gathering [or "a monument"] in order to inspire them.
>
> *(Rashi, Devarim 29:12)*

The connection seems unclear: What is the significance of the gathering — monument or *matzeivah* —which Rashi refers to? Furthermore, we recall that earlier on in the Torah we are told of a prohibition to build a *matzeivah*, for it is "hated by God"[2] (see *Devarim* 16:22). Why would Moshe's parting gift contain a prohibited action, or even a literary reference to one?

Rashi has another explanation for the term *today*:

> As today exists and is cloudy and light, so too, did [God] enlighten you, and in the future He will enlighten you....
>
> *(Rashi, Devarim 29:12)*

Again, a somewhat obscure comment by Rashi, but what we

---

1 This definition is clarified by the Sheim MiShmuel, who offers a detailed and intricate explanation of Rashi's comments. Although it is possible to understand Rashi as referring merely to a type of gathering, we employ the Sheim MiShmuel's definition here.

2 See my comments to *Parashat Vayishlach*.

can gather thus far is that on this day Moshe dies, Yehoshua assumes leadership, a new covenant is forged, and, to mark all this, some type of gathering or monument is established. Lastly, this day is bright yet cloudy.

Let us consider the reaction that the people must have had to the death of Moshe. It was Moshe who had given them hope, it was Moshe who led the valiant march out of Egypt, and it was Moshe who taught them Torah. Losing a leader or teacher of Moshe's stature was certainly traumatic. This day, despite the coronation of Yehoshua, was not a happy day; "The king is dead, long live the king" is at best a bittersweet cry. Perhaps Rashi refers to these mixed emotions when he speaks of the light and the clouds.

An alternate understanding of Rashi's metaphor is that the light and relative-light refer to Moshe and Yehoshua respectively. Elsewhere, Rashi employs this same metaphor when referring to Moshe and Yehoshua: When Moshe is told of his impending death, he tells God that a replacement must be found. "The flock of God cannot be left without a shepherd."

> God said to Moshe, "Ascend to this Mount Avarim and see the land which I have given to the Children of Israel. When you have seen it, you will also be gathered to your nation, as Aharon, your brother, was gathered...."
>
> Moshe spoke to God, saying, "May God, the Lord of the spirits of all flesh, appoint a man over the congregation who will go out before them and go in before them, who will lead them out and bring them in, and the congregation of God will not be like sheep which have no shepherd."
>
> God said to Moshe, "Take Yehoshua the son of Nun, a man in whom there is spirit, and lay your hand upon him. Set him before Elazar the Kohein and before all the congregation, and give him command in their sight. You will put your honor upon him so that all the congregation of the Children of Israel will be obedient."
>
> *(Bemidbar 27:12–20)*

This is the formal coronation of Yehoshua. Rashi explains,

> "Put of your honor upon him" — This is the ray of light on [Moshe's] face.
>
> *(Rashi, Bemidbar 27:20)*

We recall the light, which emanated from Moshe's face when he descended Sinai with the second tablets. Moshe was instructed to give a part of this glory to Yehoshua, as a symbol of the leadership he would soon assume.

Rashi continues:

> "Of your honor" — but not all of your honor. We find it taught that the face of Moshe was like the sun while the face of Yehoshua was like the moon.

The differing degrees of light Rashi uses as an expression of the leadership personalities of Yehoshua and Moshe are a paraphrase from the Gemara:

> "You will put of your honor upon him" — but not all your honor. The elders of that generation said: The countenance of Moshe was like that of the sun; the countenance of Yehoshua was like that of the moon. Alas for such shame! Alas for such reproach!
>
> *(Bava Batra 75a)*

Here, the fact that Yehoshua was compared to the moon is not seen as something great. Rather, it is a lament of the people of the generation that had been privileged to see the glory of Moshe. The light that emanated from Yehoshua was surely bright, but it did not shine like the light of Moshe. The day Moshe dies and Yehoshua takes over is the day Yehoshua shines — objectively bright, but subdued when compared to Moshe.

Now the people are the flock of Yehoshua, a great leader in his own right, the foremost student of Moshe, with the very light of Moshe radiating from his face, but nonetheless suffering from comparison with Moshe. The people therefore lamented the ascension of Yehoshua to leadership; he was great, but he was not Moshe. What they may or may not have realized was that the death of Moshe marked the end of this glorious generation which had witnessed so much: the plagues, the parting of the sea, the Revelation at Sinai, and countless other events. Certainly, some survivors were about, but with Moshe no longer around, they were simply vestiges of days bygone.

It is difficult, at times, to define a generation, because time is fluid. People of all ages left Egypt. When do we consider a generation to have ended? Perhaps the best definition of a generation is its leadership: Moshe's generation — the generation of the Exodus — comes to an end with his death. Moshe, the greatest Jewish leader and prophet of all time, was the defining factor of his generation. They were the generation of Moshe, a "*dor dei'ah*" (generation of knowledge).[1] The day of Moshe's death marks the end of that generation as well. This new generation, led by Yehoshua, which would soon cross the Jordan, had undergone a subtle change which carried philosophical and legal implications.

In *Parashat Eikev* we discussed the halachic principle that all Jews are responsible for one another.[2] This spiritual reciprocity began as the Jews crossed the Jordan and is a characteristic of Yehoshua's generation, a defining attribute of the new generation that will conquer and settle the Land of Israel. It is an expression of the common destiny of a people. Ritva explains:

---

1 See *Zohar, Shemot* 62b for the source of this term.

2 This is not simply an expression of mutual concern and care, but also includes such things as blessings. For example, if one Jew said Kiddush but another has not said it as of yet, the former is permitted to repeat the blessing which he has already made. This ruling is somewhat strange: Clearly, if the first person had not made the blessing, he would be able to include the second one in his blessing. But if he has already fulfilled his obligation, how is he able to recite the blessing again? Evidently, he has not completely fulfilled his obligation, as long as his fellow Jew has not fulfilled his own obligation as well. This is mutual responsibility. The implication is clear: the spiritual state of one Jew is interdependent with the spiritual state every other Jew. See my comments on *Eikev*, where this idea is explained more fully.

> All Jews are mutually responsible, and all of Israel constitute one body.
>
> *(Ritva, Rosh HaShanah 29a)*

Or HaChaim explains the new covenant formed at the point of transition between Moshe and Yehoshua along the same lines:

> Moshe's objective in [establishing] this covenant was to create mutual responsibility.
>
> *(Or HaChaim, Devarim 29:9)*

Now, as the Jews take leave of Moshe, a new chapter begins, one which includes the implementation of a new ideal of mutual responsibility. Thus, Or HaChaim understands the closing words of the covenant:

> The secret things belong to God, our Lord, but those things which are revealed belong to us and to our children forever, that we may fulfill all the words of this Torah.
>
> *(Or HaChaim, Devarim 29:28)*

Mutual responsibility includes that which is known, in the open. Secret acts, on the other hand, are God's concern.

This idea of mutual responsibility can explain Rashi's reference to the *matzeivah*. In *Shoftim*, Rashi explains the difference between *matzeivah* (monument) and *mizbei'ach* (altar): A monument is made of one stone, while an altar is made of many stones or components. During the time of the forefathers, a *matzeivah* was acceptable. After the nation is formed, however, the Torah proscribes use of a *matzeivah*. A *matzeivah*, Rashi explains, signifies one — an individual approaching God. An altar, on the other hand, signifies the totality of the Jewish people, all sorts of individuals gathered together to form a beautiful mosaic. During the time of the forefathers, individuals reflected the totality of Jewish life; the generation of Avraham consisted of Avraham. Our forefathers were spiritual giants, individuals who were able to approach God as individuals. But once the Jewish people become a nation, a *matzeivah* becomes inappropriate.

Arguably, Moshe was the last individual who represented the entire nation:

> As Rabbi was once expounding the Scripture, the congregation became drowsy. In order to rouse them he said, "One woman in Egypt brought forth six hundred thousand in one birth."
>
> There was a certain disciple there named Rabbi Yishmael son of Rabbi Yosi, who said to him, "Who can that have been?"
>
> He replied, "This was Yocheved who bore Moshe, who was counted as equal to six hundred thousand of Israel; for so it says, 'Then Moshe and the Children of Israel sang...' (*Shemot* 15:1); 'The Children of Israel did according to all that God commanded Moshe' (*Bemidbar* 1:54); and, 'There has not arisen a prophet in Israel like Moshe' (*Devarim* 34:10)."
>
> *(Shir HaShirim Rabbah 1:65)*

Moshe represents the entire nation; when he dies, the entire nation becomes responsible for one another spiritually. It is true that the nation is now represented by many individuals, who will need to coalesce in order to form a cohesive whole. But one of the final lessons with which Moshe leaves the people is the idea that ultimately we are one people, gathered together to reflect unity and interdependency. The one body described by Ritva is mirrored by the *matzeivah* described by Rashi (and Sheim MiShmuel). With Moshe gone, perhaps the light did not shine as brightly, and the people became depressed. On the other hand, Rashi reminds us:

> As today exists and is cloudy and light, so too, did [God] enlighten you, and in the future He will enlighten you....

On the day of Moshe's death, the light of Moshe shining like the sun could be seen, as well as the light of Yehoshua shining like the moon. But the people were told that henceforth the light will be on them. The light of Moshe was diffused. Though surely much of the discernible light now was to be seen on the face of Yehoshua, the source of Moshe's light, Moshe's greatness was his status as

God's representative. With his death that light would be spread out among the people. For that light to shine forth in its full brilliance, the people had to gather and form a unified whole. The light had now become the domain of the entire nation, represented by mutual responsibility and spiritual reciprocity.

In the future, the light of Moshe will once again dazzle us with its splendor. The method of bringing this light forth is performing the commandments. Each and every Jew is involved in this process, for bits of light are spread about among all our people.[1] If we look around and it seems cloudy or dark, it is simply because we have not as of yet succeeded in making the light shine. "Let there be light"!

1 See the introduction of the *Ketzot HaChoshen* for a similar concept.

Parashat Ha'azinu

Moshe's Song

This week's parashah is one of the last parashiyot in the Torah. Here Moshe takes a different course of action when compared to the other sections of *Devarim*. Until now Moshe either taught or retaught the commandments or rebuked the people for their misdeeds. In *Ha'azinu*, Moshe breaks out in song. It is not the first time that Moshe is involved in song; the *Shirah* after the miraculous splitting of the sea is surely the more famous of Moshe's songs. But that song was the response to an unparalleled Divine action. That was a song inspired by religious ecstasy. It was a moment of rapture; Moshe led and the entire people followed.

Here, Moshe sings by himself. The generation that left Egypt is dead, and soon Moshe will follow them to the grave. This seems like a strange time for Moshe to break into song, but herein lies the greatness of Moshe.

In order to understand this idea, let us look at a passage in the Gemara which describes an instance when someone wished to sing but was not allowed:

> When the wicked Nevuchadnetzar threw Chananyah, Mishael, and Azaryah into the fiery furnace, the Holy One, blessed be He, said to Yechezkel, "Go and resurrect the dead in the plain of Dura."

> When he resurrected them, the bones came and smote the wicked man [Nevuchadnetzar] upon his face. He said, "What kind of [bones] are these?"
>
> [His courtiers] answered him, "Their companion is resurrecting the dead in the plain of Dura."
>
> Thereupon he broke into utterance, "How great are [God's] signs, and how mighty are His wonders! His kingdom is an everlasting kingdom, and His dominion is from generation to generation!"
>
> Rabbi Yitzchak said: May molten gold be poured into the mouth of that wicked man! Had an angel not come and struck him upon his mouth he would have eclipsed all the songs and praises uttered by David in the Book of Psalms.
>
> *(Sanhedrin 92b)*

The conclusion of the passage is that Nevuchadnetzar wished to sing but was not allowed, and had he sung, his songs of praise would have fared well in a comparison with those of King David — the sweet singer of *Tehillim*. The passage is difficult: Why would God display the miracle to the heathen, if not to make him realize the greatness of God? And why would Nevuchadnetzar be struck when the idea of a God more powerful than he finally dawned on him?

The Kotzker Rebbe addresses these issues in a short comment:

> You wish to sing praise while the crown is on your head. I would like to hear how you sing after being slapped in the face.
>
> *(Emet MiKotzk Titzmach, p. 37)*

Many people, after being inspired by a wondrous sight, have the ability to sing praise. The greatness of David HaMelech was his ability to sing despite personal tragedy which would have broken the spirit of a lesser man. The angel came to hit Nevuchadnetzar. Had he sung at that point he would have indicated spiritual greatness and true humility. But in the aftermath of the blow, Nevuchadnetzar no longer felt inspired. The moment was lost.

Now we can appreciate the sublime greatness of Moshe: Surely the song sung after the splitting of the sea was a moment of religious ecstasy. That song was the first time people sang to God. The Midrash indicates that in the future this will be noted:

> "That which has been is that which shall be" (*Kohelet* 1:9). The Rabbis say: In the Hereafter the generations will assemble in the presence of the Holy One, blessed be He, and say before Him, "Master of the universe, who shall utter a song before You first?"
>
> He will answer them, "In the past none but the generation of Moshe uttered a song before Me, and now none but that generation shall utter a song before Me." What is the proof? As it is said, "Sing to God a new song and His praise from the end of the earth, you who go down to the sea" (*Yeshayah* 42:10).
>
> *(Kohelet Rabbah 1:28)*

But Moshe, like David, sang even when things were not going his way. David sang when escaping from his own son who was attempting to usurp his power. Moshe sang the moment before death.

When we contemplate the words which Moshe uses we are all the more amazed:

> Listen, heavens, and I will speak; hear, earth, the words of my mouth. My teaching shall drip like the rain, my speech shall flow as the dew, like the small rain upon the tender herb and like the showers upon the grass. Because I will proclaim the name of God, ascribe greatness to our Lord. [He is] the Rock, His work is perfect; for all His ways are justice. A God of faithfulness and without iniquity, just and right is He."
>
> *(Devarim 32:1–4)*

Of all the ways of describing God, Moshe refers to God as a "Rock." Of course, this term signifies the power of God. But when we recall that the downfall of Moshe took place when attempting to extract water from a rock, it is all the more surprising that this particular appellation is used. This understanding may be found in the *Zohar*:

> Moshe in his song first said, "The Rock, His work is perfect," referring to the occasion when water issued from the rock....
>
> *(Zohar, Shemot 64b)*

In his song, which is sung immediately preceding his death, Moshe completely accepts Divine justice: "[He is] the Rock, His work is perfect; for all His ways are justice. A God of faithfulness and without iniquity, just and right is He."

Instead of avoiding this painful topic Moshe addresses it head-on, displaying absolute acceptance of God and His will. This is yet another indication of the spiritual level that Moshe achieves.

At the beginning of *Sefer Devarim*, we noted that Moshe deals with three main issues: Rebuke, in the hope of bringing the people to a higher spiritual level; a review of the commandments based on the Oral Torah; and this section of song where he indicates that there is no remorse on his part. Moshe goes to his death with dignity, praising God and his people, as we will see in the final parashah in *Devarim, Vezot HaBerachah*.

Parashat V'zot HaBerachah

The Last Eight Verses

The Torah comes to its completion with the following verses:

Moshe, the servant of God, died there in the land of Mo'av, according to the word of God. He [God] buried him in a valley in the land of Mo'av, opposite Beit Peor; and no man knows his grave till this day. Moshe was one hundred and twenty years old when he died; his eye was not dim, nor his natural force abated. The Children of Israel wept for Moshe in the plains of Mo'av thirty days, and the days of weeping and mourning for Moshe were ended.

Yehoshua the son of Nun was full of the spirit of wisdom, for Moshe had laid his hands upon him; and the Children of Israel listened to him and did as God commanded Moshe.

There has not arisen since in Israel a prophet like Moshe, whom God knew face to face, in all the signs and the wonders which God sent him to do in the land of Egypt to Pharaoh, to all his servants, to all his land, and in all that mighty hand, and in all the great and awesome deeds which Moshe performed in the sight of all Israel.

(Devarim 34:5–12)

At the outset of *Sefer Devarim* we noted the centrality of Divine authorship of the Torah to the Jewish belief system. Furthermore, we saw the importance of Moshe's contribution: the entire Torah is believed to have been dictated by God to Moshe. These last eight verses pose a challenge to that position. For how can Moshe write after his own death, or, alternatively, how does Moshe, when still alive, write about his own forthcoming demise?

The Gemara offers a number of approaches to these verses.

> The master said: Yehoshua wrote the book which bears his name and the last eight verses of the Pentateuch. This statement is in agreement with the authority who says that eight verses in the Torah were written by Yehoshua, as it has been taught: [It is written,] "Moshe, the servant of God, died there." Is it possible that Moshe, being dead, could have written the words "Moshe died there"? [No.] Rather, up to this point Moshe wrote, [and] from this point Yehoshua wrote. This is the opinion of Rabbi Yehudah, or, according to others, of Rabbi Nechemyah.
>
> Rabbi Shimon said to him: Can [we imagine the] Scroll of the Law [*sefer Torah*] being short one word, and is it not written, "[Moshe commanded the Levi'im,] 'Take this book of the Law' " (*Devarim* 31:26)? Rather, up to this point the Holy One, blessed be He, dictated and Moshe repeated and wrote, and from this point God dictated and Moshe wrote with tears.
>
> *(Bava Batra 15a)*

On the one hand, the question of "authorship" is debated in the Gemara. On the other hand, the question of the Divine source of these verses is not debated. According to both opinions the source of the words of the Torah is certainly God. The point of disagreement is limited to the question of whether Moshe or Yehoshua was the conduit through which the word of God flowed. In a sense, the opinion of Rabbi Yehudah indicates that *Sefer Yehoshua* begins eight verses earlier, at the end of *Devarim*. However, this description is somewhat imprecise, for there is a major difference between the end of *Devarim* and the beginning of *Yehoshua*, namely the relative holiness. The status of the Five Books of Moshe, known as the Torah, is clearly superior to that of the books of the prophets.

Let us return to the Gemara passage cited above, the conclusion of which is unclear.

> Which of these two authorities is followed in the rule laid down by Rabbi Yehoshua ben Abba.... "The last eight verses of the Torah must be read [in the synagogue service] by one person alone"? It follows Rabbi Yehudah and not Rabbi Shimon. I may even say, however, that it follows Rabbi Shimon [who would say that] since they differ [from the rest of the Torah] in one way, they differ [in another].
>
> *(Ibid.)*

There is some halachic debate regarding the proper understanding of these words. Rashi explains that when the *gemara* says that these eight verses are read by one person, it means that these eight verses should not be divided into two *aliyot*. We know that the minimum size of an *aliyah* is three verses. These eight, though, according to Rashi, should remain as one unit. This opinion of Rashi has been codified in the *Shulchan Aruch* (428:7).[1]

Rama (*Orach Chaim* 669) indicates that the custom of *chatan Torah* is derived from this passage. The Rama's understanding that "one person alone" reads these eight verses indicates that the one who reads is to be a special person in the congregation.

Rambam's formulation is of particular interest.

> The eight verses at the end of the Torah are permitted to be read with less than ten [without a minyan]. Even though the entire Torah is from Moshe based on the word of the Almighty, since these verses give the indication that they were written after the death of Moshe, their status is changed and it is permissible for one person to read them.
>
> *(Mishneh Torah, Hilchot Tefillah 13:6)*

---

1 Of particular note are the comments of the *Mishnah Berurah*, section 428, note 21, which indicate that the opinion that Yehoshua authored these verses is authoritative.

Rambam is unequivocal that the words of the Torah originate from God and were dictated to Moshe. Nonetheless, because these verses give the impression of having been written after Moshe's demise, their halachic status is changed inasmuch as they can be read without a minyan.

In his introduction to *Mishneh Torah*, Rambam similarly writes:

> The entire Torah was written by our master Moshe before he died, by his hand.

Rambam's position is clear: The entire Torah, including these eight verses, was the product of the hand of Moshe.

Rashi, in his comments on the *Chumash*, writes:

> "Moshe died there" — is it possible that Moshe died and then wrote "Moshe died there"? Rather, until this point, [the text] was penned by Moshe. From this point forward was penned by Yehoshua. Rabbi Meir said: Could a Torah be missing something and [Moshe] says, "Take this book of the Law"? Rather, God spoke and Moshe wrote with tears.
>
> *(Rashi, Devarim 34:5)*

Rashi's comments are unclear, for he cites both the opinion of Rabbi Yehudah and of Rabbi Meir despite the fact that in the Gemara these opinions seem diametrically opposed. Rashi is clearly answering the question of how Moshe could write about his own death in the past tense. It is unclear in Rashi's comments which of these opinions he considers normative, or, for that matter, what is the nature of his "compromise" position.

Further analysis of the Gemara passage can allow us to understand Rashi and gain insight into the entire issue.

> Rather, up to this point the Holy One, blessed be He, dictated and Moshe repeated and wrote, and from this point God dictated and Moshe wrote with tears.

What does the expression "Moshe wrote with tears" mean? The simple understanding would be that Moshe wrote these verses while weeping. Moshe, the faithful servant of God, takes dictation for the final time, is overcome by emotion, and weeps. However, it is unclear why, according to this understanding, Moshe's tears should change the halachic status of these verses.

Ritva explains that when the Gemara says that Moshe wrote with tears, it means tears literally — in contradistinction to ink. These comments of Ritva would indeed explain why different halachic status was accorded these verses: they were, on the one hand, written by the hand of Moshe but, on the other hand, without ink.[1]

Based on the explanation of Ritva, we can reinterpret the words of Rashi: Indeed, Yehoshua wrote these words, and Moshe wrote these words. Moshe wrote them with tears, based on the word of God, while Yehoshua wrote them with ink.[2]

The Vilna Gaon understands *dimah*, the word we translate as "tears," to be pronounced in a slightly different manner, as *dimah*, meaning confusion. These verses were written by Moshe, but without Moshe understanding the meaning of the words he was writing (*Kol Eliyahu, V'Zot HaBerachah* 133). Based on this teaching of the Vilna Gaon, Ketav ViKabbalah suggests that Rabbi Shimon and Rabbi Yehudah did not offer opposing views, and their words can be reconciled along the lines of Rashi's explanation to the text cited above.

This teaching of the Vilna Gaon reminds us of the idea popularized by Ramban in his introduction to the Torah, where he describes the existence of a primordial Torah which preexisted creation, written with white fire and black fire. This Torah is said to contain a string of letters that compose the Divine Name. This teaching is found in the *Zohar*:

For the Torah, as we have been taught, consists entirely of His

1 For a discussion on the halachic status of invisible ink, see Rabbi Levi Yitzchak Halperin, *Responsa Ma'aseh Choshev*, vol. II, 14. In general on this topic, see Rabbi Yitzchak Mirsky, *Hegyonei Halachah*, vol. II, p. 100–108.

2 See the comments of Maharsha, *Bava Batra* 15a.

> Holy Name; in fact, every word written therein consists of and contains that Holy Name. Therefore, one must beware of erring in regard to this Name and misrepresenting it. He who is false to the Supernal King will not be allowed to enter the King's palace and will be driven away from the World to Come.
>
> *(Zohar, Shemot 87a)*

The source of the white and black fire may likewise be found in the *Zohar*:

> The Torah was manifested in a black fire which was superimposed upon a white fire, signifying that by means of the Torah the Right Hand clasped the Left Hand so that the two might be fused, as it is written, "From His right hand a fiery law to them" (*Devarim* 33:2).
>
> *(Zohar, Shemot 84a)*

Based on this teaching, one can understand the giving of the Torah as pieces of divinity being broken off and handed to man. The essence of the Torah is the unveiled aspect of the Divine mind, of which we are permitted to have a glimpse. This celestial string of letters was broken off letter by letter, word by word, and handed to man via Moshe. With poetic justice, at the very end of the Torah, the same form is reestablished. As the revelation comes to a close, the same primordial Torah is recalled by the unique character and status of the final verses.

Ultimately, all of Torah has an elusive aspect. Being Divine, indeed it should transcend human understanding. Our ability to fathom God should be less successful than viewing a cryptic string of letters. Through an incredible act of Divine benevolence, man was created and given understanding and choice. As God's crowning gift to man the Torah was given, its secrets uncovered and revealed to the masses.

Perhaps now we understand why at the end of the Torah, the last eight verses which maintained the Divine lettering are the domain of the individual, to be read as one unit. We are taught that even an individual may read these verses, because they remind us of the Divinity of the words and of the ability of every individual to relate to all the words of the Torah and the meaning behind them.

> We are fortunate, how good is our portion, how pleasant is our lot, and how beautiful is our heritage.
>
> *(Daily Prayers, based on Tanna D'Vei Eliyahu 21)*

> Blessed is He, our God, who created us for His glory, separated us from those who stray, gave us the Torah of Truth, and implanted eternal life within us. May He open our heart through His Torah and imbue our heart with love and awe of Him, so that we may do His will and serve Him wholeheartedly.
>
> *(U'Va LiTzion)*

Chazak, chazak, venitchazeik.

Index

Please note: This index is not exhaustive. It is intended to help the reader find topics which may be found in unexpected places.